THE IMPOSSIBLE THEATER

Herbert Blau

It is said of Tamerlane, master of Asia and conqueror of half the world, that he only once used the word "impossible"—and that was when he was dying.
—True Stories of the Supernatural

THE IMPOSSIBLE THEATER

A MANIFESTO

THE MACMILLAN COMPANY, NEW YORK

COLLIER-MACMILLAN LIMITED, LONDON

First printing
The Macmillan Company, New York
Collier-Macmillan Canada Ltd., Toronto, Ontario
Library of Congress catalog card number: 64-24008
Printed in the United States of America

The author has quoted copyrighted material from: *The Ideal Theater: 8 Concepts*, published by The American Federation of Arts, 1962, under a grant from the Ford Foundation Program in Humanities and the Arts; *Two Plays and a Preface: The Miracle Worker* by William Gibson, copyright © 1959 by William Gibson, reprinted by permission of the author and the publisher, Atheneum House, Inc.; *Eros and Civilization* by Herbert Marcuse, copyright © 1955 by Beacon Press, reprinted by permission

TO MY WIFE

for courage and her children

ACKNOWLEDGMENTS

Here and there throughout this book are gleanings from various essays I have published before, in *Tulane Drama Review, The Noble Savage, Educational Theatre Journal, Encore, Theatre Arts, The Second Coming, Arts in Society, Kenyon Review.*

Some of what I have had to say was originally prompted by a trip abroad several years ago under a grant from the Ford Foundation. A fellowship from the John Simon Guggenheim Foundation has helped me to complete the book.

The book is my own doing. I say that because the theater which lies behind it, and I trust beyond it, was a collaborative effort, occasionally a battle royal. I am indebted to all those who have fought along with me—most especially to my partner Jules Irving, who has shared all the repercussions of my pugnacity. There have been repercussions, but that has been half the pleasure of the battle.

An undaunted man in our corner has been Alan Mandell, who came to us from Canada to uphold the principle that the American theater will perish unless you are willing to work for it at least twenty-four hours a day. His devotion has released my energy for more than the writing of this book.

There is one other person to whom I owe a considerable debt—though, as I shall explain later, he has little but disdain for the theater: the critic, poet, and teacher Yvor Winters.

H. B.

San Francisco, September 1963

CONTENTS

PART ONE

The American Theater in the Cold War

1 FALLOUT   3

2 THE IRON CURTAIN   28

3 NEW FRONTIERS   54

PART TWO

In Search of Identity

4 THE BALANCE OF TERROR   87

5 IN THE COMMON INTEREST   113

6 GROWING UP WITH ENTROPY   141

7 COUNTERFORCE I: THE SOCIAL DRAMA   183

8 COUNTERFORCE II: NOTES FROM THE UNDERGROUND   228

9 THE CLEAREST GODS   277

PART ONE

THE
AMERICAN THEATER
IN THE COLD WAR

1

On the other heart, I had murder in me.

—William Gibson, *The Seesaw Log*

I play. But this is what I think.

—Wallace Stevens, *The Man with the Blue Guitar*

FALLOUT

The purpose of this book is to talk up a revolution. Where there are rumblings already, I want to cheer them on. I intend to be incendiary and subversive, maybe even un-American. I shall probably hurt some people unintentionally; there are some I want to hurt. I may as well confess right now the full extent of my animus: there are times when, confronted with the despicable behavior of people in the American theater, I feel like the lunatic Lear on the heath, wanting to "kill, kill, kill, kill, kill, kill!"

My friends, wanting to spare me my murderous impulses and practicing a therapy I respect and despise, tell me to calm down, give it time, things are happening. Things *are* happening: I want to look at them and see what's really happening. And to those who share my view of what the theater might be but defer to the sluggard drift of things, I want to say what Brecht's Galileo said to the Little Monk, temporizing in pity for those who, fixed in the old routines, scrape a living somehow—on the premise that if whatever is is not right, it is at least unalterable—"I can see their divine patience, but where is their divine fury?"

This will not be a palace revolution because in this country there are no palaces in the theater, no center of authority except the merchandise marts. I should like to say it will be one of the aims of the revolution to drive the moneylenders from the temple, but the moneylenders have never been in the temple; and where they are they remain, for the time being, impregnable. This is not to say they shouldn't be assailed anyhow, for it is the nature of rebellion, born of distress and aspiration, to proceed against hope.

One of my aims will be to badger the bluff and delusive benevolence of our Affluent Society wherever it has misguided the theater, and to urge those who believe as I do, but who haven't the audacity or sense of fellowship, to follow—wherever they may be—the true slope of their own talent and passion. I want to arouse that passion. The saddest thing, as always, is that a lot of people who should be in the temple are not, and it is to them that this book is principally addressed. If I seem to have appointed myself guardian of the Ark of the Covenant, it is not only that I am caught up in my imagery; it may also suggest that the temple still has to be built, as it must be from generation to generation—for each man on his own hallowed ground.

If I risk being struck dead for presumption, well, these are parlous times, and in or out of the theater—as a Radiation Equivalent Man—one risks being dead in any case.

Rebellion, said Camus, is not realistic. Because it is not realistic it may work miracles. To say this, however, is not to imply that the rebel is indifferent to facts or has no sense of history; if anything, he is gorged by that. Though Camus' book *The Rebel,* prompted by holocaust, followed out the metaphysical consequences of the word, what he said bears upon the state of the theater in America: "Rebellion is born of the spectacle of irrationality, confronted with an unjust and incomprehensible condition." The rebel seeks order in chaos, the danger is always excess, and the fury of reform may lead nowhere. It was Lear who also said, "Nothing will come of nothing." Irrationality may leap from the object to the one who wants to change it, especially when the object is as amorphous, and deluded, as theater in America.

If, as I believe, it is the nature of the theater to court peril, then it's a risk one may have to take if he wants to work in it honorably. There is a lot of desire and thinking incipient in our theater that is quickly cowed by the cocksure weary realism of established mediocrity. It may be true that thought collects in pools, but still water stinks if not deep. And we must talk up if we're not to be talked down to.

In the process one may have to understand one's own motives and one's own performance, and though I shall be working on the principle that the tigers of wrath are wiser than the horses of instruction, my wrath, I trust, is not uninstructed. What I shall say comes out of more than a decade of experience in trying to create *a* theater in America, during which time I have tried to understand the meaning and place of theater in American cultural history, the behavior and purposes of the people in it, and the relation of theater to other arts—most particularly in a period whose rhythm and imagery were conditioned by the Cold War.

So my call to action will also be a sort of cultural history. The first part will consist of several chapters of more or less invidious comparisons, complaints, laments, warnings, exordia, and exhortations, leading into and growing out of analysis of the American theater and the world behind it. Then there will be a series of chapters drawing upon the development of my own theater and its milieu: I mean not only the geography and atmosphere of San Francisco, and its purported renaissance, but also political and social events, tendencies in painting and sculpture, as well as theoretical problems that, for one reason or another, came up just then.

The career of the theater in which I work traverses the main events of the Cold War. This was a period of unprecedented crisis in that the crisis was endured with a most remarkable consciousness of its shape, scope, causes, and peculiarity—intense self-awareness with increasing loss of self, a penchant for motive with diminishing capacity for action. And, confronted with terrible issues, a remarkable capacity for forgetting them. Yet the period of the Cold War is also the period of the cold cannula, the surgical probe going deep into the thalamus of the brain and, colder than space, literally burning to death by cold the remote tissues of disease.

We shall go into this paradoxical era as we shall go into various of our productions that demonstrate the dilemma and its consequences for the theater, and lead us back to the issues again, with the special powers invested in the theater from ancient times.

Poets and philosophers have always used the theater as a metaphor of reality. As John Donne said in a sermon, "the whole frame of the world is the Theater." This may be reality or illusion, but the idea that all the world's a stage is written in the blood of the human race; and the multiple illusions of contemporary life, which may be its only reality, are described in the best drama as they are engaged in the Cold War. That too is an impossible affair, or so it has seemed. Yet if politics is the art of the possible, theater is the art of the impossible. "Seeming, seeming" is what it's made of.

Given Space, atomic energy, and Ruanda-Urundi, politics may no longer accept its definition, but the major theoretical concern of this book will be to explain why I define the theater as I do. To avoid claiming some wonder-working powers for the theater that it can't fulfill, let me say that among the various meanings of the word *impossible* I have in mind is the one you get when you say it raging with your teeth clenched. "So many things in the theater are discouraging," Eric Bentley remarked some years ago, "that any man of sense would give it up. But the theater is a *femme fatale,* and for those who feel her fascination the question: what is to be done? has perpetually to be asked and perpetually to be answered affirmatively."

But before that can be done, one has to know how intolerable the theater really is, for it is a form aspiring to be an institution in an age in which most existing institutions are, in one way or another, suspect.

If there are some wonders it can't work, the theater—from Eleusis to

Bali, and if we can believe Aristotle and the anthropologists— *is* a Mystery. It is not only a *femme fatale* but it knows the ways of fatality, which is the special province of Tragedy. I need not go now into the paradoxes of that form, nor into the high seriousness of the greatest comedy to suggest the theater is particularly devoted to those divisions of man's nature, seeming without remedy, that led Freud to the almost elegiac conclusions of his *Civilization and Its Discontents*. Where politics—the exercise of government for livable ends—tries by means ranging from diplomacy to wire-pulling to prevail against stalemate, the theater—by means ranging from fable to *trompe l'œil*—takes us through the formal experience of stalemate, the livable and the unbearable. At its best, it is not deluded by its denouements, nor is it disillusioned, for irony is built into the form, where people pretend to be what they are not—even when, as in "the Alienation Effect" of Brecht, they're pretending they're not pretending.

Yet the theater, because it is an art, has the potentiality of collective power without cautionary limit; it can imagine into being such stuff as dreams are made on, good dreams and bad dreams, what politics may someday come to and what politics must try to avoid. Of course, all this is theoretic. Practice does not make perfect. The institution of theater and the ideal form of theater may be at war, the necessary dialectic of the two turning into impossible conflict; or stalemate. When we complain about the absence of Tragedy in the modern world, we step right into this gulf, a corollary of the Cartesian abyss. So, too, when we complain about the theater in America. Yet we must complain because, while the theater can't carry the whole weight of the world on its back, like any other human enterprise it ought to carry its proper share. While defense budgets grow and all our skills fly up to the heavens like Claudius' words, they tell us that the pragmatic cost of our great democratic achievement is the dark backward and abysm of that one art which, born in the paroxysms of ritual, is able to express the whole rhythm of social intelligence—the most full-bodied testament, more immediately human than that of architecture, to men in an active *believing community,* moving by right reason and concerted instinct toward some valid if barely-realized purpose.

As a social art, the theater is a service that is time-serving in a way that the more private arts of poetry and painting need not be. It really—I am speaking of the form—wants to put its giant mimic shoulder to the wheel. Action moves on. It may encourage feeling and thought, but the end is communion. Human behavior in all modes is held up to public scrutiny. Or so it should be. This book grows out of the common knowledge that the theater in America is time-serving in ways that debilitate the form and, by extension and common apathy, even those parts of our culture which think themselves indifferent to it.

We have been living through a period of prolific activity and non-ideas. I don't mean outright hostility to ideas, which might mean philosophical conflict, but the systematic conversion of ideas to negotiable coin in an era of adjustment. Unimpeded by anything to think about (we think loosely about everything), the enterprise is terrific. Since the mechanism of society apparently functions without our thinking, all we have to do is go through the motions. We scrutinize what we already know. Our world begins to look like our theater.

To wit: in the last presidential election many people deplored the absence of significant differences between the two parties; not that there weren't issues, only the issues, for all the television debate, weren't the real ones. No wonder the election may have been decided by faulty makeup. Whatever your own position, take one example: which of the two candidates was unalterably against nuclear testing? Take another: which of them was in favor of admitting Red China to the UN? I am not saying the nation would have approved a debate of that kind—or even endured it—only that the real issues weren't debated.

The withdrawal of ideological conflict from the public scene would be more alarming if it didn't appear that conflict was so profound we were better relieved of it.

I am not arguing that the theater is an adequate substitute for public discussion, or that its immediate function is to be a forum. The immediate function—as our two most didactic dramatists, Shaw and Brecht, have said—is to be entertaining. But it is a forum, like it or not, and if it is true to its nature it won't be relieved of conflict, whatever happens or does not happen (excepting the final failure) at Geneva, Capitol Hill, the smoke-filled rooms, or Madison Avenue.

Naturally, part of what is wrong with the theater has, as they say, always been wrong with the theater. The present impasse in America began long before the Cold War, which impacted the impasse by making it a state of mind. Can anything be done? Well, we have had remarkable traditions of social change in this country. The trouble with the changes taking place is that they seem less determined by people in the theater than part of the mechanism, like "the peacetime uses of atomic energy," a by-product of the fission. If this observation seems an ideological adjunct of the New Negativism, I am not trying to be cynical, the situation is. I shall discuss its more benign aspects in Chapter 3, but we may compound the cynicism by euphoria. We need not count our blessings with a radiometer to know that whatever is happening in the American theater it is nowhere near what our country's resources and good will should be able to make happen; some few things are on a scale likely to be self-defeating; a good deal of it—as with the growing consciousness of the need for regional theater—is going to become established along recognizable lines; and very little of it has anything to do with the art of theater. For within the new activity, our theater remains a stronghold of non-ideas.

Given conditions on Broadway and the flaccidity elsewhere, when serious people in the theater seek new ideas or want to check their own, they still have to go to Europe. Travel is broadening, sure, but in this instance it's discouraging to have to bypass a whole continent. You go, then, to Germany and you come back talking, say, about the Berliner Ensemble or the bounty of Hamburg, or the municipal theaters rebuilt before almost anything else after the war. Many of these buildings are as smart as the Manufacturer's Trust Bank on Fifth Avenue and equipped like the laboratories of Alamagordo. I was shown around one in Mannheim, filling a large city block, by a technical director with all the pride of an Undershaft displaying the salutary wonders of his munitions plant.

My tone here may suggest I am not all that starry-eyed about what goes on in some of those theaters; and indeed, we can be sentimental about what we don't have without realizing that under given historical circumstances what we don't have won't hurt us. So I won't seem unnecessarily cryptic, let me only point out that the emotions manipulated by Reinhardt and Jessner and other great German directors were the same emotions manipulated for other ends by Goebbels. I agree with those who say that no city can consider itself civilized without a repertory theater; but when we become zealous about the idea of repertory (about which I shall say more), we tend to forget that it may not be civilized with one. The fact that Germany had repertory theaters in almost every city doesn't explain the Nazis, but it didn't save the country from barbarism either.

Nevertheless, remembering those buildings and the amazing programs in some of them, you look around at home and wonder: if a town like Gelsenkirchen could have one of the finest theater buildings in Europe, why can't a city like Chicago or San Francisco, not to mention cities less cosmopolitan or the multitude of smaller communities defaced by new storefronts, supermarkets, and the same old atrocious civic architecture, or other communities suffering the same old changeless blight, have something comparable? The German recovery is not only antiquating a lot of our industrial plants, as the Common Market may antiquate our economics, but it is also embarrassing our city planning, or lack of it.

When you do make these comparisons, however, the answer is—after some desperate mental map-looking—what about Dallas? where Frank Lloyd Wright did build a theater finally (ambiguously operating at the moment). And anyhow, give us a chance, America is young, Tyrone Guthrie is here, and the Ford Foundation is on the horizon. And you are reminded that in Germany the loose confederacies of the nineteenth century had established, as in music, a solid theater tradition in every duchy. You speak of Vilar, and you are told, yes, France could have a "popular theater" because the House of Molière is three hundred years old. We are, so the defense goes, a country still sowing its cultural oats—tomorrow and tomorrow and tomorrow will be the day; while the silos are packed with surplus.

No, I do not accept the excuse that America is still coming of age. Pleading youth and paying the damages may have been all right up through the nineteenth century, even up through World War I—after which our art had available all the enlightening benefits of disenchantment and exile; but we are now almost two thirds of the way through the twentieth century, and the least we should have learned from the catastrophes behind us is that there is nothing automatic about progress. Ezra Pound—who thought Western drama a form of "second-rate intensity" to begin with—may have been premature about the failure of American culture long before he broadcast for Il Duce and was declared insane, but as regards the American theater he has always been up-to-date: to despoil our potential wealth is worse than *usura*.

Our fiction, our poetry, our painting have already reshaped literature and art everywhere, as have our films, because for a long time we had a monopoly. Yet, though American acting has given the eloquence of provincial muscle to the British theater and Sartre has adapted Arthur Miller's *The Crucible* for film, and though the Swedes produce the posthumous O'Neill because he reminds them of Strindberg, few who have been abroad and made an effort to see, and were honest about what they saw—instead of shifting the issue to the Soviet Union and saying, look, they have their theaters, but where is their freedom?—would concede the United States has anything special to show the world, as it does in painting and sculpture. And when one entertains, as I have done, visitors from abroad, East and West, who have been sent innocently through the United States by the State Department, they are reticent and evasive until they discover that you, too, are astounded by the dearth.

Not that they don't see theater; it's what they see that is depressing, and where they see it. You don't cultivate your garden to please your neighbor, but as the Cold War takes a cultural turn, it is ridiculous to defend the blight. I don't know if there's parity in science, but those who go abroad on international exchange in theater certainly get the better of the bargain.

Let me emphasize that I am concerned, primarily, with the art of theater, not our national image. But that is not irrelevant, because the theater is a social art. On the national scene, I distrust doing the right things, even the noble cultural things, for the wrong reasons. If we recognize that our economy is not unplanned, but planned to favor the few; or that inflation is a bogey to perpetuate a loaded "free market"; or that we give suffrage to all the manipulative illusions of private property we do not have (like mortgaged homes, time-plan washers, and cars with their pink slips in the bank); or profit motives that reap unemployment with abundance; or a fabulous system of production that, curiously, makes a moral shambles of the Good Life—we may improve our chances in the Cold War by correcting these things, but we ought to correct them primarily because they are bad.

Nor do I want to be told, all deficiencies aside, what a blessing it is to be doing what I am doing in America. Why shouldn't it be a blessing, given our amazing resources? What is outrageous is the waste, the spoliation, the deceit, the subversion of our best interests by throwing our wealth, our manpower, and our habits of mind into the great collective scandal of our time—

and the fact that we have all consented by election or default to the massive illusions that make further subversion possible.

Today's newspaper speaks of a "waste of millions" in our armed forces. Even if one is for maximum defense, we could support a national theater on that waste. Yet, if Congress is persuaded that spending and a strategically unbalanced budget is good for the economy, and the government accepts going into the red as part of the natural order, I have no confidence that the theater, like the invisible worm that flies in the night, will find its way into the budget, below the ICBMs and Polaris submarines—leaving aside the question as to what part of the job subsidy would really take care of, for government money often goes in the arts to those who don't need it, to those who do the same old things with it, or to what we can do better without. For example: the productions of *Our Town* and *Carousel* that misrepresent us abroad—while the Living Theater sells paintings to get there. (That my own theater has gone abroad for the United States no more changes this point than it corrupts us.)

When the question of subsidy arises, there are always those who claim the artist doesn't want government money because of the danger of political interference. I know some artists who hold this position, too (though I can hardly believe those particular ones are afraid). Moreover, when we went to perform at the Brussels World's Fair, we *did* run into political interference. Usually, however, when one hears the argument about intimidation by subsidy, it's not the artist worrying about independence, but the legislator worrying about money. When August Heckscher announced his intention to resign as President Kennedy's special consultant on the arts (indicating that all was not going well on the job), he said: "The majority in political life still tend to talk of culture as if they were telling an off-color story."

One of the two members of the House Committee inquiring into the performing arts appeared on a television program in San Francisco. Was he interested in theater? "Hell no! I'm interested in corn and hogs." What was he doing, then, with the committee in San Francisco? "Somebody has to keep an eye on that Democrat. You don't think we're gonna let him come out here and ask those questions by himself." He wasn't much impressed either by the remark that Communist countries had an advantage over us in cultural exchange, with the Moscow Art Theater and the Berliner Ensemble serving as emissaries through Europe. "We sent Louis Armstrong," he said, "but that didn't stop Khrushchev." What he did know, no matter what the issue, was that it should be taken care of "on the local level."

Well, in stranger ways than he knows, we agree.

For subsidy isn't the issue by a wide margin. As Katherine Anne Porter said in a recent interview: "Even Saint Teresa said 'I can pray better when I'm comfortable,' and she refused to wear her hair-cloth shirt or starve herself. I don't think living in cellars and starving is any better for an artist than it is for anybody else; the only thing is that sometimes the artist has to take it, because it is the only possible way of salvation, if you'll forgive that old-fashioned word. So I took it rather instinctively."

W. McNeil Lowry, head of the Ford Foundation's program in the arts, has been stressing a similar point in more secular terms: "At its most basic levels [art] is not about money, or facilities, or public acceptance; it is about the surge of artistic drive and moral determination . . . not about buildings, or labels, or numbers, but about the artist and the standards by which he pursues his art, alone or in ensemble with others who respect the craft." Surveying the arts in America, he observed that "somehow in our country businessmen or municipal and state officials appear to think art begins with real estate." All one can say is that it is natural enough for them, that's their business. But even in Mr. Lowry's informed appraisal of this situation, there is the leniency of the benefactor toward the presumptive artist, many of whom say the same things.

Talk to theater people and see how rarely you encounter anyone who diagnoses the problem very differently; who wants a theater because the private life is not enough and the secret life intolerable; who, whether in quiet desperation or turbulent desire, in blood knowledge or brainy instinct, in derision or joy, must have a quorum; who is obsessed with something that must out in public and for which only the language of the theater is adequate. And which—like Artaud's Plague—at some crucial point might never be accommodated in a municipal building, nor reconciled with the balanced budgets and predictable stability which foundation grants—as they go beyond the individual artist to an institution—must perforce assume. In a public form such as the theater, the problem abides: what do you do with that impulse in art which is inescapably nihilistic? And which tempts the very greatest theater artists to abandon security at some point in their careers to rediscover what their art is about? In science we have learned it is profitable to encourage that impulse, and we are beginning to provide for it in the solitary arts. But in the theater the problem becomes complicated long before the point of breakthrough. As the prospect of subsidy materializes, from whatever source, we may discover a lot of tenacity seeking support—but of no other art can it be said so widely that the nose you keep to the grindstone may no longer be an artist's nose.

Whatever the nuclear connections, our "population explosion" has produced what *Life* calls a "cultural explosion." Just as overcrowding may more sharply define loneliness, abundance may seem like desolation. "A people that left no other vestige than a few leaden pipes in the earth and a few iron rods on its surface," wrote de Tocqueville, "might have been more the master of nature than the Romans." Surely, the viaticum theory of cultural regeneration is suspect: provide a container and you may not get the thing to be contained. Put up a new theater building, and some veteran of summer stock may end up running it through the Samuel French catalogue. Like some of the urban renewal we have seen, we may regret it when it happens, for it then seems irremediable.

On a higher level, however, it is not merely buildings that are being talked about, but the character of the buildings and the formal properties of the stage. This is more like it. Yet in all the talk about new stages there is also something premature and misleading. I sometimes get the impression from panel discussions on the "New Theater" that if you thrust the stage out into the audience you are automatically back in the sacred grove.

Some of the people who are partisan for vegetable platforms or *le tréteau nu,* desiring superorganic relations between the actors and the audience, are also likely to be enthusiastic about the theater practice of Brecht. They seem to forget, however, that the Theater-am-Schiffbauerdamm in East Berlin is a hideous rococo affair, which Brecht refused to have modernized because (sentimental reasons aside) he felt the anachronism of the auditorium gave another perspective, even historical depth, to the austere ironies on stage. *Arturo Ui* took place, for instance, within a false proscenium lined on all sides with penny-arcade bulbs and painted with nudes, cowboys, Bavarian church steeples and, above in the center, a liaison of helmeted Prussians. Do you want to live in a world of gangsters, or do you want to change it? In the comic-opera theater, with its beaded chandelier, caryatid nymphs, fauna, gilt, cherubs, and the sculpted swag above the frame, that question of Ui's— asked in the epilogue as he stripped his Führer's mustache—had a bizarre potency.

Arthur Miller was probably right when he said at a conference on theater architecture that the stage as we know it is "a limitation to the playwright at least to the degree that it is no inspiration to him—he is dragging it on his back half the time." But there are people complaining about the need for new theaters who are overextended by the ones they have. And, speaking of the sacred grove, we should remember that the Attic *skene* grew out of the landscape with the elaboration of the dithyramb. The rite came first. By all means, let us project new theaters and stages with every shape imaginable. And if they must be built I'd personally prefer the dreams of a great architect to those of the theater person who always feels entitled to nudge his T square. (I know, I know—look what Frank Lloyd Wright *did* when he was given the chance! but as long as we're talking big about new buildings, we must really take the risk of letting the architect's dreams infect our dreams so that something really new may, indeed, come of it.) Even so, as I look at some of the admirable "Ideal Theaters" that have been designed, and contemplate the sorry habits of mind currently embodied on our stages, I fear we're likely to wind up with extraordinary theaters like the one in Mannheim, with cascading ramps, swivel seats, a louvred ceiling for pinpoint lighting, a jim-dandy convertible theater that can do anything and—as I was told when I was there —nobody who knows how to use it.

New stages *are* new ideas, and transformed space may, like painting or music, turn on an actor as a play itself can't. It is conceivable that new theaters will incite playwrights and directors to release and exceed themselves, but aside from whether or not many will be built in short order, the question remains whether our theater artists can break out at the challenge were it to materialize. They are surrounded by modern art in all forms, but despite Proust, Picasso, and Schoenberg, they might just as well be in the nineteenth century. Miller is close to the truth in saying, "All this will be resolved by someone writing a play [or conceiving a production] which creates, out of its own demands, a shape—and that shape then will begin to dominate and to create new plays. What would happen is that a play would almost literally burst out—people would discover that, if they tried to produce it correctly, they'd have to chop down the proscenium, or they'd be so disguising it that it would be imperative that it not be there."

Yet before we hack at the proscenium like the cherry orchard, we ought to have pounded it with our fists, exhausting ourselves in the task of knowing its limits, so that when it crumbles, we know what we've knocked down and whether we have anything genuine to erect in its place. When I say this, I have no particular stake in the proscenium arch—though I have no doubt that when we've come full circle through the trapezoids and turtlebacks and clam shapes, the turntables and treadmills, ogives, ovoids, the wombs of modern theater design, the proscenium—deferring both to the Peeping Tom and the rationalist mind in us—will assert its square prerogatives.

What one does have to understand is that the stage is by nature existential, since it entertains the art of crisis. And for anything essential to take place on a stage, there must be between it and a play some mortal exchange, each testing the other's limits. Whatever its shape, the stage is a worthy antagonist, like the Action painter's canvas. To fight it does not mean to abuse it; one respects his best enemies. The theater event, religious in source and however secularized, is an affair of honor. From which no participant—including the spectator—is exempt.

That most demonic of modern dramatists, Jean Genet, illustrates these ideas with the awful piety of perversion. No blueprint I have seen recreates the stage so vividly as the actors do in *The Screens,* as they literally help to draw a new theater. Genet's play *The Balcony* caters to our fantasies in a dazzling black comedy of appearance. In Scene 5, after a series of sadomasochistic ceremonies, Arthur the Executioner, dressed in a classical pimp's outfit, is chastized by Irma, the madam, for whipping one of the whores too hard. He replies that the banker, for whom that particular fantasy had been designed, "wants to see stripes on her back. So I stripe it." Arthur assures us he is conscientious about his work:

> ARTHUR: I tried a couple of times to draw marks on her back with purple paint, but it didn't work. The old guy inspects her when he arrives and insists I deliver her in good shape.
>
> IRMA: Paint? Who gave you permission?

She is outraged by the deception, the Grand Balcony having "a world-wide reputation" for the stringent realism of its fantasies, "the most artful, yet the most decent house of illusions. . .":

> ARTHUR (*shrugging his shoulders*): What's one illusion more or less! I thought I was doing the right thing. But don't worry. Now I whip, I flagellate, she screams, and he crawls.
>
> IRMA: In any case, be careful. The house is being watched.

At which point we are snared. Having conditioned us to a drama based on the reality of illusion, verisimilitude and true confession, a process supposed to make us forget we are in the theater, the proscenium now frames us. Bated for revelation, we are baited and exposed—as voyeurs. (A student of mine described, lest we claim immunity too quickly, how a relative of hers, who hated the play and wanted to walk out, gave his reasons in a detailed and graphic account of the action. She had never heard him be so eloquent or so concrete.) *The Balcony* may be, and has been, played in a theater without a proscenium, as almost any play can in some fashion. But Genet's first stage direction shows how precisely he had a conventional stage in mind: "On the right wall, a mirror, with a carved gilt frame, reflects an unmade bed which, if the room were arranged logically, would be in the first rows of the orchestra."

Both Miller and Genet have earned the right to question the constraining authority of the proscenium arch (Genet more than Miller); and Genet, as always, makes a principle of his contempt. Normally, however, when I hear directors, playwrights, critics, and even actors inveighing against the proscenium, as though they were Samson shaking the pillars of the Philistines, I wish they'd be put out of their misery by a weight dropped from the flies. Why does one object to a play like *Our Town?* Because, for all its craft, it is a play of tedious proscenium-stage emotions, most especially when the Stage Manager is standing in front of it, or when it is played in the round.

I have seen Shakespearean drama produced in both reasonable and overly mechanized facsimiles of the Elizabethan playhouse, and even with the advantage of a great text, a good deal of what I have seen struck me as utilitarian if not inconsequential. Things have apparently changed, but what used to be wrong at Stratford-on-the-Housatonic was not the windlasses and maze of trolleys on a rehabilitated proscenium stage, but that what was cranked on was mostly the sort of *House-and-Garden* Shakespeare, replete with Venetian blinds, that has been festivalized into moral blandness, *cum* whoopee and educational purpose—with the usual Renaissance lutenists, a midsummer night's dream at the suburbs. The most admirable of the festivals have the virtue of basic fidelity to the text and a clean unpretentious quality of performance. Sometimes there is the dividend of gusto. But what I generally miss, beneath the swashbuckle of great verse and the Kulchural pitch and momentousness, is the subterranean life of the plays (a *Macbeth,* for instance, clawing bloodily at "the insane root"), and instead of fidelity or capricious updating, an immediacy of conception, by which I know that that world on the stage is unavoidably mine.

The most impressive theater I have ever seen—from the standpoint of production more impressive than the Berliner Ensemble—is the Comic Opera in East Berlin, directed by Walter Felsenstein. I mention it only because our sincerest reaction to *more* is likely to be an arbitrary *less*. It has long been evident that the economies of the Brechtian stage are expensive economies, but at the Comic Opera there are no pretenses of economy. It illustrates superbly the idea Vakhtangov used to expound to his students: "Don't try to make technical discoveries. Take the things at your disposal, give them a new stage life." At the Comic Opera, maximum resources are used maximally. In a sector marked by crudity of taste and outright propaganda, the productions are impeccable. The whole stage acts in the most sophisticated cadences, or with marvelously detailed humor; even the mechanisms have meaning. And in Berlin, that city of crisis—classically schizoid, entrancing, and intolerable— what they seem to convey is the prayer for community in the deepest and purest sense. The Comic Opera doesn't seem so aggressive as the Ensemble, and it lacks its reformatory depth; but what it salvages from the crisis of Berlin is joy; not the euphoria of the American musical or the dark ecstasy of the Blue Angel, but benevolent joy, good will, good feeling—which shines past its politics and that appalling wall while never losing sight of its presence.

By contrast, I can think of productions which have transfigured the resources of impoverishment, also creating energy of despair. One, which has partially revolutionized modern playwriting, was performed for years in Paris at the Théâtre de la Huchette, which looks like a cubicle for Existentialist brainwashing, and smells it. I am referring to Ionesco's first play, *The Bald Soprano,* whose production there was orchestrated mayhem based on discreetly realistic character study. Banalities fall with the aptest solemnity, bells ring like *le mot juste,* the Maid is punctiliously dispatched with a hammer, and—since actors are costly—Mr. and Mrs. Smith and Mr. and Mrs. Martin are doggedly interchangeable.

At least in principle. The point is that more is more or less is more, depending on what fate places at your disposal, and more importantly the urgency of what you have to say. The thrust stage, which is the newest fashion in America, may have a natural genius for intimacy, but just as I've seen actors standing virtually on top of me who seemed as distant as the moon, so it is possible for real imagination to play against the grain of a stage's genius, to transform it by drawing and quartering it. One thing is sure: the thrust stage and all its gregarious variants, which we've known about for years, have no natural genius for supplying us another Shakespeare.

Frankly, I think there's too much fuss about the kind of stage on which Shakespeare is to be produced. Poel and Granville-Barker taught us to exhume the vital stuff from the trappings and tedium of meaningless overproduction; the replicas of Elizabethan playhouses have, by physical analogy, told us something of the architecture of the plays and their cinematic flow. Well and good, we've learned those lessons: speed, spatial form, and the poetry of scenic duration—we must never forget these. Yet you do not need literal pit, trestle, and loft for a sense of structure and superstructure. Tiring house and cellarage are concepts and images, not merely places; they exist in the rhythm of the plays, in the subtext, and can be evoked if need be on a flat floor behind a proscenium. This is not to say I wouldn't like to have an Elizabethan stage; I might. But one has what one has, and the crux is whether you are there, truepenny—for me, as I have declared, the stage is a sort of battleground, a space to be struggled with, or violated, in Holy War; the prize, a vision. The text is the source of vision, but for us today the Great Chain of Being hangs by the infinitely extended and curving thread of relativity. As the poets used to say of language, we must wrench the stage into meaning. If I were producing Shakespeare today at the Globe itself, the problem would still be to make the text survive the mortal, essential, ineliminable, and Shakespearean conflict between what you think is there and what is really there—to move past the scaffolding to "the thing itself."

Which is transfixed in crisis. The theater is the Public Art of Crisis. Whatever its conventions, it is meant to be an open form—a mystery without secrets and, except as it shares the stage fright of modern art, without security measures. I think of the dramatist as a specialist in danger, who confronts it where it is minimized or evaded by others. The actor serves by being an expert in the mimicry of conflict, most particularly by self-exposure; and the director, if he is fulfilling his proper function, is a Socratic gadfly, questioning the text, the actor, and the stage itself, referring them all back, and himself, to the concrete evidence of the world. Epidaurus or Cherry Lane, *en plein air* or *rive gauche,* the hieratic sandalwood of the Noh or the rough boards of an obscure loft—the real momentousness of a play depends on what is seen, and why, what is evaded and what is plumbed, the risks taken and the commitment made, the willingness to see a text as if for the first time or with the rigor of ancient wonder, the spirit of the ensemble—and the Necessary Angel, the Imagination.

I shall say a good deal more about the craft of theater as I study the productions which will be the main focus—a pretext for the larger issues—of the second part of this book, as well as aspects of the development of my own theater—a syndrome of all the possibilities and dangers I have alluded to. Indeed, one of the chief perturbations of the twentieth century has to do with the conversion of energy to craft—the point at which art and science meet and by various reversible equations, some perfectly overwhelming in their results, make craft itself a mode of energy. In art, we are cultists of departure, devotees of process—the waiting, the doing, the going, the means. Technicians of technique. Think of Hemingway's "sequence of motion and fact"; Eliot's "objective correlative"; Kandinsky's "image" and Stanislavski's "Method"; Zen, jazz, and organic art; improvisation—the flight of the Bird and the words working among themselves, the peregrinations of Leopold Bloom and the short formidable life of drip and blob; the powerfully exposed architecture of skin and bones.

I am speaking of the best that has been thought and said. In our world of relative value, wherever the end justifies the means, we are usually with the worst, in the realm of the intolerable, with Camus' murderers in judges' robes. To the extent the means absolutely justify the end—in the Joycean Epiphany or the physicist's cloud chamber, in the Actors Studio or in *musique concrète,* in the New Wave or the old *Angst*—we are violated by order of another kind, the tyranny of "the intense inane." Our fear is the loss of energy *in* our love of craft, which is a making and a beguiling, a craftiness. One might say the Cold War is the status quo of craftiness brought on, after two promiscuous outbursts of energy in this century, by strategy and counterstrategy, an affair of technique *against* technique, in everything from guided missiles to balancing budgets and the lyric poem. The question is, what will come of this mutual deterrence: continued stalemate? progress? or extinction?

Even as the question became most intense, it seemed we were moving backward through some neoclassical prelude to a renaissance when, along with Frost's medal and Casals' invitation to the White House, Arthur Miller was restored to political grace and Shakespeare performed before a Chief Executive whose wife had shown herself to be a kind of good Queen Anne. Mr. Kennedy's monument will be a cultural center, but his assassination, and its unresolved ambiguities, seemed torn from the shrouded violence on which we rest in peace; and which still makes us fear that our *Annus Mirabilis* is liable to be an Apocalypse—at the end of the fox hunt a real beast in a real jungle.

HURRY UP PLEASE IT'S TIME!

Since we first heard that line from an expatriate American in demotic British, we have suspected the jig is up. In the days when T. S. Eliot, born on Huck Finn's river, was experimenting with theater and writing his *Notes toward a Definition of Culture,* intellectuals worried much about the Void, The Waste Land, nerve failure, rats' feet over broken glass in the cellar, the "dissociation of sensibility"—and thought wistfully about some unifying tradition with a centripetal imagery, an imaginative and conceptual mousetrap.

One must remember that when Eliot began writing his offbeat, deadpan satiric verse, he was the slightly Dadaish and dandy spokesman of a poetic revolution and, give and take a little snobbery and anti-Semitism, even the social liberals admired him. For himself—looking for a way, as he said of Joyce, "of controlling, of ordering, of giving shape and significance to the immense panorama of futility and anarchy which is contemporary history" —Eliot moved one inevitable day over the far side of protest to Little Gidding, proclaiming himself an Anglican in religion, a Royalist in politics, and a Classicist in literature. The liberals, humanists, skeptics, know-nothings, and agnostics he left behind fetched about as they could for panaceas, platforms, symbols, ideologies, myth, Hip, *satori,* and relative peace of mind.

Some of them went into our theater, and found it.

Urgency and *Angst,* however, are still the terminal conditions of real artistic life in America, as they are elsewhere—especially as elsewhere grows increasingly near at hand. We used to think that communication would solve all the world's problems; now we know it may cause some of them. How sad to discover, for instance, that foreign students, after four years in American colleges, go away hating us for somewhat better reasons. As the world grows smaller and smaller, it also looms woefully large, so that while one of our recent Nobel-prize winners, an expert on atomic particles, assures us we'll never see the end, we see all too clearly the scaly dragon of Communist China raising its sullen head; and we know, I fear, precisely what it wants. I think of Beckett's tramp, ruthless for recognition: "You're sure you saw me, you won't come and tell me tomorrow that you never saw me." Unfortunately, we are not so innocent as the little messenger from Godot and, unlike the tramp, Peking doesn't seem to suffer from lapses in memory. As Yvor Winters writes in another context: "Great planes are waiting in the yard. . . ."

Where urgency and *Angst* don't exist, or are handy-packed into platitude, you are dealing with good intentions, minor art, or just plain *kitsch*—which is mostly the case in the American theater. Whereas in poetry, a revolution had indeed taken place from the twenties through the forties (a revolution to which even its current enemies defer, having learned from it), the theater went through a partial metamorphosis (what has been called a "missing revolution") with the Provincetown and the Little Theater Movement; and after the social passion of the thirties, generally settled back to its customary brainless depression.

If I am mispresenting some of it, I am not misrepresenting much. In 1929, someone named Velona Pilcher wrote wisely in *Theatre Arts:* "I don't think it goes too far to declare that a play is no concern of a living playgoer, play-reader, producer, or player unless somewhere within it, or within the art that shall present it, there moves the reflection of these things:

Four years of World War
Frazer's *Golden Bough*
Epstein's bronze Madonna
The Prose of D. H. Lawrence
The Thought, as far as it could reach, of *Back to Methuselah*
The Mask of Gordon Craig
Einstein and the scientists
The Union of Socialist Soviet Republics
The dramatic dancing of the Diaghilev Company
The Outbreak of Peace."

To this day some of these things aren't adequately reflected in our theater, not to mention the outbreak of the second world war, the gravitational-field theory, the approach to a genetic code, the work of the Berliner Ensemble, the baked meats of Belsen, Pollock's *Totem #1,* Hiroshima, the films of Antonioni (not to mention Eisenstein), the Plague of Artaud, serialist music, and all the fractures and tensions of art brought on by our cormorant Cold War.

Little of what goes on in the American theater, for all the occasional attention to Vital Issues, seems in touch with anything that really counts, and I don't mean didactically in touch, but rhythmically, viscerally, in the bone structure, where anxiety eats like strontium 90. The sense of urgency of which I speak has many sources in philosophical and social history, but it has its American locus now at the launching pad at Cape Kennedy, where those great phallic capsules of a nation's energy, looking like Moby-Dick, are sent deterrently into the wild blue.

What do you do about the Bomb? All questions coagulate in that.

Forget it? Leave it to the politicians? Not by a long shot—in art, at the last desperate limit, it becomes a technical matter again. And technique—as Falstaff says of instinct—is a great matter. "When heroism returned to our age," wrote Yeats in his introduction to *Certain Noble Plays of Japan,* "it bore with it as its first gift technical sincerity." Thus, the final considerations of this book will be technical; that is, directed to the art of theater itself, the making, the producing, the acting out, and the ideas behind it all, from the force that through the green fuse drives the flower to the moral choice that trammels up the consequence. Technique to demoralize the technicians, the oracular gift. Would there were a soothsayer around, however, who could convert the Bomb, like the war in *Cymbeline,* to a "sanguine star," promising peace and plenty. That may not be the artist's function, but whatever his function, the "crooked smokes" of his devotion seem to climb up his own nostrils instead of rising from blest altars to laud the gods. "Sing Praise, sing Praise, sing Praise, sing Praises out,/Unto our King sing Praise seraphickwise," wrote Edward Taylor, the best of our Puritan poets. But, as they say in the more savage parts of the Old Testament, in these days there are no kings and even the best of gods are suspect gods.

As for the one God, says Nietzsche, He is dead!—and we have listened, the best of us—in Kafka, in Joyce, in Mann, in Duchamp, in Hemingway, in Faulkner, in Action painting, in atonal music, in O'Neill, in the unreconstructed Eliot, in everything from Tennessee Williams to assemblage—to the rivers flowing down to the urinals.

As we take the stage, desiring the rough magic of Prospero, we wonder: Shall the earth inherit itself? When Lawrence speaks of America being one day as beautiful in actuality as it was in Cooper's Leatherstocking novels, he adds that will be "when the factories have fallen down again." And now we have reached the epoch where the fall of factories seems more than an outside possibility, we may even conjecture that there is in our budgeted reverence of the Bomb a yearning as well as a horror—as though the fear of destruction is the incestuous partner of our desire for the soil to reclaim America again. Where finally shall that huge Redstone phallus fall when it takes off into the atmosphere? Back to the old earth whose grass will fill the cracks of cities and maybe bury us in a way that Khrushchev didn't imagine, as the jungles and rainforests have submerged the civilizations of Maya?

For some young artists there is wish-fulfillment in what we trust is only a fantasy. God is dead! says Nietzsche—and to look at their canvases or their sculpture, you feel them celebrating the triumph of Vegetation. When, as I do, you feel like punching them in the face on behalf of civilization, you are stopped by the fact that such art—the collage, the frottage, the sound blocks, the combine-painting, the Happenings, the whole iconography of feces, fetus, and demolition—is among the most formidable we have. The arms of Venus are mutilated still.

But in the American theater you'd barely know it, except by default.

A San Francisco columnist, reading the graffiti on a toilet wall, came back with an answer: Nietzsche is dead! says God. That may put Nietzsche in his place, but it doesn't relieve the tension, and it's a loss in either case. Result: many of us are still worrying about the Void and still fetching. But just as the metropolitan explosion—that civic extension of ontological *Angst*—has led to suburban conformity and "unilateral dedensification," so a good many Alienated Men have become—from Madison Avenue to the President's cabinet, from the CIO to the AEC—Organization Men, some by choice, some without becoming aware of it, some despite themselves, and some, like Mann's Aschenbach yielding up his discipline to the discipline of the abyss, for sheer oceanic release.

Discussions of the waning of dramatic art invariably come back to the absence in our time of any unifying mythology, the lack of a Ur-form of social aspiration. However, when he is charged with being at loose ends and exhorted to reflect what is harmonious in our culture, the artist is likely to say, which culture? Depending on where you look, we *have* our centripetal imagery, and we are repelled by its implications: where there is unity today, there is likely to be Levittown and the Lonely Crowd—the totalitarianism of the mediocre, half-educated and uncommitted. To which we are all committed more than we may care to be.

In her book *The Origins of Totalitarianism,* Hannah Arendt makes an important distinction: "A fundamental difference between modern dictatorships and all other tyrannies of the past is that terror is no longer used as a means to exterminate and frighten opponents, but as an instrument to rule masses of people who are perfectly obedient." Amidst the glut of energy and prodigal motion, the atomic-powered windlasses and assays of bias, the task of all the arts is to protect the residual will against the tyranny of multiplicity. With the Cold War, political witch-hunting, mass-produced and mass-publicized violence, wire-tapping, prefixless telephones, hidden persuaders, security checks, and committees on committees (following the release of the U-2 pilot, the Senate Foreign Relations Committee favored "establishing a new watchdog committee to oversee CIA"), the sheer trial of making choices and knowing whom to trust (think only of buying a soap, say, in a super-market, where even the "specials" abound)—*what words are adequate? what form? what mode of drama?* "Tangled with earth all ways, we move," writes Janet Lewis, in a small but gracious voice overheard in a garden. For the rest, our mind closes itself off against the horrible dream of truth, if it is a dream. Our instinct is to behave like Desdemona after she is incredibly assaulted by Othello as a whore. When Emilia asks how she feels, she replies: "Faith, half asleep."

And so are we all in our common whoredom, pacified by dread. If somehow you refuse to be pacified, to whom do you complain? You write a letter to your congressman, you get back a form. They tell me my vote counts, and I suppose it does; but as I pull the levers in the privacy of the cloaked booth, often on propositions and people I know nothing about—not through lack of responsibility but the impossibility of keeping up with it all—I don't *feel* it counts, and that's what counts in art. Nature imitates art; things do become Kafkesque. King David was punished by Jehovah for numbering the people; that is, for initiating the bureaucratic device of the census. Think, however, of the unimaginable bureaucracy of modern life, the innumerable ways in which we have all become records, punches on electronic cards, documents, briefs, credit accounts. What would become of us alas! if, as in Pirandello's *Right You Are, If You Think You Are!* the files, all of them, disappeared or burned? What if they don't? Can we survive the conspiracy of system, maintained by ourselves against ourselves in our own interest? Will our credit run out?

In the realm of *Realpolitik,* the power balance has led one theorist to revive an analogy between human behavior and animal behavior, to this effect: "While species that lack the weapons to do serious injury may fight all-out, those that have absolute weapons, like the rattlesnakes, confine their fighting within ritualistic limits." The ritual balance of power, the maintenance of ambiguity in perilous tension, has also been one of the major preoccupations of art in the twentieth century. Art has created its own absolute weapons and taken, as I have indicated, its own security measures. They, too, may be self-destructive. In my own theater, under the ritual influence of Artaud, we have experimented with a Theater of Cruelty—not to its hypnotic limit, but so much so that we are now saying with Hamlet before he entered the closet of Gertrude: "Let me be cruel, not unnatural."

To know whether you are unnatural, and if so how to keep from being so is another matter. If none of this seems to be a problem in the American theater at large, the more shame to it; for while it may not be satisfactory to live—as Freud said we must learn to live—in tension and doubt, it is less satisfactory, and morally reprehensible, to turn your back. And just plain ignorant to think you can do that with impunity. As the nuclear scientists have recently explained, those fittest to survive the fallout are insects.

Throughout the book, I shall be using the theater as an image of the Cold War and the Cold War as an image of the theater. I have learned from experience that to the degree politics is immobilized by the disease and obscurantism of the Cold War, the theater is liable, holding its mirror up to nature, to become addicted to what it sees in the mirror; or to be demoralized into caution, looking away from the mirror altogether, either because it's terrifying or because it pays. At its worst, the time-serving nature of the form may dwindle into tedium and cowardice. And the theater, one of the most ennobling forms ever imagined, takes part in the widespread conspiracy against the human.

In view of what I've said, don't ask me what conspiracy. If you don't know it, that's it. We are all responsible. When I call for a revolution in the theater, it is this conspiracy which is the real enemy. And though I shall be taking particular aim and dealing with practical objectives, the revolution I am after is a restoration: to reconfirm for those with whom I work, and others, an idea of what the theater might be—as I have suggested, a most ancient and sacred idea, facing facts but not bullied by them.

Beginning with the next chapter, I shall talk more specifically about the condition of theater in America and about those I want to reach. And I shall name names. But it was in this spirit—concerned with what we were doing and where we were going—that I wrote my own company from Europe several years ago:

"As regards our repertoire, we must be less concessive too. My own feeling is that we must go way, way out, further than we have gone with our most unorthodox plays; risk is our medium, and we must find a way of looking at our plays that will express, if nothing else, the strategic relativism of a company of fairly well-educated Americans in the Year of the Bomb, 1960ff.

"This does not mean looking for *a* cause or even *causes,* but rather continual searching of the text for its deepest subjective possibilities and its furthest objective references to the flux about us. It means a more vigorous alliance with the humane against all forms of dehumanization; and lest my misanthropy swallow too bitter a pill of positive thinking, we must, if necessary, be more cruelly humane as well, never relinquishing the theater's power to criticize, bitch, exhort, shock, cajole, protest, and pray. To do this we may think ourselves more libertine with our texts than ever before, but our purpose will be to fill the stage with all of ourselves, and all we are capable of imagining; deepening, extending, with all the authority and technique at our command, for the theater, in an age of dossiers, visas, and IBM cards, is one of the last sacraments of the individual's right to a public *identity*."

I don't want to push false analogies of terror, but as the two major powers bestride the world like Colossi, there are various ways—despite the Cold War, perhaps the cause of it—in which they look increasingly alike. Years ago, André Gide returned from a trip to the Soviet Union, gave up the Party, and told us what was happening: "I see already a new bourgeoisie developing in the Soviet Union from these untried masses, with exactly the same faults and vices as ours." The revolution of the proletariat has now produced an age of managers. The profit motive has begun to subvert the collective. The need to train a younger generation so they might understand the theories of Marx and Lenin, or so they might cope with scientific textbooks in the interest of the arms race and Sputnik, makes it possible for this same younger generation to read what is not officially approved.

That may yet bear fruit. Meanwhile, the Soviet theater, once the most experimental in the world, is not—under the aegis of Socialist Realism—what it once was. And the summary portent of this decline, just before World War II, was a speech made by Vsevelod Meyerhold, perhaps the greatest, surely the most courageous director of our century. The speech followed the capitulation to Stalinism of practically every major Soviet director, including Stanislavski, who redeemed himself by befriending the man whose work he personally detested, when the Party liquidated Meyerhold's "hostile" theater.

Meyerhold, who had been accused of making formal experiment an end in itself, spoke to the First All-Union Congress of Soviet theater directors in June 1939, after a keynote address by Vishinsky, who staged the Moscow trials. What Meyerhold said then led to his arrest and disappearance, the hideous murder of his wife, and the extirpation of his name from the Soviet encyclopedia, one of those erasures from history that have become a sign of the twentieth century's perverse effort to put history into servitude: "In my heart, I consider what is now taking place in our theaters frightful and pitiful. And I do not know what it is—antiformalism, realism, naturalism, or any other 'ism.' But I do know that it is untalented and bad. The pitiful and wretched thing that pretends to the title of socialist realism has nothing in common with art.

"But the theater is art! And without art, there is no theater! Go visiting the theaters of Moscow. Look at their drab and boring presentations that resemble one another and are each worse than the others. It is now difficult to distinguish the creative style of the Maly Theater from that of the Vakhtangov, the Kamerny, or the Moscow Art Theater. Recently creative ideas poured from them. People in the arts searched, erred, and frequently stumbled and turned aside, but they really created—sometimes badly and sometimes splendidly. Where once there were the best theaters of the world, now—by your leave—everything is gloomily well-regulated, averagely arithmetical, stupefying, and murderous in its lack of talent. Is that your aim? If it is—oh! —you have done something monstrous! . . . In hunting formalism, you have eliminated art."*

Stalin's death, material growth since the end of the war, and changes in the economy have begun to open doors and loosen tongues in the Soviet Union; and there are indications not only that new voices are being raised but that disgraced old ones are being heard again. A couple of years ago, in a conversation with the director of the Bolshoi, I asked about Meyerhold. His answer was abrupt: "He was part of our history." Very recently, when he was visiting San Francisco, the director of the Moscow Theater of Satire admitted proudly to having been a student of Meyerhold. When I asked him what he

* For an account of this period and Meyerhold's speech, see Nicholai A. Gorchakov, *The Theater in Soviet Russia* (New York, 1957), pp. 355–65.

was doing during the period of Meyerhold's disrepute (that was my euphemism), he said he was in disrepute too. There is an abyss there to which we might feel more superior if, during the same time, our theater had been conspicuous for its courage.

Though, as I said, I don't want to stretch the analogy of terror, Meyerhold's speech defines the sensation I have when I review the state of the American theater before, during, and after the war, and which could never lay claim to having been either so preëminent or so experimental. Theater in America is not so much a reflection of the Cold War as one of its worse symptoms, having abdicated to other arts the task of dealing with the paralysis that has beset the world. Look at the "boring presentations that resemble one another and are each worse than the others," drabber for the opulent vacancy: "gloomily well-regulated, averagely arithmetical, stupefying and murderous in its lack of talent." In America, lack of talent is perhaps not the point; one might better speak of the murder of talent suffering from lack of principle or misguided by people who should know better and not yield up the truth for which—in our more fortunate circumstances—we need not suffer Meyerhold's fate: "But the theater is art! And without art, there is no theater!"

Let me name one name now, one I respect: William Gibson. He is the first to understand the limitations of his plays, and his book *The Seesaw Log* is a moving document, an autobiography of his experience during the production of his first play on Broadway. Gibson, who is also a poet and novelist, describes how compromise after compromise led to a seizure of "irresponsible malcontentism" and finally to utter resignation: "I had crossed the line: I was no longer in my inner world of writing, where the logic was that of a lifetime, but in the outer world of show business, where the logic was only that of this production, evolved to meet the emergencies of our situation . . . if I could not have my logic, it was a matter of relative indifference to me which of the other logics we followed."

With the success of his play, he thought himself forced to grant the collective intelligence of a monster he found reprehensible by all other standards, and which almost drove him from the theater entirely. Though he has capitulated to the monster a second time, he concluded and still appears to believe what he wrote then: "One might say many enthusiastic and truthful things about the rewards of the professional theater, such as the money, and the comradeship, and the money, and the self-espials, and the money, but to me they all lay in the arms of the truth that the theater, in this country, in this decade, was primarily a place not in which to be serious, but in which to be likeable; and it behooved each of us in it to do careful bookkeeping on his soul, lest it grow, like a dyer's hand, subdued to what it works in."

No doubt he is right. But if I am to follow his advice and do careful bookkeeping on my soul, I shall have to conclude, accepting his premises and conclusions both, that I may not have been serious these last ten years; concluding that, then I must have been deluding myself all the time because, for better or worse, I have been working under the impression that, if nothing else, I have been serious, and that one must in fact be serious if he is not to see the thorough stain of the dyer's hand. Dyed one may be, in some part—for the theater is an impossible art even away from New York, its impossibility being in its corporate bones—but there is a special and obdurate kind of seriousness which is an espial of its own: to carry on the fight may mean creating, in every way possible, your own terms; to allow for self-denial of all kinds; to anticipate small audiences as you strive for large; to invite the hostility of people outside the theater and, most distressingly, those who work in it with you.

Gibson did his sincere best to see what he had seen, but nothing does more harm to the American theater than when a serious man sees its nature and possibility in the illusory terms of Broadway.

I am one of those who believes some of what he reads in the history books and some of what he is taught in school. When I was a student in courses like The Development of Dramatic Art, they used to tell me that there was great theater on the south side of the Thames, and that most of the renowned theaters of the world—the Théâtre Libre, the Freie Buhne, the Abbey, the Vieux Colombier, the Provincetown, were developed by zealous amateurs. I believed them. I still believe them. Only I learned long ago that some of them didn't really believe it themselves, my teachers. In the same way, I have always felt that one ought to get his principles from his vocation, not impose them on his vocation, the point being that what one does in the theater ought to be determined first by the nature of theater itself—not the spurious nature Gibson describes, but the natural consequences of the form as form, and by the values of the drama whose truths outlast the generations.

This is one of the ways in which I shall be using the plays to which I make reference in this book. I have lain in the soil and criticized the worm, and the worm has had a few things to tell me which I should like to report. I see no reason why I should turn to Mr. Gibson's limited experience, or to Mr. Merrick (who once took time from his myriad affairs to give us unsolicited advice), or to Mr. Kerr, or the Bureau of Labor Statistics, or John Chapman (imagine! the leading newspaper in San Francisco reprints *his* reviews), ANTA, or even the American Educational Theatre Association, though I respect these gentlemen and institutions more or less. If the play is the thing—and I don't believe it is, but we shall come to that—then it is to the play we ought to look for our principles, and to the play which one holds to be good and true and beautiful.

I realize that some of the plays to which I refer later in the book will be held questionable by many people working in and around theaters, and elsewhere, but my choice to do them comes from the feeling that they resemble those plays everybody defers to in time, and that are taught in all the courses in The Development of Dramatic Art.

If I were looking for advice on how to run a theater, I should go to Ibsen and Shaw and Shakespeare and Aristophanes first of all, to Aristotle, who really *saw* what was going on, and to the wisdom that surrounds the theater in other art forms and social and philosophical disciplines. I think there is a world of difference between the Socratic "Know thyself" and the Emersonian "Trust thyself"—but whatever the difference it is not so great as that between either of these thinkers and the dicta "Trust the audience" or "Trust the box office" or "Trust the reviewers" or "Trust my experience because I've been in the theater forty years, man and boy." When I encounter that last patronizing voice I am tempted to do what Stavrogin did to the general who said nobody tweaks his nose; or to feel as various heretics of the theater have felt in the past, that it ought to be blown up for the sake of starting all over again.

Among people I know, it is usually the idealists who are the most toughminded and down-to-earth. That is a matter of fact. It is your bread-and-butter realist who usually seems out of this world.

I think one of the best things a person in the theater can do today is to deal with it as though Broadway, say, never existed. But this is a book and not a theater, and thus—in my next chapter— I shall try to tell why.

There is a point at which you can, finally, only "Go to your bosom,/Knock there, and ask your heart what it doth know. . . ." At the same time, I am speaking as one who has a certain impatience with those who claim purity for themselves against this most contaminating of all forms, who talk of integrity but refuse to risk it, and also with those who don't go to the theater because they or their intellectual friends don't think it worthy. The idea of compromise is a tricky affair in the theater, since the form is by its nature compromised in ways that no other form is. So when I hear people claiming a purity for themselves that they could never exercise were they running a government or a theater, I am inclined to say what Shaw once said to a Labour candidate named Joseph Burgess who, refusing to compromise on a particular issue, lost his seat in Parliament: "When I think of my own unfortunate character, smirched in compromise, rotted with opportunism, mildewed by expediency—dragged through the mud of borough council and Battersea elections, stretched out of shape by wire-pulling, putrified by permeation, worn out by 25 years pushing to gain an inch here, or straining to stem a backrush, I do think Joe might have put up with just a speck or two on those white robes of his for the sake of the millions of poor devils who cannot afford any character at all because they have no friend in Parliament. Oh, these moral dandies, these spiritual toffs. . . . Who is Joe, that he should not risk his soul occasionally like the rest of us?"

Part of the eternal fascination of the theater is the way in which it puts the soul to the test, both in the play and among the people who work on it, not to mention the audience. And though I shall be using my own theater, The Actor's Workshop of San Francisco, for the purposes I have mentioned —as documentation, not as the chief subject of this book—I do not mean to claim for it any unquestionable accomplishment or exemplary behavior, for it is a work in progress, in need of revision. What I am saying would be no less true—even more so if The Workshop went out of existence tomorrow.

The Workshop is not exempt from my general charge against the American theater. Indeed, we have not been able to proceed as though Broadway never existed. That was a circumstance of our birth, when we didn't know any better. We have suffered, too, from lack of faith in our own best convictions; and I can say without qualification (there are those in The Workshop who would disagree) that wherever we have acquiesced we have failed ourselves and our mission, our responsibility to the American theater. I do not mean mere expediency, but the kind of choice where you suspect, but are not certain, that one thing is better than another. I think the only exoneration of The Workshop as a theater is that it has had the constant passion in an impossible time to do the right thing wherever it has surely known what the right thing is to do. Should that passion cease, it would make very little difference if it existed or not.

No medium imposes on those who work in it—those in particular who direct or try to direct its destiny—more possibility of errors in judgment. We have made them, more than I care to remember—our chief distinction being, perhaps, that we have made them while taking risks that the merely self-deluded and the wholly compromised would never dream of taking, or the pristine would evade in shoring up their purity against its potential ruin. And because we can feel restive about not having, at various times, risked enough. As I wrote the company in that same letter, the tangible achievements of The Workshop are these: "to have persisted through unwillingness to believe in it, outside and, more harmfully, inside; to have wrenched diversity by the scruff of the neck and made it into a reasonable facsimile of unity; to have made inferiority on some occasions reach beyond itself; to have made it possible to be guilty about compromise and, as a result, to compromise less."

One other thing, the that-without-which: to keep in the mind's eye and in practice the idea of *sacrifice*.

How wonderfully the pioneers talked about that! Lugné-Poë, for instance, wrote years ago that the idea must be dinned into people who work in the theater, which "should belong to those who love it for its own sake, the true amateurs." He added: "The amateurs: how much good they can stir up! The great mistake is to believe that any real man of the theater, author or actor, is ever a professional. The miracle which will transform the theater in France and elsewhere will take place among the amateurs and nowhere else. There can be no doubt that from the very day the 'professionals' control the stage, the theater is destined either to go astray or become entirely bankrupt."

I shall be querulous with a good deal in this book, but I have no quarrel with that. Need I add that in approving of the amateur neither of us is against money?

2

SUBTLE: *'Sdeath, and Mammon*
Must not be troubled.
FACE: *Mammon! In no case.*
SUBTLE: *What shall we do then?*
FACE: *Think: you must be sudden.*

—Ben Jonson, *The Alchemist*

Who killed the bright-headed bird?
You did, you son of a bitch.

—Kenneth Rexroth, *Thou Shalt Not Kill*

THE IRON CURTAIN

I have said this would not be a palace revolution because there is no palace in the American theater.

In France there might be a palace revolution because there is the institution of the Comédie Française. When I was in Paris a few years ago, there was an article in the Comédie in the same edition of the hebdomedary *L'Express* that contained Sartre's epitaph on Camus. The article began: *"Le Théâtre-Français traverse une crise. Une de plus."* We can well envy a country— whatever its political troubles—which can enjoy such a crisis; it's a grand habit. Far be it from me to complain about the Comédie; the French complain enough. Though it is forever in danger of becoming a museum, the Comédie is still the place to hear the full trained diapason of the classical rhetoric, the ethical valor of voice, and to see the realism of Molière *presented* realistically. But the paramount value of the Comédie is that it exists. There. To be attacked.

One discovers on looking into the traditions of the French theater that certain of its revolutionists—some of the most *avant-garde*—begin their careers by vilifying the Comédie and end up directing it; or like Jean Vilar, running a competitive national theater on other principles. Their aim: like Mallarmé, to purify the language of the tribe; like Copeau, to scourge the stage of its corruption and do reverence to the bare boards; like De Gaulle, to recover *gloire* by driving the Republic back to its fundamental truths. These truths are never self-evident, they have always to be renewed. Sometimes the means are charismatic and a little tyrannous, and the dialectic may not be confined to the theater alone.

By now, reform is traditional in the French theater as in French politics: from Robespierre's summons to the poets to commemorate the Revolution, through the pitched battles between the old guard and the new over Hugo's *Hernani,* to the riot in 1896 over Jarry's *Ubu Roi,* an assault on the French bourgeois as savage, for all its farce, as Marx's *Civil War in France.* "Ah," rhapsodized one spectator, "but the première of *Ubu Roi* was a grand evening, and historic indeed. Since then literature, art, politics have been saturated with Ubu; the scent of Ubu is everywhere; one fights for Ubu." Ubu, the big turd, is still being fought for, but bids fair in the age of deodorants— winning the day everywhere from Düsseldorf to Dallas—to take over the boulevards. Ionesco's *Rhinoceros,* written in the tradition, made it to Broadway after having been comfortably situated at one of the national theaters.

There was a relation between the reported crisis at the Comédie and the one in Algeria—a cultural stasis causing atrophy in one and terror in the other, about which the Algerian-born Camus, inspired voice of the Resistance, had been silent unto death. Renewal may be costly or ghastly, a *ratonnade,* but institutions can be purified if they exist and if, fundamentally, they have meaning. In a famous open letter urging Copeau to "spend no more time kissing the earth or laying foundations" and to accept the leadership of the Comédie as his destiny, Granville-Barker tells of being present at a performance when the spectators started booing the actors for "heaven knows what administrative misdemeanor. . . . But a gentleman rose in his stall and, facing the brawlers, called out, *'Respect pour la Comédie'*; and the noise soon died down." It's the intensity of that respect that stirs up the noise in every generation, as it did in the recent crisis.

To contend with it, André Malraux—novelist, art historian, hero of the Spanish Civil War, as of the Resistance, now minister of culture and honored guest of the White House—divided Gaul into two parts. He left the right bank Salle Richelieu in conventional hands and turned the left bank Odéon (which Henry James once called "that remote and unfriended establishment") over to Jean-Louis Barrault, another descendant of Ubu, who is also devoted to the Catholic Claudel and the cynic Anouilh, and whose wife is the most enchanting actress of French bourgeois comedy.

These complications suggest the odd, but rich, cross-fertilization of the French theater, as does the fact that another house was turned over to Jean Vilar to be used for a "theater of insolence"—though Vilar's lack of sympathy for the De Gaulle regime was manifest. Moreover, angry at the Comédie for producing too much Feydeau and neglecting Racine, Malraux had also been planning to give a theater to Camus for the production of French and Spanish classics. Whatever it is, then, at any moment in history, the Comédie is a constant measure of departure, idiosyncrasy, experiment, and quackery, a locus for worship and animosity, like Paris itself, to which we have no equivalent.

Perhaps it's better that way. (Malraux's revisionism seems to have made a bourgeois of Barrault, and Vilar has since resigned from the TNP.) Yet I doubt it. I don't mean my remarks on the Comédie to be mistaken as merely francophile. No culture—as we see in every French dramatist from Jarry to Billetdoux—can be so paralyzingly bourgeois as the French. Our Babbitt is a beatnik, a paragon of disaffiliation, compared to Flaubert's Monsieur Homais. Nor do I mean to be sentimental and simplistic about a world we never made and only contemptuous of the one we did. The French have their boulevards as we have Broadway, though—as we have seen—there is a dynamic on the boulevards affected by their proximity to a national theater. Whereas a Barrault or a Malraux may want to purify the Comédie, which is an institution, who wants to purify Broadway, which is an economic and pathological condition? Where would you begin? By burning at the stake in Shubert Alley the four or five cunning ladies who, along with David Merrick, hold dominion over the Broadway stage?

To talk about Broadway *is* mainly to carp; but we must carp and carp louder, not for Broadway's sake, but because it remains the chief referent for theater in this country and, more outrageously, the chief aspiration for young actors, directors, designers, and playwrights. Bless Broadway, it will survive, if anything does. And nobody would spend his good time beating a dead cow if there weren't so many who still held it sacred, or fed up to the teeth, still buzz like dumb flies around what *they* tell you is a carcass.

Though the Broadway theater is now more than a $45,000,000 annual business, statistics are increasingly available to explain why the more disillusioned producers are predicting, again, only a few more years for the Great White Way; or why one has said that "because of increased costs of production and the step-ups in contracts with the theatrical unions, the serious play will be driven out of the theater"; or why the *Business Review* of the Federal Reserve Bank of Philadelphia, graphing a boom on nationwide spending for the performing arts, adds: "But all is not well in the . . . industry. Its silver cloud seems to have a leaden lining. Performances begin with *P* and that rhymes with *T* and that stands for trouble, as the song from 'The Music Man' might go." The trouble seems to be every year, but *The New York Times* reported recently, again, that "Broadway is ending its most disastrous season in memory."

As for the Road, that national extension program of Broadway, the Broadway Theatre Alliance says "that only blockbuster attractions like *My Fair Lady* and *The Music Man* could prosper." And Walter Kerr adds: "If you once had twenty-five theaters in Chicago and you now have three, the theater is dying; and you can't get around that." Even San Francisco, once considered "a great theater town," is looked at warily by touring productions and frequently detoured. Though Kerr thinks the dying may be cyclic, prior to a rebirth, no wonder the Alliance is discontinuing operations.

Not that people aren't making money. Ernest Martin, producer of *Guys and Dolls* and *Can-Can,* is tired of the same old complaints, in which, for obvious reasons, he doesn't believe: "There's too much self-deprecation and complaining in the theater. Why don't we say how good we are for a change? I suppose it's in the nature of the business. . . . But I think we should stop knocking our business." And Mr. Martin's complaint has substance. Theatrical investment firms have shown that money can be made, if one studies the profit-and-loss records of the people involved in the production, the proposed budget, and other industrial factors, such as what star is available, whether Macy's new theater club will offer it to its members on their charge accounts, and whether Helen Thompson of the Play of the Month Guild, having been shown it in advance, approves of the script.

Commenting on this practice, Herman Shumlin says: "I'm all for the clubs. They're good if they bring people into the theater. There is always the possibility, of course, that they could dictate terms if they get too big, but if they get to a point of danger we can step in and say 'hold it.' " This is not hypocrisy, it is, as we say, a solution. Lest Mr. Shumlin, who has a reputation as a producer of "serious plays," be left holding the sandbag, one should remark that this watershed psychology has never worked in business or politics, as the gasping history of the twentieth century shows—for the point of danger, and no return, is the original lowering of the dykes.

After the pieties of those who want to give us the best that compromise affords, one is refreshed by the pristine profit motive of David Merrick, who has the brash grace to really mean it. And Mr. Merrick expresses my sentiments perfectly when he says: "My feeling is that there will have to be more disaster before all elements in the theater wake up."

Nevertheless, let's stop knocking the business. "We cannot say," as Edwin Posner, chairman of the American Stock Exchange, observed after the big fallout at the market in May 1962, "that this will be the low because who knows where emotions go"; but even if "these are times—if you'll excuse my being trite—that try men's souls, we'll live through it, just like we've done before."

Yet while "the figures, the statistics, the earnings, the dividends and the general healthy state of the U.S. economy," according to Mr. Posner, show that "stocks are rapidly becoming realistic," theater statistics, brought up to date, show no such trend—and turn into lamentations. The Golden Year of 1927–28 is invoked, the year before the movies, when 264 productions played in 80 theaters. Now, only 32 theaters, many of them threatened by midcity rents, demolition and conversion, featherbedding, shallow stages, and obsolete equipment—and only about 50 productions, most of them either musicals or otherwise stupid. Ten years ago, a production of a straight play might cost $60,000; today, $150,000. Musicals? *Sound of Music* was delivered to Broadway for $486,000, *Camelot* for $600,000. All this leads to slower return on the invested dollar, and so on—as is the wont of statistics, not obscuring the real issue because plenty of people, even on Broadway, know what that is: are we talking about business or are we talking about art? and what are the minimal relations that must obtain between the two in this institution before we are talking about nothing at all?

A weekly take of $29,000 was apparently not enough to keep Brecht's *Mother Courage* playing in New York. This was one of the surrenders to the law of supply and demand that led Howard Taubman to say that "Broadway is free enterprise gone mad"—although he also places the blame on the theatergoer for wanting "a gilt-edged guarantee that the play he attends is successful and will entertain him." There is more to it than the opportunism of producers in a Barnum & Bailey economy; it is a cultural problem of huge proportions. Still, what we are really inquiring into in this book is the state of mind in the American theater that led anybody to think that the production of *Mother Courage* on Broadway, after all these years, could be an artistic event of any importance—especially if, like *The Threepenny Opera*, it *had* been successful.

The pathos is evident not only in the trade papers or the theater pages, but also among specialists in American culture. Commenting on an interview with Walter Kerr—in "The American Character" series of the Center for the Study of Democratic Institutions—Edward Reed reviews the ordeal of the Broadway producer. Without denying that there are plenty of mere real estate operators around "looking only for their percentage," he adds, "The fact is that the theater, which is generally considered to be a commercial as well as an artistic enterprise, has been drawn and quartered by an array of economic complexes, fallacies, and paradoxes that no practical businessman would put up with for five minutes." He agrees with Kerr that changes in theater architecture, space staging, re-exposure of the dramatic event and of the actor in his unencumbered presence, digging "back to the root of the theatrical sensation as such," might help restore an audience to the theater. "But," adds Reed, "one may ask whether a thoroughgoing revitalization can ever come about while economic lunacy prevails."

So far, so true. Kerr speaks of the actor "standing there, like a sacrificial bull, in the center of an arena. . . . It is as though we are all assembled not for a bull-fight but for a man-fight, to see a man torn to shreds interiorly by going through an enormous crisis, like the most devastating crises we all go through. . . . I am more and more interested in the notion of the human condition being viewed as a sacrifice by a number of people gathered to share in and support this sacrifice." It is just such a conception of theater as I have in mind, but one must always ask at the moment of truth, what are you sacrificing for? There is communion and communion. And though one man's altar is not another man's altar, one could ask how a man who holds this conception of theater could admire some of the plays he does or participate in anything like *Goldilocks*.

Still, I have no doubt Kerr really wants to "imagine how the theater can be thrilling again"; and though I know little about Reed, the tone of his commentary shows he, too, is serious about the whole business.

Yet both of these earnest men are contributing in their own way to the general lunacy, which Kerr defines earlier in the interview: "I would say there is no American theater at the present time. There is a New York theater." Even if that is so, by Kerr's own testimony that theater is dying. A couple of questions later we learn he is not very familiar with theater outside New York, but he assumes that at its best it is like off-Broadway and he is certain the "resurgence of little theater groups does not yet represent a vast rebirth of theater."

Unfortunately, he is right.

But after saying of the theaters outside New York that "they are essentially small operations," Kerr drops the question—we must be big, big—and any further possibility. Given his influence, it is a negligence we can ill afford. For aside from assuming the New York theater deserves the maximum energy of restoration, it encourages the congestion of talent there that makes its death pangs, even if cyclic, all the more appalling. And even the Center for the Study of Democratic Institutions perpetuates the kind of authoritative thinking that makes the free flow of theater through the country—which needs talent even more than money—needlessly difficult. In New York, there is no question of minimal relations between the institution of theater and the art of theater, for there seems no alternative to economic lunacy. If you concentrate so much wealth, so much talent, so much organizational energy, so much publicity, so much critical concern in one city—so much of it unusable, and the rest debased or impotent—what else can you envisage but the theatrical parallel to those cemeteries squeezing the parkways to Long Island, in which the dead are piled upon the dead?

And for what?

Go through the entire history of the Broadway theater and ask yourself, as Edith Isaacs did long ago, is it really worth it? Advising the insurgents of the new Tributary Theater movement, she said: "There is no excuse for their following the example of the trade theater which has developed too few notable playwrights, distinguished actors, fine theater companies, and altogether too few even of the stable fortunes which have been its goal, to make its past way seem the way of material or spiritual wisdom." As for its present way, can anybody really serious about the welfare of the American theater not be embarrassed by it artistically, furious over the way it wastes our natural resources and—unless one is reconciled to perennial emptiness or defends it as natural law—forlorn over the betrayal of every dream that ever arose in its vicinity?

This is not a rhetorical question only because there are still too many who agree with Lawrence Langner's posthumous declaration that "The actual fact is that during the past 50 years, we have developed the most important and exciting theater in the civilized world. . . . We have no reason to bow our heads or feel subservient to any other country in the world as far as our theater is concerned. We have what they would all like to have—a free theater in which writers can freely speak their minds without interference from government or the authorities." Which perhaps shows how the half-rebels of one generation (Mr. Langner was one of the founders of the Theatre Guild) can become the naïve Establishment of the next. In the arts, government interference is an old-fashioned, silly, and inefficient way of limiting freedom. We are paying tribute, but it is not the kind Mrs. Isaacs had in mind.

The ticket-scalping scandals of Broadway, and the self-defensive pieties over the "ice," are not only a natural outgrowth of its economy, but an inevitable extension of its values, as reflected in the plays, the style of production, and the behavior of the people who work there; and I mean the very best people, not merely the outright swindlers.

Even as it shrinks on its own premises, we have too much of Broadway all over the country. For some people in the American theater, far from New York, there is virtually no other idea of what a theater might be, certainly accessible in action. When we say American theater, it is the image people think of. As for audiences, whatever is not brought to them by the Theatre Guild subscription, the theater clubs and automation may soon make possible. In due time even, the Lady from Dubuque will be able to spare Broadway its missionary work by picking up her tickets for the latest in New York at the box office on Main Street. (This glad tiding, by the way, comes not from David Merrick but from Edward B. Young, vice-president of the Lincoln Center, who said they were considering nationwide ticket distribution modeled after the electronic system used by the airlines!) Frankly, I'm not too optimistic about changing the habits of this particular Lady from Dubuque. I worry more about those in the theater who, knowing better, feel we must capitulate to her taste and rule out serious alternatives as second-best.

In a preface to two other plays, William Gibson says: "The Broadway audience is a given. It has grown monolithic; a generation ago, when thirty plays could be produced for what one musical comedy costs now, they could survive on fractions of this audience, but *The Miracle Worker* must attract a thousand theatergoers a night or close; there is little choice here."

That being the case, one wishes Gibson would see there are more than two logics, that of the isolated writer and the twisted logic of the monolith, which will soon be supported by the computers, those new neutral agents of thought control. But he concludes in his preface: "The Broadway audience is the nation's; it is our only audience which exists in numbers sufficient to support a complete theater, from playwrights to ticket-takers; it is therefore the audience to which every germinating talent in the theater is drawn. All other audiences—off-Broadway, at our universities, in little-theater communities—are second-best and temporary substitutes. It is not dominant in the American grain to regard less money, less glory, and for that matter working conditions or less technical finish, as preferable to more, merely for the sake of internal scope."

What I worry about is that he will be believed—and not only on Broadway, but in the universities, off-Broadway, and the little theaters. In actual fact, he has been anticipated in these places for years. But what about that American grain, which moves in many directions? In the opening monologue of his book on the subject, William Carlos Williams speaks through his hero, Red Eric: "Rather the ice than their way: to take what is mine by single strength, theirs by the crookedness of their law. . . . I, then, must open a way for them into the ice that they may follow me even here—their servant, in spite of myself. Yet they must follow." One of our greatest poets, Williams has written some plays against the grain Gibson describes, and chose to work as a doctor so he could do it.

I see no reason why one shouldn't ask of artists in the theater what artists in any other medium take for granted: less money, less glory, less technical finish—if necessary—for the sake of the truth that is in them. (Since it's not without precedent, I should add there may be, with patience, the money and the glory too.) If this seems harder in the theater, then we must be more stubborn about it. One of the stranger paradoxes of the American grain is that artists such as Gibson, with a genuine yearning for belief that prompts him to write a play with uplift like *The Miracle Worker*, should refuse to believe at some crucial point, if not in miracles, in the unfathomable capacity of artistic faith buoyed up by collective will.

But then, despair is circular. And in the history of the American theater we have seen a lot of faith sunk by will that was not collected.

In the May 1962 issue of *Theatre Arts*, the new provisional editors,* re-calling the magazine's origins, reprinted the first editorial by Sheldon Cheney, written in 1916, in which he speaks of "a new generation of artist-workers," experimental playhouses creating small but appreciative audiences, and the new magazine's desire to seek out "the creative spirit" wherever it touches work in the theater. "It begins modestly; but there is a good fight to fight. . . ." The provisional editors, reaching back to this optimistic revolutionary impulse, comment: "Sadly, none of the 'experimental playhouses' to which Mr. Cheney was referring has survived. Sadder still, his editorial can in conscious irony stand the test of time. Change several references, revise some of the language and you will leave unchanged the awful pertinence. The

---

* I say provisional because they didn't last long. The whole farcical story is too dreary to tell here, and it has since been told by Gordon Rogoff [*Tulane Drama Review* (Winter 1962)]. But briefly: under Rogoff, *Theatre Arts* revived a dissonance it had lost after it began operating as a Broadway house organ. Alarmed, the old guard returned, padlocked the door, and the old broadcasts resumed on a sort of halfway frequency; that is, since one can no longer ignore Brecht, say, or theater in France, there are articles on such subjects. But instead of *Pantagleize* or *In the Jungle of Cities*, the play of the month is, as of yore, *The Unsinkable Molly Brown*.

speculators are still in the playhouse. Even when the artists are allowed in for a hasty glance, they are never quite certain that they are artists—or indeed that the theater is a home for art."

Cheney ended his editorial with a postscript: "We intend not to be swallowed by the movies."

The new editors—misjudging the immediate enemy and their own tenure—ended thus: "We continue modestly; it is still a good fight; it demands your engagement; and we shall not be swallowed by television."

One wishes they would have added, since the fight is now not only a good one but a much harder one, that artists and theater-workers insult themselves by standing around waiting to be "allowed in for a hasty glance"—the assumption still being, even among these intelligent men who were about to be dispossessed (they may have since changed their minds), that New York is immovable Mecca. It is this expense of spirit on a waste of shame that inadvertently provides more rationalizations for people in the theater who talk differently but are really with the Philistines and Walter Kerr, who is perhaps the most stylish of the daily reviewers, but finally an out-of-town buyer of orthodox persuasion and academic connections.

The temptations to total despair are such that Richard Gilman could write, during the brief Emancipation, "there is no magic in our protests that the theater is perennial, that its loss would be unthinkable, and so forth." Gilman was writing from "the boundless unhappiness and ennui induced by a theatrical season in which I saw more than a hundred plays and spectacles only three of which aroused me to more than a temporary acknowledgement of some isolated and hermetic act of skill or passion."

As one project or another gets going in New York—a playwright's theater or a new acting company—one is glad to have a Gilman, or a Simon, or a Brustein there to provide for the minority which reads them the ballast of informed criticism, however acerbic. They can praise and praise splendidly (see Simon's eulogy of Zero Mostel) and they can be encouraging (even in the undeluded and qualified approval of the Living Theater by Brustein); but they are mostly swallowing hard. And one can see from the gravity (and periodic silence) of Brustein that despair over our theater is linked to resignation over the debility of our entire culture: "As long as the majority remains enfeebled in soul, nerve, and intellect—demoralized in spirit, seeking release in fantasies and opiates—the work of the serious playwright will remain a minority expression, recruiting its spectators from among that 'aristocracy of character, of will, of intellect,' which Ibsen hoped would resist the cultural degradations of the democratic dogma. The voice of the people is still the voice from the TV box, and he who would have it otherwise must first start a revolution in the consciousness of modern man."

Things are too dark for me to quarrel with the cultural diagnosis; in fact, I tend to share the view that men have almost never shown themselves capable of any high degree of general culture. But if the job does seem impossible, I would have it otherwise. One of the things I admire about Norman Mailer

—for all the jockeying for power, the postulation about orgasm, the crap about cancer—is that he "will settle for nothing less than making a revolution in the consciousness" of modern man. And in his loud way he has done his small part. I honor him for it. Moving by increments still takes large ambitions, especially today. As for the theater, where we have so long settled for next to nothing, it would seem the best way to start a revolution in the consciousness of modern man is to do what you can to start a revolution in the consciousness of people whose ears you may have. I am speaking not merely of readers, of audiences, but primarily of workers, those who must do the job. In the profession itself the human waste is incredible, as are the self-delusions, the dodges, the exacerbations of the rat race.

Gibson says that theater reform must begin with more teachers like Annie Sullivan in the kindergarten. Good. But as it's tricky to die into this world, you can't wait around for others to change it, or for the next generation to become enlightened. Besides, education has its own problems, and I have heard the schoolmen also ask what could be done until the whole culture improves. On the other hand, zealous men are trying to deal with the problems of education as I am trying to deal with the theater, acknowledging the power of the enemy and the treachery of the terrain, but not surrendering on any front. Nothing can be more discouraging than education in America, but things are happening in education as they are happening in the theater. And the wrong things are likely to happen there, too, if our most enlightened people are waiting, say, for curricular miracles to train our Annie Sullivans.

No revolution proceeds down a single track; there are arterial routes into every part of society. One campaign supports another.

Take the unions, which are monoliths too: in a vicious context they are bound to be impossible, as they are on Broadway. But there are reformers in the unions as there are reformers even in industry, anxious to restore the radical basis of our democratic institutions, and a proper dynamic among them. They all suffer from idiot competition and ingrown selfishness. They are all beginning to know it. More practically: the structure of the theatrical unions is changing. Formerly the stagehands passed jobs on from father to son; now the officers are younger, with not quite the same stake in the old battles for equity. No doubt, the featherbedding remains and, since the unions are very conservative and work by common law, they stick to precedents (or demands) that have already been established. But in a fresh context, where relations are gradually developed from the ground up, it may be possible for the unions, though their laws are prohibitive now, to be more reasonable as they cannot be reasonable where the terms of irrationality are fixed.

If this seems utopian, it is also in the more authentic American grain, and as regards the unions, what I have said is based on the experience of my own theater.

It is packing and false euphoria in an unwholesome environment—such as that in which off-Broadway developed—that gives the impression of a grab-bag, on which the mercenaries close in. And since, instead of an institution, you have primarily a showcase, there are only rather glassy grounds upon which anybody can be consistently reasonable. The rules are as capricious as the traffic, and some of the enterprises which aspire to permanence suffer the suspicion of ubiquity. It is hard for the real thing to bargain when it includes so much that is demonstrably false.

Off-Broadway was never so dazzling in its contribution to the American theater as its best days made it seem, but as the big producers now move downtown to reduce costs to the level of what was once off-Broadway's most extravagant fancy of a budget, even its best friends, such as Howard Taubman, say it is a "sweat shop. It's a weak breed for the professional theater to depend on." And Ward Morehouse reported to us in the provinces at the end of 1962: "*Most significant development of the entire drama year*: The near collapse of the entire off-Broadway movement."

So breaks the bootstrap of a makeshift dream? And if the dream fades—will we remember very much of what it was about?

Certainly there is zeal and occasional excellence in and around Broadway. Who ever denied it? There is more than anywhere else because in some places there is absolute zero. But—speaking of sacrificial bulls—at what a bloody cost! And I mean now not only puerile shows and financial loss, but the cost in human dignity: actors walking around behaving like the roles in which they hope to be cast; playwrights butchered by play doctors; grown men simpering in chorus lines; intelligent women with four years of training in college theater spending their summers playing second lead to an incompetent Hollywood ex-star in some idiot's delight; directors outguessing atrocious scripts as they step over box-office names and old friends (who flopped once too often) to slipping careers; acknowledged stars waiting for another custom-made part in which to pass a tedious year or two punctuated by television engagements while they dream of repertory and the great classical roles; or, after years of expectation, an aggregate of rabid luminaries, the very best, in reverent and somewhat erratic ensemble, doing the most sophomoric O'Neill, while the lesser lights of America's great purist academy of acting do their scenes, and stand and wait; and everybody dependent on a few newspaper sages, most of them barely equipped for their jobs, who are not ogres but virtually embarrassed by the power they wield and constantly trying to deny it, though the demoralization is such that better-informed people read them first because they affect box office, and then as if they knew something.

Look closer at the pathos of that playwright. He is a tenacious soul who hangs on for years on option renewals—hoping his one play will get that break, writing it over and over at the whim of any agent or director or star who shows interest (and considering at the outset nobody *but* a top-drawer director or a top-drawer star), though it may be a play started in a playwriting class at the New School in 1950. Finally, by scrounge and scratch, the necessary $150,000 is raised, the play does previews on the road, where it is rewritten out of all recognition, until the playwright doesn't even recall why he wrote it (or who); there are bad reviews in Philadelphia, an old pro or a new specialist is brought in to save the money—not the play, which is disfigured beyond redemption—and it creaks into New York for a solid three-day run after more bad reviews (the success story of *Seesaw* is not the mode), the investment too large now to call it quits.

Or there is the writer I knew who said he would do anything, ass-kiss or pimp, to get at least one play on Broadway. He is now moderately famous, and others are kissing his ass. To call such types artists is to impose more on them than pity allows.

Dostoyevsky's characters had a way of debasing themselves on behalf of the spirit, but what price debasement here?

And if in the midst of it something decent survives, a good performance or a worthy play, a resounding tinkle in the tarnished brass, you'd think it was the music of the spheres. To shift images and return to the fury of Brecht's Galileo: "How does a pearl develop in an oyster? A jagged grain of sand makes its way into the oyster's shell and makes its life unbearable. The oyster exudes slime to cover the grain of sand and the slime eventually hardens into a pearl. The oyster nearly dies in the process. To hell with the pearl, give me the healthy oyster!"

As for this particular oyster, it makes life more unbearable for itself by secreting nonsense.

This actress, we are told, "can do anything"; so she does it over and over in what amounts to the same play—or, when the chance to do "something different" arises, we discover she hasn't the training for it. This director, we are told, is "so full of emotion"—which means he is full of one restricted kind, like the actor who says he is "a feeling actor not a thinking actor"— which means there are huge areas of experience in which he feels nothing at all. Or: the theater is advancing: after years of oppressive subjectivity, we are going to create "an actor who has gone beyond the training of his psychological instrument and has really set about training his theatrical instrument." So the voice teachers are brought in and the body-movement experts and the fencing masters—all to be desired—but nobody asks what psychology we have been dealing with all these years, whose instrument has been surpassed. Beyond Freud? Broadway has, to my knowledge, rarely been anywhere near him—either the reality principle or the pleasure principle; not to mention those weird instruments, the aions and mandalas, of Jung.

And when something resembling a genuine pearl does appear, it is difficult to assess it in that scene. This accounts for the initial extremes on Edward Albee's *Who's Afraid of Virginia Woolf?*; on the one hand, it was reified into a masterpiece; on the other, it was assailed as if it were a national scandal. In part this was the fault of the sort of buildup the scene encourages;

in part, it was due to the fact that, there being nothing even remotely so good, it dominated the scene of which it became an emblem.

Even before the success of *Virginia Woolf,* Albee was the ripe subject of press agentry, was posed in the Sunday ads so as to recall O'Neill, was invited into the stately magazine section of *The New York Times* as the inside spokesman of the Theater of the Absurd (with whose leading practitioners he has much less in common than meets the eye), and in some schools was already being taught in classes. The writer is not his publicity, may not even be responsible for it, and one prefers Albee in the creative-writing programs to the Lajos Egri or Kenneth Thorpe Rowe manuals. His gifts are the real stuff: he has toughness, savvy, dark humor; and accepting the premise that the world is in an awful state is, I think sincerely, trying to find a form for it.

If his work corresponds to the new market for instant decadence, that is not wholly his fault either. In the preface to his first volume, which included *Zoo Story,* he spoke with the good modesty of a novice still astonished by quick success. The preface to *The American Dream,* however, goes after the tabloid reviewers who took him to task for alleged "defeatist *content*" and nihilism. Now: though *Zoo Story* serves up a gratuitous patsy to the suicidal hipster and his shaggy-dog story, the play has the undeniable virtue of going back in a modern image to the archaic condition of Western drama: in this world either that's my bench or yours, however we may be taught, and believe in, the value of sharing. Reducing that conflict to a deadly game (the psychopath's "I'm crazy, you bastard" preëmpts the legacy of our holy demonism), Albee puts the question: do you believe sufficiently in what you are to kill for it?

It's unfortunate that the question was put to the wrong guy, leading us to a maudlin conclusion. And worse, that the tone of this conclusion infests *The American Dream,* with its surface of satiric deadliness that appeals to the legacy of reverse Momism in our anti-culture. Aside from the fact that the play is baldly imitative and ridden with the clichés of anti-drama as with the clichés of nonconformism, Albee speaks in his preface as though the vulnerability of Tennessee Williams had taken a cue from the manic-aggressiveness of Allen Ginsberg: "Every honest work is a personal, private yowl, a statement of one individual's pleasure or pain; but I hope *The American Dream* is something more than that. I hope it transcends the personal and private, and has something to do with the anguish of us all."

It's not the anguish one minds, nor even the yowl. We are all entitled to that, and can hardly avoid it. Even *Time* celebrated the Age of Anxiety and Guilt by featuring Edvard Munch's gibbering skull upon its cover. Nor do I begrudge Albee his rankling against the invincible ignorance of most reviewers. Yet if he had really written the play he thought he had written, what did he expect? And if it was, as he says, his "intention to offend," what about the reviewers from the *Times, Post,* and *New Yorker* who are quoted on the back of the book with his approval? The strategy of prestige quotation one understands; we have all done it. But I'm afraid his yowl is not quite a *Howl;* and the danger for him, as for American art generally, is not rejection but *assimilation*—which may be why Ginsberg, a good poet turned huckster in self-defense and distrusting his own ambitions, feels compelled to take shelter in Chile and India. Think of the difficulty Mort Sahl has been having since *he* was made into an institution by *Time.* The *avant-garde,* embraced by status, has trouble remaining *avant.* Albee, too young to have been in the vanguard, was born with an offbeat spoon in his mouth. And Broadway is beginning to love him for it.

I would stay out of the controversy over *Virginia Woolf*—because it confirms Albee's talents—except that it may lead to a more important point. I happen to agree with those who dislike the play because it creates a cosmos of the unexamined adolescent hostilities of the other plays, and because the outrage and personal anguish do play into the hands of an audience which gets its kicks from being abused and which, believing nothing, likes to believe it can take anything. (I am not objecting to sado-masochism in the drama, which has its place in a world-view, like death and taxes.) Nonetheless, if *Virginia Woolf* is not "a classic example of bad taste, morbidity, plotless naturalism, misrepresentation of history, American society, philosophy, and psychology," it is a belated copy of that savagely cerebral anti-rationalism, that voraciously inspired bendiction of crap which, from Jarry to Beckett and Arshile Gorky, is one of the richest traditions of modern art, compelling us to remember that "Love has pitched his mansion in/The place of excrement." But shock tactics are a nuisance if they are not a vision.

What I object to in the play is the assault on values that have never been profoundly honored in the American theater, or experienced by Albee. The academic put-down is smug, the abuse of women suspect; and even the fecal matter is the uninspiring detritus of a great inheritance. To cite Yeats again:

> Know that when all words are said
> And a man is fighting mad,
> Something drops from eyes long blind,
> He completes his partial mind. . . .

Of the subjects which compose his conceit of American life, Albee has said only the words which have become such platitudes of the offbeat that they are now safely on records. We are only too ready to deride what we have never known. As for the off-Broadway environment in which his yowl was cultivated, it reminds one of the joke about the difference between the American bohemian and the European bohemian: the European becomes bohemian *after* he is educated.

Sure, there are exceptions, but in that environment, madness is likely to be a posture, the smashed icons are not the Thrones, Powers, and Dominations, but the grovelers of Academe and the store dummies of Madison Avenue—and all one needs to be a visionary is a very partial mind.

Still, if it weren't certain to be toured and my theater could get the rights to *Virginia Woolf,* we would produce it—for in the process of looking for an American play to perform each season, one is thankful even for partial mind. And Albee is likely, if put on, to be more than that. It may be, as Richard Schechner wrote in his diatribe against the play, "The lie of his work is the lie of our theater and the lie of America," but the quality of his work suggests he has to live through the lie to go beyond it. Moreover, if we accept —as Albee's most intellectual critics tend to—the "ontological speculation" of Genet, we may have to seek reality by acting over its provisional lies, including our own.

On Broadway, this is now impossible because the nature of the lie is obscured by premature celebrity, and so many superior and antecedent lies have been excluded. By the time they reach Broadway (e.g. Brecht), the true lie is a false truth. In the context of a permanent theater, however, where Genet and Brecht may have informed the evolution of a company's work, or where more than one limited psychology has been available, the lie of Albee may be more properly measured, and it may not be essential to attack him like a sacrificial *pharmakos* in our rage against the viciousness of the tribe whose values he incarnates as he assails them.

The argument over *Who's Afraid of Virginia Woolf?* aside, of the various off-Broadway writers moving to Broadway, or remaining off-Broadway for that matter, Albee is the one most likely to turn out a genuine pearl. Which— given all the unsuccessful secretions—doesn't change very much the condition of that oyster.

Let me repeat: the Broadway death image is not mine. I don't think Broadway will die, but at the moment I couldn't care less, and I don't recommend staying around in expectation of a corpse. Or, whether it is ready or not, a rebirth. I know the old saws about the theater being an Ancient Whore and a Fabulous Invalid (in that setting, *Androgyne* is the word), but they strike me like the mollifying response to the atom bomb, that every century has had its disasters—utter obtuseness about the present issue. What one regrets with all the uncertainty built into the *art* of theater is the miasmic perpetuation of the milieu by so many talented people making their way, darkling, or in great expectation, to so little accomplishment.

To be perfectly truthful, I could say like those who are above complaint that I don't mind myself an evening of relaxed poshiness with the expense-account spenders, dressing up and Sardi's and all that. Nor is there any reason why, as we raise the old banner of Decentralization, we should exclude New York, which badly needs some permanent theaters of its own. Perhaps the Actors Studio will provide one, perhaps Elia Kazan at Lincoln Center. Perhaps one of them will become at last a national theater in vital proximity to our graveyard. And some other solutions are quite urbane: it has recently been proposed, for example, that art theaters be developed somewhat like art-film houses—each appealing to a minority audience and financed by investors attracted by what Wall Street calls "a balanced portfolio of distributed risks." Our minorities are, indeed, sizeable, and adjusting our economics to that fact will perhaps give rise to a series of modest-sized theaters with moderate prices, each specializing in a particular kind of play.

I don't really see this as significantly different from what off-Broadway attempted—its economic laws succumbing to the economic lunacy of the total environment. I don't know what would keep these new art theaters—to the extent that they are located in New York—from becoming mere show-cases, the actors drifting off to those nearby greener pastures. But good idea. We must be hard-nosed about art. Perhaps we will have a spate of such theaters with sound investment plans. In a revolutionary era, when social thinkers—observing the new polity of Europe and the emancipation of Asia and Africa—are saying that after the senseless interruption of two world wars we are moving at last into the twentieth century—I am prepared to believe anything. I am prepared to believe even in the reformation of Broadway.

The sickness of theater in New York is bound up, however, with the larger metropolitan pathology. Several years ago I was standing on a balcony over-looking Central Park with one of the country's pioneer city planners. He looked north of the park, to the blight on one side and the new syndicated apartments on the other, and said, "That's criminal." Then he looked south, toward the raising bones of a new skyscraper, and said, "That's suicidal." Just as we can see the City, skin cleansed, congealing in a madder future, walls toppling every twenty years over their escalating clauses, renewal projects relocating slums while the cars pile up to Mamaroneck, so we can see practically every development in the New York theater—from off-Broadway to Lincoln Center—as a holding action or another stranglehold on the waiting minions.

Everybody knows some residual drive for status, perhaps among the new managers, keeps the great industries in New York, when most of them have taken options on land in places like Rye and Tarrytown. In the forties all the talk was of Decentralization, and Jean-Paul Sartre, shocked by the congestion when he visited, predicted there would be no more building in the City. Then the boom.

What draws the elephant draws the flea. Just as small industries circulate around the behemoth to provide services, so a lot of the best energy in the American theater still circulates around Times Square, behaving like mer-chandise and dreaming on breakthroughs but reluctant to make that break. Everybody knows how absurd it is. At a time when the Department of Labor is worrying about 4 to 6 per cent unemployment, far be it from me to recite the old figures about 90-what? per cent unemployed. What do you say about a profession, however, in which most of those who *are* working are ashamed of what they do, or have learned to blind themselves to its inconsequence? What do you say about those actors and directors who go to Equity meetings to speak up on working conditions or racial discrimination or the United Nations, but who then appear in one fraudulent drama after another, dramas that demean them as people, or vacuous musicals that impact the very condition their union was born of, and who—asked by the President what they can do for their country—would have been hard pressed to find an answer unless they gave up their careers?

I mentioned Herman Shumlin before not because he is more villainous than other producers, but because he is more virtuous, and because his reasoning is the higher echelon of that debased hope which keeps making the rounds, as it makes the situation more contemptible, right down to the rank-and-file.

When Louis Kronenberger quit drama reviewing after twenty-three years, he wrote: "How could one not feel relieved when so much of one's job was not merely dull but degrading; not just clumsy but cheap?" He concluded the essay on his retirement by saying that "whenever the producers, or the Powers That Be, want a civilized theater world, something to match what exists in other forms—even high-cost forms—of art, I feel sure they can bring it about. One prerequisite, to be sure, is Powers That Be who are civilized themselves."

If this seems beyond fondest expectation, those Powers untouchable (after all, Mr. Kronenberger didn't seem to touch them in twenty-three years), it seems strange that equally hard to reach are the people who suffer most. I mean those in the labor markets of New York and Hollywood, some of whom by TV residuals and an occasional long run have become as acquiescently bourgeois as their audience (one of the metamorphic symptoms of midcentury America), some waning in will under the debilitating labor of making those rounds, playwrights with their plays, actors with their very selves, even the reviewers in the nocturnal masochism of their profession. For all the conspicuous consumption in the investment theater, it is balanced by the conspicuous waste of human resources. In a prosperous period of rising unemployment, the following—from the union magazine *Equity*—describes the personal, mythic and phenomenological consequences of constant unemployment:

> And I, . . .
> The ad of myself selling myself,
> Smile very coca-cola, exceedingly pepsodent.
> Surely,
> I should slap a halo
> Sideways on my head,
> for under my armor of smile
> I scratch a hair-shirt of an earlier era
> When I hawk What-I-Am
> at your glass door. . . .

To work at all the actor may have to concede a lot of principle, if there is any left in the mass humiliation. A relatively prominent character actor revisited our theater after a winter of TV filming in Los Angeles where, as he put it, "only the dollar and nothing but the dollar counts." He added, looking past us to New York, "my profession no longer exists." This man was making, however, more than a living at some surrogate for his profession, and had a modicum of reputation. What about the rest? Whereas a painter or a poet might even choose to avoid public consumption by consuming himself in any old pad, like Kafka's Hunger Artist, you usually need at least two to make a theater, for all the adage about some boards and a passion. So there's no recourse. Or so they say.

Sacrificial as they are, many people in the theater are not sacrificial enough. Who hasn't heard of the young actor who works all night at Riker's so he can sit all day at Walgreen's and wish there were repertory theaters where he could perform with permanence. Well, things have improved, we hear. Now he works as often as he can at the "soaps," so he can afford to do something "significant" off-Broadway, while he wishes there were repertory theaters where he could perform with permanence. Wake up, stupid!—if you're going to hold a job, hold it where it will do you some good. And perhaps there will be more of those theaters, more permanent, in due time. No other self-respecting artist, no painter, no poet—those who would endure any hardship so they might work out their own destinies—would put up with the delusions of those people in the theater who might have worked a lot more at their art if they had *chosen* to suffer the obscurity they suffered anyhow.

It is incredible how many workers in the theater agree with Herman Shumlin that "Economics is everything that is wrong with the theater"; or the unions, or the movies, or the mass media, or the proscenium arch, or the Play of the Week, or fear of creeping socialism, or the fire laws, or the decentralized hangover of Puritan morality, or "the youth of our country's culture," or the fact that there is only one shining knight in tweeds to go around. The recent operational grants of the Ford Foundation, providing a measure of stability and in some cases real estate to a number of theaters outside of New York, may, along with Tyrone Guthrie, validate the rest of the country for those who cluster around Broadway like displaced persons so long interned they can't move out of camp even when the barbed wire is clipped and the shackles loosed. We shall see. Money also talks sense. Somewhat. But there are many, too long benighted, who may still not see the handwriting on the wall, which has long declared who is really responsible for the failure and fatuousness of the American theater.

For, my dear colleagues in art, let us face it: the biggest impediment to the growth of theater throughout America has never been, as the cry goes, economics or stultified communities (though they do their part), but the timorousness and self-deceit of people *in* the theater who are always deploring lack of subsidy and want of opportunity to do "meaningful things"; who dream of companies "like they have in Europe," but wouldn't go beyond New Jersey to find one; who are tame, submissive, and even ignorant of the way their art, often never practiced, has been debased in this country; who let themselves be humiliated and humiliate themselves before the meat merchants of casting offices; who, prey of agents, prowl the studios and seek out showcases rather than create stages in places all over the country that would welcome them; who drift away from meaningful opportunity when it confronts them because it doesn't pay enough or because it looks impossible or because the new is really intimidating or because surrender seems more profitable; who take one quick shot at it, and then surrender; who are not artists because they have forgotten to think as artists, or never did. Many know they have sold out, and they follow the normal recourse of the delinquent in blaming their delinquency on the conditions that prevail, thereby impacting the conditions. Some, deferring to the fact that at some social point the theater *is* a business, put it into premature collusion with big business. Some, convinced it is a business and chiefly a business, are available at a price for any show, converting what are sometimes rare skills to the most corrupt ends, of which even the spirit of their union—whose protection, as mere jobbers, they really need—wouldn't approve. Some, who really have the welfare of the theater at heart, desire to make it a civic venture before they've provoked a civic need, not to mention a primal artistic impulse *in themselves*. Either they start a project pretentiously and fail dismally, or more frequently they abandon it at the first resistance or earliest "better" opportunity. *What has kept America from creating a significant theater up to now is that our talented people, and they are legion, have never stayed together long enough to do so.*

And it is not only the actors, not only the last generation. Recently a young director came to us on a graduate internship from one of the major university drama departments. From the outset it was clear he was not only talented but had uncommon executive ability, and we were anxious to make a place for him. But before the season was over he said he was going to leave. He had an offer of a job. Now, I don't want to simplify the motives involved—from a restive wife who wasn't yet acting to a sense of estrangement from the Beat younger members of our company. ("I went through that stage," he said, "when I was nineteen, *with* beard. Now I'd rather wear a tie." No sweat; we understood.) He had some reservations about the way our theater functioned. Good—stay with us and help improve it. No, it wasn't entirely that. He sincerely respected our aims. What then? It seemed the main problem was this: having decided (hastily, I think) that directing was not the one talent which was death to hide, he wanted to learn administration. Why not here? "A slick outfit," he said, "can teach me better what I need to know." What did he want to know? How to produce. To produce what? He didn't know.

The job, as I recall, was to be resident stage manager of a new playhouse in Florida which took in touring shows. "You know, musicals," he said, a little embarrassed. "I said slick, but I feel I need to know it." But why? "I can't say the money isn't important." Let me say I think the money was secondary. And since he is more purposeful than most, I have no doubt he will learn what he wants to learn. "Someday, maybe. . . ," he had started to say. Someday, maybe, he will put it all to good use—but, as he admitted then himself, the odds are very much against him. One can imagine the subsequent career; in this case, because he has first-rate ability, not frustration but very probable success—and the money (I mean this) always secondary, until he becomes a serious producer, when he shall be forced to concede that "Economics is everything that is wrong with the theater."*

Though economic causation remains a weighty motive in this mammoth art, there are too many claiming economic strangulation as a pretext for what they really prefer to do anyhow; who would do just about the same if they were handsomely subsidized. It is one thing to go out and make money, no pretense; another to go out and make money when you pretend you want to make art; still another, perhaps the widest duplicity, to make a little bit of money so you can make a little bit of art.

Only a few years ago Brustein, describing Broadway's inducements to Suburbia—the status appeals of stage décor, the interior decoration of the theaters, the 2 P.M. matinee, the 7 P.M. curtain—said: "Broadway apparently is willing to do anything—short of setting up branches in the suburbs like the large department stores—to tap that large audience which hovers on the borders of the city." Now we hear, however (*Equity,* May 1962), how "Theater Goes to the Shopping Center." Under the guidance of the new triple-thinkers of the agencies, the purveyors of socioanagogic meaning by subliminal means, we have the play that is charted on graphs (two beats and a seduction, pause, then an Oedipal pattern): the Playboy comedy; the highbrow musical (with social themes and a few songs you can just barely not hum); and the group therapy of Inge and Chayevsky, built rather on the basic course in Home and Family Living. To salve the aspirations of the more daring producers, there is also *Death of a Salesman.*

Even a truly significant play, like *Salesman,* may be incapacitated by the atmosphere of its production—and I am not speaking of amateurish production. In certain settings, under certain producers, you can only expect of drama immaculate aisles of canned gestures and branded intonations, the processed pabulum of the theater's old palpable grasp of significant action; the theater like a health-food bar.

Still—as is always the case—those who cater to the will of Suburbia are those who profess to believe in the good judgment of a popular audience and the progressive elevation of taste in our democracy. If they are not liars and scoundrels, they are protecting their despair by self-deception. Nevertheless, it's possible for an honest man, as the whole nation grows suburban, to see in the rising standard of living, in increased social security, a very great

* Things have moved even faster than I expected. Since I wrote this, he has become assistant to one of Broadway's serious producers.

opportunity. Dullness is the liability of the Welfare State, but need it be so?

And is our image of the suburbs correct? The skeptics of the Left think them too conservative; the alarmists of the Right think them too liberal; the people who live there read all the books about the apathy of Organization Man. For years, our muckrakers and social theorists, surveying the concrete jungles, drummed into us the pathos of anonymity—alone, alone, all all alone; our novelists and poets confirmed this image. So, believing what they'd read about themselves, not wanting to be sealed-off victims of the urban blight, Americans—forced by the population explosion to move from the cities— tried to build communities based on the old egalitarian principle of brotherly good will and togetherness. The next thing they know they are being analyzed as conformists.

There is, indeed, something pathetic about it; but as Undershaft points out to Major Barbara when she sneers at the "better fed, better housed, better clothed, better behaved" residents of his munitions suburbia, there may be hypocrisy in longing for the vigorous deprivations of the working-class district. Similarly, there may be hypocrisy—since we are not prepared to pay the price of social regression—in longing for the baggy-pants comedians, the razzmatazz musicals, the burlesque houses, the pep, the boffo humor, the wiggly "symmetrical digits" of Mae West, and the cue-stick vulgarity of another era. Take the ex-burlesque comics off television and you put a lot of men back on the picket lines. And, though it is deplorable the way the highbrow serious drama of Broadway directs itself to the diffused democratic prejudices of the middle classes, would we really prefer the end of FEPC, their blandness to some degree making it possible? No. And there's even greater hypocrisy in pretending that these are the only alternatives. Shaw doesn't. But, then, he asks that we be willing to use the same means that brought us creature comfort to blow up society.

And if that's a solution too perverse to understand, it's still possible to imagine a theater that does not merely puff it up like our daily bread, and reduce every antagonism, every complaint, every controversy, every little nuance of our countless irremediable bigotries to the well-tempered palaver of a panel at the temple, or the demagoguery of the dead-white homogenized center.

The cultural drives of Suburbia are with us, and they will be provided for, for they can be paid for. True, the people there are neutralized and vulnerable; they can also be underestimated and made still more vulnerable to more neutralization. This is often done by the men-of-good-intention with their someday ambitions, who unwittingly cooperate with the tranquilizer-peddlers. I shall say more of this in connection with the universities, but my immediate concern is not for the housewife in search of distraction, but the theater artist beguiled by expediency, the provisional measure becoming fatality.

When theater does go to the shopping center, it is usually run—I am sad to say—by just such a young man as I have described, grown older, a little more experienced in producing and, when confronted, aggressively defensive. Inside, his hostilities will grow in proportion to his self-betrayal, and while the suburbs stand there ready to be shaken up, he will secretly want to blow them up.

Of the other people involved in such schemes, what else can one say except that they, too, are well-intentioned and really want "to provide living theater," except they have forgotten what makes it live—if they ever knew. Actually, under their aegis, and in this environment, the notion of "living theater" is an extension of the mirage of "interpersonal relations," as if there were inevitably something more valuable in "direct contact" with "live actors" behaving like fools rather than, say, an intelligent film or a good book.

One could go on endlessly about the pieties substituting for vision on and around Broadway. Take one more: the most illiterate people in the theater are always canting about the theater existing for the play. The play is the thing, the playwright comes first. Well, let us say a little more about our plays and playwrights.

Actually, it is not only the dopes, or the unqualified vested interests, or those zealously Waiting for Subsidy who would think me too severe about the lack of accomplishment in American drama. Arthur Miller, for instance, in a fine talk on "The Playwright in the Atomic World," points out that America has created "a kind of dramatic style" in the past few decades. On the basis of his correspondence with Europeans and his own experience abroad, he says that "it is often admitted that if there is leadership in the contemporary play since the Second World War, at least in terms of international public appeal, America has it."

If public appeal is the principle, maybe. Nor do I deny we have a kind of dramatic style; I have catalogued some of it. But Miller has himself been a good critic of that style, which "has all moved now to a dangerous extreme of triviality. It is a theater with the blues. The genuine original cry has become a rehearsed scream of a self-conscious whimper." The fifties, he said, "became an era of gauze"—and that, as with the genuine original cry, the very best of it, say the plays of Williams and the direction of Kazan, not the slipshod ladies and threadbare psychology of their followers, also whimpering in the movies.

Miller might also have said something about the meliorist corollary of this Hot-Spell-and-Miltown psychology, with its summer houses and clinging vines, adjusted to the suburban-egalitarian-theater party "Jews-and-Negroes-are-just-plain-white-Protestant" orthodoxy of Broadway. And, lest we forget, homosexuals too—speaking of Integration. Though it generally turns out that it is not sexual perversion but rather the outer signs of an inner grace, maintaining our Puritan heritage. One would like to see not only the real dark at the top of the stairs, but what would happen when the good lady unbuttons her blouse, if he really *is*.

If every reflection on their themes inclines to condescension toward our playwrights, is it that we have forgotten how to praise? Or is there something really ominous in our theater's epidemic of secular charity for spasms of planned neurosis, or its tender flushes of humanitarian love performed with all the reflexes of marketable instinct?

Certainly the question is loaded. The tendency has been much analyzed and rightly deplored. Could it be that the exasperation and patronizing tone of Brustein, Tynan, Mary McCarthy, or the writers of the quarterlies, are more than the sour griping of the snobs and academics? (Academic, egghead, not-a-theater-person: thus we live with our sins.)

It's not the preaching one minds—Brecht preaches, Shaw preaches, Lenny Bruce preaches—but the felt adaptability of belief, the tepid relinquishment of conviction, or the downright absence of it.

In the atmosphere of the bull market, surely it is to be expected that American playwriting will suffer from the kind, often the same degree, of inhibition that even the most emancipated of Soviet writers experience today. In Moscow, a novel is published; it is time, we see, to talk about the forced-labor camps—but can anybody say what is really wrong, what and who are responsible for the forced labor? How much different, really, is the New York stage? No wonder Tennessee Williams threatens every other year to stop writing for Broadway altogether, only to end up nursing his bile off-Broadway amid the ante-bellum rigging and Venus flytraps of impending adjustment.

Is it now only the atmosphere of the bull market? Or is there something in the sinew and nervous system of American playwriting, infected so long by the bull, which prevails against the possibility of consummate vision from the gifted older writers of a former dispensation, as it does against an Albee, with all the lore and technique of the *avant-grade?*

True: Miller, Williams, Hellman, and Odets (don't we think of him as washed-up already?)* would seem to have as many years before them as Ibsen did when he embarked on the most formidable part of his career. As Harold Clurman has pointed out, they have a right to fail, to falter, and be silent. They need time even to waste. Nor, since an artist is his own competition, need they be urged to compete to keep up false pretensions. By nature and desire they are surely as earnest and productive as the rest of us. More. But, as we think of Ibsen virtually beginning his career at their age, do we have the same expectations about them? We can't demand a masterpiece every time out, but how many masterpieces do we have, really?**

---

* Odets died of cancer on August 15, 1963.

** On January 23, 1964, Miller's *After the Fall* was produced at Lincoln Center after years of great anticipation. Its honorable truce with history would be no less onerous if Miller himself hadn't virtually declared it a masterpiece. He seems to think he is pioneering a new form. But in a theater where *Marco Millions* is still admired, whose better judgment can prevail? Where nature is so demoralized, it takes real artlessness to believe there is anything original in the disjunct mechanics of *After the Fall*. As the language fails the large ambitions, so the open stage (I'd guess, I haven't seen it) exposes the play as a domestic drama shifting minor perceptions with the skill of a television camera. What is really saddening, however, is the failure of a man who

There are moments and intuitions in all these writers that I embrace with pleasure and fraternity, but can we really say we go to any of them a second or third time, for that larger wisdom or deeper solace, that vital trepidation that comes from knowing you may see what you didn't see before, the shock of recognition we still have in Ibsen with all the anachronisms? There are a few of their plays I should not want to be without, but even if there was only one Ibsen in Norway, even if the classics of other eras were surrounded by junk, does that really make the state of drama in a country the size and wealth and promise of ours any the less oppressive?

And I am speaking not as an academic (although I am that too, and proud of it), but as one who has produced some of the best of these plays and is constantly trying to justify to himself and the most intelligent people in his company the "obligation" to produce some more.

There is, indeed, an oppressive academic attitude toward these questions, but that was inherited from Broadway. It accounts for this ludicrous paragraph from the preface to a new anthology of *American Dramatic Literature* (isn't the word *hyperbole*?): "The serious American dramatist can now be successfully compared to the best of American novelists and story writers. The struggles of the human individual against the impersonal destructive forces of society have become as evident in Sidney Kingsley or Arthur Miller as they ever were in Frank Norris or Theodore Dreiser. The fears, emotions, and terrifying responsibilities of men in war described by Stephen Crane carry the same forceful impact in the plays of Arthur Laurents or Herman Wouk. The isolated loneliness of man and his attempts to find meaning in life are vivid and tragic in Eugene O'Neill just as they are in Fitzgerald or Hemingway. And the destruction of a sensitive woman in a society that she cannot understand and to which she cannot adjust her principles is as fascinating in Tennessee Williams as in Henry James." (!)

It has been a habit of literary criticism to deny to the fiction of the liberal

---

was in the center of some of the most significant public episodes of our generation to tell us anything about them we hadn't already deduced from the mass media—or discounted there.

So near to Broadway and so dependent on its values, Lincoln Center has yet to declare itself a free city. As for Miller, the windy self-justifications of *After the Fall* may be partly due to his approaching the auspicious occasion of Lincoln Center as the anointed sage of the Broadway scene. The whole atmosphere seems to be one of the plushiest sacrifice, replete with agents, the star system, and publication in the *Saturday Evening Post*. As the deepest sincerity may go the way of its environment, so conviction pales in pontification. As for the most notorious part of the play, its poltergeist is not Strindberg but Tennessee Williams. One remembers Miller's criticism of the gauzy dramas of the fifties. There it is again, the "rehearsed scream of a self-conscious whimper"—Marilyn Monroe as Maggie the Cat, undone by what *mendacity*?

If, as the case goes, Miller had to get this play out of his system in order to go on, let us hope he will find a way to distinguish between what he has done and what he aspires to do. For more on that, and an assessment of his previous work, see Chapter 7, written before *After the Fall*—as were my comments in the text on Lincoln Center.

democratic tradition the cogency and resonance of form one feels in the European novel. But whatever it may suffer in that comparison, the American novel is a very mineshaft of profundity when compared with our drama. Even to compare the dramatists mentioned—to set the ineluctable honesty of O'Neill beside the flannel-footed pedestrianism of Wouk—strikes me as some kind of—what? it's too stupid to call it blasphemy. But it is not unsymptomatic of the peculiar standards forced upon the academic mind with some investment of scholarship in the American drama by that more or less impoverished subject.

Nor is it irrelevant, for all the respect one accords O'Neill, to harp upon his limitations, for some of the respect is doltish, as is the claim that American drama is still in its nonage because it was idiotic until O'Neill. (Actually, since it was less pretentious, it was probably more entertaining.) If it is in its nonage, there is good reason for it, for our other forms have flourished in the meantime. Fortunately, either Faulkner was forgotten in the catalogue above or no parallel could be found, though it should be apparent to anyone with any kind of standards that we have nothing to match him for dramatic power in the American theater; and—to shift arts—nothing to match the achievement of Pollock, de Kooning, Still, and the American School of painting, even if you contest the achievement or may want to quarrel, as I shall, with where it has taken us.

Make all the excuses we want, there are times when the most negative judgment of our theater seems like mere understatement. "I have searched my thoughts for some time now," wrote the designer Peter Larkin, "to know why all my good artist friends and my good sculptor friends don't have the slightest use for the kind of work I do, theater work. Though I know they're an ingrown, contentious, nasty lot, this reaction bothers me." It outrages me, but when we swallow our pride, we know they have solid ground for their disdain. In England, the Puritans closed the theater in 1642; in this country, where stage plays were considered impious and profane and put in a class with other "rude and riotous sports," the theater took some time in developing. When it did, our best artists would have nothing to do with it, and not only the painters and sculptors. Whereas in other countries, no man of letters would think his career complete unless he had written for the theater, here our highest dramatic instincts went into fiction and poetry. With two exceptions: T. S. Eliot, who got out as soon as he could, and Henry James, who equivocated.

The reigning powers of our New York theater may think neither of them a great loss, but their careers are instructive. Eliot always understood that the health of a society, like the health of other forms, is reflected in the health of the theater; and if his later plays—accommodating themselves to the boulevards out of desperate principle—turned out rather listless Menanderish comedies, his early experiments are only now beginning to be realized by others. Sweeney adumbrated Ionesco. As for James, who was zealous about writing for the theater—"my *real* form, which I am capable of carrying far"—our custom is to think of him as too genteel for the rough-and-tumble of the theater or, more recently, suitable for occasional adaptation. Yet it has always been my conviction that there is more virility in the flick of an eyelash of one of James' characters than all the posing of the equivocal studs of Williams and Inge, and more *drama* in the most inscrutable parenthesis of his darkest period than in a whole Broadway season. Shaw thought his giving up the theater was a great loss. And as the style of those devious dramas coming to us now from Europe pervades the scene, we may one day be ready for the technique James developed from Ibsen.

As for the generation of writers since World War I, except for a couple of left-handed indulgences, Faulkner didn't write for the theater, Hemingway didn't write for the theater; Harte Crane, with the greatest command of Elizabethan rhetoric since Melville, didn't write for the theater; Scott Fitzgerald didn't write for the theater; and today, when a really good writer is prompted to look at our "distinguished American plays," they strike him as relics of structure left over from Newtonian habits of mind, stock ideas on a dilapidated bicycle. He'd not only rather see a good movie, but probably shares the feeling that a single film like *Marienbad* or *La Notte* has more that is germinal in it than the whole American repertoire since the end of the war.

Need it be so? I insist upon not believing it. But you couldn't even argue the point with many people in the American theater, who haven't the slightest idea how much of their world has been left out of their theater. Virtually resigned to the dominance of film over "the living theater," Gilman says: "Actuality may be the highest good; when actuality becomes unreal we will settle for true shadows." But nobody really wants to be forced into a choice among forms, even when, as with Yvor Winters, you feel compelled to place forms in a hierarchy. It is no more satisfactory, indeed, than choosing between actuality and true shadows.

So far, in my review of the state of the American theater, I have been making very few distinctions of this order. I have been speaking mainly of the perfectly obvious—what every fool knows, that the American theater is a mess; and what a good many fools avoid, that they are responsible for it. And who, when they are finally footsore and heartsick, ready to settle for second-best, turn to those alternatives to Broadway which are beginning to appear on the horizon.

There, in the provinces, we shall at long last find balm for "the live actor." When I hear certain people talk, however, about "the live actor" (is there a point to the redundancy?) and "legitimate theater," I am tempted to say, like Gloucester's natural son in *King Lear*, "fine word, 'legitimate'!" If what we presently have is legitimate, "Now, gods, stand up for bastards."

3

The center of power still remains here; while to the west of it true elements of the great people to whom the future control of the continent belongs are gathering together almost in secrecy.
—Alexis de Tocqueville, *Democracy in America*

The Romans, deprived of power and freedom, asserted their privilege of licentious murmurs.
—Edward Gibbon, *The Decline and Fall of the Roman Empire*

This is an American job, not just a New York job. I want someone who knows and cares about other parts of the country. It's a job just down your alley.
—Harry Hopkins to Hallie Flanagan

NEW FRONTIERS

As everybody looks west once more, the prospect of Decentralization revived, we must ask what it is that we want to decentralize. No doubt we want to do a little bloodletting on Broadway so our country's youthful culture can enjoy a lot more of its aging talent. But one questions the real seriousness of some of those who suddenly discover the provinces after the Ford Foundation, say, has put some grubstake on the trail. If I sound like an old homesteader protecting his claim, it is only because I think it should be recalled that those alternatives to Broadway have been there a long time, and because, since there is not at the moment that much loot to be had, I'd like to encourage those who are waiting to see how it goes to come out and join us now, for better reasons.

What we want to avoid first—lest Decentralization extend Mr. Minow's "vast wasteland"—is bringing to the rest of the country those attitudes which, willingly subservient, are frustrated anyhow around New York. Though the new homesteading may not involve quite the old risks, it is subject to some of the old anxieties and self-doubt: if you have stayed away from Broadway or choose to leave it, it may be taken as a sign that you are either not serious, hence amateurish, or too serious, hence not with it. Or, as Mr. Langner remarked, you may be among those who "are being influenced by the sick

European *avant-garde* theater. . . ." Such people, he added, "are seldom given an opportunity to function in the normal healthy American theater, nor do they want it."*

Albee's success may soon change that. When the change has taken place, however, one may expect those under the influence of the European *avant-garde* to be even sicker. You may not find God on Broadway, but there are (I'm told) a few serious angels around. And I agree with those members of the Broadway Establishment who have been dealing with sour grapes through the years: if you really have talent, Broadway can use you. The danger is it *will* use you, and you too can be a member of the normal healthy American theater.

Actually, you don't have to go to Broadway for that. When he was Secretary of Labor, Arthur Goldberg—foreseeing a renaissance on the New Frontier—reminded us that, in addition to all the orchestras, opera companies, and string quartets around the land, there were more than 5000 community theaters. (I have heard reports on little theaters ranging up to 30,000!) Why, then, do we worry about Decentralization, which would appear to be an accomplished fact? Is it only that most of these theaters are not professional? I don't believe it. I think the trouble is that most of them are normal and healthy, and in my more manic moments I am convinced that if 90 per cent of them were to disappear overnight, there might be an improvement in American culture.

Putting aside our Freudian concern lest one man's health be another man's sickness, when I hear such statistics or when I am told by a past president of the American Educational Theatre Association that more people are participating in community theater than in any other collective artistic enterprise in human history, I am not inspired—for it all has that spooky dietetic resolution one sees at a banquet in the look of a man who has learned to live with his coronary.

The artisans and guildsmen who worked communally in the Middle Ages were building cathedrals; and though I am no amorist of that period, the question is *What are we building?* Or rather, since so much of it is *fait accompli, What hath God wrought?*

For Mr. Goldberg has the scene, if not his statistics, straight: multitudinous theaters incarnadine the landscape. They have bled and been bled so long most of them no longer know what they are and what they might be. They have almost nothing to say on their own and await orders of the day from the latest issue of *Theatre Arts* (perhaps demoralized a little by the recent reversing trend of that magazine).

That same past president, who runs a community theater of longstanding reputation, grew nearly apoplectic when I asked similar questions and voiced

* The rapprochement in culture between the two major powers is demonstrated when this is set beside Khrushchev's remark, reviewing abstract painting, that it does not appeal to "normal healthy people."

similar charges, and in the process made some slighting remarks about the Samuel French catalogue—which, aside from its few useful services, provides inanities for high schools and little theaters. (During the McCarthy period, Samuel French had announced a playwriting contest in which one of the conditions was that French "reserves the right at any time to declare ineligible any author who is, or becomes publicly involved, in a scholastic, literary, political, or moral controversy.") He had previously denounced as "garbage, nothing but garbage," certain plays I had praised, including one by Samuel Beckett. Rising now, however, to the defense of Samuel French, he said that same play was now in the Samuel French catalogue (where it is no longer garbage, I assume) and (if this wasn't the millennium!) his wife had produced it recently in a studio production.

Which is the customary way: infiltrating from abroad, true subversion turns out like high fashion. We take our corrosives for protein like Tiger's Milk cut by fruit juice. Just as Giraudoux is lubricated by Valency and Duerrenmatt shaped up by Vidal, in the enchanting little theaters of America directors with the souls of interior decorators turn *Waiting for Godot* into a fairy tale and have a ball with *The Bald Soprano*. "Everything goes slowly, everything happens by degrees in the provinces," wrote Stendhal, "life is more natural." By which he meant how deadly life could be outside of Paris. His tone went with Vladimir Nabokov on his tour of America in *Lolita*. Nevertheless, my Call to Order is meant not only to send people west, but also to arouse action among those who are already there.

For the true substantial dream of the American theater is still Decentralization. It is, in fact, Manifest Destiny. If it seems again to be coming on apace, it is because, like the crab, we had crawled backwards. And once more we must ask why—if engineers can reverse the course of rivers or irrigate the deserts—we shouldn't be able to turn the Tributary into the Source.

There are those who feel the task of rejuvenation is hopeless. There are those, like our past president, who will be outraged by my disdain of the vast deadwood around the nation. In this, I include much of the educational theater which, according to the ancient testimony of Sheldon Cheney, once "poured knowledge and courage, expertness and ideals, into the little theater movement."

Later in this chapter, I shall want to discuss some of the new possibilities of educational theater. But, by the farthest stretch of self-defense, would anybody looking for courage in the American theater make the same case today for the universities? Expertness of a sort, yes; knowledge of a sort, yes. But what happened to all that idealism? For the carnage of those high ambitions —often in very nice buildings—also incarnadines the landscape.

"Moral apparently:"—George Bernard Shaw said it—"those who make half revolutions dig their own graves."

When the Little Theater Movement started after World War I, a chorus of brave and visionary voices told theater people to stay where they were and create their own theaters. Some of those voices remained in New York, but the old yellow-covered *Theatre Arts* took on Decentralization as its primary mission. Whole issues were devoted to the Tributary Theater, with experimental playhouses, sophisticated repertoires, and regional passion. There would be the Metropolis, but inspiration would come from the provinces. In those days, the editors (first Cheney, then Mrs. Isaacs and Stark Young) refused to accept the distinction between the professional theater and the amateur. Not only Lugné-Poë, but Granville-Barker, Gordon Craig, everybody who was anybody in the modern theater was conscripted to declare the intrinsic vision of his personal soil.

Lee Simonson was saying that the Broadway theater is a boarding house, the community theater is a home. "As to a national theater," Kenneth Macgowan wrote in *Footlights Across America,* "if we are ever to have one it will certainly not be found on our feverish Broadway, or in that synthetic capital, Washington. It will have its roots in every state. It will live nationally as American life lives nationally through its local and characteristic institutions." By the end of the thirties, Cheney wrote of the Little Theater Movement in his history of the stage: "Immature still, no final achievement has come out of them—but what is a decade or so in the history of an art? At least they have been significant of a deep and strong current in the national art life, have been important as destroyers and innovators, have given to the country its most promising institutional stages . . . and have brought the spirit of youth to expression."

One feels on reading back through those issues and those books that there was *in the American theater!* a natural alliance between theater and exaltation, that the word *art* was not reprehensible, nor eggheads suspect, and that he who chose not to cross the road to the Metropolis was not plain chicken. In fact, as the editors appraised each month "The World and the Theatre," there was positive glee when they could report the success of some inauspicious venture opposed to what they were calling the Trade Theater. Example: "The truth is that there was never a more completely amateur theater than the Cleveland Playhouse unless it was the Moscow Art Theater. There were never actors more entirely amateur in their approach than the Clevelanders, however professional in their training. Frederick McConnell, the director, has had not one but dozens of offers for work in the New York trade theater. So far, he has scorned them. But if he ever should produce for Al Wood with Jed Harris as stage manager, he would still be an amateur. And to know what that means is to study and understand the record of the Cleveland Playhouse from its first days in a packing box, and also to know that some day we will again divide the theater not into professional and amateur but into amateur and trade."

Scorn. And temerity. And refusal. The missionaries of *Theatre Arts* printed little theater budgets, advised on costs of hardware and muslin, suggested ways of saving money (best way: Imagination), but they never made money the issue—and, indeed, when they did raise that issue, they told the directors of the Tributary Theater, in communities and on campuses, that since theater sails anyhow on the high seas of chance, the best way to be lucky is to be wise. And that did not mean, as Mrs. Isaacs said, following the example of the Trade Theater, whose "laws must obviously be altered if the theater is to progress to permanence. Obviously, too, they can be. You have only to look over the history of the trade theater to see how often these laws have been remade in an economic crisis and to realize how easily they could be altered to meet a successful, a really successful artistic rebellion."

Mrs. Isaacs was writing in the year free enterprise went crashing in the Great Depression. A number of our economic laws had to be altered, often by improvisational means threatening the Constitution. Since the end of the New Deal, mobilization, reconversion, and the creation of a "dual economy," sluggish to the point of recession and bolstered by permanent defense, have put a limit to mere determination about social change. But only a limit. One of the deleterious effects of the policy of Containment is that it becomes more than geopolitical—a psychic atmosphere. Outright conformity aside, one result of the new Moral Realism, which is the better part of the general feeling of helplessness in the Cold War, is to deprive many of us of all sense of rebellion. But if the thirties could learn to say yes out of economic necessity, it would seem possible to learn to say no out of biological absurdity. Of those who have learned to say it, some have renounced the whole works, and withdrawn to await the last syllable of atomic doom. But the huger choice is to say no and stay with it, rather than capitulate to "forces" so abstract and remote as to be beyond even the "experts" to whom we turn them over.

I have been sufficiently tainted myself by the European *avant-garde* not to be subverted by the American spirit of perfectibility; but as regards the modern theater, we all know that everything in it worth a damn was born not only of positive determination, mostly by amateurs, but of foolhardiness beyond belief. It was such foolhardiness, seized by proletarian urgency, that took the theater through the thirties. ". . . we were carrying on a task that was almost against nature!" wrote Harold Clurman in *The Fervent Years.* "Do not mistake me: I believed that this impossible task had to be carried out by us—since if it wasn't, by whom would it be? But, my idealism did not preclude my seeing that in a very real sense we were fools." That disastrous period gave birth to the Group, and the Federal Theater looked fair for a while, as part of the public works program and in collaboration with local theaters all the way to Treasure Island, to alter the economics of the Trade Theater, with multiple companies and simultaneous openings, and a general boost to the morale of the profession, despite all the charges of featherbedding that accompanied the more scandalous charges of subversion that eventually canceled its subsidy.

Those responsible for the Group and the Federal Theater were also convinced that a really successful artistic revolution could alter the nature of things, and though both enterprises perished in the disillusion of the forties and the silence thereafter, much of the boldness and scope and authority in the serious theater we do have comes from people who were trained by them or remember their example—though we need not be sentimental about what was actually accomplished and though much of what they produced would be embarrassing today.

Nor need we misrepresent what will alone can do. "For ten years I had been an idealist," wrote Clurman in describing the collapse of the Group. "Despite my knowledge of the facts, I had been impelled by the feeling that if one's will is strong enough, and if one's desire is sufficiently hot, these alone could mold events. When will and desire, however, no longer correspond to facts, when facts do not provide them a sufficiently substantial basis, when will and desire become isolated forces, they induce a kind of madness, cause pain without grace. My will and the collective will of my fellow workers were not sufficient to establish a Group Theater that might endure despite the jungle life, the drought and famine, of the Broadway theater in the early forties." Still, as he also pointed out, hardly anyone attached to the Group "had abandoned its ideals or lost faith in its hypotheses and practices." For myself, when I ask why some of the better-paid people in the market place don't join the revolution, and am told that revolution is only for the amateurs, I always recall how Margaret Barker turned down a manager who had asked how long she thought she'd be busy with her present engagement: "If our play is a success—twenty years. If not—twenty years." Or when some ambitious actor hems and haws about giving up the TV gravy or—as recently happened—rejects a season of repertory (which, naturally, he always wanted to do) for the outside possibility he will be *seen* in the national company of a third-rate Broadway play, I recall Morris Carnovsky's answer when, after opening in *My Sister Eileen,* he was asked how it felt to be with a success: "I have been with a success for ten years."

Those ten years were ample to justify my absorbing the Group in a discussion of Decentralization, which is not only a geographic matter. What the Group represented was up to that time, not even excepting Eva Le Gallienne's repertory theater, something essentially foreign to theater in New York. It was more companionable with the spirit that infused the Little Theater Movement and that was during the twenties broadcast in the universities. Yet it was *in* New York, and the imagination of professional theater people was such that, whatever sacrifices had to be made, they were still to be made there. The situation, we trust, is changing. If the Group failed, it failed with the environment, and the times, and because a group needs nourishment from other groups, not only in the theater, but in every other agency of society as well; it is the basic principle of organic life. In the absence of such collective encouragement, the only alternative would seem to be subsidy.

Which is the problem we have inherited. The military policy of Containment—the social symptoms of which extend from the anonymous sexuality of the Twist to the deadpan thuggery of our new Masscult Heroes—has paradoxically made more money available. Now, however, that the prospect of various kinds of subsidy seems less remote, the question remains whether the groups formed or forming around the country will return to the mainstream from which the Group came (I am not speaking merely of its sociopolitical character, but that too), and from which each of them can nourish each other. Now that the cultural explosion, a product of excess leisure, is inducing civic officials to provide art centers and business leaders to convert tax deductions and oil-depletion allowances into new theaters, will the new groups which play in them be willing to exercise their independence in a society which now seems less hostile to what they represent, as it grows more indifferent to what anything represents? It has become a platitude of our compliance that, with the class wars fought and social security established there are no good causes left. Anybody who inquired (even before Birmingham) will know how absurd that is—and one may ask whether a breadline is any greater inducement to social action than a shelter program. One may even ask, as the labor experts are doing, whether we've gotten rid of all the breadlines.

Let us grant the point, however, and its corollary: the causes are gone, the theater is not a pulpit. If there is no need now to get up on a platform, will our new theaters be willing when there *is* (you see how absurd!) a clear and present danger? And will we know how? For even the best of us have learned, confronted with issues too harrowing, to invoke craft against commitment, by making a commitment of craft. In a similar way, the public invokes culture as a substitute for the ardors of understanding and responsibility for action. There is bound up in the manufactured prosperity of the arts—the flood of paperbacks, the astonishing record sales, the Sears, Roebuck gallery, that theater at the shopping center, the statistics of the Stanford Research Institute which tell us more people are attending cultural events than baseball games—a lot of good public will, there's no denying. While for the present Mr. Goldberg's renaissance will surely go begging among the bureaucrats, one day the good offices of earnest men like Senator Javits and Representative Thompson may even produce the miracle of government subsidy. Let us take warning, however, from Hallie Flanagan, when she summed up the murder of the Federal Theater: "If this government theater had been less alive it might have lived longer."

The recent discomfiture of an investigating committee by the outspoken Women for Peace may indicate that, for the time being and despite the Minute Men of the Radical Right, a new Federal Theater would not have to worry about a Dies Committee. However, at the moment, whatever else is in the offing, we haven't the slightest prospect of such a theater. What we do have and may develop will undergo, as I have suggested, more subtle forms of intimidation.

These are inherent in the conspicuous virtues of the New Frontier—whose policies are being continued in the altered personal style of President Johnson. There are those who feel that the Texas pragmatism and congressional know-how of the new President may set wheels in motion that Mr. Kennedy's eloquence couldn't budge. For it was one of the liabilities of Mr. Kennedy's administration, with all its superior potential, to be done in by its own expertise. There were antennae everywhere, and tons of facts. It seemed a card-index administration with an ethical sensibility, informed by Harvard and computer based. President Johnson may conduct more of the nation's business by the buttonhole techniques of the Senate cloakroom, but he felt impelled to keep Mr. Kennedy's advisors, and no politician can avoid today the roadblocks that became marked in constitutional democracies after the war—and by the ambiguities of social progress in this period.

As much as it knows, the government sometimes knows no more than the next man (witness the Bay of Pigs), but the image of knowhow, backed by the new style of "research and development," is kept up. (The astronaut's famous prayer before Congress had the usual thanksgiving for research and development.) This was even true during the know-nothingness of Eisenhower's term of office. As for the electorate, having very little to say in its own right, and informed—as Arthur Schlesinger said to his fellow historians —by media that have as much relation to reality as the shadows in Plato's cave, it is also full of experts. What else could we expect from all those paperbacks, those extension programs, the swamping of colleges, the foreign films, the quiz shows, the readers' subscriptions, and the public information services of industry, labor, government, and private lobbies. If there is no class warfare, there are the new status groups and all the old vested interests, with more course credits and all sorts of technical proficiency, yet in the ensemble producing, in de Tocqueville's words, "a small, distressing motion, a sort of incessant jostling of men, which annoys and disturbs the mind without exciting or elevating it." The New Frontier—even in Johnson City, where the difficult is done immediately and the impossible takes a little time—is peculiarly susceptible to this motion; balancing with precision the claims of every interest group, it sometimes resembles a Calder mobile that can't move at all.

In culture, when it does move, there is the long procession past the Mona Lisa. The Kennedy's no doubt had more valid rapport with M. Malraux than Mr. Johnson is likely to have, for his tastes seem to run to the cow-and-cactus brand of painting. Out of deference or indifference, Mr. Johnson will probably not resist the cultural trend, but when we assess the new interest in the arts encouraged by the Kennedy's, it feels somehow symbolic that when Frost appeared at the Inaugural, he was blinded by the glare. For there is the feeling—as Karl Meyer and others have said of the Philharmonic Hall at Lincoln Center—that you are going to have official architecture for official art. Or, after Miller, Behrman, and O'Neill at Washington Square, when the curtains do part at the permanent home of the Repertory Theater, you will see the curvilinear prow of a set by Boris Aronson, with an Agamemnon in the poop sounding like J.B.

Now, there is no reason the Establishment shouldn't have its own auditorium and its own art—which may transcend, with luck, official expectations. There is perhaps no reason the most dissident art should be sponsored at all—

except that provision for dissidence is supposed to be one of our most cherished beliefs. That being so, we can't help wanting a little subscription to the idea that the opposition, not merely the jostling, has a right to be heard; and not—to the degree we justify dispossession by saying it has always been so —twenty years later. Nevertheless, that distressing motion is more subtle even than our dissidence sometimes knows. There you are, reconciled to neglect, determined to burrow from below at the Babel above, like a voice from the cellarage—when the long arm of benevolence touches you.

The paradoxes of recognition never became clearer to me than when I was in East Berlin several years ago, calling on Helene Weigel-Brecht at the Berliner Ensemble. Weigel, primly potent in a black ankle-side gown, her glasses breasted on a chain, served tea. Then she picked up the phone and called Elizabeth Hauptmann, Brecht's secretary and collaborator, to come over and meet me. We had corresponded briefly. When Hauptmann arrived, Weigel introduced me as the director of the first American production of *Mother Courage*. Hauptmann, recalling, smiled. Then Weigel said, "And he is here on money from the Ford Foundation." End smile. Severe Prussian set of jaw, proletarianized: "Any strings attached?"

I have since learned you don't have to go to East Germany to be asked that question. My theater has received a series of grants from the Ford Foundation, and though that makes me no expert on the ulterior motives of capitalist beneficence, I can say this much: If the Foundation has—as people have warned us—any intention of subverting our independence, then it has given no explicit evidence. Nor, when one wonders at what point in a theater's intransigeance support would be withdrawn or withheld, I would say at this juncture even the Foundation doesn't know. For the Foundation is, like any other institution in this ambiguous period, yawing with the cold wind on the New Frontier, and trying to define its own character. I have no doubt that were we to have another McCarthy era, there would be more uneasiness among the trustees about who was receiving how much for what—as there was when Robert Hutchins' Fund for the Republic ran into trouble and was declared by Henry Ford II "a wholly disowned subsidiary." If it could be shown that our theater has a reasonable quota of what the Justice Department might consider fellow travelers, I suspect giving might be curtailed, as it possibly has been elsewhere, I don't know; there are a couple of curious omissions. Or if the vigilantes of the Birch Society were to take over the country with their machine guns, I foresee far less generosity to us, especially as we have more or less expressed ourselves in public on their solid American virtues. We must remember that during the McCarthy period there was no subsidy to the theater of any kind. Symptomatic of the period was ANTA, with a congressional charter barely worth the parchment it was written on.

The attack launched against the Federal Theater at the end of the thirties was part of a general assault on independent thought and progressive legislation that continued through the security measures of war and on into the "permanent war economy" of Welfare Capitalism. In that assault—it is important to see this—the theater was one of the first things to go. "Were they afraid?" asks Hallie Flanagan at the end of *Arena.* "Were they afraid of the Federal Theater because it was educating the people of its vast new audience to know more about government and politics and such vital issues as housing, power, agriculture, and labor? True, these issues were dealt with in only a small fraction, less than 10 per cent, of Federal Theater plays. Still I could see why certain powers would not want even 10 per cent of the Federal Theater plays to be the sort to make people in a democracy think. Such forces might well be afraid of thinking people." By the beginning of the fifties, even Brooks Atkinson, writing from within the Establishment, was forced to declare that the hoodlums and the Yahoos were in control of our cultural life, as they were in Russia.

Let us face it: they are still largely in control; but there is a double thaw.

Still, the problem of cultural endowment is different as the State is different in character, and as the source of endowment has changed. We are not dealing with government sponsorship, but with the munificence of private enterprise, which can once again be looked at with muckraking skepticism. Just as the philanthropies of the early twentieth century were partial atonement for the pillage of the Robber Barons of the nineteenth, so the profits of postwar Reconversion, almost unmanageable, were fed off into cultural foundations as tax deductions. With trusts so large and dividends so accumulative they could barely be spent, these were no mere fringe benefits. (I recall reading several years back that one of the foundations had about forty-eight times more money than when it began giving it away.) During the 1962 stock-market depression, the foundations were among the corporations that freed money so the economy could be restored to normal; when everybody was trying to sell, they bought. It was an act of faith. Which is to say the foundations are not merely reflections of public guilt and a means of tax write-off. (Nobody can tell, for example, whether the proposed tax cut would encourage cultural giving, by freeing money, or discourage it, by making deductions less urgent.)

As Daniel Bell points out in *The End of Ideology,* although business may be "more manipulative and security-conscious," it is also "less pecuniary and acquisitive" and "has achieved a certain social-mindedness and become decent, at least to its 'exempt' personnel. . . ." There's the hitch, of course—meaning, perhaps, those who shape up. Yet it is certainly to be expected that the Foundation, this midcentury development of industrial philanthropy, and with a board of directors composed mainly of hard-nosed businessmen protecting the dividends of valuable family stock, will be vulnerable to the pressures of opinion like any other capitalist institution—and we must recall that even the Supreme Court, whose record on civil rights has improved, battened down its democratic hatches during the McCarthy storms.

The psychology of foundation grants is worth a study of its own. They are a peculiarly American phenomenon to the extent they have gone, in the theater and the academic world, to people like myself, who were brought up to believe there were three villains in the universe: Herbert Hoover, John D.

Rockefeller, and Henry Ford; and whose sense of history was outraged by Ford's "bunk." Now we find it the natural condition of talented estrangement in our body politic to be catered to, financed, and sent on the Grand Tour. Or, as with our theater, provided with operating funds. If that is the new secret weapon of the Establishment, I prefer it to neglect, and if there is a Grand Strategy to assimilate protest, I am willing to take my chances. After all, Sophocles was a general and Shakespeare accepted—nay, would even have filled out in triplicate forms for—a coat of arms.

Nor am I claiming immunity when I say this. Since the theater is an institutional art, the Foundation is intent on steering you in the direction of stability. There may be that point at which money, accumulating, has no alternative but to be virtuous; but whatever gives you stability will inevitably change your character. As Scott Fitzgerald used to say, the very rich are different from us; a little touch of affluence takes you a slightly different way. Up to now, the Foundation's practical advice has been invariably sound; but it is not obliged to prevent stability from becoming a drag. That task is ours. And if there is any pressure, under our grants from the Foundation, to become other than that for which we originally came to its attention, it is more likely to come now from the community than the Foundation. For the community did, indeed, after much provocation and civic alarm, dig up matching funds for the grants Ford had tendered provisionally. And there is consequently the feeling in the community that it can now determine our nature. Surely, the community has always determined our nature to a degree, even when we were a most "hostile" theater. But when you think of the simplest, most unadulterated, and grossest forms of pressure, they will invariably come not from the mere Yahoos but from those who, having encouraged you for what you did years ago, may stop giving you encouragement when you change your course; or rather, when you persist in it—because that persistence may carry you past what they bargained for.

We recently had a manifestation of this from one of the more ponderous of the reviewers in the area, whose support, I must admit, we have welcomed with that compromised contempt that is another aspect of the theater's time-serving social nature. It was at the end of a nearly slanderous review of a play of my own. I am not arguing its merits; let us say the play was even *that* bad, God help us! For this reviewer it appeared to be in that tradition of inscrutable or seminarish or obscurantist plays, probably inept as a result, of which we had done a good many. I don't think Martin Esslin would classify my play in the Theater of the Absurd, but I am thinking, and I gather the reviewer was thinking, of playwrights ranging from John Whiting to Jean Genet. The anti-intellectual rumblings had begun in previous reviews, were seconded elsewhere, and we were being warned that the public was tired of them—though I should say we had been doing concurrently plays by Shaw, Shakespeare, Jonson, Chekhov, Osborne, Brecht, Williams, and O'Neill, as well as some other new plays more or less straightforward in their deportment. Now this reviewer felt compelled to say openly to me and my colleagues: you have been "well-endowed by the Ford Foundation, presumably to bring 'community theater' to the Bay Area"; none of this "precious" stuff you have been doing is community theater, and you better think of giving us what the community wants.

Even if this reviewer did represent "the voice of the community," the point missed is that we had never accepted money from anybody on the grounds described. True, we saw ourselves as a community theater, but a community theater in the sense that the manifestos of the Little Theater Movement thought of theater: one which would be governed by no codes dictated by *ex-cathedra* smugness, and which would fight the barbarians at every turn, moving as well as we could discern them over the real dramatic issues—to an act of communion at the risk of outrage. And we do not see how we can do this unless we refuse to accept anybody's predispositions about what is and what is not community theater, and unless we seem from time to time mere "destroyers and innovators," afloat in the mad abstract dark. Nobody, we learned, is more offended by experiment than certain clerks of the New Literacy who, knowing a little bit about everything, feel privileged to know it all. They are the worst censors.

And beware of the smilers, too. The standard critique of the Group Theater came from one reviewer, very well-disposed of course, who wrote: "It has been bound rather than liberated by its idealism; and it has needed more than anything else the counsel of a genial and skeptical mind." Who is this mind? Clurman rightly suggests that "genial and skeptical mind" is the devil's mind.

As for the Foundation, having investigated us with its usual care, it recognized us, we assume, for what we were and what we aspire to be. Our cards were on the table, our behavior out in the open, our principles in our program notes. We made no deals. Nevertheless, the fact that even one rather silly and officious journalist thought fit to censure us registers somewhere. You promise yourself you will ignore the reviews, but the promise—given the reality—is in vain. Bad reviews keep your audience away as much in San Francisco as in New York, and until a theater is assured of a full subscription which will take it on faith, they will continue to threaten. So be it. In the unbalanced *Realpolitik* of the theater, let the censure, the animosity, the patronization be registered—the trick is not to cease and desist in being what you must be, as though the theater, that massive, incurably form-failing communal art, were a single indomitable being playing his own shuttle across the woof of his necessity.

That is no mean trick. And that passion may be derived more from our own generation's counter-rage for identity than the collective determination of the theater movement of the twenties. It is as though we need constantly to invoke ourselves into being, against disbelief in the possibility of a collective life, and as we memorize all the lapsing theaters of the twenties and the thirties, and the dearth of purpose out of which we were born in the period of the Silent Generation.

While the Group and the Federal Theater emerged and foundered, what had happened to the little theaters and their mentors at the universities? Perhaps the extent of their achievement was always overrated, as the Movement may have been given to premature flushes of self-celebration. By 1929, doubt had set in as to what had truly been accomplished and where things were going; and Mrs. Isaacs was calling—we see on reflection—for an artistic rebellion that had presumably taken place. As in the current revaluation of off-Broadway (though, in my opinion, the achievement of the little theaters was infinitely greater), observers began to realize that all the promise had not been consummated. The "destroyers and innovators" had either disappeared, waned in will, or went themselves to Broadway, where they became more or less compliant members of the Establishment.*

In *Advance from Broadway,* published in 1941, Norris Houghton points out that "The most talented boy in the university theater will be encouraged— even by those who profess to have lost their faith in Broadway—to try his future along Times Square." (The usual piety, quite American, is: "He must see for himself"—what is clear to any blind man from a distance.) Houghton adds: "Frederick Koch, most ardent regionalist of them all, will tell you within the first five minutes about every ex-Playmaker who has succeeded in the big city." And his followers, never quite believing in their real achievement, are still name-dropping, and still sending their prize pupils to the Metropolis. (In the early days some, like Paul Green, returned and put considerable ability into symphonic dramas on American history and folk plays that, seeking a *polis,* attracted tourists and gave us *Oklahoma!*)

Though Augustus Thomas had once warned in *Variety* that "the Little Theater rebellion" would have "the 'legit' by the throat 10 years from now," by the end of the twenties Barrett H. Clark was so outraged by the borrowing from Broadway and the reversal of Decentralization that he wrote, "If I had a really good experimental play, I would try to sell it everywhere on Broadway before I sent it to the little theaters." Still, as St. John Ervine pointed out, the Movement had made itself felt on Broadway and was getting back dilutions of what it had inspired. The trouble was, he said, that "Broadway, in improving the quality of its productions, had taken every man and woman of quality out of the little theaters which, alas, were left in the fearful guard of, I will not say, unthrifty knaves, but of pretentious and incompetent and ineffective egoists who imagined they were making a world when they were merely making a mess."

Frankly, I don't see very many of them any more who even imagine themselves making a world; and I'd prefer the mess to the uninhibited servility

* Some—even the most visionary—may always have been members at heart. Robert Edmund Jones, one of the heroes of the revolution, had written in the old *Theatre* magazine: "I have never seen one of the so-called 'Little Theaters' that I would exchange for a chance to work on a Broadway production. I am heart and soul for Broadway. . . ." But that was in 1917, before his own disillusionment and the breakthrough of the twenties.

which makes many of them aspire now to the slickness they have seen on tour. But St. John Ervine's purpose, in urging a revival of enthusiasm and invention on the little theaters, soon becomes plain. "The Broadway theater is living on the bones and blood of the little theater and is now in fine fettle [he was writing in 1931], but unless the little theater soon recovers from its anaemia, the Broadway theater will presently sicken, too, and we shall be in a very sad state; for the Broadway theater depends for its life on a continuous flow of good corpuscles from the little theater."

Though he differs from other critics about the "fine fettle" of that year, the prophecy was fulfilled. Yet, in his calling for a revival in the little theaters, the presupposition was (and it was the same in Mrs. Isaacs' summons to an artistic rebellion) that Broadway is the God-given terminus of all enterprise. There is still the assumption of tribute to be paid, and it is that antiquated notion of Tributary Theater, once so inspiring, of which we must rid ourselves today if a genuine revolution is to take place and Decentralization is not to reverse its course as it once did.

And it is not so impossible as it seems. This is not some new provincialism. New York will no doubt continue to reign supreme among our metropolitan cities, but the population explosion has shifted the continental axis, and the same things that make it easy to get to New York make it just as easy to get away. Beyond that, we have begun to see not only the need but the inevitability of major centers of culture throughout the nation, along with the new concept of the megalopolis, which will make San Francisco, for instance, the terminal point of a metropolitan area extending to San José (people are already commuting to Los Angeles). Sociologists and regional planners have predicted this drift, as well as those who started immediately after World War II to relocate themselves. I am not referring merely to shifts in the labor force, or to the migration of artists, but to industries and even baseball teams. A tribute to the continental tilt is the regional-theater program of the Ford Foundation, which could have been predicted even before the Foundation thought of it, and was. And when the reviews start coming from the other end of the country, and from the Midwest, perhaps even the most recalcitrant will realize that there are not only a few regional theaters out there, but a lot of people who never wanted to go to Broadway, really. *The New York Times* says so. The statistics say so. And statistics never lie, nor reviews.

Yet it will take more than a tilt and an exodus to make a revolution—even as the gods cooperate in their relentless geologic way.

Within America—aside perhaps from the Method, which is the natural orthodoxy of the American actor—there is very little theater culture to pass on. For artists working in the theater, there is no real give-and-take, nothing to set us off and nothing to be set upon, except that in which we *do not* believe. I am talking of plays, ensemble groups, style, ideas of production— and just plain ideas, with all their attendant forms of seeing and believing. In my own apprenticeship, when I was most desperate to learn whatever could be learned from any source, there was practically nothing—I do not exaggerate—*nothing* to be learned from Broadway. And there was in this country virtually no place else one felt compelled to go to learn, excepting one's own unaided resources, fortified by the literature. It's an unhappy theater in which one can learn more from books than he can by watching the stage.

Where one should learn from books, too, in the university theater, they are not always trusted. With all their facilities, the university theaters should be the radiation laboratories of the American drama; yet they remain—with few exceptions—backward, gouty, and intimidated, turning out students whose careers, even if successful, perhaps especially if successful, are mainly destined to triviality.

When I went with an engineering degree to a graduate school of drama, my scientific friends tried to dissuade me by saying only the worst students are in drama departments. They weren't wholly right, but they weren't that wrong. Again, plenty of talent—this was right after the war, and there was a lot of it waiting to get at itself. Now, an actor needn't be an egghead, but I see no reason why, wanting the spontaneity of innocence, he profits from self-enforced ignorance. You can tell me all about the strolling players and the Funambules, but such speculation is in vain, for our urban and egalitarian culture is not merely La Strada. An actor needn't be an ideologue either, but he is obliged to be a citizen, and is no more exempt than the rest of us from being the best one he can. Also, I suspect there was a cunning about the itinerant actor that, outside of the profession today, social security checks have made somewhat unnecessary. As for the familial unity and tradition of craft to be handed down, in our theater it doesn't exist.

And everything else aside, a university is a university.

If Hamlet's advice to the players doesn't suggest the value of intelligence, Chekhov's advice about Hamlet—he said the role couldn't be played except by an intellectual—does. And there is the fine story of the great Viennese actor Josef Kainz, who said he couldn't play Prospero because Prospero had to be a great man, and he wondered whether a great man would become only an actor. Perhaps not. And it would surely be unfortunate if Prospero were not played for want of great men. But Kainz's remark shows the kind of perception that helped make him a great actor in roles he thought himself worthy of—and which one still sees today in the dignified intelligence of Austrian actors. I saw a production of Camus' version of *The Possessed* in Vienna that for sheer grasp of ideas would be unthinkable in America, where even our oldest actors still feel like kids.

Usually it's not innocence the college actor wants, but course waivers. Playwrights? Given the climate of most drama departments, I have serious doubts whether they should be there at all. As for our scene designers, they ought to be artists, see-ers, rather than mechanics or great levelers; and our directors, whatever else they are, ought to be men of brain.

What was missing, though, was not so much erudition as *adventure,* the sort of thing one finds today in a wind tunnel or marine biology. Not that there wasn't activity. As in America at large, there was all the apparatus of full production, but where were the New Frontiers? The art of the theater was not made a personal or moral issue, nor was there any real dissidence in theory or practice, any impulse to be heard by shattering the sound barriers. If there was complaint, it was generally about roles, or Aristotle's *Poetics,* whose recurring modernity we could barely understand. What seemed experimental was merely niggling, an affair of dimmers and what they used to call "styliza-tion"; at its worst meaning enlarged gestures and fake speech; at its best imitation of the old innovation, the scene done in three modes—naturalistic, symbolic, and constructivist, *The Time of Your Life* on a seesaw. One didn't take to heart, however, the fact that each of these modes, having analogues in social and philosophical history, once constituted a revolution in the con-sciousness of men, for which artists did battle and went to prison.

I pick up the very latest anthology of modern drama, just received, and read in the introduction Zola's rallying cry: "Our theater will be naturalistic or it will not exist!" Having learned that it will exist anyhow, the students hardly cared what it existed for.

Eric Bentley—whose anthologies have done more than all of Broadway to enliven theater in America—tells how "after a moving performance of *Rosmersholm* at the Yale Drama School, [he] heard the students comment on everything except Ibsen's lines and Ibsen's meaning. The young men and women could lecture you on lighting, costumes, *décor,* acting, direction, but it seemed not to matter what was being lit, costumed, decorated, acted, and directed." That was at the other end of the continent about a dozen years ago, about the same time I was going to school. Apathy was general all over, like the snow over Ireland at the end of *The Dead.*

In the most evasive way, the play was the thing, and it didn't make too much difference, really, what play. (I don't remember hearing the name of Brecht until shortly before I left the department.) Those who went out to run thea-ters, in colleges and elsewhere, were taught or believed beforehand that there should be a "well-balanced season" (favoring the comedies, if possible). As for the world around us, there was some generalization about the relation of theater to society, mostly in other periods. The best of our professors (the students thought him too academic) did encourage some of us to work on a Living Newspaper on the Bomb. But in actuality, the physicists on campus were more political—as many of them were more artistic, and still are.

How prophetic did Ibsen need to get?

Let me be clear: this was right after the war when direction had to be restored. What I describe may not have been entirely the fault of the depart-ment—presumably one of the best. Nor were the students wholly at fault. This was the dawning of the Silent Generation, whose atmosphere was anticipated by the very profession of theater in America, infested by com-merce, grown speechless with impotency, a profession in which "The best lack all conviction, while the worst/Are full of passionate intensity."

But has the situation changed that much? Not long ago, I lectured at the

National Community Theater Center, where most of the students had been in college drama departments. If anything, they were more startled by the notion that a theater artist is committed in the ways I have suggested; if not startled by the notion, despairing of the chance to act on such conviction. More recently, I attended a series of auditions in Chicago for students wanting to go into the professional theater. What they wanted from the theater, what they had to contribute to it—aside from more or less talent, and more or less training—few of them knew, or said. I can't believe they were incapable of asking such questions of themselves, or me; only in the theater it rarely occurs to anyone that somebody would be interested. Instead, they asked the regional theater directors present about salaries, working conditions, and so forth. How much good it would have done us to have been asked: what is your theater up to? why does it exist? what does it have to say? what kind of plays do you do? how? and why do you do them?

But in Chicago the students did their scenes or showed their drawings and, opportunity being scarce enough, kept such questions (if they had them) to themselves. In such a profession—who dares use the word *art?*—a job is a job. There are always exceptions; more books being available now, the students have read some of those my contemporaries should have been reading. But given the dispirited training and the conditions that prevail, even some of the exceptions go the way of all flesh.

Scene: a metropolitan college; a large drama department in an enviable theater plant. The annual musical review is in preparation. A lot of resources are put into the production. An announcement reads: "No message, no moral, just GOOD CLEAN FUN." Well and good, joy, who could object? Only—though some serious plays had been done—there had never been any message or moral to which anybody had been devoted, nor, on the whole, any other kind of fun from which to seek relief. This was the same season that began with *Auntie Mame.* Distracted from distraction by distraction, we need diversion. At the same time, in the student magazine—where the stories, poems, and drawings were at the heart of the matter whatever else their faults, however clumsy the humor—a story called "Ain't We Got Fun?" was being censored for obscenity. *Auntie Mame,* I suppose, is also GOOD CLEAN FUN—only when will educated people learn that it is usually the good clean fun which is obscene?

Now, frankly, I think the students deserve their musical and will survive *Auntie Mame.* Scout's honor: I am not against fun. It is my firm belief that every season (it is implied in the very word) ought to have its bacchanalia—though bacchanalias, as Aristophanes shows, are wilder, riskier, more seminal. What is disturbing, however, is the justification of the junk by the argument that "we first have to get them interested in the theater" or that students need to be trained for the *kitsch* because that's what awaits them outside. Which is like saying we ought to train our literature students to teach the *Saturday Evening Post* or our musicians to prepare for Lawrence Welk. When I am told that such things are done, moreover, "to serve the community," I am confounded, because the community is overrun with such service. And when was it a college's function to serve the community by conforming to its worst taste? To pass on a heritage in which you believe is one thing, but must we have the *ethos* of Dick and Jane, the Ur-figures of the elementary schools, brought up to the college level?

Most disheartening are the remarks about such performances by members of the faculty—professors of our great humanistic tradition—who are impressed with the talent, the pacing, the skill: "Why, it was absolutely *professional!*" So were the Mickey Mouse clubs, with their faceless desecration of the most gifted children, who wind up with mature facelessness in "our great native art form," the Broadway musical. The new teaching machines are excellent, the circulars say, because students are now "dial-orientated." I think we cannot justify anything in a curriculum that encourages this tendency.

Is the theater a serious academic discipline or is it not? Nobody is really offended by harmless diversion. Relaxation, fine. But I am talking neither of exceptions nor of rules; I am talking of theater as a way of life. I am saying that teachers ought to have convictions. And I am saying that people in responsible positions are not practicing faithfully what they ought to be teaching if they are not. I am saying that students ought to have convictions. They ought to know, for instance, what those with their wits about them have learned—that, as in the past, the funniest plays are likely to be the most deadly. Take Aristophanes: the hilarity of *The Clouds* and *The Frogs* was part of a resolute effort by a political conservative to keep the Athenian Empire from destruction. There was no more joyous (and expert) production in America the year the Piccolo Teatro di Milano brought over *The Servant of Two Masters.* Yet when I was in Italy and asked Paolo Grassi, one of the directors, why he had decided to found the Piccolo (which, by the way, means *little*), he said, "Misery! I am speaking of misery—miserable people!" *The Servant of Two Masters,* in the Piccolo's interpretation, was one of the first fruits of the determination to do something about it, by going back to the roots of the native drama, to the *commedia,* with its boundless improvisational energy, which abhors dial-orientation.

There are any number of intelligent people working in college drama who for one reason or another capitulate to all this. Whereas other departments are searching out anti-protons, it takes drama departments a long cautious time to catch up with the anti-drama. Thus, much after certain developments become established in the market place, a drama conference takes as its theme "The New Drama and the New Play." In the days when college drama departments were being formed, it used not to be so—and in a few strongholds it may still not be so; but surely, while other developments are taking place elsewhere, most of the drama departments will be producing the old *avant-garde.*

In a survey in the *Educational Theatre Journal* (March 1962), Theodore Shank indicated that during the preceding ten years there had been a trend "toward the production of fewer *Broadway* plays and more *standard* plays."

Yet, according to the survey, the distribution of standard or "classical" plays seldom goes beyond Shaw, Shakespeare, and Noel Coward. As for the foreign plays, New York's increasing reliance on them, Bentley's anthologies, the Dramabooks of Hill and Wang, the offbeat authors of Grove Press, and the sophistication of the *Tulane Drama Review* have had some effect. But for all their notoriety, Beckett and Brecht are still largely avoided, as are Pinter, Whiting, Albee, Adamov, and Genet, not to mention unknown playwrights. Professor Shank's conclusions: "Instead of a spirit of experimentation which would lead the college theaters to present dramas which are not frequently produced, the same conservative spirit which has been prevalent in the commercial theater seems to exist." Though not necessarily immune to box-office pressure, college theaters generally have more proportionate subsidy, fewer expenses, and far better buildings, and one would think they could take risks when they are still risks—if only out of academic obligations comparable to those compelling research in other fields.

As for "student needs" (that evasive old bogey), one learns when he teaches either poetry or physics that students are turned on by the new to look into the old because, nothing having been held back in the present, they want to discover the first principles behind the latest phenomenon, because they want to see where their hunches and perturbations came from, or because, sensing something still missing, they want to know how all that energy or beauty was lost. The really new play gets close to where the student lives, just as the classics do when they are approached not with updating strategies or antiquarian respect, but for what is immediate, meaningful, residually beautiful, and incriminating in them. Some of the students with tremors of dismay about their backwardness search out courses in other departments, and if you keep your ears open around the drama departments, you may discover some students reading Ghelderode and Frisch before their teachers, carrying the texts around as they rehearse *Auntie Mame*. Again, things are improving: this year, between sessions of good clean fun, the department even risked a Brecht.

When the university was guardian of the arcane, integrity was a matter of individual discipline. In science, which the popular mind—for all the priming by mass magazines—relinquishes to the realm of Mystery, pure research can proceed relatively unimpeded. But the theater is a public art that invites community. And community, whatever its blessings, invites adulteration. True, adulteration may appear like Spenser's Duessa, in the lineaments of the utmost propriety. As the university assumes more of the aspect of a cultural center—with poets-in-residence, creative-writing programs, art festivals and galleries, and enlarged theater premises—the campus theater may extend its radius only to find it has run into a neat circumference of model villages and commercial malls. And a whole set of attendant values that could turn a potential civic theater into a gathering place for nonplused and plumbeous civility.

It mainly depends on the way policy is first established. It's hard to do later what you should have done now. One can read back over the principal addresses at conventions of the American Educational Theatre Association to see that a good number of eloquent men are trying to spur on experiment, to encourage new plays, to urge the student into other departments "to extend his awareness," and "to emphasize the high—the *very* high—importance of the theater in education," as well as to dissipate the drama teacher's sense of inferiority vis-à-vis his colleagues in science by reviewing what he can do even for nonprofessional students: "You will be making them sensitive and integrated human beings who can grasp and enjoy existence in the perfectly normal course of life."

This genteel passion is admirable, as is the belief that out of the "myth" of educational theater, "out of the traditional academic adversities of impossible space, limited time, sketchily trained personnel, and a begrudging administration, out of these ashes, our Phoenix, the American theater will—despite them all—rise!" If they are not exactly rattling platitudes they are not cracking nature's molds either, or getting at the inveterate blandness, the mealiness, or the generalized good will of teachers who have never been entirely sure what educational function they serve, or students whose careers remain professionally nebulous, unless they decide to teach also.

However you look at it, rhetoric betrays, and it is the "integrated human beings" one distrusts. Integrated with what? One rarely feels in the literature of such conventions, as in the departments themselves, that out beyond the curriculum is a world which may be too disordered to grasp, too spurious to join, in which existence is a leasehold, and in which a "perfectly normal course of life" is next to impossible.

Education can hardly proceed in any of the liberal arts unless one has a grasp of the unsettling wisdom of Bob Hope at the commencement exercises of his son. Certainly no "sick" comedian, Hope told the graduates who were about to go out into the world: "Don't go!"

As of now, not even the trolley colleges are likely to be by geography and disposition civic theaters, and there's perhaps no reason they should be. Perhaps, to begin afresh, they ought not to produce publicly at all, but concentrate on internal growth among the students (and the faculty too): cell groups of actors, new plays, improvisation, choral work, mime and masks, song and dance, acrobatics, *reading* texts. If the students on tech crews didn't have to build huge sets for public performance and then waste more nights pushing those sets around, the departments wouldn't complain so much about lack of time for training; and the students could study art, literature, history instead. And the theater work needn't be all laboratory—hell, there are plenty of students to see the students. None of this would take the place of the theater conservatory for the strictest professional training, but it would go a long way toward repairing the schizophrenia that now exists in the colleges between begrudging academic standards and half-baked theater training. If four years were spent on real work at close quarters instead of in the public eye, the students might then really be prepared for what seems the next major development in the American theater: professional theaters on campuses.

For there are visionary men in the universities trying to reconceive their function in view of the population explosion, the ambiguity of metropolitan limits, collaboration with industry and trade unions, and even the vanishing margins between academic disciplines; who see no reason the arts should not have the same privileged and active status in education, without the impediment of mere pedantry, that engineering and medicine have. Such status is untenable without the standards of those other professions and performance of work that does not make a mockery of the exemption from academic routine, and unless there is an urgency to bring what is discovered back without compromise into public service.

The idea of endowed companies on campus is not novel. (F. Cowles Strickland had this in mind when he initiated an artists-in-residence program at Stanford after the war.) What has not been satisfactorily explored is the form they should take to be warranted. They should certainly not be there as a pretext for inviting Maurice Evans and Helen Hayes, or to transplant Broadway and summer stock. To produce plays "more professionally" is not sufficient justification, however much one approves of better performances. The course such a theater might take might be better indicated by saying that, whatever they perform, they need the kind of autonomy granted to and the imagination of the atom-smashers. This implies they will look upon rehearsal and performance as modes of inquiry, not only flirting with but exploding into the unknown. The danger of insularity and secretiveness arising from such autonomy is in part mitigated by the necessity of performance—the inherent gregariousness and exhibitionism of the theater. What is done may be strange, but it is done to be done.

To achieve anything like this, it will be necessary to exorcise prejudices in two directions: among educators who distrust the pedagogic value of a theater that does not exist solely for student performance (though they do not raise the same eyebrows about the laboratories); among theater people who consider acting or directing on campus a professional sellout (though what in the world they'd be selling out, given the state of their profession, one could hardly guess). The academic novels inform us that the artist at the university is liable to pangs of self-mortifying guilt. The campus may, indeed, seem a retreat, and for some artists, needing to make a living, has been no more than that. But those who fear contamination by academia are not necessarily any more independent. Those who teach may certainly be overburdened with courses and committees, and the loss of energy I can appreciate, having led such a divided life myself. But when I hear complaints about the debilitating, conformist atmosphere of the university, I am inclined to feel I am listening either to those who are easily intimidated or frighteningly conservative (if not simply anti-intellectual), as certain brooders on artistic liberty are likely to be.

Whatever the politics of Academe, the lassitude of departments, the economics of publish or perish, the failures of involvement among professors, it is a haven of utter license compared to the economic and mental slavery most of those in our theater have known. And what an environment it could be! As imagination may extend the powers of research and scholarship by its very presence, shaking up stuffiness, it is possible to conceive of a theater on a campus which is locally dissident, clarion, substanced by ideas born of hard solitude in other disciplines, challenged by the criticism of colleagues worthy of respect, and in turn testing those ideas and weighing criticism by engrained conviction and practice, in the open, unscholarly, but no less exacting the forum of the stage.

Such a theater would be a boon to any Extension Program, and would be worth financing for that alone. Productions could be toured to areas which do not have or could not afford themselves to support a theater of stature. If, however, John Ciardi is right and the universities have been taken over by the deans—well, so far as most drama departments go, there's no great loss. My own feeling is that nothing substantial is ever administered out of existence—if those concerned are alert. The deans may be a trial in an age of managers, but the administrative mind flourishes where busy work is necessary to cover up the fact that little else is happening, as in schools of education. In pedagogy, excess deanship is a variant of the lapse of content in dyslogistic technique.

Before university theaters presume to the status of civic theaters, however, let them better serve the university, performing with educated distinction. As some of these theaters are currently run, even a good part of the faculty and students—who deserve a theater too—don't attend the productions. This was true, everybody proceeded to tell me, at one great Midwestern university at which I was a visiting lecturer. The department had dwindled to ineffectuality from being a bastion of Decentralization in the old days; and in this instance— having no more power as a department—had to *rent* the quite satisfactory theatrical premises on the campus. When they produced, they felt obliged to produce not what they judged to be essential for the university (could they presume to judge, though they are being, as presumable specialists, paid to judge?) but what they thought would help to pay the rent. This meant luring the "community" of a rather prosperous town. What lured the community, if it did, alienated the faculty and students. Where experiment was carried on, it was mainly initiated by the students, though to atone for past sins the department is now starting a very little theater for rather *avant-garde* plays.

One doesn't finally like talking out of school about these things, but the facts are there, and they are insupportable.

At the beginning of the preceding chapter I spoke of the peculiar dialectic carried on between the Comédie Française and the *avant-garde,* a dialectic which in the work of Copeau reached out to the provinces.

Copeau was not an unknown director when he decided to leave the Vieux

Colombier to take a small group of young people with him to Pernand in Burgundy—an action which later influenced the summer "retreats" of the Group. Copeau was respected not only by theater people but by the most exacting of literary people, such as Péguy and Gide, with whom he helped to found the *Nouvelle Revue Française*. He had been a literary critic, wrote plays, and later, as a Catholic man of letters, was an ally of Claudel. When he went to the country it was, as Granville-Barker put it, to "begin again from the beginning," and he did that so religiously that Granville-Barker had to beg him to "spend no more time kissing the earth or laying foundations. . . ." Before he returned he had not only replanted the art of the French theater but had laid the basis of a "popular theater," on which he wrote an important essay.

Copeau had hardly been impure before going to Burgundy. The manifesto of the Vieux Colombier, which he left when he felt a sterility in his work, also comes out of a *tabula rasa* disposition, a desire to start from the ground up. For Copeau the renewal of theater meant not only the stripping down of the stage to *le dispositif fixe,* the bare platform, but also the renewal of man in the theater. The actors, too, had to be laid bare or "exercised": "If I have the patience and the strength," he wrote to André Suarez in 1913, "in two or three years these actors will have almost become men."

Copeau died, greater in aspiration than achievement. Like most men of his fervor, he was disgusted by the recalcitrance of theater as a medium and the impiety of some he could not reform. Yet his manifesto for the Vieux Colombier reshaped performances on boulevards all over the world, even as it has been forgotten by many of the little theaters in America to which it gave original principle.

The practice of Copeau followed a path back to the classical tradition in its purity, and every major figure in the French theater since, from Louis Jouvet to Roger Planchon, is indebted to him. In his letter to Copeau about the directorship of the Comédie, Granville-Barker described the process of renewal: "You wanted to 'kiss the soil' and regain strength. Well, you construct and perform, you and your actors, one quite primitive play, very simple, very genuine; that is kissing the soil to some advantage. The next day you gave us Molière. It does not become a mere Englishman to speak on the subject; but if that was not a truly traditional performance, with all the spirit and strength of Molière conserved, and all the dead redundancies of the so-called tradition cut away, then I never saw or imagined such a thing." Some of the heirs of Copeau, who went with him to the provinces, are still there.

In 1960, I saw a performance of *The Imaginary Invalid* at Vienne, a Roman town not far from the industrial city of Lyon. The production had been sent out from the regional center of Saint-Étienne, directed by Jean Dasté, who had married Copeau's daughter. The troupe was playing in a municipal auditorium, a plain building in peach stucco erected within the retaining walls of an antique theater and looking like it had been put up by the WPA.

As we walked toward the building on a winter evening, we could see the darkened stone and broken slabs of the Roman stage. When we were told there would be a nine o'clock curtain, more or less, we went for chocolate at a café nearby. There were three men, looking like Cézanne's card players, but throwing rubble green dice as they drank wine and beer.

We returned to the theater and took our seats in a sort of mezzanine. In the corridor were a couple of firemen, burly in their buffed helmets. In the gallery some schoolchildren were squawking and throwing spitballs at their more genteel friends who sat with their parents in the orchestra. The ceiling of the theater had been painted to resemble a sky rimmed with sprigs of spring flowers. There was no pit for the piano beside the stage; the lighting instruments, with transformers to boost their power, swayed on their stanchions in full view. The bared boards of the main floor, the shabby touring set, the faded etching of Orpheus and Eurydice in the lobby at intermission, the portrait of Mounet-Sully, the candy vendor who hawked his wares, the first impression of heavy makeup and overplaying, the tacked sash of Angelica's costume, the unbuttoned laughter of the adults, the whoops and whistles of the children, the barely heated auditorium—it felt like an opry house on the Comstock Lode or like Saturday morning when the talkies first came in, an event with its own chaotic substance.

It would have been little more than picturesque if it weren't that the production, which was always the engaging center of the event, pointed back to the sources of Molière's art in a way that the Comédie didn't. It reminded you that Molière also kissed the soil before coming to court, that what he brought to Paris and Versailles must once have been broadly slapstick, and that if it became civilized, it was never tame. Dasté's troupe brought the elegance back to the provinces as well as the gusto. If behind the wit was the gamy invention of the strolling players, amid the clamor a masked pantomime was performed with exquisite timing and humor. Some of the performances might have seemed cruder on another stage in other circumstances, but Vienne was the place for rough edges. We hear that Copeau was finally more priestly and the Vieux Colombier more austere, but the performance that night was in the elemental spirit of *les Copiaux*.

Let me not, however, misrepresent my feelings about that production. I am not implying that a provincial audience is necessarily more responsive than big-city folk, and I have seen some abominable productions in backward places. Though I certainly wish more of our theater had a similar animation and intelligence, and so uninhibited an audience, I am not forgetting that in Vienne the only other public competition was a ruin. What was impressive, however, beyond the performance was that it was made possible by a man who had resisted not only a lucrative career in Paris but also the recipes of the boulevards, just as Roger Planchon, a much younger man with the additional motive of his Marxism, was doing nearby in a proletarian suburb of Lyon. They are working in a tradition summarized by Michel Saint-Denis in his elegant lectures *Theatre: A Rediscovery of Style:* "I have never directed a play I did not like. I have never directed 'boulevard' or 'West-end' plays. I must say that I have never been asked to. The theater is divided into very definite families." Of course, in his relation to the heritage of the best modern theater, Saint-Denis was not only a disciple but also a nephew of Copeau. As for the rest of us, we have only their mutual example. Which—like the revolution of the twenties—we are only too anxious to forget.

Saint-Étienne, I should add, is no center of urban sophistication. They say: We must not rush our audiences too fast. Long before he became a vogue in middle-class America, Brecht was being produced by Dasté in front of the coal pits, for people who had never or rarely seen a play. They say: We must always remember the audience. Let us remember them by all means. But let us not insult them with the trimmerlike illusory "needs" of well-adjusted community. Also: in our own cities, let us not exonerate them. In discussing my own theater's development, I shall say more about audiences; but when we talk of Community, let us remember, too, that those Broadway audiences are largely transient audiences. Back in their own cities, people who tell you they "just love the theater" are party to the duplicity of it all. I am not speaking of those who will probably never have anything to do with the theater, those who unashamedly prefer TV, but those who have TV "only for the documentaries which the medium does so well, you know"—people who know better or pretend to want better, and who might do better if they weren't indulged. There are enough of this kind to support a major theater, without subsidy, in any city in the country, if we didn't encourage them in their hypocrisy.

In his autobiography, Guthrie speaks of similar conditions in the British Isles as "the provinciality of provincial towns," where the middle-classes "ape metropolitan manners and tastes, and will only accept artists who are recognized successes and 'celebrities.' Exactly the same principle," he says, "applies in the United States. It is not the suction of New York, but their own provinciality which draws the cultural life out of other cities." This includes some of the dynamic junior executives who head up civic arts committees and the people who needn't stay home to ape the metropolitan manners of New York, but who can well afford to go there for that purpose. Our euphemism for such people is the term *cultural leader;* while they are sure to be at the opera, they are also the chief patrons of the new suppertheaters where you can drink your way past a second-rate star in a second-rate musical long off-Broadway, and think *Stop the World, I Want to Get Off!* is the most offbeat musical since the defanged version of *The Threepenny Opera.*

Cultural renaissance or cultural inferiority? For all this said, and though he is surely welcome, we must finally ask the question: Why was it necessary for Sir Tyrone Guthrie to organize a theater in the middle of America?

If it has something to do with the provinciality of provincial towns, it also has something to do with the lack of courage and leadership, for all the talent, in the American theater. But things are changing. The cultural leaders are greeting the talent and together they will do what a secretary recorded as the intention of a recent arts conference: "to disperse art through the country-side." As someone said in amending that phrase if not the intention, the countryside is not an aesthetic sponge, much of what is dispersed is not art, and besides it might be better to leave a little of our innocence intact. (In England, Arnold Wesker—who was better motivated—learned something of this kind to his dismay. Believing what he wrote in *Roots,* that there were blunted lives all over England, he started to do something about it with passion and self-denial. But many of the better artists, all of whom respect Wesker, refused to go along with his project to enlighten the provinces by saturation bombing of their unprovided sensibilities. Too much Wesley in the Wesker. They tell me it made for a migrant population in the Midland pubs. For among the cultural weapons of Centre 42, a proletarian enterprise, were folk singers assigned to descend on the pubs with poetry and music. But sentries are posted, and when the call went up that the folk singers were coming, the drinkers cleared out as if it were the blitz.)

If what is happening in the American theater—the fostering of regional groups; Shakespeare festivals, and now Shaw; improvised comedy in the bistros; new theater buildings; provision for repertory in the arts centers; the patronization of foundations and the formation of state art commissions—is an incipient revolution, it is also the resurgence of a revolution that failed.

That revolution started in the twenties, and it not only failed in the theater, but it failed—despite the New Deal, the Fair Deal, and Welfare Capitalism—in education, medicine, and civil rights. If the administration is faced today with a sluggard Congress crawling over rotten rules to the issues of Medicare, federal aid to the schools, and desegregation, it is because we are suffering the lost zeal of our radical animus, born of a tradition of dissidence that is always in danger of dying. Our sociologists tell us it is dying now from benevolence, from affluence, from automation, from the reign of the generals, from over-grown unions, from all the fringe benefits of an old sellout.

All of this can be documented, and all of it can be argued against. As Henry James wrote in *The American Scene:* "The living fact in the United States *will* stand, other facts not preventing, for almost anything you may ask of it. . . . If you have luckily *seen,* you have seen; carry off your prize, in this case, instantly, and at any risk."

Still, there are more than enough facts to win an argument and a good deal of complication that appalled James in the prophetic nuances of his fine perceptions. They cannot be dealt with instantly any more, though we must still take our risks. Henry James could go away; the Lost Generation could go away; we are tempted to go away. But in a world closing down on us, with much of Munich looking like Main Street, the Ginza like the Bronx, and juke-boxes only thirty yards or so from Henry Adams' beloved cathedral at Beau-vais, even expatriation pales. The experience of a couple of generations has brought us back to cultivating our own gardens. In the theater, any way you look at it, we must not only do it ourselves, we must do it here—but we must do it with the intelligence that once caused our best artists to leave home.

And the chief thing for us to do is to start creating real alternatives in "popular theater" to the community theaters and the shopping centers which reflect not the spiritual power but the moral stupor of our cultural explosion. The model may presently be French or German, but the desire is universal, and we once had a fair start on it. I am thinking of a theater of regional centers, widely recruited audiences (in collaboration with schools, churches, unions, industry), workshops, critiques, lectures, tours, youth conferences, a full public life growing around what must be its basic premise, a substantial repertoire—as Vilar might say, plays fit for the cathedral not the crypt, cutting past the surface tastes of both actors and audience to the deepest roots of community.

If you can't start big, start small. If you can't start with money, start without money. It has been done before and—to repeat what must never be lost sight of—no other artist would think it strange. Such a theater has to be developed at every level, and perhaps it will create a climate for the hypostatic powers of a great playwright to take root as well. Maybe we shall have to wait in any event, as Wallace Stevens once said of poetic drama, for a terrible genius to be born. But there's a lot of ground to fertilize while we wait. I should like to see realistic theaters, ritual theaters, acrobatic theaters, Beat theaters, Zen theaters, Übermarionette theaters, concrete theaters and abstract theaters, poetic theaters purifying the language of the tribe, and pure mime doing without it: theaters of the marvelous and theaters of the mundane, Agitprop theaters, absurd theaters, and even square theaters—so long as that is a real point of view and not our current accommodated fatuousness. "Give me a point on which to stand," said Archimedes, "and I will move the world." But there must be a point.

As for the regional theaters now operating, of which it has been said their existence is the major achievement of the last decade, they must now strive to deserve the attention (and the money) they have received. They must encourage, not only be the example of existence, the newer theaters which are arising. Some of these, like the Guthrie Theater, may be born to greater notoriety and endowed with greater material resources. Along with the Lincoln Center Repertory Theater they may set the pace for us—though we shall all be running for nothing if art doesn't win. We must convince those working with us—some of whom will have relapses of malaise over being far from what really counts—there is no reason the theater shouldn't experience, as a kind of Counterforce, the excitement of discovery one senses at Cape Kennedy. We must believe we are capable of adventure and even *grandeur*. Antoine, after all, was a gasman before he became one of the fathers of the modern theater; he might have been one of the visitors to Genet's Balcony, a mere phantast, dreaming on Power.

Though I have a personal stake in a permanent theater of identifiable character, I can even imagine a circuit of such theaters, first in given areas, and then all over the nation. Nothing like ANTA's well-meaning but impoverished (and fortunately abandoned) notion of a forty-theater circuit or forty circuits of theaters (I forget which, but no matter, for they would have been little more than minor leagues for Broadway). In such a circuit, actors might be exchanged, new plays given successive or simultaneous productions, and other productions might be toured as they were first imagined by companies each with its own distinction. The universities, with their good plants, could be the geography of such a circuit, especially if they develop companies of their own. Ideas would flow with the people; there would be a dynamic in performances, competing styles, things to argue about and to learn from. Obviously, it all requires leadership and willing sacrifice in the groundwork—and to begin with, recognition that it can't wait on subsidy, publicity, or the reformation of our entire culture, but may be a condition of such a reformation.

It may be presumptuous to believe these things, but it is what Jimmy Porter called pusillanimity to believe anything else—and unless we do we shall be going, however industriously, through the same old distressing motions. It may turn out, sadly, that we do not ourselves have the requisite gifts for a renaissance, but we, all of us, need to rid ourselves of the idea that what we do in the provinces is mere biding of time, a training ground or a tryout for the Metropolis; and that our primary function is to serve up to the community, by making plays available, what the community already has elsewhere.

Every theater that has ever struck the imaginations of men knew that the play is not the thing—but a continuum of plays, conveying a significant view of human action in a particular time, and passing on a heritage of perception. I shall describe in Part Two how these ideas grew upon my own theater; but if we are not able to do the full job ourselves (that is, the founding directors and actors and designers, for these theaters are, though some have already lasted as long as the Group, still young), perhaps we will impart a tradition of inquiry and daring to the younger people working with us or turning to us now for guidance. And to encourage them to stay with it, rather than believe with some of their elders that the real things are occurring elsewhere.

The Cold War has been punctuated by "revolutions of rising expectations." But the colonial revolutions of our age are something new in the world. Nobody can but cheer when plutocracy and false privilege are overthrown and freedom is achieved. Yet, if we must be moral realists, we should see that some of these colonial revolutions lack, because of the speed with which values are transformed and rejected in our age, the articulated moral fervor of our own. The anarchy begins in some cases after freedom has been granted by controlled historical process; then the power struggle begins. The chains off, there is a swift clamor for economic parity and industrial development. It is all understandable, desire moving fast as the times. But though these revolutions have their spokesmen and their heroes, and I do not mean to deny them ideals, they do not seem to speak with the natural religion of a Jefferson or even the egalitarian outrage of a Tom Paine. Some are plain tyrannies, some barbarous, some perversions of their democratic intent. And a Jean Genet seems to know more about them than U Thant. Maybe it's no more than we all deserve for allowing so many to be so repressed for so long; speaking of Counterforce, we live in a time when both nature and humanity seem bound to revenge themselves, like some loosed ravening beast, on the inhumanity of us all.

I do not believe this is too large a context in which to understand what is happening in our theater. I am acquainted with the historical skepticism which sees the downright economic motives behind the moral eloquence of the Founding Fathers. But, mired as I am in the negativism of the European *avant-garde,* I should like to get some of that self-evident principle back into the atmosphere of our art. In our theater there are old grievances, but there too—desire moving fast as the times—there is too much clamor, particularly among young people, for economic parity and industrial development. They are talking about new theaters before they have made any commitment to the self-creating power of theater. Building theaters and encouraging De-centralization may solve a labor problem, but unless it does more than that, unless it gives actors more than the security of season contracts, and even a number of varied roles, it will be another half-revolution, leading to a new variant of the usual quiet desperation.

The theme of the Group Theater, with its revolutionary concerns, still remains pertinent: "What shall it profit a man if he gain the whole world, and lose his own soul?"

Because there aren't that many jobs available yet, we have the immediate task of getting theater people to behave like artists instead of drugged pigeons in a chicken coop. There was a time when it seemed both brave and necessary to go to New York. Actors had to have actors to play with. I have pointed out that there were always theaters around, but let us say they were too inept or the actors overlooked them. Now, however, a few decent theaters are clearly there and new resources are at hand. True, none of these theaters has the reservoirs of talent it needs, and thus it is no revelation when somebody writes that the regional theaters don't have casts to match those on Broadway. Given all the talent congested there, no wonder. First things first: the talent must move. We must attract it by offering a drive and sense of audacity that is not true of the theater they have known. Young people coming out of the universities must be told squarely that even the absence of salary—which, yes, we all deserve it, though it may not be there right away—is not sufficient reason for yielding their art to the rat race.

Let them take jobs, let them be apprentices (they'll wind up doing it, fruitlessly, in summer stock); if they don't like what we have done, let them create their own theaters—there are places all over the country ripe for them. But let them not wait for the system to accommodate them when, after making their rounds, they are already deformed. There is nothing sadder—

and we have had this experience with a few who have come to us on Ford grants—than to encounter an actor of genuine ability, one who must have had extraordinary promise, whittled down by twenty years of being second or third fiddle to "stars" with not half their natural talent; and who—now that TV and radio, plus a reasonably good salary on the grant, permit them to do what they have always wanted to do—are not quite up to it any more. And I am not speaking of others who were never so "successful" to begin with; or those, trapped in the rat race, who are forlorn, after much searching of conscience and pocketbook, when they tell you they would really like nothing better than to join you for a season but, you know, my agent, the residuals, I'm up for a couple of parts, you know.

There are, indeed, rising expectations in the American theater. Developments here are matched by increasing awareness of what is going on abroad. Through the common marketing of previously unobtainable plays, a wider repertoire and a potentially wider audience have been made available. Now that the theater seems a little more literate, novelists and poets are turning to the writing of plays. Painters and sculptors are lurking backstage, thinking about design. It is encouraged too by the drift of the artist, after years of underground research, back to poetry readings, direct address, the public forms. "*I want! I want! I want! I want!*" cries Bellow's Henderson, in quest of the full intellectual and sensory embodiment of the American Dream. Bellow himself is one of those who now want some boards for their passion. The private life having become too monstrous after all, the theater is the most expansively objective of all forms to which an artist longing for social existence might be drawn.

Some of the new interest in the theater by our writers is not unmixed with the desire to pick up a quick buck by taking respite from what they consider the more labyrinthine problems of craft in the novel or lyric poem. (Well, they shall learn.) The foundation grant has been an inducement. But whatever the reason, intelligence is being wooed and badgered into our theater, and it will take intelligence to keep it there. Up to now, we have given very little evidence that we have it. But what we must do is create an atmosphere in which our best artists—at the *beginning* of their careers—will think quite naturally of working in the theater, as distinguished men of letters do elsewhere.

It once almost happened in our "missing revolution." That revolution was given impetus, a widening of horizons, by theater artists who had gone abroad. The same thing seems to be happening today. Many of us have now had the chance to see what the best companies of Europe have achieved and to study their work.

What have we brought back?

Listen to Kenneth Macgowan and Robert Edmond Jones as they returned from Europe in the early twenties to tell us about Reinhardt and Jessner, and the Vieux Colombier, about *Masse-Mensch* and the Theater of the Five Thousand, about black drapes and the Linnebach projector, about the

Redoutensaal and the Cirque Medrano: "It is hard to escape the belief that this ferment means something. Something for life and from life; something for art and from art. Something immensely important to the sense of godhead in man which is life and art together, and life and art fecundating one another." Who talks like that today in the American theater? Who says as one project after another is announced: "Just how much this may mean is perhaps the test of your belief in the theater. It is the conviction of some of us that there has resided in the theater—and our hope that there may reside once more—something akin to the religious spirit." Who asks: "Can the theater make itself—in a new sense—religious?" Or, if the man of the theater finds no religion in modernity, "what can he do? Is it possible that he can create the spiritual in the people by creating it in the theater? Can he see the vision himself; and, if he sees it and embodies it, can it make over the people?"

Make over the people? Who will presume?

The faith expressed by Macgowan and Jones is the same apparently simplistic faith that was expressed in the manifesto of the Provincetown Playhouse by George Cram Cook. Harold Clurman described, in *The Fervent Years,* the occasion on which Robert Edmond Jones made an impassioned but very shadowy definition of the theater for the young people who were forming the Provincetown. Clurman didn't understand it, but he remembered it. Is the path irretraceable? Do we need some of that—what?—naïveté? Or, having gone through a second war and the ambiguities of Korea, the Berlin Crisis, the suspense of Cuba, and the terrifying doubts born of too much knowledge, too much despair, too much indecision, too much equivocation, too much relinquishment of power, too much denial of value—do we have the will to restore the excellence of vision to our theater, to ask those great naïve questions of it? In our superlatively helpless sophistication, do we have the power to become as little children again, and play, play for keeps, because we are the guardians of a sacred institution?

Or is it too embarrassing to think that way?

Would arrogant levity help us? "The apostolic succession from Aeschylus to myself" (who else but George Bernard Shaw said it?) "is as serious and as continuously inspired as that younger institution, the apostolic succession of the Christian Church." Writing as a drama critic, Shaw said of the people about whom he was most conscientiously uncharitable—who were seeking not merely subsidy but official honors: "Now for their gentility and knighthoods I cared very little: what lay at the root of my criticism was their deeper claim to be considered, not merely actors and actresses, but men and women, not hired buffoons and posturers, however indulged, but hierophants of a cult as eternal and sacred as any professed religion in the world."

Are we to believe him? Or do we exonerate our delinquencies by smiling at the old cad, who was always kidding?

PART TWO

IN SEARCH OF
IDENTITY

. . . it is difficult to settle or even discuss these problems in an atmosphere of intimidation.

—President Kennedy on the Cuba quarantine, 1962

Eppur si muove! [*And yet it does move!*]

—Galileo Galilei

THE BALANCE OF TERROR

Not long ago I was able to begin the first rehearsal of Brecht's *Galileo* by reference to two articles juxtaposed in the morning's newspaper. One reviewed the proceedings at a symposium of science called "The Flow of Life." The subjects covered were the unifying mechanisms of energy conversion, the nature of decay and death, and the prospects of evolution. The astronomer Harlow Shapley reflected on the hundred thousand million billion stars in the universe and said that if only one in a billion of these stars is a sun similar to our own, the chances of life in the universe become immense. Citing experiments in molecular synthesis—the creation of self-replicating matter out of primitive chemicals and radiant energy—he said: "They prove that you don't need either miracles or the supernatural to go from the inanimate to the animate. . . . Life in our own galaxy is inevitable." Not only is it inevitable, but according to Theodore Dobzhansky, professor of genetics at the Rockefeller Institute, who also spoke at the symposium, "Man may now, if he chooses, introduce his own purposes into human evolution."

Next to this article was one on the publication of a book by physicist Ralph E. Lapp, *Kill and Overkill: The Strategy of Annihilation.* The book certified what everyone suspects, that the United States has stockpiled "enough nuclear explosives to overkill the Soviet Union at least 25 times."

And vice versa. Dr. Lapp observed that never before in history did so many people look like so many sheep going to slaughter. In the same paper was a review of a novel, *Fail-Safe,* about which one of the authors said: "We talked with scientists, missile experts, and political theorists, and we came up with the definite impression that war by accident is not probable or likely, but inevitable." Sidney Hook and others have since taken the book to task for crying havoc prematurely, but poor fiction or irresponsible prophecy, it puts on record the persistent tremor of most everybody's silent thought—especially as the stalemate, with its partial test ban, goes beyond the control of the two major powers.

In the lead column on the front page was an account of Red China's invasion of India, launched the previous day.

In the background of these temporal events was the Ecumenical Council of the Catholic Church, called by the late Pope John XXIII in response to changing physical and social conceptions of the universe. The next day's paper carried a story on the debate over liturgy reforms, including the use of modern languages instead of traditional Latin in the rites of public worship and the Mass. (In Brecht's play, Galileo writes ironically to his spiritual advisor: "The argument in favor of the Latin liturgy—namely that because of the universality of this tongue, the Holy Mass can be heard in the same way by all peoples—seems to me less happy, since the blasphemers, who are never at a loss, could object that *no* people can understand the text. I heartily reject cheap lucidity in sacred matters.")

The debate on liturgy reform was, of course, a very minor item of news beside President Kennedy's speech announcing the "quarantine" of Cuba and the decision to board all ships bearing nuclear missiles to that island.

The alert was sounded. As usual, but with more than usual consciousness, we rehearsed in an atmosphere of unbordered discovery and immediate trepidation. The Cold War, which had gone its impossible way through crisis muted by crisis, was back in the realm of Brinkmanship. By noting this, I am not presuming to judge, even by hindsight, the late President's decision, nor did I feel then with Bertrand Russell—also quoted that morning—that we would all probably be dead in a week. Nevertheless, even if Lord Russell was not right, we were conducting our rehearsals of *Galileo* with specific attention to that possibility, which circulated around our work like a fissiparous cloud. Whatever becomes of this cloud, I review these circumstances to show the extent to which I feel our theater is a work in progress.

Our career has always seemed to me—paranoia be privileged—a manifestation of the Cold War, impacted with unnegotiable anxieties and always on the edge of survival. It took some time, however, before most of those working in the theater could see things in this image, or relate what they were doing or found impossible to do to what was happening in the world. They were not abnormally insular; they were simply behaving as people in the American theater are accustomed to behave. The theater was a carapace in which one secreted his fear and trembling, muffled his indignation, and relieved outrage by innocuous subjective ejaculations. If it wasn't therapy, it wasn't collective action either—which had gone out with the thirties. For some, in dread of anything else, it was no more than show business. *Art?* If art wasn't invoked to forestall the intrusion of real crisis, the word was otherwise embarrassing, as in the rest of the American theater.

Whatever we haven't accomplished, we have progressed rather far; for when we met at the beginning of the fifties to discuss the formation of a studio group, it would have been next to impossible—if we had talked of producing at all—to have placed the art of theater and our own craft among the symptoms of the Cold War. Possibly there would have been bemused and patronizing attention. More likely it would have been disruptive because some of those involved would have considered it merely tendentious, meaning bad—though John Foster Dulles was precisely at that time enunciating his policy of "Peace or else"; and though several years later we were to do the first production in America of Brecht's *Mother Courage,* of which one reviewer said the "anti-war crusading seems . . . pretty old hat." He prefaced this by saying: "Perhaps the fault here lies that Americans are sufficiently naïve to believe there are still causes worthy of defending, and that to some, war can still be the great adventure. . . ."

A little more than four years later, that same reviewer did a Sunday feature on Martin Esslin's study of Brecht. Noting the complexities of Brecht's thought and technique, he said: "He requires a special audience. Indeed, it was my unhappy experience as dramatic editor to criticize the Actor's Workshop's American premiere of 'Mother Courage' not in terms of 'epic theater' and 'alienation' but merely as a rather uninteresting production, and what an uproar that lamentable and admittedly inexcusable naiveté provoked."

A criticism of the production in terms of "epic theater" and "alienation" may not have made it any more interesting, any more than rehearsal of a play in terms of current events guarantees excellence in performance. The actual quality of our production of *Mother Courage* is lost in time, along with the controversy which, if minor, was almost unprecedented in San Francisco theater history. What is of interest is that there *was* a controversy. I can't say the controversy carried all the way over to our production of *Galileo,* but its meaning was not lost, for the lessons were maintained in the continuity of our theater—and there was some controversy over *Galileo* for other reasons.

A production is a refracting glass, the locus of all sorts of issues—theatrical and cultural—which may be lost sight of in the process of rehearsals. It is easy to think this is just as well. Eliot once said, thinking of Henry James, there are artists with minds so fine they are unviolated by ideas. That doesn't mean they don't have any. In any art, the day-by-day doing is mostly technical, working it out. But the final cause of technique is discovery: what for? There are conceptions and conceptions, and the doing may become an Idea.

If it has become habitual with The Actor's Workshop to suffer remorse of conscience when it forgets why it is doing what it is doing, or can't control it, there was a time when we barely knew what we were doing, or why. I should like to explain why this was so. If, as purpose grew, we could not quite fulfill it, practice exhausting theory, practice did generate theory. And it will be the aim of this part of the book to explore how, in a working theater, the press of theory, the problems of craft, the conflict of personalities, the choice of plays, the production concepts, and the whole practical administration of the theater—including relations with a developing audience—interfuse with and mirror each other, becoming an emblem of the times.

Occasionally it seemed a very shaken emblem indeed, resembling those last high-valency elements on the periodic chart, with their vulnerable half-lives. For the fact is, when I speak of the behavior of "the company," I am referring to a relatively small nucleus of people determined to make an enterprise of enduring substance out of what may often seem (even to them) a theatrical operation of conventionally surpassing difficulty. They give a necessary mooring to a large group of transients who go in and out of San Francisco, or are miscellaneously available to the theater, with varying degrees of fidelity and opportunism.

Even the loyal equivocate. This was, however, much more so in our early years, when they were not too sure what they were involved in. Take our production of *Mother Courage*: I wrote shortly afterward that in reading the play "for the first time, the company—most of whom had not been in a Brecht play before [some had not even heard of him]—felt that Brecht had done precisely what they had been told he would do. They were alienated; they were also bored." Because of that and because of resistance to what was considered a policy of "experimentation for its own sake" (sad to say, we have hardly ever been *that* experimental), some of our better actors refused to be in the play. "On the other hand," I continued, "because Brecht was new to the company, by not having to use some of our more experienced but obdurate actors we did avoid some of the snarls that would have arisen through antagonism on their part to the qualities, procedures, and values of an unorthodox play." It's hard to imagine such resistance now, but it was then I started to be aware of one of the real ironies of the American theater, not only in New York, the extent to which "many of its best actors *prefer* to dedicate their talents to plays that insult their intelligence."

We had something of the same experience in our first production of Beckett, and when we did a scene from *The Balcony* in our studio several years before it was produced in New York (we could not get the production rights ourselves), two of our maturest actors walked out in protest. However, by the time we did *Endgame,* almost everybody in the company was ready to jump into the ashcans. Since then, we have developed *aficionados* of the Absurd. Genet is still repellent to some, but he would hardly have the same effect today. Aside from our educational campaign internally, he has received the blessing of notoriety in New York. San Francisco is not yet so cosmopolitan, or its actors so independent, that Big City opinion doesn't count. Later

I shall discuss this situation, and I shall say more in another context about *Mother Courage,* but it is clear that it no longer seems unorthodox, and that since its production the company, reviewers, and audiences have been better prepared for *Galileo.*

Because it embodies, more or less up-to-date, the major concerns of our theater, I should like to devote the rest of this chapter to that production. To repeat: craft and life, life and craft. In talking about *Galileo* and, later, others of our productions, I shall be concerned not only with what we had to think about to do the play, but also what the play caused us to think about, which affected in turn the way it was done. Thus *Galileo* will serve as a pretext for further reflection upon the dilemma of theater in the Cold War, and will focus some preliminary notions about the dramatic form. Looking out on the world, we shall then look back on the play. As much as the Cold War informed our production of *Galileo,* it also deterred us from producing it according to the Rules. While it posed for us some crucial problems of technique, it also defined a new relationship to Brecht—whose influence on the American theater has grown by leaps and bounds since our production of *Mother Courage,* when he was relatively unknown here.

Let me not be mistaken: the ground we cleared for Brecht was negligible beside the bulldozing of belated recognition. Books on Brecht, essays on Brecht, Brecht on Brecht, David Merrick on Brecht—if the propaganda mills behind the Iron Curtain were to expend all their subversive wiliness on behalf of Brecht, they could hardly achieve what paperback saturation and the extravagant tolerance of the new purchasing power have done in the last few years. Consumption is not conspicuous, it is voracious. Status anxiety has turned into a compulsion that stops at no enemy. Sometimes the higher the price the easier the turnover. When we chose to do *Mother Courage* the rights were for the picking, the royalty picayune considering the litigation that came when the play's European reputation finally made a dent on Broadway and two productions were announced simultaneously. In due time the legal wrangling was over, and *Mother Courage* came at last to New York. But appetite, a universal wolf, had perhaps waned in the waiting; perhaps it was the production. Anyhow, after the financial failure, one wondered whether and when there would be a next Brecht on Broadway; but yes, art prevails, Merrick gave us *The Resistible Ascent of Arturo Ui.* The breakthrough came, of course, with the ingratiating *The Threepenny Opera* at the Theater de Lys and Louis Armstrong's recording of "Mack the Knife." And last year there were simultaneous productions of *A Man's a Man* off-Broadway.

For those who were previously *in,* the desideratum was a pilgrimage to the shrine of Brechtian production in East Berlin. The missionaries have returned (myself among them), proclaiming the miracle of the Ensemble's achievement; the theory of Alienation is waved as a reproach to the Method with its psychological addiction ("We must conquer the ego," says one recent convert); and before we had seen very much at all of the plays, we had that relatively official tribute to Brecht, the anthology called *Brecht on Brecht,* dripping with un-Brechtian reverence, and convincing precisely those whose lives and values the plays put in question that Brecht was a charmingly roguish charter member of the American Civil Liberties Union. The model-books are studied and the dogma—drawn from somewhat opaque and diffuse polemic—spreads. Well and good. Brecht's dogma is far better than the customary daffiness, and even misguided devotion may be an improvement, like the plagiarism of retarded freshmen. I say this having demonstrated my own carping share of piety on Brecht's behalf. Whatever he deserves, however, the fact is Brecht became fashionable even before he was done. And when we undertake a production of one of his plays today, that reverence may be an impediment.

While I am aware we may profit from passing on a tradition—haven't I complained we have so little to pass on?—we know the liabilities too, also demonstrated by the Comédie Française. When the Comédie is at its best, there is a subtle dynamic: the myth of style lingers in the crooks and crevices of some reliquary gesture by one or another of the older players, like a racial memory. The detail is passed on to the new *sociétaires,* while something of the spirit evaporates into history. It is sad but inevitable. When a vital new director takes over the reins, his function is to spur the haggard conventions in another direction. The style is re-examined, not modernized. When there is genius, something of the departed spirit is rescued from history—and the tradition is comforted by true ghosts.

I am sure that in the process many things are still being done as they were done by Molière. Many are not. What was basic in the two productions of Molière I saw one year—a new version of *L'École des Femmes* and an old one of *Tartuffe*—was a realistic approach, not stylized or *commedia*ized, as often happens in America. Now, while it would be wonderful to know, too, exactly how Shakespeare was played by his own actors, I am not one of those convinced that either Shakespeare or Molière was necessarily played better in his own day—especially Shakespeare, whose plays are less "classical," as his language is more bountiful and coined. With our technical resources and modes of acting, I can imagine our doing—the word is inadequate—better productions than were done at the Globe, although I'd prefer to say (without encouraging the tendency to skip over the problem by resort to novelties) the whole question sometimes strikes me as meaningless. For one thing, we simply don't have the same relation to a culture or a tradition as exists at the Comédie. And, whatever is passed on, Shakespeare's day is not our day. If Shakespeare played his Roman dramas in Elizabethan costume, I'm not convinced at all that is the most illuminating way for us to see *Julius Caesar.* Roman costumes, I should add, are not the point either, nor is modern dress. If it were in the grain of Shakespearian drama to have been thoroughly ritualized in performance, the theaters of his day might have been less prodigal with their prompt books, and the drama might have come down to us through families like the Japanese Noh.

With Brecht, the "tradition" is so close, and in Europe often so supervised, as to be intimidating. And the more I work in the theater, the one thing I am most disinclined to hear is how a play *should* be done, even from Brecht, who wrote prescriptions. For me, the problem is to see the text free of premature orthodoxy, without dialectical prejudice, and preserving certain first principles that can be deciphered in the most recondite of his theoretical essays: that reality is full of contradictions, ever new; that the critical faculty must remain alert (even to deficiencies in Brecht's own text or ambiguities subverting his supposed intentions? what did *he* do with other plays?); and that the drama is directed to social change. That last is the mission of Epic theater. The degree to which theater of any kind effects social change, or whether it does at all, is certainly open to debate. My own feeling is that the plays form themselves around a particular tension that can be posed in the terms of this problem: a conflict between belief in the possibility of change through art (distrusting static conceptions of human nature) and rage over the adamance of actual behavior (which imitates itself in the search for freedom). In *A Man's a Man,* for example, we may be convinced that what happens to Galy Gay, brainwashed into a fighting machine, does happen, and it can happen to us. However, should the war occur that none of us ever wants, we may not be convinced we could have avoided it.

In America, Brecht's socialism presents a special problem, too. One of the reasons for the failure of socialism as a political movement in this country is that its ethical will could not function when confronted with the ambiguity of practical dilemmas. Recourse to war may be a capitalist delusion, which can be unmasked and demystified by analysis; but was there anything short of war that, admitting the possibility of previous errors, could have stopped the Nazis once those errors were made? There are stranger things in political necessity than are dreamt of in Brecht's logistics. His *intuitions,* however, tell us that human nature (which his theory denies) knows this and, whether it wants change or not, cannot always change for the better. "Priapus is Priapus," Galileo says of the grinning god of the demonic id, and the question remains, as ever, whether the ego can be conquered—even if that were desirable. Where id was, ego shall be, until id restores the balance of power. Or, as in the case of Azdak, it is banished from the Republic—Azdak's own garden—lest it become subversive.

Ganz normal, as they say around the Berliner Ensemble.

Can these paradoxes be ignored in performance of the plays? I don't think so—if one wants to be honest with himself. And before describing some aspects of our production, I should like to pose some other questions (or contradictions, to use Brecht's term) about *Galileo* in view of the frightening complexity of our lives, whatever our rational passion for change. His political commitment aside (and I don't intend to leave it aside), Brecht shares with every major artist of the twentieth century the knowledge that our world lays multiple claims upon us, and that disaster usually follows upon simplistic choice or paying one tithe at the expense of another. Or—in any case. For, in the twentieth century, the subterranean monsters of history looked as they surfaced more incredible than anything ever submerged in the depths of the psyche.

Look at this contradiction: Galileo says that the function of science is to ease human existence; Galileo also says, when pressed to it, that the truth must be followed regardless of where it leads.

Ibsen has shown us the mortal danger of that position. He has also warned us we may not be able to do anything about it. All men desire to know, said Aristotle in his *Metaphysics*. The shock occurs when Science, rather than remaining a disinterested virtue, becomes an empirical vice, like gluttony. Not all our discoveries are blessings, whatever our concern for humanity. The old fables, such as Pandora's box and the apple in Eden, warn us that there may be something illicit in the very process of knowing. And our own age, splitting atoms, has developed new parables on the terrors of inquiry. Which is now bound up fabulously with the political conflict.

It is not only the Bomb. As James Real and Harrison Brown have pointed out in *Community of Fear*: "Thus, no matter what is possible must be pursued. Can a gigaton (a billion tons of TNT) bomb be built? We must do the work and see. Can climate over the Soviet Union be altered? We must experiment. Can the earth be burned, broken, kept from rotating? Can all life be eliminated? Can we make the oceans boil? All of these questions must be considered. If we don't consider them the Russians might, and if successful they would have us at a disadvantage." Even if the political motive of free inquiry is not always posed, the war machine whirrs in the background as every potentially immoral investigation man can imagine is carried out in the name of pure science.

The course of action would seem clear: change the motive. But are we not then stricken with the additional fear that even if these experiments were conducted out of the most disinterested motive, they might not be any the less nefarious in the end? Do we not tend to feel we are living out a disturbance in the balance of nature for which, someday, we may have to atone? What is the solution? To stop the experiments?

But, we exclaim in impatience (the mind cannot bear too much paradox), Brecht wanted to show that Galileo was wrong to recant. The purpose of science is still to ease human existence. True. That's the argument. But what does the drama show? We must ask that, and the argument should be able to withstand the questions reality prompts from us. Such as: Why does human existence invariably deflect our purpose? At the moment, however, I am inquiring not only into Brecht's play but also into the problem of drama, not only didactic drama, in the contemporary world.

Toward the end of the play, Galileo foresees the time when, as a result of his recantation, the gulf might grow so wide between science and the bulk of humanity "that the sound of . . . cheering at some new achievement would be echoed by a universal howl of horror." The implicit rhetoric of his self-denunciation is that we must prevent this from happening. But how? You can't second-guess history. It has already happened, had happened when Brecht wrote it, could happen again, and one wonders not simply what we can do about it but what the scientists and politicians can do about it. Between a risk and a certainty there may be no doubt, but there are a considerable number of apparently responsible people who are not equally convinced what is the risk and what is the certainty, as President Kennedy's stand on Cuba and the public reaction to it demonstrated. One may observe, as Hannah Arendt did early in the fifties, that mankind's future never "depended so much on political forces that cannot be trusted to follow the rules of common sense and self-interest—forces that look like sheer insanity, if judged by the standards of other centuries." When we look for the true communal experience of our lives, it turns out to look like powerlessness.

Even to consider the fate of drama in these circumstances seems absurd, but there's no doubt it loses its majesty and conviction to the extent that what seems so is so—precisely because it aspires to be a communal form. Will and Necessity: these are the chief motive factors in our conception of drama. But what happens to the form when it seems not to make a difference any more whether man has free will by nature, in view of the staggering impasse which virtually deprives him of its exercise? Much has been said, too, about the degeneration of the idea of the Hero. Brave as he was, an argument could certainly be made that John Glenn was a capsule hero, expendable and replaceable, like a superbly machined part of an automated process. Our first Negro astronaut tells us, in fact, that once you're up in orbit, it's like driving to a supermarket. There is, surely, a misleading modesty in this, which I understand a little. When I was in the paratroops, I used to console myself about the danger by remembering how many others would be making the same jump, which was largely automatic, with all the safety devices tested. The danger and fear are real nevertheless. What is different is that the imagination of the deed is diffused through a system. Our new heroes are team heroes. While they restore a sense of adventure and project new models of courage, their choices are often left on the ground. And they do not focus the idea of heroism—despite President Kennedy's comparison—like a Columbus or even a Lindbergh, who were, in a crucial sense, loners.

As heroism is diffused, so villainy is diffused. Having come to understand more about the radically metamorphic nature of Evil, we wish we had the power to give it a more distinct and indubitable shape. In revulsion and frustration, we wish there were clear and present devils. This is not only true in the pathological witch-hunters of the Right; you see the symptoms in the left-wing protestants. And even in the most independent spirits. Just about the time of the Cuban quarantine, the morning's newspaper carried an interview with novelist Nelson Algren: "The brass, they're crazier than ever. They don't even have to go to war now. But they're at the levers. . . . A military machine, under no matter what flags, is an insane operation." Those are my sentiments, but is he wholly right?

Personally, I am appalled by our Defense Secretary's options, ranging from strictly limited nuclear war to Armageddon. But has anybody given— short of urging what is obviously not going to happen—a more foolproof guarantee against global suicide? Certainly his view has been convincing to rational men. Working on the assumption that nuclear war may be irrational but not inconceivable, McNamara would apparently welcome the day the Russians achieve "second-strike capability" because he thinks it will bring a more stable "balance of terror"! The absurd truth of the matter is he may be right. I don't want to believe it. (And even as I write, this policy seems to be going through a subtle transformation, leading past the economy measure of relinquished shipyards to a new propaganda for peace—based on the intelligence that the Soviet economy is harder up than we thought, and the CIA report that it is even behind us in conventional weapons.) I wish he were more uncompromisingly pacifistic and could see his way clear to recommending even unilateral disarmament, but I am not certain he isn't doing more (even in the wiliest change of policy) to keep me alive than my wishful thinking—though I shall not cease and desist in thinking so.

I proliferate these paradoxes to get at a major distinction between the reality and the drama which reflects it, and then some. "We all have our ideas," says Reinhold Niebuhr, "of how to escape the nuclear dilemma. Many of these ideas are Utopian and irrelevant." As one might expect, he renounces "the strategy of fleeing from difficult problems by taking refuge in impossible solutions." One impulse, however, of every major drama is to take refuge in impossible solutions. Or, to put it another way: to refuse to recognize the impossible as impossible until the solution is shown not to be a solution. The Utopian solution may fail, but in the maturest drama it is, somehow, represented, whatever may be true of politics.

Inherent in the idea of drama is the theme: *thinking may make it so.* By contrast, politics is as politics does, putting a limit on such thinking. One of the virtues of President Kennedy was that he refused to be beguiled by the apparent success of any single political action. One of his defects was that there were certain actions, quite dramatic, he did not think political. (Like taking a Negro child by the hand and leading him into a segregated school.) One of the first things he did after the Cuban "success" was to puncture any euphoria brought on by the Soviet retreat by reminding us that one major mistake on either side "can make the whole thing blow up." And even with an atmospheric test ban in the offing, he had promised to sacrifice our cities, if necesary, to the defense of Europe.

Are these merely words, or are we to take them seriously? If we take them seriously, what are we to think of ourselves? If the principles of maximum deterrence and massive retaliation are not lunatic in fact, one is certainly justified in looking askance at a world that can, without too many shrieks of horror, accept them as rational or necessary.

Seeming, seeming. One of the prices our theater has to pay for such a world is that no illusion it can create—even by anti-illusion—can comprehend entirely the illusions we live by. There are those who feel that freedom's most slavish imitation of the Nazis was the barbarity of saturation bombing, which continued that reversal of the course of history which began when a civilian population was first indiscriminately slaughtered. Is it beside the point to wonder how many rational men, including Brecht, were opposed to that? Now we are able to contemplate, as though it weren't to begin with a moral crime, the extermination of millions, the chief problem seeming to be the mathematical decision as to whether it will be this many millions or that many millions. It is as though, reverting to the reasoning of medieval theologians, the choice to resist evil pure and simple could not be made— but rather a choice between a lesser and a greater good.

That one equivocates at all is the most appalling paradox. Seeing all sides of every question, we diminish if we don't utterly paralyze our capacity for action, putting our lives in question. The great intellectual achievement of the twentieth century is the way we make it seem reasonable to put our lives in question. And we must not forget: even some of those who asked publicly whether the action were really necessary were not certain President Kennedy was wrong to risk nuclear war in the Cuban crisis. Those of us who questioned the action publicly (not to mention those who thought the risk was immoral to begin with) were most certainly in a minority. Given such tensions, no wonder most of our drama seems tame.

The President spoke of a major mistake on either side causing the whole thing to blow up. That we can hardly know when we've made a mistake impacts the climate of puzzle and dread. If experts can't judge, how can the theater presume? In actuality, it doesn't. The theater doesn't so much judge as take "a reflective gape" (Henry James' phrase) at the flow and disruption of human purpose. And it documents that gape in action. It embraces the shape of crisis—kisses the Medusa's lips. The theater enables by re-enacting; it renders and it stands in awe. That may be a rude awakening, woe producing wonder, but energy is restored and inertia overcome. We *feel* less powerless. We see what we have seen, but what we see is suspect. We may see a Utopian solution, or we may laugh like hell. We may do both. In Brecht, as in all dramatists worth the conflicts they pose, appearances deceive. They are also precisely what they appear to be.

What is important when confronted with appalling doubt is to be able to argue out the risks, so far as possible. That's the least we have a right to ask of our politics. The chance is politics won't comply, which we should have known. One alternative is the disaffiliation I have mentioned, to scorn politics, and to deal with the impossible by refusing to acknowledge its claims. As Karl Shapiro puts it, quoting Henry Miller, "The only thing for nonenslaved men to do is to move out to the edge, lose contact with the machines of organization which are as ubiquitous in this country as in Russia. 'Instead of bucking your head against a stone wall, sit quietly with hands folded and wait for the walls to crumble. . . . Don't sit and *pray* that it will happen! Just sit and *watch* it happen!' " Shapiro tells his students "to cultivate an ignorance of contemporary political and military events because they do not matter." The result, at one extreme, may be the scene of *The Connection*. As Shapiro poses it, it is by no means an unjustifiable, dishonorable, or irrational position. Refusal to participate is a risk worth argument. But the trouble with the drama is that it always comes back to those risks which cannot, for all the argument, be argued away. Which may be what we mean when we call it a social form, whose specialty is crisis, haunted by paradox.

If the hero makes us brave, his drama makes us cautious. This is no less true in Epic theater, with its passion for change and its anti-heroes. When Galileo says that he has betrayed his profession, we cannot ignore what he explicitly says; yet we cannot take his words entirely at face value. Whatever their objective "message," it is undermined by masochistic self-contempt. I say this at the risk of being charged with corrupting Brecht by psychology, although we must remember that to discount psychology as a material factor is to pervert social reality too. Psychology is one of the conventions of drama, like plot or rhetoric.

Brecht had doubts which were never fully reconciled in the play. There are also perturbations descending from the puritanically debauched and antic influences of his younger days; for instance Rimbaud and the Berlin Dada movement. Peter Suhrkamp, his West German publisher, is right in saying that political dogma provided "the cure for the anarchy and cynical nihilism of his early plays." But, though his form grew more rational and less demoralizing, dogma was not a total cure. Brecht's Marxism no more exempted him from the doubts that we all share, and the contradictions, than it overthrew the artistic integrity of his work. What Marx and Rimbaud, say, had in common—and what provided a link between Brecht's addiction to the elliptical and the arcane and his commitment to the analytical—was that they all believed that "the tradition of all the dead generations weighs like a nightmare on the brain of the living."

To *do* a play like *Galileo* means getting at all doubts, those which are worked out in explicit paradox, and those which are simply there, unaccommodated by dramaturgical skill. You can try to cover them up or you can reveal them. We tried to reveal them. The production may have cracked under the strain, there were those who felt so; but for me that risk was preferable to an uncritical and safer certainty. And I found it significant—though publicly the production was very well received—that the one reviewer who really saw what happened was from the leftist *People's World*. Praising the production, the reviewer found it tainted by the "cynical absurdities of Genet."*

* The divine fury of Galileo's social passion intersects at some level of art's irrepressible nihilism the social passion of Genet's fury. In his edition of Brecht's plays, Bentley quotes a passage from Rimbaud's *Season in Hell*, which Brecht appropriated for *In the Swamp* and which shows how he anticipated the creative malignancy of Genet: "*Je suis un bête, un nègre. Mais je puis être sauvé. Vous êtes de faux nègres, vous, maniaques, féroces, avares.*"

Galileo, we must remember, was written over twenty years ago. Like all of Brecht's work, it has been changed with the times. History is the prime mover. Yet, for all the analogies, a Brecht play is not a Shakespearean chronicle, with its psychological network deepening even the lowest character. *Galileo* stands or falls on its central character; the rest, even the Pope, are minor figures of middling interest and satirical substance; except for the Pope, they are only mildly engaging to actors—and the fault, I contend, is not theirs. There are vacancies of feeling I do not think can be rectified by praising, as I once did, its quiet intellectual beauty or invoking the theory of Alienation, for the play makes demands which are also conventionally realistic. If the actor supplies the feeling, he is in danger of overacting; if he doesn't, the moment may be insupportable and dull, whatever it is "showing." To supply an "attitude" toward the character may assuage your interest in Brecht's method, but it may not make—to those skeptical about prejudgments—a more convincing character. Nor is there a perfectly constructed argument. At its best, however, the play has a cumulative power invested in the career of Galileo, and certain scenes are very subtly plotted.

Take this one: when Galileo is waiting with his daughter to present his book to Cosimo de Medici. In the reading it seems simple enough. Galileo is given the courtly freeze, at the end of which he is handed over to the Inquisition. But there is one short sequence in which the Lord Chamberlain appears to say the Prince cannot see Galileo because he has to go to the riding academy. (I am referring to the version prepared by Brecht with Charles Laughton.) The excuse is transparent, but why, the actor playing the Chamberlain asked, did he then go back upstairs before he returned to tell Galileo that the Inquisition wanted to see him in Rome?

When one studies the scene, he realizes that the simple action is surrounded by significant political maneuvers. The Inquisitor has suddenly appeared in Florence, backs turn on Galileo. The Chamberlain's rebuff was not just a poor excuse, it was a warning to Galileo not to persist in announcing or teaching the research he could very well continue in private. When Galileo didn't withdraw, the Chamberlain returned for instructions and was apparently told, since Galileo would not take the warning, to go ahead with the arrest. Though he is late in trying to escape, Galileo—who seems naïvely insistent through the scene—has been quite aware of the danger. His caution almost slips by us, but we learn unexpectedly that he has before coming to the palace arranged for horses to take him to Padua.

Not only do the actors have to be aware, then, of the lucubrations behind the scene, but the Chamberlain is confronted with a fair problem on the scene. How do you tell a great scientist, without seeming melodramatic and heavy-handed, that the Prince can't see him because he must go to the riding academy? (I bring it up because the actor brought it up.) One of the things that came to mind as a parallel was the task Pierre Salinger had the week end everybody in the administration remained in Washington, preparing the announcement on Cuba. When the press asked Salinger what was happening, he had to be able to say, without blushing over the inadequacy, that most of them were down with the flu. Naturally, the press wouldn't call him a liar; from obvious evasion they were able to make more or less the right deduction —according to unspoken rules of the game. In Galileo's case, knowing the rules, he backed out too late.

It is the kind of scene which takes us back to psychology through intricacy of plot. The demand is not, for the actor of the small role of the Chamberlain, one of self-exploration—but knowledge of the text, of the world, and what was objectively happening. What needs to be acted is easily acted once what is required is known; and it does not take an actor of any special emotional range to make the scene work. Which may, indeed, be discomfiting to an actor whose social passion is not such as to satisfy him with demonstrating the dramatic point rather than that range. (Despite what they say, in Brecht, type-casting often works best, even if it appears to be an anti-type. Beyond this, there is an enormous qualitative difference between what is required of the actor playing this Chamberlain and the actor playing the role, say, of the Captain in *King Lear,* also involved in a major political conspiracy, who appears for the barest moment to say: "I cannot draw a cart, nor eat dried oats./ If it be man's work, I'll do't." There must be a wealth of personal distinction in that Captain—rugged, prideful, competitive—a man of destiny in small. He serves himself as much as the plot. An actor can chew on it.) With Galileo, however, the *internal* psychology is quite subtle. He apparently suspected before he came that there was danger; it was confirmed almost immediately by the rebuffs. Yet why did he persist so long? His behavior cannot be explained by plot alone, but has to do with what I take to be the most compelling thing about Brecht's drama—his study of a man of scientific imagination who thinks with his body and who, when he has made a discovery, must "boast about it like a lover or a drunkard or a traitor." As he says to the Little Monk: "That is a hopeless vice and leads to the abyss."

This is the romantic aspect of Brecht's realistic character, the poet in him. But Galileo is not a poet, to whom we are inclined to grant license; he is a scientist, from whom we expect responsibility. Or rather Brecht does. One of the problems we have in interpreting the play is that he seems to demand more responsibility from him than he can reasonably bear. And the "message" that comes from Galileo's self-denunciation seems to carry the weight of a lot of afterthought.

We do know that Brecht revised the play after the Bomb was dropped on Hiroshima. In an early version, Galileo's recantation was exonerated as an act of cunning which spared him for the writing of the *Discorsi,* the great treatise on Motion. Many years after the first version, conducting rehearsals at the Berliner Ensemble, Brecht was reported to have told his actors that Galileo must be exposed as a social criminal. The recantation was not a great historical achievement but "the 'original sin' of modern natural sciences," of which the atom bomb was the classical end-product. What is more, we were to understand that by recanting Galileo put science back under the jurisdiction of Authority and the forces of reaction, impeding for more than a century the social revolutions of the Enlightenment.

So the thesis is developed. In Epic drama, the manuals say, the stage shows forth the action; the audience is estranged, put at a distance, given arguments. The proper study of mankind is man in his social role, alterable and altering: "The world is what it is becoming." We had read the lessons: narrative realism, by all means, but art thrown back upon nature, above all— meaning we would submit the narrative to the changes that time brings *in our own circumstances.* Estrangement moves in reciprocal ways: history made legendary; legend informing history; history correcting legend, here and now. Brecht altered his play to conform to history; he revised other people's plays in the light of it. When we looked at Brecht's play as he looked at others, our own historical skepticism was aroused, and we began to wonder. (Just as Lionel Abel must have wondered when he said: "If Brecht thought that Galileo should have undergone martyrdom, then his thinking can be called gross.")

An Age of Reason, says the lyric, might have begun. Might. A vigorous, belly-loving, middle-aged, impoverished man who sees a New Age, Brecht's Galileo also raises the classic question: "What *is* the scientist?" The historian of science, Georgio de Santillana, says it is the question inevitably raised whenever we see thought intimidated, either by the Holy Office or the Atomic Energy Commission. "It is usually the scientist who is taken by surprise by a redefinition of his activities coming from the outside." Brecht shows us this process: the man of science, lionized and by no means unworldly, is suddenly baffled by Policy and Reasons of State. "And the result," adds Professor de Santillana, "is always one more turn racked up on the old screw. By subjecting the scientist as a cultural being to the administrative suspicion that usually attaches to questionable adventurers in international traffics, *we have simply brought one step further the process of secularization of thought.*" (Italics mine.) In other words, the danger of intimidating the scientist is that thought may become vulgar, his ideas merely exploited. Today we don't suppress physics for the gravest of moral and cosmological reasons, or simply to protect a power structure; we rather encourage it to benefit the power structure.

Now, Brecht shows this process, too; and he would probably share Professor de Santillana's feeling, comparing the Oppenheimer case with that of Galileo, that there is a structural analogy, that in the general symptoms "we are dealing with the same disease." But he would hold no brief, it appears, against the secularization of thought. The carnival scene is supposed to show how Galileo's ideas reached the market place to liberate the people—but should it not also show the old danger of partially informed freedom turning into license? If we put the action into the crucible of inquiry (showing *all* the contradictions), we must ask whether there is any guarantee of social virtue in a populace informed by ideas which, in the process of sifting below, are necesarily adulterated. If that were so, *Life* magazine is performing a public service of unparalleled scope. I should add, for the record, that in trying to show these contradictions, the positive desire to overthrow the social order inclining toward anarchy, our carnival mime overthrew it too soon. There were startling moments in a Brueghelesque scene, but it became, I felt, violent and overdrawn beyond our original design. "*Les malheureux sont la puissance de la terre.*" Our problem, which we didn't manage, was to sustain a sense of the people's dignity as we showed the latent distortions in their power—conditioned by what we have learned in the twentieth century of the way social revolutions can be perverted.

As for the final judgment of Galileo, we are not convinced that the self-denunciation is the whole case, nor is Brecht convinced, for he has Andrea say before leaving with the *Discorsi*: "As regards the author in question, I do not know the answer. But I cannot think your savage analysis is the last word." One of the difficulties with the analysis is that it *feels* superimposed, for all its power—and the indictment weighs like an equivocal sentence on the brain. It seems compounded of post-mortem Marxist guilt and instincts left over from Brecht's own early theater of cruelty. Listen to the wish-fulfillment in the words of Garga, the negative hero of *In the Swamp,* at the end of that play: "To be alone is a good thing. The chaos is used up now. It was the best time." It is the voice of the Absurd (though, like Brecht, "*holding on to the money*"), and its demonic presence never really disappears—no more than empathy—from the drama of Brecht. The truth may be concrete, but it is also elusive; and the chaos is never used up.

Moreover, the contradictions of our world and our nature exacerbate it. "I believe in the brain," says Galileo. But the flesh believes in itself, and the flesh is weak. (Another social reformer, Tolstoy, wrote: "The flesh rages and riots, and the spirit follows it helpless and miserable.") Who knows whether, when shown the instruments, he could really hold out? "Unhappy is the land that needs a hero." True. But when the land *is* unhappy—as in Hungary or East Germany—what then? In America, the "lesson" of Galileo's crime is further complicated by the fact that, whatever the analogy, a House Un-American Activities Committee is not quite a rack. Arthur Miller could refuse to name names with some impunity. Galileo says to Andrea that his power was such he might have resisted the authorities. But with the screws tightening, who can say? Giordano Bruno *was* burned at the stake. History does qualify, like torture. Sartre, in his play *The Victors,* graphs the neurological shudders of this issue. There may be reasons for bearing it out to the edge of doom, but they would demand a metaphysics of rebellion that Brecht, for all his early nihilism, could never quite accept. (One of the things about him that makes Ionesco furious.)

Galileo is, for the most part, a restrained, slow-cadenced, thoughtful play, the low emotional key of which leads us to the abyss nevertheless. Before dismissing Andrea, Galileo declares the paradox that is most haunting because it seems to characterize the twentieth-century experience of what the

Renaissance called "novelty"; that is, scientific discovery itself: "This age of ours turned out to be a whore, spattered with blood. Maybe new ages look like blood-spattered whores." There is a short existential leap from this to the dramas of Beckett and Genet, which seem to be written on the premise that new ages not only look like but *are* blood-spattered whores, no maybes about it.

In recent productions at The Actor's Workshop, we have been leaping back and forth over this blood-dimmed distance. In subsequent chapters I shall go back to show how we got there in the first place. In talking of our repertoire, we are likely to say we represent all points of view; but the major conflict in our work has been defined by alternating allegiance to the social consciousness best represented by Brecht, as opposed to the ontological consciousness of Beckett or the scabrous anthropology of Genet. This has been qualified most recently by malaise over the feeling that they are all, *mutatis mutandis*—cultures crossed at the deadest level of the great Oversoul—essentially un-American. But we shall come to that.

It was not, then, a "Brechtian" production we were after when we chose to do *Galileo*. With *Mother Courage* we were reverent, or tried to be. We studied the theories and struggled to the limit of our naïve resources to deploy ourselves in "Epic style." In approaching *Galileo* quite differently— after years of pondering Brechtian notions—my trust is that to be irreverent is to be more faithful. We are certainly more critical; and that, I take it, is what Brecht is finally after.

For Galileo's crime does not discredit his belief in the brain any more than it did the *Discorsi;* one of the great pleasures of the play is that we see the brain admirably and joyously and muscularly in action. It is the virtue of Epic theater that it puts the critical mind back in the center of the drama—whatever specters, devils, and darkness inhabit the periphery and netherworld of conscious behavior. At the limits of man's perception, within and without, there may be mystery; but there is a lot of terrain justly governed by man's intelligence. Reason may not be enough, but it is not in vain.

Our production was designed to suggest these controlling limits. In conceiving it, we worked out from the center—the actor there, with his rational wit about him. What he used was to be real, substantial, worn—and made beautiful by time. Things became more abstract as they became more decorative or emblematic, or as the eye moved around the borders of the stage. The scenes became more abstract in their composition as they passed from the good natural rapport of Galileo and the young Andrea to the more artificial circumstances of Florence and Rome. When we evoked the material splendor of the period—in contrast to the plebeian earthiness Brecht favors —the purpose of the staging and the production elements was to declare the point of view from which we were seeing it. Thus, the costumes of Bellarmin's palace were opulent beyond propriety: the garb of the princes of the Church —who were also, according to Brecht, the representatives of secular authority

—was velveted and empurpled, regal; the women's gowns were exaggerated in their elegance, but not arbitrarily—they were taken from the highest, most daring fashion of the period. Where they were grotesque, they were grotesque like our own most *outré* fashion (e.g., shaven pates and green hair, sculptured coiffures; we found parallels, by the way, in *Vogue*). When he came from Florence to Rome, Galileo had passed beyond the pedants of the Medici to men of exquisite breeding and intellect, who were also sensualists. There were, as Cardinal Barberini points out, grand ladies of pleasure, with prelates circulating among them. In short, the aristocracy of *la dolce vita*.

To correspond with this, there was a further progression to abstraction. The lights came up on a group downstage, the first image of a set of masks —the animal masks of the ball covering faces in high makeup; above them, descending and spreading like a gold spider, a chandelier. In a stream of music (composed electronically in a broken canon) the guests passed and stopped, as if in another dimension, estranged from the more realistic motion of Galileo, who arrived accompanied by Virginia and Ludovico. The guests applauded soundlessly as the stage froze. Virginia and Ludovico moved toward the music and were absorbed in the stream—their motion slowed and very graceful. Barberini and Bellarmin emerged from the sound barrier—the dove and the lamb. When they replaced their masks, after the battle of wits ending in the silence of Galileo, he too retarded into the dimension of artifice. Yet the more oppressive the atmosphere became, imposing its will on him, the more conscious one may have become that his theories would subvert the fixity—for the chandelier, its discs moving ever so imperceptibly, was constructed as a mobile. Later we saw the Inquisitor—who has been the true guiding spirit behind the scene—perfectly stationary beneath it. The music then seemed consonant, realistic, as if the dislocations were waiting to be resolved in his presence, while his immobility was contradicted by the motion above him.

Throughout the production, our effort was to get more by more, and by certain planned incongruities. Renaissance properties were sculpted in a modern idiom; the naïve lyrics were in the dissonant context of electronic music; a panoplied curtain, lined in blue, unfurled from above the audience —on it, lyrics and legends were projected. When the curtain was flown, becoming a canopy again, we saw abstractions projected in the background, vaguely extrapolated from the scene. On the side of the proscenium, framing the stage, were two giant tapestries. When certain projections appeared on the lowered curtain they were meant to be read as part of a triptych. The triptych presented three mythic options, each integral and beautiful on its own terms: a Ptolemaic universe featuring a Vitruvian man, racked by perfect geometry; a Copernican universe, sun and earth whirling with the turbulent repose of an Action painting; between them, projected, a series of photographic images of Einstein's space—alluring in extension or blank with potential. The curtain lifted like a scroll to reveal the story of Galileo, played out in the center of a world proceeding through the baroque, profuse in impressions, and which had to accept, for all its braininess, what Camus declared "the desperate encounter between human inquiry and the silence of the universe."

Given the desire to incorporate that desperate encounter, the final contradiction, there were aspects of the production which may have seemed too opaque for Brecht, depending on how you look at the world. As Galileo says to the Little Monk who moves him with an account of the rationally ordered lives of the Campagnan peasants, "Sir, my sense of beauty is wounded if Venus appears in my universe without phases." So, too, my sense of beauty (and history) made it necessary to ask questions and assert contradictions that a more standard reading of the text would avoid. Beyond that, we were trying to extend Brecht's conception of the habit of science as a physical impulse and, at the limit of rational inquiry, an aesthetic matter, last judgments returning to intuition. (Einstein, too, said of a certain proof that he distrusted it not because it was wrong, but because it was ugly.)

"Do not be hasty in your conclusion." If the play, born of a theater of political action, takes a position, that is its most impregnable one. Plays less partisan are more tendentious. For what Brecht gives us in the end is not a position but a way of arriving at a position if a position is possible. His Galileo is important for his debt to history and history's debt to him, but also because he reconfirms for us, beyond his own weakness, a way of looking at things that survives its limitations. Andrea, following the lesson of the master, shows the little boy in the final scene that the shadow is not a witch but an old woman ladling a pot. The boy sees, and goes on—*despite* the evidence of the senses, which Galileo says is a very seductive thing—believing what he believes.* Science falters, the facts change, the heart has its own reasons—but the principles of inquiry remain. Who can quarrel with Galileo's caution to his assistants: "My intention is not to prove that I was right but to find out *whether* I was right. 'Abandon hope all ye who enter the realm of observation.' Perhaps they are clouds, perhaps they are spots, but before we assume those phenomena are spots, which would suit us, let us first set about

* Carl Weber told me that Brecht cut this scene because he felt it disturbed the play's balance by making it seem that Galileo had won. Frankly, it never occurred to me to think of it that way, which seems to miss its irony. I would say, rather, the scene shows the extent to which Galileo—for all his scientific wisdom and worldliness—had overestimated human nature, whether Brecht believes in that or not. People do not necessarily believe the evidence of their senses. They may see it is wrong to be superstitious, but they are superstitious nevertheless. The boy sees the shadow and shouts, as Andrea passes over the border, old Marina *is* a witch.

To my knowledge, the scene was never produced before we did it. But after the play was on, we eventually cut it too, not because it disturbed the balance, but because it apparently seemed redundant. If I were to produce the play again, I would try to find a way to make its point with more force—because Galileo did not win. Today those boys are better educated; they may even become learned men, like those who refused to look through the telescope. They will now look, however, and go on believing what they believe.

proving they are not—fried fish. We crawl by inches. What we find today we will wipe from the blackboard tomorrow and reject—unless it shows up again the day after tomorrow. And if we find anything which would suit us, that thing we will eye with particular distrust."

We crawl by inches. If one wanted a cue for approaching a Brecht play, or any significant play for that matter, he needn't look much further. The passage is a definition of method. The humility has the confidence of imaginative discontent. The habit of distrust is not, however, the discipline of distrust. Some of us crawl by inches because we don't know how to proceed. There is no method, and there is no direction. Confidence is not a datum, a natural attribute of talent, status, training, or belief; it is rather what we long for. Even when all is permitted, we waver.

It is a condition from which a theater created in the 1950s was almost bound to suffer. Inclinations do not make a position; and for years we told ourselves and our audience we were not a partisan theater, not because we didn't value partisanship or because it was entirely true, but because we weren't sure, in many areas, what it was possible to be partisan about. One reason is that we were living in a period in which our sources of information were either restrained or suspect—at the same time as we were flooded with news in which our perils and our blessings were very mixed.

I have described the circumstances in which we began our rehearsals of *Galileo.* On the day the play opened, it was announced—for all the world as if it were planned by our own publicity department—Mariner II had brushed Venus, after going 182,000,000 miles through space.

Generally overlooked in the natural wonder of it all was the report that NASA had thrown up a blockade around the scientists of the Jet Propulsion Laboratory responsible for that historic event. The science correspondent of the San Francisco *Chronicle,* usually reasonable about security matters, wrote: "NASA officials decided some weeks ago that propaganda value for this genuinely superb space achievement could best be exploited by a full-dress Washington ceremony. It would also afford political leaders holding NASA's purse strings a chance to take bows before the assembled press corps." It was conceded by NASA, he said, that no classified information was involved in the information blackout.

Well, granted the need to jockey for position in the Cold War, one can even understand a blackout for maximum propaganda. But on the front page of the newspaper, opposite the account of the flight to Venus, was an Associated Press report on a monograph by Supreme Court Justice William O. Douglas, who warned us that the nation was becoming warped by ignorance. Justice Douglas said the "common sense or informed judgment of people, which we trust in theory," has been perverted by censorship, secrecy, and exploitation. "The new centers of power," he said, "are in the hands of those who control science; and one who traces the controls back to origins often finds the Pentagon in the central position. . . . Those who finance the scientific revolution usually control those who work for them."

He was repeating the alarm sounded by President Eisenhower in his farewell address in January 1961, when he described the military-industrial colossus as something novel in the American experience—moving beyond politics into our spiritual life. By implying that the scientific-technological elite was in servitude to the Pentagon, he was to signal the entrenchment of the Warfare State which President Kennedy inherited. Though both Eisenhower and Kennedy were aware of the perils, the limits of security have been virtually impossible to define. The instruction of the citizenry is largely dependent on the mass media; so, we are reading the shadows on the wall. The result is public hallucination.

(My father used to read the newspapers from end to end, advertising, classifieds and all, and then pronounce his verdict: "They're all lying." Yet, like most Americans who felt the same way, he also believed what he read in the newspapers. Who can keep up with it? Only the psychotic perhaps, like Grandma Iva Kroeger, the trunk murderess, who draped a plastic rosary over the prosecuting attorney and said to the reporters: "Why don't you people print the truth?" She was accusing them of misrepresenting her age. When the reporters pointed out they had used the date she previously gave them and asked her to explain the change, she refused with a cunning smile: "One astrology never tells another astrology her true birth date." Medieval science was never so arcane as our own, nor truth so Mayan as in the Cold War. Of course, what I report about Grandma Kroeger, I read in the newspapers.)

It is in this atmosphere that all the work I have done in the theater has been done. What we have been trying to develop in our theater is a counter-atmosphere in which the special properties of the dramatic form, devoted to crisis, are enlisted against the epidemic of mystifications. This does not mean we are developing a political theater or a polemical theater or a theater limited to social issues. I should hope that anything we do has some such concern, but our main dedication, in an era of weird bureaucracy and statistical miasma, is to the spirit of theater itself—communal, playful, protestant, and life-giving. For fear of being didactic, however, one may simply be irresponsible. And more than one of our productions has been motivated by the urgency of the battalion runner in Faulkner's *A Fable,* who looks about him and says: "This is terrible, I'm going to do something about it."

In actuality, every drama takes a position. The most anemic Broadway farce is a testament; there is a soapbox in every play. If, as Nietzsche says, architecture is the oratory of power by means of form, the theater is the oratory of action by means of form. It is not only critical but epicritical. We hear in the most silent gesture the rhetoric of provisional behavior, the passage of what is done and what is not done. What we show prescribes. "Bless thy sweet eyes, they bleed," says Mad Tom to his blinded father, agape with the incredible wound. Is it a benediction, or is the blessing revolted? Bless what bleeds. Almost unbearable—but you might have to live it both ways. We see what might happen if what *is* happening weren't so palpably true.

Yet a great play is a true lie. The greater it is the more it disarms our disbelief: "What, art thou mad? Art thou mad? Is not the truth the truth?" That lie is indelible. If not true, it should be.

What was, what is, what shall be. Impressed on the present, by dint of fantasy, is a past and a speculative future. Every memorable play is a diary and a prophecy. And bearing down on the accumulative uncertainties of the world as we think we know it now, every prophecy helps. It makes no difference, as Spinoza cautioned, that "prophecy never rendered the prophet wiser than he was before." He who shouts "Woe, woe, woe to Jerusalem!" may be nothing but an alarmist (or doom may descend anyhow) but he keeps the rest of us alert. It is the duty of the theater, encarnalized and gregarious, to honor the prophet. And to perform that duty, there are two ethical imperatives: Speak out! Act!

I stress a way of thinking about the theater, because for me it is a way of working. *Galileo,* because it is a play with political bearing, specifically incites the kind of thinking I have been doing in this chapter. But the same considerations have come to prevail more and more around whatever productions we do—not by enforced procedure but as a general state of mind, an *atmosphere.* There is, I should say, nothing particularly inspired about recommending awareness of one's world as a ground for performance: it would only seem natural. The density of a play depends, however, on the kind of question you are willing to ask about your world, and yourself; and the prophecies you are willing to make. Speak out? Act? Unfortunately, we are dealing with a profession where opportunities are so scarce one fears giving offense. It is an occupational hazard of the theater business to be forgotten. To avert this disaster, one keeps his mouth shut, files away his anxieties and his questions, grins through those rounds.

There's nothing inborn about apathy. If it comes of surfeit, it may also come of rejection and insecurity. Even when talent is exercised in the American theater, there is something furtive about it. Actors are driven into studios when there are no stages. There are advantages, no doubt, to the development of craft; but craft may sneak around the public issues, and the hermetic society of the studio is likely to be an unsatisfactory community in the end. Take one of the basic freedoms of the studio: Improvisation. For all its liberating utility, it tells a tale of paranoia. The studio is only an example, a somewhat belated one, of that underground activity which has been almost the salvation of modern art. Yet, though it may have the satisfaction of prophetic undertones, one aspires to a completer life and a less darkling voice. There comes a time when the voice from the cistern, whether worn by repetition or become a mere cry in the common air, may have very little left to say.

The Actor's Workshop began as a studio (it is still in the name) but evolved rapidly toward more explicit social engagement. That has its attractions and its dangers; the deeper life may disappear. Our voice is still a long way from being a majority voice, and possibly should never be. What is involved in our evolution, however, is not only more social awareness but the desire for larger audiences and a more genuine community. Despite this, we remain attentive to that voice from the cistern; and periodically, when community seems too pleased with us, we issue solemn warnings to ourselves about learning to live with failure. That there is a piety to it I don't deny. There has been evangelism, and not everybody complies. Commitment has its sluggish currents. There is spindrift and defection. There are those new to the company who are puzzled by the "intellectual" to-do, and some of our older people—prideful of accomplishment and less resistant now—still think privately it might be better if we just went about our business—that is, produced plays people liked—and let the world take care of itself.

As for the hip younger people, they already think us square. Which puts those of us who have been through the mill of more than a decade on our mettle. It is a new complication in the running and erratic dialectic of our growth. But in the atmosphere that has developed, the company is attuned to crisis, and more responsible to it. Whatever disenchantment sets in once the diurnal tasks are performed, one feels the striving for purpose. It has always seemed to me an appropriate image of our condition that San Francisco is built on the San Andreas Fault. Even the sense that some undefined destiny has been betrayed from time to time would be impossible if there were not increasingly a fundamental stake in the shifting ground.

This atmosphere was not set forth as a mandate at the beginning of our career. It rather arose out of a sustained indecisive effort to understand what a theater is about. The play is the thing, for the moment. Now, however, each play has behind it a history of other plays. Not only was I able to refer to the morning's headlines at the first rehearsal of *Galileo,* I could also place the production about to begin in a continuum of other productions. Some of these had strains of feeling and thought very different from those normally associated with Brecht, but which are in Brecht, too. Out of the corpus of previous work inevitably came the critique of Brecht's methods and ideas which determined what we did with *Galileo.*

We had gone in recent years through every subterranean passage of the Theater of the Absurd. Though they outrage categories, the instincts of playwrights such as Beckett, Genet, and Ionesco would seem to be opposed to the bold, declarative, Marxist character of a Brecht play, descending from the *Lehrstück,* "designed to clarify the ideas of the authors and of all those taking part, not to provide anybody with an emotional experience." Ionesco has attacked Brecht again and again. (The continuum is enlivened by the fact that Ionesco has also walked out on Genet. Said he: "*Je suis un blanc.*") If Brecht urges us to take a stand, many of the plays we have been doing have warned us that it may be impossible to take a stand; that in an atomic world fission is a property of belief as well as matter. Beware of ideology.

"Nothing to be done." That's hardly the way a play should begin. However, a generation of incinerators, Hiroshima, and deterred deterrents lies between *Waiting for Lefty,* with its affinity to Brecht, and *Waiting for Godot.* And one of the illusions we've had to improve the quality of is that social problems are social. They are that, perhaps, but more than that. (Recommended reading: *The Maids* as a minority view of our relations with Cuba.) It may be all right in wish-fulfillment to get rid of social evil, as Giraudoux's Madwoman does, by pushing all the capitalists into the sewer, but it's another thing to get them anywhere near it to do so. In the Warfare State, the dirty business is everybody's business—what is good for General Dynamics is good, so he thinks, for the small shopkeeper in Houston, who is also living off TDX contracts. It was easier, if not better, when the rakeoff was more exclusive. You could spot the enemy by the size of his stomach. Odets was saying: "Come on, let's do it—*now!*" But it was done when it was done, and done imperfectly. The New Deal was negotiated by experts, but it was improvisation nonetheless. Giraudoux, an elegant ironist, was saying: "Wouldn't it be nice *if*. . . ." Which is a way of putting the real issue into somebody else's head. Genet is saying, the issue murderously out in the open: "Look out! it's going to happen, it *is* happening—those knives are real!" Only Genet, like the Envoy in *The Balcony,* is a master of obfuscation, and a pervert to boot. Can things be really that bad? we muse, fingering the selvage of *his* illusions, safe as only voyeurs can be.

One of the curious things about some of these plays is the way, reflecting the stunning paradoxes I rehearsed before, they also put life in question. For Brecht's Galileo, as for Mother Courage, there is never any doubt that life is worth living—even when he is most contemptuous of his recantation. "I still like to eat," he tells Andrea, referring to a goose ambiguously sent. But there is another view of Galileo's recantation, which introduces Camus' essay "An Absurd Reasoning," in *The Myth of Sisyphus:* "I have never seen anyone die for the ontological argument. Galileo, who held a scientific truth of great importance, abjured it with the greatest of ease as soon as it endangered his life. In a certain sense, he did right. That truth was not worth the stake. Whether the earth or the sun revolves around the other is a matter of profound indifference. To tell the truth, it is a futile question. On the other hand, I see many people die because they judge that life is not worth living. I see others paradoxically getting killed for the ideas or illusions that give them a reason for living (what is called a reason for living is also an excellent reason for dying). I therefore conclude that the meaning of life is the most urgent of questions."

For Brecht, predicating action on the changeability of man's nature and institutions, the stance is Marxist, the mission is social reform; for Camus, predicating action on the belief that "the one truly serious philosophical problem . . . is suicide," the mission is to discover how "within the limits of nihilism it is possible to find the means to proceed beyond nihilism."

The polarity is not absolute. Brecht's mission is not his meaning. There is the disparity, so troubling to many, between social purpose and what is felt uncontrollably beyond purpose. And Camus—before his silence on Algeria and the sudden death which Sartre called a metaphysical scandal, confirming the Absurd—was a man in social combat. Sartre, unintentionally mediating between the two, understands why Brecht created his Epic form, as a manifesto against the egocentricity of bourgeois theater, which "wants . . . an image of man according to its own ideology. . . ." Having aligned himself with the Marxists (and rejecting Camus' political silence), Sartre believes with Brecht that "to act, which is precisely the object of the theater, is to change the world and in changing it, of necessity to change oneself." Fine. But he also believes that Brecht, refusing the bourgeois demand for subjectivity, "was never able to make a meaningful place in his work for subjectivity as it should be."

Yet there's the rub: what should it be in a form aspiring to public assent, especially if it is calling for public action? Like the victim in the Penal Colony, we are all racked by the conflict between the Self which wants to remain inviolable and the avatars of Authority to which we must yield in social obligation. We have no Oresteian trilogy to appease in civic unity and hymeneal celebration the furies of our underground. Our comedy is beastly like Aristophanes', but a good deal blacker. Desiring to speak out clearly, we find ourselves like Beckett's Clov, confessing mournfully: "No one that ever lived ever thought so crooked as we."

So how be clear? It may be possible for a Marxist like Planchon, who knows precisely what he would like to say about the function of the Church in Shakespeare's *Henry IV* to a proletarian audience in industrial Lyon. Planchon's monks are unquestionably religious caterpillars, like the Pope and Cardinal in Anouilh's *Becket*. But in our company, in San Francisco, as I write this, a particular group of people are doing a play in which a Catholic priest supplied us with part of the costume as well as instruction in the ritual for a scene in which the Church is shown as the center of both worldly and ecclesiastical corruption. It wasn't the first time our secularism has received gracious assistance from the clergy, so much that I said to our spiritual advisor when he departed: "Someday we'll call you, Father, when we're not being anti-clerical."

It wasn't only this kindness (the Devil has power to assume a pleasing shape) that makes it impossible for me to believe Planchon's churchmen any more than I could Anouilh's. Their simplifications of history come to the same point from different ends of the political spectrum. Brecht's church-men are much more convincing. ("To take satirical aim at the worldly interests of high dignitaries," he said, "seems to me cheap.") Nevertheless, in our society—where the edges of value are so blurred that mortal enemies barely know each other for what they are—some of Brecht's intentions seem beside the point, oversimplifying our felt reality. Or at least, there are those further contradictions.

The demystifier may be right, but were we not told to trust the evidence of our senses?

Moreover, many of us—including the painters and sculptors who have come to work in our theater—have been thinking in an idiom foreign to the objective character of Brecht's later plays. In brief, they are nonobjective in their habits of mind and very nearly nihilistic in their sense of reality. They feel something like that at the taproot of Brecht's drama. But while they admire much in a play like *Galileo*—certain things which would astonish Helene Weigel and the members of the Ensemble—they think much of it is square. On the other side, our "underground" plays, through which we have become connoisseurs of dark corners, were not made to be "popular" plays. When they become so, we wonder. Nevertheless, as we burrow into these plays, we can't help but think how far down can we go before it's impossible to come back? Why should we come back? Well, that's an instinct too—the need to come out of the catacombs and found your church on a visible rock. Through all the turmoil and anxiety of theater art, there is something that resists the monstrous, the deracinated, the cloacal, the cabal—and responds to Brecht's Galileo when he says, "our work is exacting, who would do it for less than the population at large."

When we first began that work, however, it was strictly for ourselves—random, cellular, nonplused. The first principle was, simply, to provide a situation for work, of any kind.

5

*Men are no longer bound together by ideas, but by interests; and it would seem
as if human opinions were reduced to a sort of intellectual dust, scattered on
every side, unable to collect, unable to cohere.*
                    —Alexis de Tocqueville, *Democracy in America*

*The Group has a well-defined attitude toward human problems and affairs, and
while I'm sure that such a formalized policy as this is by no means necessary to
success in the theater, it is necessary to me.*
                    —Franchot Tone, speech to the Town Hall Club, 1938

IN THE COMMON
INTEREST

In a curious mixture of sincerity and misrepresentation, a biography of
The Workshop, prepared a few years ago for publicity purposes, reads as
follows: "Begun in 1952 without stars, fanfare, real estate, or capital, The
Actor's Workshop is an act of imagination by two professors at San Francisco State College, Jules Irving and Herbert Blau, native New Yorkers who
are convinced that the destiny of the American theater lies as far off-Broadway as possible, in permanent companies dedicated to ensemble playing."

As an account of developed values, the passage has merit; as an index of
what we believed when The Workshop began, it does no more than identify
a couple of important symptoms of our origin: that the founders were earning
their livings as college teachers and that we had left New York. But, though
Irving had been on Broadway from childhood and though he might have
continued a career there, his departure, mainly to escape the rat race, was
no real sign of artistic rebellion; mine less, for I never saw a Broadway play
until my eighteenth year to heaven. When I finally made it, without a critical
principle to my name, I even enjoyed *The Moon Is Blue.*

So let us beware of education.

I left New York with a degree in chemical engineering, and though I had
aspirations as a playwright, they were mainly informed by a quick reading

113

in my senior year of the Bennett Cerf anthology of modern American plays, the bloodless distinction of which must have given me courage, though I thought they were great then because they were collected. The theater was a postgraduate indulgence I could afford on the GI Bill. Privately I had every intention of returning to bubblecap towers and the Second Law of Thermodynamics, which I understood only when I began thinking seriously about dramatic form.

There was a lot of naïveté lurking behind that "act of imagination." True, by the end of 1951, Irving and I were working for advanced degrees and had been teaching for more than a year—he in theater, I in English—on the college level. However, we had developed no general aesthetic separately or between us, nor had we stayed up all night holding revolutionary conversations on the place of the theater in American culture. Social views? Aside from some study in business administration, Irving had spent most of his time in the theater, whether in college or on Broadway or overseas, in the Special Services cast of *Brother Rat*. It was not promising. He is voluble, with a bright, bantering mind, and the sort of political nature that doesn't suffer needlessly from playing the game because he never took it to be anything else; but he is not political. As for me, despite my technological background, I had a small history of social action, a superb collection of *PM* saved through high school, and had been something of a Wallace progressive when I was editor of the daily at NYU—though my editorials usually consisted, like *PM*'s, of liberal slantings of news and opinion pilfered from *The New York Times*. Thus fortified, I could be very contentious.

The drama is not, however, by nature a liberal form. It has a rigorous economy and an aristocratic past. It is neither Keynesian nor ameliorative. This doesn't mean it hasn't its own kind of democracy, but even today my liberal friends are caught wishing for what it won't offer when it is most profound. Take the controversial notion of *Catharsis:* whatever it may be, it is not social legislation. I'm not even sure it is morally edifying. If Plato would have banned art itself from the Republic, what would he have thought of its most mysterious affect? If Iago is not right, one still has to ask the question, is he wrong? And as for the morality of *Othello* as a work of art, it has always struck me as one of the most frightening moments in all art that, after *seeing* Othello put an end to himself, we see Iago—with threats of punishment that can hardly match the crime—*walk offstage*.

These curious considerations came later. It was only as I began teaching that I understood some of the lessons from those histories of dramatic art that I mentioned in the first chapter, and that I began to look upon the drama itself as a means of livelihood, in every sense. Personally, I was living a double standard in those days. There was a schizoid split between the principles I had acquired in my study of literature and those I thought possible to exercise in the theater. Because I wasn't that ardent about the theater, I wasn't that grieved by the cleavage. Not only did I not expect deeper resonances of experience or revelations of formal beauty in the theater, but like Harold Clurman prior to his founding of the Group Theater, I suspected either that "there is something inferior in the theater per se or there is something wrong about the practical theater of today that escapes me." And unlike Clurman, I wasn't sure I couldn't live without the theater, for I constantly wondered why I bothered with it at all, since I often found myself bored when I saw plays, grew annoyed (because I knew they were right) when my friends in the Creative Writing Program disparaged the best of American plays, and fretted to be back in my study.

Among my teachers had been Yvor Winters, the poet and critic, who thought the drama an inferior form to begin with, the theater too silly to be corrupt. It was Winters, a much-embattled absolutist, who taught me that the most abstract ideas were worth fighting about and that poetry was a matter of life and death. (The world is dominated, he feels, by those who "Judge definition the most fierce of crimes.") We fought about the theater, but I was upholding a cause in which I didn't really believe—though I couldn't deny the attraction of the stage and all its gregarious surroundings, to which I was drawn as I condemned them. I certainly preferred the English lyric to the American play, as I still do, but you couldn't perform a lyric—or could you? Maybe you can't. But it was a while before we began to consider questions like that at The Actor's Workshop.

Shortly before we talked about a studio of our own, Irving described, with the baited energy that is the other side of a canny poker player, the theater he and a teacher of ours were planning for a town near San Francisco. It seemed to me the best of all possible theaters under the circumstances, a very admirable prospect. Despite my misgivings, the theater as an institution was still too novel and glamorous to keep me from asking too much of it. (A lot of my ambivalences might be explained by the fact that I had just married an actress.) No repertoire was discussed, but I'm sure the intention was to offer the usual slate of comedies and musicals, a serious drama for relief, with a classic thrown in. And I wouldn't have been prompted then to offer any objections. Literally, they intended a *stock* company. That plan, however, needed $20,000 or so, and I recall saying in what must have seemed a moment of invincible ignorance (if not envy for my being left out) that we could start a theater for next to nothing.

I'm certain I didn't know what I meant.

Though I have since come to suspect myself of submarine proclivities, a certain affection for the abyss, I do know that when we started The Workshop in 1952, it was with no dissidence in mind and our hearts in a relatively conventional place. Somebody had called 1951 the year of World War II.5, but we weren't making any social protest; and though there was plenty of *Angst* aghast in me, I kept it pretty well concealed, like Dostoyevsky's Underground Man. For I would hardly have thought then that it was the theater's function to do something with "that cold, abominable half despair, . . . that acutely recognized and yet partly doubtful hopelessness of one's position, . . . that hell of unsatisfied desires turned inward, . . .

that fever of oscillations, of resolutions determined for ever and repented of again a minute later" which is the perverse dignity of the buried life, too outraged to really take shelter. And if I had at the outset pressed the claims of the buried life, the people in our group would have despaired over me.

The Human Condition had almost nothing to do with the founding of The Actor's Workshop, except by default. In a nation spending billions on guided missiles, able to create an entire city almost overnight to release energy for the annihilation of another city in an instant, whose affluence was such that it could in wartime supply two armies on two fronts in less than two years with so much surplus that it was almost forced into dropping holocaust unimagined by man so it could get on with the Reconversion; in a nation which could in a few years think seriously of digging a Randy "big hole" underground so that a 700,000-ton blast could be set off in secret, and which was at the moment financing a limited war in a remote land for reasons that almost nobody understood, Irving and I each plunked down about eighteen dollars a month and rented a loft behind a Judo Academy and went about our ingenuous business. We asked no existential questions; we were recouping no cultural losses, toppling no icons, breaking no classifications, rewriting no history, assuaging no ontological guilt, shattering no systems—as the Underground Man says scornfully—"constructed by lovers of mankind for the benefit of mankind." There was a little Sartrean nausea when we discovered rat shit in the garbage beneath the stairs, but we swept it all away, garbage, shit, and all, in the common interest. There was something inviolably American in that, which has never left us.

Though I could remember from my study of physical chemistry part of the proof for $E = mc^2$, we believed that twice two does make four, and if we had any doubts they were mainly speculative. We were not committed to the Absurd. There was no spite, no sickness, no Messianic rage, no Quest for Identity, no demonic style. There was no style at all, and though I was teaching a course in literary form, very few ideas about it so far as the theater was concerned. If revolution is an affair of logical lunatics, we were at the time very practical young men of the theater—the lunacy was yet to come. And, in varying degrees and with some agitation in the cellarage, with *Angst* over the *Angst,* all the rest.

But for those in our company who like their lunacy pure, like a fifty-megaton bomb, it was never sufficiently deranged.

Unlike the Group Theater of the thirties, then, we were not prompted by social idealism, nor did we consider ourselves "a training ground for citizenship." We had no "common cause with the worker," or—for that matter—identification with any class. No more than the young man of *Awake and Sing* did we want life printed on dollar bills—but we had a few more than he did, and we'd lived through a period in which the desire for social justice had gone through all the lettered agencies of reform and turned into a proliferating bureaucracy, stimulated by our marvelous capacity to organize for war. If we thought about it, we knew that not all the great social issues had been solved by the New Deal, but the rhythm of picketing had dissipated, and the litany of Moral Realism encouraged us to live with our sins—until, perhaps, the omnipresent issue of Segregation raised its ugly head in Little Rock.

If there was no clear social motivation to our work, neither did we have any collective sympathy with the Dispossessed; that is, with the Alienated, the Disaffiliated, the Angry, the Beat (who were gone, gone, gone in San Francisco about the same time we started making the scene); with all those who had made the problem of Identity, the strategic defense of Self against the minions and dehumanization, the primary issue of their lives; who were as much disgusted by the debilities of the Welfare State, here or in England, as they were by the terrors of the Bomb; who considered Medicare a *non sequitur* in a world that was diseased in soul. And some of whom—while pondering the twentieth century's history of torture, murder, brainwashing, saturation bombing, fireballs, fallout, and the threat of "spasm response"— could respond to that generation of Europeans who had made despair a way of life. For them, the political game is a *shuck,* the social order is bunk, the social contract a fraud, drawn up to kill us off. If one insisted on working in the theater (another shuck) rather than taking to the hills, it was one's duty to fight outrage with outrage.

While we were still in our loft, we were, on a practical level, sealed off from these sentiments. When we chose, however, to become a real theater and were faced with extinction every day, the general peril and our own became fused, and we wondered whether there wasn't, indeed, a conspiracy against us. As we began to realize what we were up against, economically and culturally, and as we improvised our way through a most eclectic repertoire, what we learned was that the questions we weren't asking had to be asked. Since we weren't, like the Group, inspired by the social urgency of the period, we had to ask ourselves by what else we could be inspired.

This aspect of our growth was defined several years later by a trivial altercation during our rehearsals of *Mother Courage,* a play which brought us all face-to-face with the implacable countenance of the Cold War. I was going rather hard at an actor who had been puzzled by some direction. It had something to do with the idea of Alienation, which I began to badger him with all over again, extending the immediate issue into the social context. Whereupon he said to me: "Cut it out, you're not Brecht." "That's all right," I answered, "when we started I wasn't even Herbert Blau."

I might have saved a little face, but the perennial nagging question remains: *Am* I Herbert Blau? And though the game of "Who am I?" can be a drag, I am not sure I am suitably identified yet by all the credit and courtesy cards that have my number. What isn't down on paper is up in the air. And fallout is only the worst of it.

As we gathered for our first session, the security measures of warfare had turned into the peacetime "torment of secrecy." Ten days after President Truman ordered work on the H-bomb and Albert Einstein had warned of total annihilation, Senator McCarthy waved a list before the Women's Republican Club in Wheeling, West Virginia: "I hold here in my hand. . . ," he said, and incriminated 205 unnamed people in the State Department, with General Marshall explicitly mentioned for good measure. The Age of Obfuscation had reached its political apotheosis, and took its toll on the theater. It was at the end of 1951—the atmosphere having grown so paralyzing in New York—that Brooks Atkinson remarked we were emulating the totalitarian countries by yielding our cultural life "to the Yahoos and hoodlums." He spoke of "something elusive and intangible" draining the vitality out of the theater; it seemed to him that people were playing it safe and that the "ignorant heresy-hunting and the bigoted character assassination" were succeeding. But it was a strange period. For as Atkinson was writing this passage about the American theater, we were confronted with the irony of Brecht and Felsenstein developing two of the greatest theaters in the world in one of its most repressive sectors, East Berlin.

What were the prospects in San Francisco?

Land's end. A sort of populated Darien; the landlocked harbor overlooked by Mount Diablo; 800,000 people—small enough to be embraceable, yet metropolitan, too; with the highest incidence of alcoholism and suicide in America; a gilded boom town grown urban on a fissure, suburbs sprawling over nine counties of the Bay Region; 3,000,000 people in the vicinity, two great universities nearby, and a trolley college of high caliber; a great park of eclectic fauna; a Chinese ghetto which feels affluent and no conspicuous slums; sick comics in the bistros and a Bohemian Club of unregenerate squares; its Barbary Coast infested with interior decorators and Alcatraz still dominating the views; withal, a city reposeful and august, the old Pacific Union Club on Nob Hill, home of the railroad kings, lording it over the new arrivals: the students, the dockworkers, the doctors of the Kaiser Plan, the Hadassah ladies, the vagrants from the valleys, the junior executives of the new Playboy set, the Beats from Tangiers and North Platte, all the questing intellectuals, and those who simply want to retire in a city whose weather is so equable you may complain of missing the seasons but feel imposed upon anywhere else; a turreted, towered, scalloped, hilly city, Mediterranean in western baroque, the old buildings being erased by freeways and the troughs filled in by Redevelopment; below its splendid bridges, a city with a nervous graciousness, upholding a worldwide reputation for a culture it doesn't quite have, though what it has is, by the standards of other American cities, impressive—a city that is a myth, with the golden opportunity to live up to it.

If we were living at midcentury, as Eric Goldman put it, in "the nagging realm of maybe," San Francisco seemed to me the perfect geographic setting. There was a kind of weird Keatsian "negative capability" in that prosperous postwar town, with full employment expected, medical conquests in the offing, rocket engines nearing perfection, and Space looming before us, while across the Bay they were developing an anti-proton. A friend of mine, a distinguished scientist who works at the University on cosmic rays, was called in to run some tests to certify the isolation of the new particle. His wife, who has acted with our company, tells the story of waiting for him to return, which he did several hours later. "Well? Well?" she said. "Well what?" he said. "I couldn't see the goddam thing."

It was a city of prospects and ambiguities, the left-wing longshoremen in a monopolistic union; a resort for homosexuals; a place for fashionable women, and psychiatrists, everywhere; three hours behind New York, yet three thousand miles nearer the Orient with its rising revolutionary sun— and when The Workshop started, a queer sort of "shooting peace" in Korea, not a "cease fire" but a "seldom fire"; while GIs hung their laundry on tanks and were getting up pheasant shoots.

Negotiations in Panmunjom had been going on about five months when we began rehearsals of our first play in our studio. Now and then the question would arise: Are we or are we not at war? And what for? The UN, hedging, called the battle in Korea a "police action" and the North Korean attack became a "bandit raid." There was not yet much talk about brain-washing, but a new generation of Americans was getting an education in the *rigor mortis* of power. Just before the turn of the year, Hanson Baldwin wrote in *The New York Times* of the coalition of Russians, Chinese, and North Koreans, that they were either "(1) primitive men who have not yet outgrown the swaddling clothes of savagery; or (2) men whose god is power unhampered by restraint, who regard murder and cruelty as necessary techniques for the achievement of absolutism." A Chilean diplomat told the UN that "cannibalism" is Soviet dogma. If this were so (and most of us were prepared to believe anything to the extent we believed nothing), then all the more appalling was the apathy and capitulation of American prisoners of war, especially in comparison to the behavior of other troops who served in Korea for the UN.

Never before in our history had such widespread and flagrant national betrayal taken place:

> The Dhow, the Gizee, and Rhee
> What do they want from me?

In the most idiotic days of World War II, it was still possible for an infantry soldier to climb Monte Cassino and feel he was doing his part to save history from the barbarians. But Korea—with its bleak, unreal terrain—seemed an unlikely place to make the world safe for democracy. Description of the landscape and the strange objectless maneuvers read like the setting and action of a Beckett drama. And, indeed, the GI who fired his rifle into the air because he hadn't the slightest inkling as to why he was fighting to save rice paddies fertilized with human dung later became an ardent spectator at our productions of Beckett and Genet.

This was the fag end of a war which was no more surrealistic than any war, but seemed so—as the Chinese delivered Christmas boxes with ribbons and booby traps. And it was stunning in portent for the future, once what MacArthur called "the bottomless well of Chinese manpower" launched its first *jen hai* offensive. In 1951, reports from Eniwetok and Nevada, containing the word *thermonuclear,* suggested that progress was being made on the H-bomb. But discounting of human cost by the Chinese after their entry at the Yalu foretold what their attitude toward nuclear war would be in their later ideological conflict with the Soviet Union. Cymbals, gongs, drums, then thousands rushing advance posts, falling, with thousands more after them. It was a panic. But the Korean War, like anti-communism, the bogging down of disarmament conferences at Geneva, failures at the Summit, kept the bulls trotting on the market.

Prior to the Korean War, Churchill made his "Iron Curtain" speech at Fulton, Missouri. There the Cold War was christened, and *The Christian Science Monitor* wrote about American foreign policy: "Nobody seems to be sure what is going to happen. And few are sure what should be done, no matter what happens." This was when we were beginning to realize with a boom that if the war had ended, there had been no victory. Of course, there were those who had foreseen the conflict with the Soviet Union even before the occupation of Berlin—and were encouraging us to fight that war as soon as possible. (Someone remarked that if the Berlin crisis hadn't developed, it would have been necessary to invent it.) But while President Truman had assured us that "We aim to keep America secured inside and out," China had fallen to the Communists, and the Russians announced they had exploded their atom bomb. A couple of months before The Workshop started, a second bomb was exploded and the explosion announced by Stalin, whose diplomacy had hitherto been more sequestered.

From that time forth we rocked and rolled with "the balance of terror." When Dean Acheson proposed a broad disarmament plan in 1951, it was possible for Vishinsky to say to the UN: "I cannot restrain my laughter"— and for Khrushchev, some years later, to bang his shoe. Meanwhile, self-righteous over these displays of boorishness, we did more than our proper share to keep the arms race alive. Our economic life depended on it.

On the final Sunday of 1951, summing up the year, James Reston wrote that all factions, East–West, Republicans–Democrats, had become victims of "events" and were "trapped by the consequences of their mutual hostility." Nobody, he said, seemed able to break the circle of mutual terror. "Indeed this town [Washington] has scarcely enough energy left after the last five years to carry on the 'cold war,' let alone end it." He was wrong about that, as he was wrong about the jeopardy of the economy of Western Europe if we rearmed Germany.

The German Recovery was one of the astonishing developments of this period. In *The Fervent Years,* Harold Clurman describes a visit he and Aaron Copland made, in 1926, to the great Hofbrauhaus in Munich: "As we entered a side entrance, the huge throng of beer-bloated, smoke-stewed,

heavy-seated Germans frightened us so that we actually beat a hasty re-
treat. I could not say why, I am not sure now, but I strongly suspect that
Munich and its famous beer-hall were then already in the grip of the rising
Nazi movement. I was totally apolitical at the time. . . ."

It is a good thing symbolic readings are subject to error, for I was in
Munich a quarter-century later and, so far as the Hofbrauhaus is concerned,
the scene hadn't changed. Yet, traveling through Germany I couldn't help
feeling, though I am no more vindictive than the next man, that somewhere
in the spiritual reconstruction the step of penance had been missed. In
November 1951, the assistant U.S. High Commissioner left Germany feeling
Germans weren't trying hard to make up for the Nazi past, citing anti-
Semitic disturbances and the presence of ex-Nazis in the cabinet, one of
whom was saying that "Hitler is to a great extent the consequence of the
Versailles Treaty. . . . Germany is no more guilty than France of World
War II."

It was part of the texture of the time, its passion for paradoxical subtlety
(I remember saying something like this to a class) that Hitler, Mussolini,
Churchill, Peron, and Roosevelt were being compared as manifestations of
the demagogic technique born of the mass movements of the twentieth century. I shall say more of this kind of subtle thought in my own work, but
that the Recovery had been made in peaceful coexistence with certain notorious specters of the Nazi period occurred to me again in the huge irony
of a small notice in a London paper: ordered by the court to get rid of his
holdings, the munitions king Adolph Krupp couldn't find anybody with
enough money to buy him out. So the House of Krupp was restored to its
proper owner and very recently celebrated its 150th anniversary. The *Times*
reported: "Everyone"—ministers, ambassadors, employees, and two thousand invited guests—"had kind words for the House of Krupp." Theodor
Heuss, former president of West Germany, was the main speaker. He said
there was nothing "basically sinful" in the firm's past. Only "hatred spurred
by war" had created an image of Krupp as an "annex to hell" while huge
munitions firms abroad were seen "in the hands of heavenly angels."

I don't know what company Mr. Heuss kept, but outside of Shaw, one
normally doesn't hear a good word for munitions makers anywhere. For
propriety's sake we generally keep them out of the way, like the Mummy in
Strindberg's *Ghost Sonata*. May choirs of angels sing round them all, for
as to a more proper disposition of the House of Krupp, I'm not qualified to
offer an alternative—and as a citizen in good standing of a "permanent war
economy," I was committed as early as 1944 by Charles E. Wilson (in a
speech to the Army Ordnance Association) to keeping my big mouth shut.
Total preparedness was to be a datum of our lives: "The role of Congress
is limited to voting the needed funds. . . . Industry's role in this program is
to respond and cooperate . . . in the execution of the part allotted to it;
industry must not be hampered by political witch-hunts, or thrown to the

fanatical isolationist fringe tagged with a 'merchants of death' label." (Italics mine.)

"Security some men call the suburbs of hell,/ Only a dead wall between," says a Genetic character out of Jacobean drama.

Years ago, T. S. Eliot had written with irony of people "assured of certain certainties." Now, every necessity increases the uncertainty. In January 1952, with Korea hanging fire, McCarthyism broadcast, names dropping in medieval rumor, government employees scurrying for security among the top secrets; charges of favoritism, bribery, and corruption, the whole mink and deep-freeze syndrome leading eventually to the expulsion of Sherman Adams; the Dostoyevskyan ambiguities of the Hiss case in the background; Klaus Fuchs, Browder at Fordham, and the unsettling pathos of the Rosenbergs; with basketball fixes, juvenile scandals, sex perversion, cheating at West Point (and not only cheating, but no remorse, since—as the culpable cadets, including the coach's son, said—everybody is cheating)—what was it possible to believe, to trust, to go upon? "Wrongdoers," said President Truman (whose Secretary of State would not turn his back on Alger Hiss) "have no house with me." But crime, it could be argued, was an American Way of Life—an inevitability of our political system, a necessity of the economy; even in its most brutal forms it could be defended as a route of social ascent, a kind of bloodletting for the underprivileged. The new criminal, we are told, is a reflection of deep changes in middle-class morality, a status seeker, like the businessman who drives a Cadillac to impress the neighbors and has a second car charged off to the needs of the firm.

While the Kefauver Committee warned of a national crime syndicate, "an elusive and furtive but nonetheless tangible thing" (how Artaud would have loved that, or the early Brecht), sociologists were becoming aware that crime, like neurosis and even madness, was a qualitative matter, a matter of degree; that, in a bewildering economy in which vested interests overlapped, in which even the commonest man fudged on his income tax, and in which this man's normal activity was that man's righteous indignation, and that man's righteous indignation a mere veil for personal guilt—how the vices revealed each other! So-and-so's babysitter, we read, stole several thousand dollars hidden in the bedroom and went on a spree to New York. But what were several thousand dollars doing in the bedroom to begin with? Skeletons were rattling in the china closets, and there were black sheep in the best families. Aside from any weakness of personal will, how many factors in American life contributed to the fall of Charles Van Doren?

Even if President Eisenhower had been a moral giant he might have floundered in the midst of all this—and at his best he only resembled that Colonel Manly in the first play written by an American, Royall Tyler's *Fashion:* the rugged fighter in worsted, with a ready smile, a firm handshake, and good sound American ideas, unborrowed—as is the wont of American intellectuals—from Middle European sources such as Weber, Kafka, and

Freud, with their instinct for the labyrinth, their darker revelations, their irony, their paradoxes, and their sense of doom.

If all the best minds of our generation didn't become hysterical, naked, taking to dope, still there was a lot of experiment with it (e.g., Huxley with peyote) that is only beginning to show its reputable proportions in the LSD market at Harvard. National advertising concerns were taking full-page ads to express public shock at the Kefauver revelations, and what they meant for traditional American morality. And though there was a let's-get-in-there-and-fight air about some of them, there was also a disquieting desperation as the cocktails shook. In the Cold War it became habitual, for all the amenities and annuities, not to prepare too much for the troubles ahead, for if they really came, that was it. So one played it cool. The psychiatrists called it "selective inattention." The jitters of the twenties and the jitterbugging of the thirties had turned into the splay-footed faceless shuffle of the Bop, non-touch; and in the sixties, the detached solidarity of the Twist, there and not-there, being *in* with Alienation. While all our sins seemed to be collecting in pollinated and bottomless pools, it wasn't clear whether the decline of value had reached its nadir or whether we were on the brink of rediscovery. But what could anybody say about religion when Mickey Spillane, who had created Mike Hammer to rub out the commies, found God?

In self-protection against the dubious absurdity of it all, everybody had his hooker—as they were to tell us several years later in *The Connection*. Ours, it seemed, was The Workshop. And if we began with temperance, it was hard to tell where the hook ended and rational intelligence began. The best that can be said about it was that we, too—some of whom had been stagnating in silence—were collecting in our own polliniferous pool. The temperance was neither a golden mean nor a habit, rather the considered spirit of the baffled times, which mused on lost possibilities of action.

A year after The Workshop was founded, Adlai Stevenson said in response to ex-President Truman's criticism of Eisenhower's foreign policy: "We must take care lest we confuse moderation with mediocrity, lest we settle for half answers to hard problems. . . . I agree that it is time for catching our breath; I agree that moderation is the spirit of the times."

From the discretion of college students who wanted to know about pension plans on graduation to the liberal smirking and catching of breath when Stevenson, with his patrician wit and shoehole humility, said things in public that raised the tone but took the radical edge off certain views left over from the New Deal, one could show that America was indeed taking pause, talking things over moderately in one prolonged coffee break. Revolutionary things were brooding; but in politics, with the coalition of Southern Democrats and Northern Republicans, party lines had broken down; and aside from a couple of mavericks like Wayne Morse, there were times you could hardly tell where anybody stood, for stands were being taken with objectivity, detachment, caution, reserve, level-headedness, in committee, buoyed up with statistics and bogged down in Rules, the apparatus of Congress beginning to creak behind the need for legislation, while reactionary senators from backward states wielded their seniority to keep things from moving, except when the Pentagon turned on the hysteria.

Gone were not only the perfervid days of Roosevelt and Hopkins with their unconstitutional go, go, go—but it might have been some very ancient polity of which one read in de Tocqueville: "I can conceive of nothing more admirable or more powerful than a great orator debating great questions of state in a democratic assembly. . . . Hence the political debates of a democratic people, however small it may be, have a degree of breadth that frequently renders them attractive to mankind." He was speaking of us! "All men are interested by them because they treat of *man,* who is everywhere the same." One of the virtues of Stevenson was his attempt to restore this tradition; but though he gave us the best political rhetoric since Lincoln, there was nobody to debate with, for it was not by debate that one was elected; and if he was treating of *man,* he was doing so in a country where most men were interested in particular men—themselves; if they were not "everywhere the same," they were trying desperately to become so.

What de Tocqueville admired in the colonial debates was the momentariness and monumentality of great issues, their relevance to mankind. But who reads the *Congressional Record* today because it speaks to mankind? The *Congressional Record* barely even speaks to the issues. And so fuzzy were the issues and the parties that Eisenhower, we remember, was very nearly drafted as a Democrat. Everywhere in the country, know-nothingness, which thought it had heard it all, appeared to be reaping its temporizing harvest.

But, Pozzo says, "Let us not then speak ill of our generation. . . ."

If alignments were breaking down in a plague of half-heartedness, on the queer margins of American life they were building up again. In the early fifties, picking up the dialectical diminuendo of the forties, the New Conservatism was speaking with authority even among the liberals, and the voice of reaction was beginning to fill the land. With the Radical Left just ceasing to grieve over the thirties, the Radical Right was saving God and Man at Yale. When Robert Taft died, Everett Dirksen became the Republican majority leader of the Senate. It was Dirksen who, along with J. Parnell Thomas and the Dies Committee (this is what we had learned to call "guilt by association" in reverse), helped kill the Federal Theater by calling its plays "salacious tripe." By the end of the fifties, Barry Goldwater, looking past the halfway measures of Eisenhower to a less compromised conservative presidency, would be backing the virulent loudmouths on behalf of the military. And encouraged by the example of the expired McCarthy, the voice of the cuckoo would be filling the land: Dr. Fred Schwarz would be imported to protect us from the commies by analyzing them in his clinics; and the Minute Men would be whipping out their machines guns to keep California safe for democracy.

Meanwhile, in those first days of The Workshop, we were not even members of the Radical Middle.

As we sat around our coal stove in the loft we had rented, I recalled the opening line of E. A. Robinson's poem about the Wandering Jew: "I saw by looking in his eyes that he remembered everything." And I thought it wasn't so much that we had nothing to say as that we had to find a way of saying it that wouldn't sound hollow, for we also thought we had heard it all. Yet we had a lot to learn, and there was a lot we didn't remember.

For the time being, though Irving and I talked impressively, it was mainly —as they said in committee—procedural: we would pick a play with good parts for all the actors and rehearse it until it was "ready." We said very little about the world outside, or what sort of play. Like our politicians, our group was cautious, politic, and already committed to being uncommitted, or at least cagey about revealing commitments. It was an affable bunch, well-educated, and though there was no palpable fear of each other, still it was in the rhythm of the time to bide it. All of the men had been in the service, we all had jobs, most of us had families. What would we, if we wanted to protest, protest about?—except the Bomb, and you don't protest your nightmares, at first.

The Revolt of the Moderates was consummated with the election of Eisenhower; and we were an obscure symptom—even though we had voted for Stevenson. It is easy and commonplace to parody President Eisenhower with his smile, that moral decency, his golf, his Mamie, his platitudes, and his lack of syntax. Proprietor of a devastating arsenal, he was Big Daddy as gentleman farmer, who carried his big stick to church on Sunday and protected us from those Bolshevik atheists with *their* dirty bombs. But as Samuel Lubell has reminded us, "The process by which we transfer our virtues and faults to our politicians is not unlike the interplay between an actor and his audience. . . . Throughout his Presidency, Eisenhower has been the understudy for the people themselves."

Alas! If Eisenhower led us before the end of his second term to experiment with nihilism and to explore those dramatists who despair of communication and scorn the possibility of social coherence; who tell us when Brecht says, Do something! that nothing can be done, and *then* explode in protest—it's because we were always afraid there was an emptiness behind the emptiness.

For while the personal warmth was a saving grace, and one knew there was as much gospel as brass in his invocation of St. Luke on behalf of armaments, you had eventually to agree with Norman Mailer that Eisenhower seemed "a President so passive in his mild old panics that women would be annoyed if one called him feminine." With a cabinet of eight millionaires and a plumber, if he didn't exactly resemble the masquerading Powers of Genet's *The Balcony,* a general *without* cothurni, we could never forgive him the fact, given the syntax and the platitudes, that he *was* speaking for us. Indeed, if the Cold War was reducing thinkers to silence, Eisenhower told us, from the time he conquered Stevenson, that in America it made no difference if we had nothing to say. Or how we said it. Style *didn't* matter. And Vice-President

Nixon, Big Blubber, was demonstrating how it was possible to succeed by improvising one's principles.

Pragmatically speaking, then: if, when we formed our Workshop in 1952, it was without "stars, fanfare, real estate, and capital," it wasn't because we had principles against them, but because they simply weren't available to us. Since then we have had stars (and prefer to do without them); we have had a modicum of fanfare (which we try to exploit, even while we distrust the way it rushes us beyond ourselves); and we are always seeking real estate and capital, like any other growing enterprise in the Cold War.

And, though we have closed down on them, we are still improvising our principles.

Since Irving did all the directing in those days, when I was away from rehearsal my wife would answer questions about me by referring to my "other work," which always sounded somehow abstract and sinister. It was. And while persisting in my own netherworld, that awful center of infernal spirits, I saw the terrors of the present through the despair of the ages. I remember trying at the time to write a poem about the cobalt bomb, which invariably turned facetious the more I saw it as the apocalyptic extension of Original Sin, which meant nothing to me as dogma but everything as metaphor. It wasn't that I was intellectually wrong, only the enormity of it all was such that when you did think about it you could only laugh or rage, or pick at your liver in silence.

My literary study was rife with outraged melancholy. Behind in my reading, I had quickly grown intimate with Yorick's skull and all the old chimeras of the atomized soul. My eyebeams had twisted over the devotional skepticism of John Donne, with all his haunting paradoxes, like "a bracelet of bright hair about the bone." And my mind had been collecting images of estrangement, not only from the fury of the patriarch Oedipus at Colonus (I was less than twenty-five at the time) and the monomaniac Ahab plunging his Pequod into the blind Atlantic, but from the probings of Freud, the unmaskings of Marx, the chthonic inquiries of Jung, the "gay science" of Nietzsche, the demonic principle that was our legacy from the deification of Milton's Satan, the whole Romantic Agony, and all the accumulated disinheritance represented in phrases and titles like these: *The Waste Land, The Hollow Men, The Beast in the Jungle, The Drunken Boat, The Circus Animal's Desertion, Zero at the Bone, The Iceman Cometh, The Dance of Death, The Lost Generation, The Lonely Crowd, The Age of Anxiety, Escape from Freedom, The Miscellaneous Man, The Stranger, The Outsider, No Exit, The Secret Life of Walter Mitty, The Dangling Man, The Victim, The Trial, The Burrow, The Idiot, The Sound and the Fury*—who couldn't make his own list? signifying nothing, and I do mean Nothingness, to the last syllable of recorded doomsaying.

Clurman was familiar with the imagery and had read a lot of these books when they were first published, but he was able in the thirties to put Eliot aside as bloodless or Kafka as irrelevant. In the trial of the Republic under the New Deal, redress was possible. Even at the chastened end of *The Fervent Years,* he could still invoke the optimistic side of Whitman: "I think it is to collect a tenfold impetus that any halt is made." Myself, I was just picking up on the dark side of Whitman, the suppressed passages of *Leaves of Grass* that resembled the bar sinister of the heroes of the Underground (it seemed ironic but right, for instance, that America's poet laureate should be a homosexual), and I was reading with rather morbid relish Dr. Josiah Trent's report (in *Surgery, Gynecology, and Obstetrics*) that Whitman at his death was "a veritable pathological museum." There was the beginning of a Litany of Fallout in the revised diagnosis, a recitative for shelter programs: "Pulmonary tuberculosis, far advanced, right; atelectasis of left lung; tuberculosis empyema, left; bronchopleural fistula, left; disseminated abdominal tuberculosis; tuberculosis abscesses of sternum, fifth rib and left foot; cyst of left adrenal gland; chronic cholecystitis and cholelithiasis; cerebral atrophy; cerebral arteriosclerosis; benign prostatic hypertrophy; pulmonary emphysema; cloudy swelling of kidneys; history of hypertension." In a period studying coronaries, the hypertension may have seemed the worst of it; but it was also very Jacobean, and I thought of it when we came to Beckett's Hamm.

As I acquired my apocalyptic vision, however, encouraged by the best that had been thought and said, I refrained from introducing it wholesale into The Workshop, which was meant to be a healthy coming together of sorts, mainly of relatively experienced actors who were tired of playing in little theaters or with college groups, there being no alternative in San Francisco. It was clear to me that every major artist of the twentieth century would see the Bomb as the superemblem of a lot of diseased energy and internal chaos in society at large, but I didn't make an issue of it at first for fear I would be incoherent if not irrelevant. Whether they could articulate it or not, some of the others may have been feeling things similarly; but it was symptomatic of the period that when suicide walked abroad, it wore a normal face. Perhaps out of vanity I felt like the astrophysicist Sir Arthur Eddington on "the theory of the exploding universe," which, he admitted, "is in some respects so preposterous that we naturally hesitate to commit ourselves to it. It contains elements apparently so incredible that I feel almost an indignation that anyone should believe it—except myself."

So it was a while before the worm gnawed at the body politic of our rehearsals.

As for the communal instinct of theater itself, I was of two minds. Given this vision of things, the theater—which posits social coherence—seemed an impossible enterprise. Yet, because it was the one art which made its way to the platform, it might give latitude to my outrage. Nevertheless, though I had read my Jane Ellen Harrison by then and written myself on the Ritual Origins of Drama; though I had thought about Aeschylus in Athens and the hieratic plays of Yeats, behaving like a dream—Eternal Gesture creating an Emotion of Multitude; though I had responded to Eliot on the Auditory Imagination and was prepared to believe the drama began as a drumbeat in the jungle—I didn't think it appropriate to issue such a manifesto as George Cram Cook did to the Provincetown Players in 1916, for it would have sounded pretentious: "Primitive drama, the expression of the communal or religious life of the organic human group, the tribe, had spontaneously the unity of a pure art. There may be two hundred actors dramatically dancing the conflict of winter and spring, but all that all of them do in that drama springs from one shared fund of feelings, ideas, impulses. Unity is not imposed on them by the will of one of their number, but comes from that deep level in each where all their spirits are one. The aim of the founder of the Provincetown Players is to make all hands work from that level and to do it by recreating in a group of modern individuals, individuals far more highly differentiated than primitive people, a spiritual unity underlying their differences, a unity resembling the primitive unity of the tribe, a unity which may spontaneously create the unity necessary to the art of the theater."

It wasn't that I didn't believe this, I do; and it has since become possible to enunciate to our company our relation to the aborted revolution of the Little Theater Movement of the twenties. But, though I spoke of our naïveté, this pronouncement required the kind of naïveté to which we had to return—which one saw, say, in the mystical ardency of Robert Edmond Jones; a naïveté which persisted through the work of Eugene O'Neill, for all his reaching after doctrines and dogmas, and in the profoundest despair. Yet there was always something in the work of O'Neill to which I, at least, had to become reconciled. Later, I found myself directing him as a sort of penance; and I didn't like myself when, with Eric Bentley, I talked of trying to like O'Neill. Ponderous as alluvial mud, O'Neill moved in a mainstream, like Dreiser or Marsden Hartley, pachyderms of spirit. In the centrifugal days of the early fifties, it seemed embarrassing to speak of "spiritual unity"; and if there were "one shared fund of feelings, ideas, impulses," it needed a sorcerer to invoke it without a good deal of artistic and intellectual rehabilitation.

On re-reading *The Fervent Years,* I envied that "sense of theater in relation to society" Clurman developed after hearing Copeau, in discussions with Strasberg, in a directing course with Boleslavsky, with his friends Sykes and Copland, and in the *ambiance* of the New Playwrights Theater, whose new playwrights were John Howard Lawson, Mike Gold, and the unfallen John Dos Passos. What I was envying, of course, though it included the Depression, was the impetus of an entire cultural revolution. As I said before, one need not overrate the accomplishment of the Group or the Federal Theater, or the New Deal for that matter, to feel nostalgia over the period. Whatever the delusions discovered by hindsight, there was adventure, and the exhilaration of social action that seemed to work. We have had nothing so exciting in America until the Freedom Riders and the civil-rights demonstrations.

The aesthetics of the forties and fifties—what I was taught, and what I taught—told us that art was deprived of complexity by making it a forum. There was a no man's land between art and politics. Ezra Pound was a symbolic figure. When the Bollingen Prize honored the poetry of an acknowledged traitor, many of us could be offended by the attacks on the jury for making that paradoxical award. The attacks still seem onerous, because in a certain sense the award was logical and inevitable, the consequence of certain theories that went back to the nineteenth century, when the most ingenious talent was going into the creation of an art which pretends to be about nothing but itself. Pound's poetry was the most idiosyncratic expression of this tendency; his politics a perversion of his constant struggle against the brainwash in American life, which encroached upon "the right of every man to have his ideas judged one at a time. . . ." In his guidance to Kulchur, Pound taught many of us how to read. But recently he has confessed: "My method of opposing tyranny was wrong over a thirty year period. . . ."

Pound's story is one of the pseudo-tragedies or absurd dramas of this century. As "the last American living the tragedy of Europe," Pound was part of a more harrowing story that has still to be properly told. For in the era of Absolute Art, while poems, behaving like music, were vibrating toward eternal silences, monsters were moving toward the ghettos; and while there is a considerable difference between, say, Cubist skin-spreading and the Buchenwald lampshade, there is a revealing analogy between the absolutism of art and the absolutism of politics, in both of which—by incantation and perfect reason—we eventually came to the uncontrollable mystery on the bestial floor.

During the forties and fifties, when we were reading back over that mystery, our instinct was to keep our politics out of our art. Many of us had no politics. If the American theater of the thirties, infected by politics, seems naïve in retrospect, the one thing we can say is that there has been no extension of range since then by keeping our political noses clean. And surely less excitement. *Waiting for Lefty* we can see (they could see it then) was no great play, but when Odets read it to the Group, Luther Adler said "The Group has produced the finest revolutionary playwright in America." The first performance is a great moment in our theatrical lore. And Clurman summed up the spontaneous roar of "Strike! Strike!" by saying "It was something more than a tribute to the play's effectiveness, more even than a testimony of the audience's hunger for constructive social action. It was the birth cry of the thirties. Our youth had found its voice."

Which it subsequently lost with the fall of Madrid in 1939: "Concurrently with this event," wrote Clurman, "came an almost unrecognizeable change in the spiritual scene of American life. A certain flatness, a falling off of inspirational force, a kind of treadmill progression subtly characterized the environment from this time till the outbreak of war in September."

Saroyan's *My Heart's in the Highlands* seemed to reconcile the old passion for "a sound, affirmative nature" with "the need for unity, good behavior, and humorous condonement of our sins." But Clurman grew impatient even with *Time of Your Life,* for all its sentimental affection for human failing, because of the Arab's refrain: "No foundation; all the way down the line." The refrain hardly had the foundation or the force it would have in the dramas of Beckett and Ionesco or the revivals of the early Brecht; but Clurman was still looking in Odets' *Clash by Night,* with its "noxious atmosphere," that seems so genial today, for some sound "portents of a clearer future." He found something in the young couple of the play, but even they "represented a kind of ideologic afterthought rather than the creative center of the play, which, no doubt about it, was pessimistic."

The pessimism grew through World War II, which was being fought as *The Fervent Years* was being written. The war's lampskin exposure of the limits of perfectibility put a damper on "the inevitability of the struggle against evil" which made Clurman, early in the Group's career, impatient with the violent ending of Paul Green's *The House of Connolly.* It was about this time that Odets was becoming silent in Hollywood, and soon after other members of the Group were either assimilated or blacklisted; or blacklisted, then assimilated. John Garfield, who played the boy who didn't want life printed on dollar bills, was to die in an aura of congressional investigations, which were blamed for it; and to a generation soon to adjust to the daily possibility of extinction, youth seemed passé. The elder statesman of the Group, Morris Carnovsky, put the case—taking refuge in Shakespeare and questions of technique: "If I was a little bit sanguine about the importance of theater as a social force, why—so I learned my lesson. Not too long after that came the McCarthy business, and some very depressing stuff happening in this country. . . ."

The effect on the profession was profound. Among our handful of actors and those who presently joined us were several who, having been worn down by the rounds, had had it, and were no longer tenacious about their careers, much less social action. Some, who had worked in educational theater, had heard enough of the hardship to stay away. Our first mission was to establish the grounds upon which we could believe in our own talents, encourage rapport, and subsequently act together to recover the passion lost in the interregnum of cynicism between the demise of the Group and the beginning of the sixties, when foundation money, the Kennedy administration, and our own achievement raised a lot of hopes.

On one occasion—after we had left the loft—I had an argument with an older actor who, having joined us presumably for what we were doing, soon wanted us to do something else. "That's what the audiences want!" I said what we want comes first, audiences second. He has a fierce temper, and as we proceeded to go round and round every aspect of the theater—plays that didn't build audiences, our naïve idealism, my academic attitudes—the argument grew more violent until he said, "Listen, you son of a bitch, I've been in the theater twenty years, so you listen!" I mustered my year's experience and said, "Twenty years? That's just why I know more than you." He nearly went out of his mind. I don't blame him, but the fact is that what I said was true. For one of the sad things about that very talented man's twenty years is that he didn't know what to respect in them, or what to learn, beyond the routines of craft.

I remember vividly his audition for the company. He did that pantomimic exercise of the tailor threading a needle. It seemed a marvel of concentration, easy, deep. And it might not have been possible without that example of internal technique which the Group, adapting Stanislavski to the American rhythm, gave us as a legacy. There was one other factor: at his best this actor has that manic grouching charm one finds in the Jewish temperament. He could very well have been one of those East Side players who Clurman said were probably the best actors in the world. When we argued, however, he was not only a frustrated actor, he was a frustrated intellectual. Yet when he is not bursting with spleen (and most hostile to ideas), he can be very intelligent. And what is behind most of the arguments we have had since then is the New York phobia. Having failed to make it there, he can hardly believe it could be made here. Nor can he believe, though he has done some roles as well as they have been done in America, that he has the power to be a better actor than most of the "successful" ones he admires, not to mention the second-rate performers he looks up to when they come in touring companies through San Francisco, actors who aren't fit to be on the same stage with him. The Workshop gave him reason for a new dignity in his art, but the sense of failure was so deep behind that pantomime, to this day affecting his craft, that now and then, there are relapses of self-destructive fury.

What is important in such a man is that he represents a large number of vagrants sucked into the vacancy that followed the collapse of hope in the theater after the thirties. The actor I mention has the chance for fundamental identity with a theater he believes in, I think, past all hostility. There are many others whose very experience since then—where they worked and how they worked, if they worked—has turned the real meaning of the Group into a total loss. If the Group could not persist because times had changed, the discrepancy between idealistic will and objective facts driving it to cross-purposes, fury, to "pain without grace," then many had inherited that pain without grace, forgetting entirely the original guiding madness—the ideals which, by a new exertion of will in a new generation, might change some of the facts.

Wherever, in the fifties, anybody tried to revive the spirit of the Group, unless those involved were all very young, it had to be in part an archeological expedition among the ruins. There was a dazed and thwarted period behind us. And the career of the actor I have described affords another example of that lapse of the sense of history one encounters in the American character. One of the plays he kept urging us to do was *The Happy Time*. Though his sense of behavior on stage is conditioned by the Group, his sense of what should and should not be done in the theater was such that the Group, whose history he knew far better than I, never existed. For while the Group believed in positive action, its optimism was not the positive thinking (or commercial good cheer) disillusionment thinks it wants.

In those first days in the loft, when we referred to the Group or any other famous theater, we were very careful of grandiose aspirations. A couple of the somewhat older hands among us then had seen a lot of zeal come to nought in the enthusiasm of the thirties and the WPA projects in San Francisco. The Federal Theater played some of its last performances below the Bay Bridge at Treasure Island. Other groups had come and gone, municipal theaters could never get off the ground, repertory companies had failed from presuming too much too soon; and the little theaters our people had known had no interest in revolution. Besides, we wouldn't have known what to do with a forum if we had had one then. (Several years later a Beat joint in North Beach would have a Blabbermouth night for those who wanted to sound off: it was not so much a forum as an escape valve, which ranged from potted anarchy to nonobjective howls. But it was lively; if you really didn't have anything to say in public, at least you could flip—and when it became a fine art, taking off on everything and changing nothing, you had something approaching Lenny Bruce—or Beckett's Lucky.)

Following the formula de Tocqueville had discerned, our actors were not drawn together by *ideas* either about life or art, but by mutual *interest* in an opportunity to work with better people than they had been working with. The older among them were mainly looking and seeing, skeptical of the outcome; and when Irving or I did in a slip from caution mention the Abbey or the Moscow Art Theater, I could feel an inward scoffing. Perhaps we were too sensitive. We were both in our twenties; aside from some plays produced in the university, I was almost totally inexperienced in the practical theater, and the actors knew it. Even my wife, who had been trained in New York and gathered her ideas about theater there, laughed when I first began to insist we *could* make a theater in San Francisco.

The lack of adhesive ideas, however, was an impediment. Though Clurman started out with less concern about politics than I had, he was swept up— as were his actors—in the fusion of the new aesthetic of the twenties with the radical politics of the thirties. With the Great Crash came the dire necessity of social protest. Moral salvation and political salvation became one. Talking like an Odets character, Clurman told his friend Aaron Copland in the summer of 1929: "I'm sick of this dervish dance they've got us doing on steel springs and a General Electric Motor." They wept together for the trouble ahead. It was inspiring. Meetings were held, techniques were discussed, fanaticism aroused, actors organized, and Clurman (who had moved in the ambiance of the Provincetown) sought with Strasberg "a unity of background, of feeling, of thought, of need, among a group of people that has formed itself consciously or unconsciously from the undifferentiated masses."

But that was a period in which the word *masses* meant something honorific and urgent, and Clurman could even in the most disillusioned days of the Group, even as late as *The Fervent Years,* use the word *togetherness* to express an ideal. To us—for everybody but the squarest squares—it had become a pretext for parody. We were practitioners and victims of that bare suffrance of language that arose out of its abuse and exhaustion by sociology, psychology, and the mass media, as well as the sloganizing of the thirties—the sort of thing satirized by George Orwell in his essay "Politics and the English Language." If the Group "clamored for greater occasions, for closer embrace, for a more rooted togetherness," and if Waldo Frank was the oracle of a new America, instructed by Mexican nationalization and the Soviet experiment, we lamented the loss of unity, sought (while distrusting the phrase) peace of mind, and feared that "separateness" was the natural condition of social man. And David Reisman documented our fear, giving us an up-to-date version of that revolt of the masses which others had predicted would lead to estrangement, malaise, and suicidal loneliness. (In a society where the heroes of Odets' early plays are now clipping coupons, it may lead —as Herbert Gold has shown in *The Age of Happy Problems*—to death in Miami Beach.)

Reisman is a representative thinker of the Cold War epoch. Turning issues about as on a spit in the barbecue of some suburban yard, he is the sociologist of the *via media,* of the age of nonpartisanship. He is free of the old liberal platitudes, but he has his own rough sociological beasts, autonomously directed. The early edition of *The Lonely Crowd* explored the shadows of affluence while trying to confirm the general good health of things. But as the computers got to work on the relative salvation of mankind by first and second strikes, his view darkened and he saw the Cold War not as a manichaean struggle but as "the failure of a way of life." The ambivalence was characteristic of those intellectuals who did not renounce America altogether as an armed madhouse, and go off to Tunis, Kyoto, or Big Sur to await apocalypse.

The distrust or critique of language had become, in either case, our chief mode of inquiry. The tradition descended from diverse sources—say, from Hamlet (who knew a hawk from a handsaw, but was scornful of words, words, words) through Flaubert's *Dictionary of Accepted Ideas,* through Wittgenstein's *Tractatus,* to Ionesco's *Jack, or The Submission:* "O words, what crimes are committed in thy name." It is reflected in the addiction of some literary people, atoning for the crimes, to the stoic or ecstatic dumbfoundedness of nonobjective painting, to the *sesshins* of Zen, and the final end of jazz—to swing or be stoned, man, depending on which end of the horn you're on. At its glorious extreme, the old adage flows out of the Symbolist cornucopia: Silence is golden. In the drama, there was a growing interest in Mime.

The objective: *not* to speak out, but to avoid saying what you knew couldn't hold up in the general decay of language, value, and civilization itself. If every poem renews the language, the words working among themselves, every newspaper corrupts it, the words working for the power elite. Though there were plenty of poets, there was incomparably more newsprint; and while some of the poets were trying to reactivate the language by making a mess of it, some of the others—trained in the academic tradition of the New Criticism, careful of excess, full of tensions, paradoxes, icons, architectonics, and the seven types of ambiguity—were growing weary of it all.

Having developed a sense of Evil along with their cabalistic techniques, they were beginning to feel duped by their own wiliness. Not yet able to accept the raging infancy which distorted Blake's Innocence, they pondered lost passion. (Or, like Richard Wilbur defending *Ceremony,* tried to be Augustan in a time of fallout.) When psychiatrists now speak of moral blandness as the characteristic neurotic symptom of the period, the poets, who had been the first to diagnose it, begin to wonder about themselves. Was this the end of inquiry? Of all that critical technique? To be tranquilized, too? If I may cite de Tocqueville again, he described with uncanny prophecy that general malaise of the fifties by which they felt trapped: "If society is tranquil, it is not because it is conscious of its strength and its well-being, but because it fears its weakness and its infirmities; a single effort may cost it its life. Everybody feels the evil, but no one has the courage or energy to seek the cure. The desires, repinings, the sorrows, and the joys of the present time lead to nothing visible or permanent, like the passions of old men, which terminate in impotence."

Only in the last couple of years, with the Negro revolution, has the power of mass action become inspiring again. But even so, the spirit of gradualism rules over a possessed minority, the action oscillating between passive resistance and threats of violence.

In art, the breakthrough, like the cure, is easier proclaimed than accomplished. And among the poets who aren't claiming millenniums too soon, the malaise—born in the twenties to a dying fall and nurtured through the crippling ambiguities of the Cold War—remains. Robert Lowell, the most exciting poet of my generation, writes at the conclusion of a poem recently published:

> Young, my eyes began to fail.
> Nothing! No oil
> for the eye, nothing to pour
> on these waters or flames.
> I am tired. Everyone's tired of my turmoil.

Not only do we suspect the falsity of our public truths, but we are experts in the detection of our private phoniness. The best informed of our artists suffer from excess of knowing, in inverse proportion to the public density. W. D. Snodgrass, in an essay appended to *Heart's Needle,* writes on this autobiographical poem: "I am left, then, with a very old-fashioned measure of a poem's worth—the depth of its sincerity. And it seems to me that the poets of our generation—those of us who have gone so far in criticism and analysis that we cannot ever turn back and be innocent again, who have such extensive resources for disguising ourselves from ourselves—that our only hope as artists is to continually ask ourselves, 'Am I writing what I really think?'. . . ."

I am defining a tone. A rhythm of mind. Few of our actors had read much poetry or even heard of the New Criticism. (And it was some time before we came to Ionesco's *Jack*.) But the poets were only more outspoken; the actors breathed the same psychic atmosphere. With them it took the obverse form of diffidence with ideas, fear of complexity, or a suspicion of ambiguities that leads to further ambiguities by default of intelligence. I am not going to make this an occasion for an assault on the limitations of actors as a species, for they are finally the most self-denying, the most generous, and the most vulnerable of artists, for all their legendary narcissism. We must love them for that, without losing sight of their special liability to the chronic indecision I have been describing. Actors or not, burning the books is no solution, even when you haven't read the books. And all the parables, from the gospels to Faust, tell us you don't return to innocence simply by renouncing knowledge— even when you really possess it.

The depth of sincerity in Snodgrass' poem is convincing precisely in proportion to his acceptance of the sad fact that he "cannot ever turn back and be innocent again. . . ." Though there were not many real opinions in that period, each man was still insisting on his sincere right to his own. To claim sincerity, however, is no verification of opinion, or even of sincerity. What we were able to bring to those early sessions at The Workshop was an analytical attitude toward the texts which was surprising and engrossing for the actors, but at some limiting point—when analysis darted from the text to them or their deranged world—became intimidating. Especially when it was accompanied by moral fervor. Claiming sincerity, some of them evaded both the issues and themselves by invoking the old smokescreen that an actor shouldn't think too much. Perhaps so. Which usually prevents some of them from thinking at all, reducing the feelings about which it was possible to have opinions.

Irving and I had neither the authority of a Strasberg at close range nor his psychiatric instincts. Nor was this particular group of actors either so zealous in self-inquiry or so submissive as I sometimes feel they become at the Actors Studio, where the emphasis on inner life—a salutary thing, a necessity—is such that you will find young people from Oregon and New Mexico being utterly true to themselves in the unregenerate rhythm of the stripped id, with its New York accent—which is somehow the sign of truth and virility; though the White Negro is now taking the stage away (witness *The Connection*) from the inferiority complex of White Protestant America. Both of us from New York, with a feeling for the dynamics of that city, we were dealing in temperate San Francisco with that same sense of inferiority. Only it felt no reverent obligation to defer to us and, as Irving would say, "put a cap on the emotions" when we behaved with the gratuitous energy of a Kazan or did pry like Strasberg.

Still, almost all actors in America, even the least experienced and the most threatened, know they must base their work on personal inquiry. Their training may actually be quite artificial, but internal technique is in the atmosphere of their profession and they speak its language even if they don't have much of it—as young people who have never read them inherit a natural disposition for Marx and Freud. As Marx and Freud can be frightening in their depths, so Stanislavski can be intimidating behind the mechanism of his theory. And while our actors might invoke him on units and beats, the objective division of the play's action into actable components, they were uncomfortable with his depth psychology and *his* moral fervor, forgetting he had written a chapter on Ethics in the Theater. In that chapter he said: "Do not come into the theater with mud on your feet." Who could avoid it? We were all doubtful cases. It would seem that Stanislavski was not so demanding after all. Consciously, however, our group was quite content not to bring the mud into rehearsals; the trouble was that we left somewhat more of ourselves outside than, I think, Stanislavski intended.

Moreover, our sort of discretion kept us from seeing (as they also fail to see at the Actors Studio, perhaps from too much mud) that there was behind Stanislavski's technique the task of finding that vague, true path of which the Master had spoken so often. "In other words, one must train one's self, *one must think and develop morally and give one's mind no rest.*" (Italics mine.) True, there is in the technique itself the same necessity for preparation that one needs, say, for psychoanalysis; free association and the recording of dreams require a practiced discipline. But with Stanislavski, as with Freud, it was a moral discipline; they both liberated the id, but revered reason. (It was a while before the liberated id turned into a fully disrupted psyche, both morality and intellect discarded in the rubbish of history, destroyed by two wars, *pure feeling* emancipated for both carnage and recovery. In painting, for instance, there was the outbreak of abstract emotion, which the theater is beginning to emulate. More of this later, for we weren't even dreaming of anything like it, yet.)

The experience of the Group Theater—with Stella Adler's recharting of Stanislavski's technique, as well as the rabid know-it-allness of the thirties—stood curiously between Stanislavski and some of our actors. If some of our generation worried about thinking too much, they had had warning from The Group, whose "directors had once practiced the art of self-criticism on their own productions and had analyzed each of the actors' performances for educational purposes. The actors were apt pupils; they didn't necessarily become better actors; they became shrewd critics. With this new instrument of criticism they made deft incisions into each other's work, into that of the playwrights (who came to loathe them for it) and all other actors outside. After a time almost everyone in the Group worried over everyone else's performance. At times there was an invisible silent slaughter going on among the

Group actors." So they gave their minds no rest; and though there were more awesome reasons, it was part of our folklore, too, that the Group failed because it talked itself to death.

"People don't seem to talk to one another enough," Clurman said in one of the informal meetings that preceded the founding of the Group. "We are separate. Our contacts are hasty, utilitarian contacts or escapist. We must get to know ourselves by getting to know one another." And they did. Togetherness banished separateness. The summer retreat, the critiques, the disputation were endemic to the Group in the swing of the period. And even Franchot Tone, who would shout "I am an American!" on the Fourth of July, when nobody else would shoot off firecrackers, was affected by the rhythm. The members of the Group did get to know each other, almost too well; and some of them, like Strasberg, haven't stopped talking yet. I do not say this in malice. The Group's talk and rapport gave America its first ensemble acting company of any distinction. When Franchot Tone complained that the Group actors at their summer camp acted only when they didn't talk, Strasberg answered: "Yes, we talk a lot because we are not simply rehearsing a play; we are laying the foundation of a theater. Our theater is more than just a matter of getting one or two plays produced."

It is one of the principles I have already enunciated for my own theater, and it is indebted to the Group.

By contrast, we did not get to know each other at first; we got to know the texts, which intermediated. There were those who wanted to go out and have coffee together, but in those days one had the feeling that the old liberal ideal of "communication" was a dodge; that one went out to have coffee because he didn't really believe in what he was doing; and that one talked over coffee, as we did when we did, about almost everything but what counted in our lives, to the diminishment of our art. Thus, when we did begin critiques in our studio, the resistance—subdued, mute, or self-protective—was fierce; and when I did begin to talk up and elaborate ideas behind the plays, some complained to Irving that they were being lectured at. Now I am a good lecturer, but if I was lecturing, it was hard to be at my best; and though in time the company became more receptive, even zealous, about seminars and critiques, the atmosphere was so seeded with distrust that we are still atoning for it. As I wrote to the company as late as 1959, rehearsing some old desires for more experiment: "In the process we must begin to talk again—there *hasn't* been enough talk among us—of collective style, of method, of plays and what they mean. Not that talk will make method, but neither will silence; and for all the satire at its expense, there is method in method. I must admit my own fault here, for . . . I somewhat adjusted my own directorial procedures to a certain impatience on the part of some of our people with discussion; this encourages the premature."

The formation of the Group was the fruition of an artistic and ideological ferment. There was a swirl of ideas and human urgency, of reformist conviction and technical desire, of acting method and social action. By contrast, though most of the nine people who were in our first play were college graduates and some of them, with Irving and myself, were college teachers, I had the impression we were proceeding in an intellectual and artistic vacuum. True, the place was jumping around us with those happenings that were named the San Francisco Renaissance—the new jazz, the poetry readings, the austerely slapdash followers of Still and Smith at the Art Institute, the Beats, the *City Lights* magazine and the bookshop named after it. But, if we were soon identified with them, we were never strictly part of that scene.

Irving and I were relatively new to the city, and though there were some painters and poets among my friends, again I was leading a double life. When, in 1957, I testified at the *Howl* trial as a "literary expert" for the defense, I had never met Ginsberg or Ferlinghetti (who was actually prosecuted), or for that matter some of the other experts, Kenneth Rexroth, Mark Schorer, and Vincent McHugh. Those I did know—the novelists Walter Van Tilburg Clark and Arthur Foff and the critic Mark Linenthal—were colleagues in the Creative Writing Program at San Francisco State College. In the thirties, Clark had coached basketball and acted in a little theater, but while he reminisced amusingly about that, he was more or less reclusive; Foff, my closest friend at the time, wouldn't have cared for the theater at all if I weren't in it, and kept his distance so effectively he is now in Damascus; and Linenthal, with whom I had gone to graduate school, talked far more with me about modern poetry, which I preferred teaching, than about the theater. None of them was involved in The Workshop's organizing phase or in a definition of its principles. It expressed nothing important for them or for any other artist.

In time, The Workshop became a locus of artistic interest in the city. Rexroth became a critical admirer, and other poets and novelists (e.g., James Schevill and Mark Harris) have been attracted to write for us. One of Ginsberg's friends, the painter Robert La Vigne, became our resident designer. But at our origin, we moved in the ambiance of things, not with them. And actually, unlike those artists who helped inform the Group, those who came to work with us or circulated in our ambiance were very different, if not hostile, in their points of view. As for my own view, I should say that while I could testify against the harassment of *Howl,* I could not really testify *for* it. Fortunately, it was the strategy of the defense to have each of the experts cover some aspect of the poem's techniques or traditions; under the instructions of the salty trial lawyer Jake Erlich, we were going to murder the district attorney with erudition. (When Al Bendich, the young ACLU lawyer who had boned up on all the obscenity cases in the history of literature, tried to suggest a strategy to some of the academic people who had met for a briefing, Erlich interrupted: "Turn it off, Al, these professors are all red-blooded Americans. If the D.A. gets smart, they'll let him have it"—smashing fist into palm—"right in the fucking face.") While Rexroth, who thought it a better poem than I did, placed it in the tradition of apocalyptic literature, I gave witness to its affinity with Dada, "the art of furious negation"—the intensity of that negation, said I, keeping it from total despair: "It is a vision that by the salvation of despair, by the salvation of what would appear to be [sic!] perversity, by the salvation of what would appear to be obscene, by the salvation of what would appear to be illicit, is ultimately a kind of redemption of the illicit, the obscene, the disillusioned and the despairing. . . ." The rhetoric of my testimony came out of the darker musings of my study, that dialogue with the depths, that was coming up more and more in the plays we were doing by the time of the trial.

In 1952, however, there was no such dialogue in public. I did hint at it in the rather silky noncommitment of the program notes to our first play, Philip Barry's *Hotel Universe;* but these were written after the play was rehearsed. The play was chosen because it had substantial roles for all the actors, and because it could be done in modern dress around the unused brick fireplace across from the stove. Yet, though there were no more urgent specifications and the choice almost an accident, I can't help feeling it was also an appropriate choice, given our collective state of mind—for the play reflected our own spiritual drift and a certain soft tolerance about intellectual fuzziness like our own. As the notes said: "Barry's bewildered and badgered characters are representatives of the Lost Generation made famous by F. Scott Fitzgerald and Ernest Hemingway. It was Barry's own generation. . . . The innocence of essential understanding of this period was a product of disillusionment, reeling standards, and the incertitude of life in an atomized universe."

We find these characters—elegant, effete, and exiled—in what used to be a small hotel, now an estate, on a terrace angled "like a wedge into space." The universe is Einstein's, the atmosphere is fantastic, the psychology is basic Freud, the action a kind of psychotherapy, with a muted jesuitical stink. The notes, as they went on, might have been describing a prototypical play of the fifties, Eliot's *The Cocktail Party,* "no chorus and no ghosts," as Eliot said, but concealed origins and an air of chic mystery. With Hell, Purgatory, and the Beatitudes designed into the living room, we learn to make the best of a bad job: "Barry, with his Catholic heritage, could not permit his creatures merely to wander laxly through the universe, decadent and unredeemed. The moral listlessness of the opening scenes is transfigured in a ritual of rebirth that is a curious and not altogether tenable mixture of the orthodox communion and the psychiatrist's couch."

The play was written in 1930. While there was an optimistic tinge to the miraculous, "The ambiguity of this catharsis, together with the *haut monde,* sophisticated weariness of his characters, offended the socially conscious critics of the proletarian thirties. The play was rejected and suffered a general neglect that its qualities of style, genuine wit, and refined earnest groping with the problems of man's fate did not entirely deserve. . . . However much we may regret the ultimate obscurity of Barry's thought," I concluded, "we cannot but admire his dramatic sensibility, precocity, and his desire to find peace

—for the lost souls of his age and, no doubt, for himself." Indeed, the malaise of the opening scene has an unusual grace for an American play; and the inexplicable guilt of the characters for a young boy they had seen commit suicide has been a memorable image. Again out of apparent expediency—but why this?—we revived the play some years later when we were pressed for a production at a theater we had temporarily rented. And still later, traveling in Europe and fighting a lover's quarrel with the existential position, I remembered that scene in composing a play of my own.

Performed in the loft, the "production" was meant to be an exercise. It played after a couple of months of rehearsal to an invited audience of fifty, for one night, and that's all. Before it began, I made a short talk to the guests explaining our moderate aim: to provide the circumstances in which actors could practice their art. The guests were enthusiastic. We asked them to sign a mailing list. Urged to do the play again, we refused and went on to another project.

Irving and I watched the "bewildered and badgered characters" of *Hotel Universe* in front of our "fire exit," a dirt-encrusted window, with egress against a low wall and a blank alley. Before we left the loft, over a year later, we had formed a "partnership," and were totally liable. Even Lloyd's of London refused to insure us.

6

GROWING UP WITH ENTROPY

Thoughts beside a dark window:

There is an actor in the center of an acting area. Say all you want about exhibitionism, if I understand anything about human nature and profited from my experience in the theater, the first thing an actor in the center of an acting area wants to do is get the hell out of there.

The drama (and to some extent this book) explores the question of what keeps him there. "There is a doctrine whispered in secret," says Socrates, "that man is a prisoner who has no right to open the door and run away; this is a great mystery which I do not quite understand." Neither does the drama, which conspires in the secret and perpetuates the mystery. In the sort of drama we name a tragedy what keeps him there seems to be the psychic cooperation of various necessities internal and external—he stays because he must. In comedy, he stays because he's too foolish to go. Stuck out there in full view of whoever cares to look, without any compelling Destiny or Rational Purpose or Categorical Imperative, he begins to act feverishly, conning us into believing that he is up to something. But it's all really much ado about nothing—a phrase which hits to the heart of comedy and the improvisational lunacy behind its civilized voice.

East, West, it makes no difference. Confirmation of this psychic tug-of-war

141

comes from that most ghostly and hallowed of forms, the Japanese Noh drama, where the actor's entry down the *hashikagara* is a technical feat of no mean rigor. Restricted by an ornate costume, his field of vision narrowed by his mask, the actor must be resolute even to reach the stage. As one theorist puts it, "A step forward for him means to advance with resistance against a power that seems to pull him backward. This requires great spiritual power and concentration on the part of the actor." In the Noh, of course, the actor hasn't the ameliorating advantage of "personality"; but then the mask protects him from stage fright and personal shame.

Nevertheless, it is this special quality of exposure that made me say earlier that the actor is the most selfless of all artists. Others master their medium by serving it, but their medium is outside them. At their best they manage somehow to get into it. The actor is his own medium at the disposal of others, oracle or spirit, but also more fallible beings—dramatist, director, and audience. The greater the actor the greater his resilience, his awe, his capitulation—as it apparently was with Duse. The poet serves his language but also supervises its continuity; the actor is the body of the word. The word may live when the actor dies. The actor acts to be acted upon.

So the director must first learn to treasure his actors, as he treasures the drama itself, even if their submission is aggressive, as it often is. Stanislavski, who gave the actor that fine advice to "Love art in yourself and not yourself in art," venerated Chekhov, but he knew of the theater that in the beginning is the actor. From him alone comes the play's middle and end. If the actor must live in sin with his character, the director must live in sin with the actor. He must take him, in faith, with all his imperfections on his head.

If behind the drama is what the anthropologists call a *dromenon,* a nuclear action out of ritual, the actor is in touch with the archaic energy behind the provisional form. He may not even know it. There is conflict, an issue, a choice to be made. The will to stay contests with the will to run. (As that great runner Falstaff proves, that is no small will.) The director's action consists of realizing the specific world in which this conflict is to occur, organizing its traffic, making it a figure of the conflict, and using every resource of his psychology and his stage to compel the actor back to his own tensions, rhythm summoning image and image rhythm, to make him want to run and will to stay, without letting one impulse triumph easily over the other.

Rhythm and image may accomplish what introspection won't. If there is rapport among the actors, you may feel out the characteristic motion of a drama as a child rocks back and forth to sense the turning of a rope before jumping in. There are the recurrent and necessary forms of activity in any play, of the mind or of the body, or mind and body jumping together: the garrulous congregation of rustics at a public house in Synge, released into snooping by the appearance of a stranger; the ceremonial comings and goings in Chekhov, the name-day parties, the theatricals, the gatherings around a swing, the discussions near the orchard that encourage public confession of solitary feeling; in Duerrenmatt, the impeccable lunacy of the coffee table, the proceedings somewhat cuckoo but very civilized, as murder has been in our time—the stage littered with corpses and devastated ideas; in *Volpone,* the awakening to gold and the visitations of the birds of prey, "the cunning purchase" and "the sports of love," according to the deadly rules of free enterprise.

In *The Iceman Cometh,* the bums in Harry Hope's saloon must sleep on stage for about forty minutes, in full view of the audience, before waking up. The drama needs them to be lively and raucous almost immediately. The scene is sluggish. The actors find it hard. They want to *adjust* themselves psychologically after deep slumber. Then an image, which O'Neill repeats through the play: it is in the very look of the room, a subterranean chamber to which a deep staircase descends from the world above. When they sleep, it is not restful; it is like being at the bottom of the sea; they are suffocating. When they awake it is like surfacing, they are not groggy. What a relief! They can splash and snort and breathe. Here are all their cronies, still floating. They can rehearse their pipe dreams to general approval rather than the censor of sleep. Will and energy are released, image becoming rhythm as in a poem.

The objective: to reach behind the torpor to "the force that through the green fuse drives the flower." To become that force. As our lives become more bloodless and charted, our power invested, the problem is how to release energy, to restore the organic, to make ourselves available to ourselves. Back in the past, there is something abandoned: the child in the man wants to make images. To play. From Nietzsche to Dylan Thomas, that is the revitalizing lesson of our Romantic heritage. Freud, who inherited the Romantic curiosity about childhood, became pessimistic when it seemed there was an elemental conflict, insoluble, between the desire to return home, by playing the child, and the rational commitment to culture and progress. Nevertheless, he took seriously Jesus' admonition: "Except ye become as little children, ye can in no wise enter the kingdom of heaven."

The theater—even classical theater—authenticates the Romantic vision. Nietzsche said, moreover: Live dangerously. In our age, how could we help it? And as we stood beside our blocked exit, watching our actors perform, we were doing that, whether we knew it or not. And as time went on, the growth of our theater, always perilous, and my conception of what the theater is about, figured in the actors, began to inform each other.

Still, we had learned from all the catastrophes of Romanticism—in the lives of artists and in politics—that it takes more than pure will to recover the lost boy, and that the more you proclaim the kingdom of heaven the sooner you are likely to tumble over a cliff, or be tossed into the street. It was the pride and glory, as well as the curse of Romanticism, to go after the Ideal directly (the kingdom of heaven diffusing in the "white radiance of eternity"); but as they plunged into the abyss, what the great figures of that movement left us was the image of "unorganized innocence: an impossibility." Whatever course our organization took, it had to provide for that, as we try to provide for it today in the technique of acting.

Today we teach the actor not to go after emotion directly, but to let it come through *doing* something, to see all desires in the form of action, described by a verb. So Oedipus wants "to rid Thebes of the plague"; Madame Ranevsky wants "to save the cherry orchard"; Major Barbara wants "to save souls"; Hotspur wants "to pluck bright honour from the pale-faced moon." The very form of dramatic action is full of innocence and moonshine intent on purpose. These infinitive phrases, however, describe the Grand Design of action, the Superobjective—what always breaks down, or comes through to dazzle our eyes. In the playing out, the actors are urged to break this Superobjective down into smaller units of action to control the course of feeling: "A *conception* is forthcoming," Stanislavski wrote, "a *reasoned form* arises and in combination they stir your *will*." But he warns against "arid calculation," as he warns against method, which is only the ground of inspiration. Still, disciplined actors have happier accidents, they are the Parian marble of the moving forms. But feeling *must* course, and there is always the chance there won't be enough—indifference is the bogey, or inhibition, or what the trade demands. What we became aware of very specifically as our theater grew was the relation between the actor's personal limitations and his professional plight—which no method could deal with entirely.

I have already discussed the economics of acting in the American theater, the hawking of What-I-Am through the glass door. Let us look further into the relation between this merchandising and the craft itself.

"This is a rough business on kids, what it does to them psychologically," said Bert Lahr in an interview. "It affects them terribly because there's not enough jobs to go around. It's their ambition. It's their goal and they study. [Part of the American Dream: education. If you can't work, you can learn to be a genius.] I see it. They go to school and nothing happens. And they work in summer jerking soda, and they hang around, until finally they're thirty-five or forty, and it's the same damn thing. They've wrecked their lives. . . . Everybody wants to be an actor. But I do know this. I've seen a lot of these kids that the schools turn out. I've worked on the stage with them and I wanted to break their hands. The scratching they do and no idea of deportment. 'What motivates me to do this or that,' they say. I said, 'You go over and get the pot. You want to get the pot, that's what motivates ya.' Everything is cerebral—you go over and pick it up. 'Get me that drink.' 'What motivates me? How will I pick the cup up?' 'Ya pick it up! Bring it over here.' How would you pick it up? How do you pick it up every day? But you don't scratch your ear when you're pickin' it up or make a big thing out of it. So they get these kids all distorted with their theories of acting."

It is a charge we've all heard. Yet in putting down the excess of Method, Lahr is speaking like a natural Methodist. Stanislavski said the psychotechnique is designed "to put us in a creative state in which our subconscious will function naturally." Concentration was fundamental, but he was not talking of somnambulism. Yet I don't want to minimize the riches of rumination, or the difficulty, for all that Lahr says from his experience, of picking up the pot under other conditions. Stanislavski—a nineteenth-century mind with an old-fashioned rhetoric and twentieth-century intuitions—could believe in the objective world, the world *out there,* unreliable perhaps, but *real.* And to induce a natural flow of the subconscious, he recommended doing what comes naturally in that world; that is, to ask yourself, as Lahr says, what is it that you want to *do?* (Lahr is also of another generation, and he laments its passing: "The art is gone now, out of show business. . . . They've seen everything. . . . I think the clowns are done." If not done, in the domain of dark humor, in Beckett, Ionesco, and the clownerie of *The Blacks.*) But the Superobjective of the actor's life intrudes on the particular objective of his art. When he doesn't know what he's doing with one, it's hard to know how to do the other. And the problem of motivation becomes muddled by the fact that, increasingly, he doesn't really believe in the world *out there.*

So, in the hermetic society of the studio the actor perfects his craft against the day, crawls into himself like Kafka's creature in the burrow, as defense against a life that may not exist for him and in guilt over the failure to function, to be a whole man in what is after all a public art. What tortures the actor with whom method is an obsession is not only the Method but also all the paradoxical anxieties of a culture that has no place for him, but tells him he'd better be an expert as well as an artist, just in case. Which, in the curious perversion of the passion for perfection, devoids him of spontaneity; in the terrible desire for craft, makes for crassness; in the awful urge to be natural once again, makes him itch. It is a form of brain fever, from which Ivan Karamazov, who pondered too much on the event, may have died.

Properly seen, the Method actor (and I am generalizing about hybrid forms) is not substantially different from the Action painter or the poet who lets the words take their own head or the musician who won't *compose* music. They share the same aesthetic heritage and the same "ontological insecurity." When modern artists began to perfect techniques to defend themselves against the technicians, internal technique was canonized in acting as it was in poetry—and the narcissistic apparatus designed to release feeling seemed bound to destroy it, by letting it run away; or to cramp it, like therapy. (As in all human affairs, the instruments invented to solve problems tend, by the fact of their existence, to complicate the problems and invent more. There is no necessity in this, just tendency; psychiatrists, for instance, create patients.) For all the trumpeting about spontaneity, the young actor, like the young painter, resembles the speaker of Donne's sonnet, confronted with death. It's in the atmosphere of his time and it's in his art. So many demons have tried to conquer it or put it out of commission, he "dare not turn [his] dim eyes any way," for fear somebody is already there. Cézanne said: "The thing is to paint as if no other painter had ever existed." But he went often to the Louvre. The impulse to get rid of the past entirely comes out of the fear the present is impossible. The actor may not run away, but he may barely be there, the more he thinks he is.

Around the college where I teach, somebody was recently scrawling on the walls: BIRD LIVES. Let us hope so. The person who has been doing the scrawling is probably registered in the Creative Writing Program, but I bet he isn't writing much. The young painter who learns quickly to despise de Kooning because it is one of de Kooning's ambitions, as it was Picasso's, to solve all the problems is like the actor who will not if it kills him borrow anybody else's gesture. So what remains? The inviolable Self, What-I-Am. If Bird lives, he lives within. The young artist knows another dimension of Sartre's idea in *No Exit*: Hell is other artists. The actor who plays himself is only the most specific expression of this idea.

I am not talking of mere introversion, or mere selfishness—a conscious withdrawal from contact in performance. I have seen actors who believe in organic relations and think they are playing *with* each other, actually *using* each other for stimulus, like properties. I reach out to You to be sure *I* am there. The ontological problem becomes a mode of acting.

Given this tendency, the collective self is a fiction, along with the world *out there*. The actor's technique becomes a reflux in which, if feeling moves, it circulates as within a closed system whose energy is depleted in public. Or, if it is tapped, performance—and the drama itself—may have to be scaled down in size. For all that such acting seems organic, sensitive to what is tactilely there, there is a remarkable unawareness of the total environment, and a very narrow margin between the "private moment" and false pride.

Take the young actress who turns off when she feels the other actor— whom she watched closely when she was *offstage*—is "indicating." This may, in fact, be true; or it may be provisional—the other actor, working from without, knows he is playing "results," but is testing an imagined form into which he is trying to build a character by degrees. In either case, her turning off doesn't encourage the organic in the other, for organisms depend on relationships. "Stay with me," says the singer Ray Charles, "and I'll find you." But no—voice lowered in protest to a whisper, searching out the stage for "true stimuli," the actress may step over the line chalked by the stage manager to mark a door, in order to scratch what will be an elegantly set table, for suet; she will respond in character to the accidental fall of a hammer offstage or to a murmur in the auditorium; but the one physical fact to which, relentlessly concentrating, she will never respond is that all the other actors on stage are talking louder.

There are conditions, of course, in which she can be very responsive. Let another actor whisper in return, and in a moment the two will be disappearing into each other. Indicating maximum honesty. The absurdity is a cognate of the fear I have described. Still, the kind of actress I have in mind is capable of her own sentient beauty, one can't deny it; it usually consists of "moments" or comes out in a reckless pursuit of a line of action to some physical conclusion, even if it means throttling the other actor for stimulus.

What we desire, however, is the rarer abandon of genuine intercourse, actors playing to each other in responsive passion—as they are, in their own way. There may be need for method to achieve unity, but the paramount need is charity, not condescension; not aloofness, but giving. The precondition of this is the actor who is willing to engage, and willing to let go, all ways. One of the virtues of a Brecht play is that it urges the actor who has something deeply subjective to say not merely to cut it off, but to say it. Which, really, is the meaning of Alienation—to make your passions bold and public.

There used to be a time when we worried about actors who tore a passion to tatters or climbed the curtains. Nowadays, with everybody taking a class and becoming craftier, I am personally delighted to find an actor who *can* tear a passion to tatters; or, as the prologue at the Cocke-Pit reported of Edward Alleyn, one who is a "Proteus for shapes, and Roscius for a tongue. . . ." There are extremes, naturally, and among your garden variety of actors a generous amount of useless passion, disembodied or smoldering like James Dean—casual-carnal hip and feminine athleticism, motorcycle Praxitelean. But modern acting generally—whether through the coolness of Alienation or immersion in the Studio or the scaling-down of intimate theater—tends to be reticent when it is not psychopathic. And it is the correlative of the well-adjusted audience's recoil from too much feeling. One sees the inevitable solution to that on television, where the real emotional investment, like the real technical skill, is in the advertisements not the drama, which is gauged down to all tastes while the volume is souped up to sell the product.

I remember the dismay during our production of *King Lear* when Michael O'Sullivan very nearly beat his brains out while exclaiming: "O Lear, Lear, Lear!/ Beat at this gate, that let thy folly in/ And thy dear purpose out!" The impression some had was that he had blown his top too early. Perhaps so. We considered this criticism very carefully, but decided not to change the action. For there is sometimes in the observation about what an actor is "overdoing" the implication that he doesn't know what he is doing. Or couldn't control it. O'Sullivan could have played the scene with more restraint, but we were after bigger stakes. The danger was excess or hysteria, and occasionally he may not have avoided it. But for us, the action was an image, precise as he could make it. If it was not a safe emotion to be striving for (I notice that Morris Carnovsky was criticized recently for straining too hard in the same scene), we were directed to the melodramatic fury by the text. Even if it were an editor who instructs Lear to say those lines while *"Striking his head,"* one could feel the inevitability of the gesture in the rhythm—and in the frustrated malevolence of an absolute monarch who had been told for eighty years that he was "everything" and who had just called upon Nature herself (who he had every reason to expect would listen) to scourge his daughter and make her barren, and there she was still scornful, still thwarting, stripping him of his knights; a dispossessed king who would at the climax of his rage desire to spill all the germens of his manhood in self-extinction. Strike his head? Why, even Willie Loman might do the same.

To do less might satisfy our conditioned sense of proportionate emotion, but it would be something less than Lear. We may discover more about this problem when, as will be the case, we revive certain neglected dramas of the Jacobean and Romantic periods, such as those of Byron.

Peter Brook is reported to have said during an underplayed run-through of his production of *King Lear*: "in a concert hall there is a taut silence; everyone is listening for *and* perceiving subtleties. You see this level of acting, in thirty years this is the way all Shakespeare will be played." That may be true. I understand what prompted it—the whole tradition of realism in the English theater, ranging from the Shakespearean correction of Marlovian rhetoric to the current assault on the stereotyped and trippingly-tongued readings of the Royal Academy of Dramatic Art. There is also Brook's interest in the *nouvelle vague* film. But I am not sure I should like to see all Shakespeare played that way; and the one thing that does seem sure about the Globe is that the groundlings would have found it very strange.

Brook is not, true, talking about a performance that would be all mute and mumble, but a storm is a reasonable facsimile of a storm in Shakespearean drama, whatever else it might be, and though I acknowledge the difference between thunder sheets and actual forked lightning. In an age dreading promiscuous explosion, I can respect the desire for reticence. And there are virtues to understatement demonstrated in the generally low key of the Berliner Ensemble. But understatement is, as we encounter it in America, a strategy that needs looking at askance. The low key may be subtle or exact; it may also be simply frightened. With violence stealing the headlines, with power so venereal we keep it locked up, we withdraw, we compensate, we turn off: so much energy out there; so little to spare here. Occasionally an actor, out to prove himself, does not pluck bright honour from the pale-faced moon, but virility from the orgone box. The result: not demonic courage, the rage of innocence, but a visceral twitch. There is, however, another kind of power that I should like to see restored to our theater. Brook knows Artaud very well; he would probably recall that mad seer's description of the Chinese actor who practiced his art by howling against the desert winds. It is the discipline of the demonic. The modern actor, Artaud adds, has forgotten how to scream.

Earlier I said I didn't understand the Second Law of Thermodynamics until I began to study dramatic form. The law is concerned with the symptoms of Entropy, that tricky ratio of modern science which, like the Thomistic demon, measures the unavailable energy of the universe. "The dead beast kills the living me," says Herakles in *The Women of Trachis*. Entropy dwells upon that process. We construct systems to recoup the losses.

The oldest forms of improvisational drama result from the energy man applies to his anxiety to keep him from running away. One of the charming aspects of such drama is the illusion there is no such thing as Entropy, especially if you run faster than the beast. Or dress like one. In the Old

Comedy, with its Comus or hymeneal feast (*and its archons who paid the bills*), energy is reversible and man indefatigable, though the caprices of fortune buffet and batter him. This spirit is preserved in traditional farce where the character can take as many lemon pies as you care to throw and keep rebounding through the swinging door. Comic heroes, like old soldiers, never die. (*Neither do they pay the bills.*) They rise up from the battlefield like Falstaff—and what should have been dead mutton is solid fantasy. The comic hero comes back. He has resources. Or so it appears. They buried the old knight in the interest of Progress. And by the time the drama reaches Ibsen, not only has the nature of comedy changed, but man has either the illusion that he doesn't want to run away, that he is quite comfortable in the theatre of life, or that he wants desperately to run but doesn't believe it possible—determination of behavior is overwhelming (*and economics is becoming all, with a box office paying the bills*).

I am speaking of the Ibsen who came down from the mountains for his "social plays" with characters that Wedekind called "tame domestic beasts." It was by reflecting around this Ibsen that I began to see the shape of our own enterprise, the dangers involved and the conceptual leaps we might have to take.

We worked on *Hedda Gabler* in our little studio. For want of space, Irving, who directed, wedged the action between two walls. It seemed quite right As I wrote in the program: "Hedda's dramatic reality, although not her personal fulfillment, is in the tight suffocating bourgeois parlor which Ibsen equated with the outer world. . . . Ibsen deliberately limits his scope; he is clinical; he refuses to go beyond the patholigcal condition. He makes no ethical judgments, but within his restricted scene he manages to expose, with meticulous care, the nervures of a special disorder, attached to place and time."

Yet, as *"Banzai!"* shouts came up from the Judo Academy below, and a body hit the deck, ruining the silences, I was reminded of the wilder life secreted in the parlor, the trolls grinning in the corners. And I would recall the fabuolus lie of Peer Gynt to his mother, in which he describes himself riding a great buck on the top of the mountains, faster than the wind, then plunging to the fjords, down, down, and down to meet his own image rising from the water, stopping suspended in air, and instant before the crash. Fantasy becoming truth, Peer is the incarnation of unavailable energy, the self-possession of an age poised on self-destruction. The bourgeois parlor can't contain such power. And we were hardly up to it then. But the conservation and use of power in an age of power became, incrementally and in my mind, a mission.

It wasn't power, however, that marked those early "exercises"—there was no real point of view. What we had, rather, was a lot of pace, gusto, and surprising animation. With so much that was sluggish around, our guests were impressed.

The first play I directed was, like *Peer Gynt,* about an actor who ran away,

Synge's *Playboy of the Western World*. Our loft was about as shabby as the public house, but we reveled in the nutted speeches and "the springtime of the local life." We found the rhythm of the shebeen and the humor in the hypocrisy of those pagan Christians in the blighted West, who solicit the lie they reject when it threatens them. "Is it killed your father?" says Pegeen, lowering her broom with wonder as Christy cowers. "With the help of God I did surely, and that the Holy Immaculate Mother may intercede for his soul." Immediately the stranger becomes "mister honey." After all, who can help but admire a man who killed his father, since he has acted out our deepest fantasy. And so long as the dead man supports it by remaining at a distance.

If we were to do the play now, we would probably brood more upon that. And we tried then not to stint on the cruelties in the gap between the "gallus story" and the "dirty deed." When Pegeen, for instance, tried to loose the lassoed Christy from our fireplace, to which he clung in peril of his life, she, who loved him a moment before, really let him have it with a hot coal. Nevertheless, at the time we were more interested—perhaps rightly—in the gaiety and the romance. (One remembers *Playboy* is a drama that caused riots, but even Brecht, who did a version, couldn't restore the natal shock.)

As for our energy and gusto, which seemed appropriate here, the danger was that they might be gratuitous in other plays. For they were, as I've implied, not so much the result of stylistic perception or an intuition of our later effort to do noble battle with our demons, but rather an extension of Irving's driving temperament, or of mine, to which the actors responded. Despite my studious melancholy, in public we both thought fast and moved things quickly, and some of the urgency of those early productions was sometimes nervousness, sometimes impatience, and sometimes—our actual fund of good humor aside—overdrilled and overpaced. (When we became better established, there was a period when we were charged with slickness.) The fact is, too, we were not yet emancipated from that taste for high polish and no flaws, that anxiety over the gaps, which in the theater we had known made things look professional. We were picking up our cues, and urging the actors to do so.

That was less superficial than it seems. And now that we are far more concerned with organic motivation of pace, say, we find ourselves employing all kinds of tricks, stratagems, and psychological subterfuge to induce the actor to do what he might do more naturally if we simply said, "Pick it up." Now that we let it flow more, it is sometimes flat. It would take a good deal more experience to learn that the theater is one of the most conventional of arts, and that precision, fluency, and pointing were no less sincere than feeling things out—and may be sources of discovery. "I want the *soul* of Beethoven," said the violinist. "How can you know the soul," said Toscanini, "if you play him so slow?"

Here, of course, is an an aesthetic crux to which we shall keep returning: art and chance. What we would have to restrain eventually would be the temptations to the attractive and seemingly adventurous orthodoxy of chance, the indulgence of relativity. The art of theater flows in the bloodstream of the individual but, because it is eminently social, it implies, somewhere, a normal pulse. The human organism is relative enough without our making a fetish of it. One need not measure out a scene by tapping time with a ruler, but we might remember that among the techniques discussed in *Building a Character* was that of getting to the truth within by superimposing a rhythm from without, and there are exercises performed by the pupils of Stanislavski in which clapping hands is a more incisive way into an action than free association.

The issue is not simple, and I shall take it up again in connection with other productions. Nobody wants to move fast merely to give the audience an impression that something is happening when it is not. A performance, like a poem, has to be earned. But there are interminable evasions in internal technique that we want to understand, and Robert Lewis put it well when he said there is nothing more phony in the American theater than the fear of phoniness. Among the worshipers of the Berliner Ensemble are some who would be astonished were they to see a rehearsal conducted by Erich Engel or Manfred Wekworth; for, with all the trial and error of almost unlimited rehearsal schedules, there is the customary German deference to the director, who can orchestrate a performance at will down to the last syllable. Actually, the natural is a matter of convention and conditioning. And I have seen actors at the Ensemble and other theaters execute cheerfully and faithfully, with no apparent loss of dignity or Self, directions so explicit they would paralyze most American actors. It is a matter of social cohesion, too, of mutual trust and a common aim. The Brecht Ensemble obviously has something to say in which they all concur, and they want to say it accurately— even if it means the cardinal sin of acting as we know it: accepting somebody else's reading!

We were developing the common aim, but slowly—and it had more to do with our plays than with methodology. Although our loft might have been more of a laboratory, it never became a labyrinth. We called ourselves an actor's workshop, but from the beginning we had the instincts of a theater and not a studio. We did scenes and had critiques, but we did not, for better or worse, become obsessed with craft independent of production. Producing became a habit. If that has faults, so does endless training; and we were spared the debility of vexation without representation. What work the actors did on themselves—and I don't mean to minimize that—they did on roles they had to bring to performance. There might have been more personal exploration, but the acting was neither hermetic nor glib. And if there wasn't stylistic unity, there was the feeling of an ensemble which had to be, as the company grew and others left, constantly renewed.

It was an intelligent collaboration rather than a style, which is a conquest of form born of recurring perception. Sought too early, it may look like idiosyncrasy. If style isn't a conquest, it becomes a convention. By playing together we grew intimate, but we were too uncertain of ourselves to have a style. And though we sought meaning in our plays, there was no distinct policy behind their choice.

Despite the toughness of *Hedda Gabler* and the swagger of *Playboy,* the main determinants of play selection were casting and a vaguely academic responsibility to the modern classics. As for scene design, if we jerry-built a metaphor out of necessity, we also copied photos from *Theatre Arts.* We had neither a designer nor any conception of "total theater." But if I was surprised to find myself so close now to the center of a stage, I was starting to think about such things and about the relations between the play we did and those we might think of doing. In the company critiques, we argued about "offbeat" plays and "popular" plays, and what a potential audience would want to see. We were by no means far out, but some of the actors feared we would be. And I was prone to say then that we might have to educate an audience as we educated ourselves.

Some good analytical work had been done on *Hedda Gabler,* a very close slow reading of the text. And the "company," enlarged by auditions, was very attentive when I did an exegesis of Lorca's *Blood Wedding,* whose surrealist imagery and symbolic clusters, the lyrical development of the narrative, were considered deeply *avant-garde.* (I think it is symptomatic of the American theater of the early fifties that most of our actors, almost all of whom had studied drama in college, had never read Garcia Lorca; some had barely even heard of him.) Up to that time, *Blood Wedding* had only, so far as we knew, been performed once before in America, and not successfully; and we managed in our production to dispel some of the platitudes about ethnic distance that always come from *aficionados* who may have seen a bullfight or two. Though I would hardly claim the performance was purest Andalusian (the music was purest corn), it did convey the heat, the passion, the ominous murmurs of the wedding, and the blood vengeance. The drama moved convincingly from one plane of reality to another, the impersonal Woodcutters chanting the unspoken sympathy of the community for the lovers (who had violated its code but fulfilled its fantasies), providing a transition in a rhythm close to nature to the more entropic presences of the Moon and Death. And the acting, uneven as it was, went in some performances a considerable way down to "the dark root of a scream."

If we weren't doing, as the poet said of his poem, what we *really* thought, we were doing some plays in which you hardly had to think at all. Arthur Miller has said of American drama that it "is pre-eminently active, relatively unreflective as such. It deals with nothing it cannot act out. It rarely comments on itself; like the people, it always pretends it does not know what it is doing. It must *be* something rather than *about* something." Here we have a populist variant of the iconographic fallacy developed by modern poets and painters: the thing *is.* It is not *about,* because what can be said about anything when there are, in a world rejecting absolutes, no reliable principles of evaluation? If all is becoming, then process itself is the final value, and the intensity of the felt life in that process. It is the basic theory behind modes of art ranging from

Pound's ideogram to Pollock's totems, and can be very complex. Well and good. Experience is the final test, and "The rest is silence." Only, to the extent that the process is "relatively unreflective as such," you may neglect to act out a good portion of experience that has been held valuable through the ages; and there may not really be pretense involved in not knowing what you are doing. Whatever is, may be right—but it may not be very much.

So it was with *I Am a Camera,* the John Van Druten adaptation of Christopher Isherwood's *Berlin Stories,* and *Summer and Smoke,* by Tennessee Williams. Once again, they were chosen because we could cast them. *Summer and Smoke,* transplanted from Dallas and failing on Broadway, was produced at the Circle in the Square about the same time we did our production. Although the arena stage can with some losses accomodate almost any kind of drama, it is especially suited to plays of unheroic emotion and introspective action. It also has the power, because of the eternal attraction of personality, to deflect attention from the shallows of a drama to the hollows of behavior. There is always plenty to watch, and it does have, with certain plays, the compelling density of a television screen. Both *I Am a Camera* and *Summer and Smoke,* which profited from being seen up close, had a sensibility in common with the TV plays of the Fred Coe stable. Both plays came out of the irresolute atmosphere of the late forties and early fifties. If they were not quite running away, then—like *Hotel Universe*—they were dramas of drift and vague apprehension, but more secular. They were what you might expect from an era that had very little to say, or from an American theater that felt it had very little right to say it, and at its most sincere just wanted to be let alone, like the people such plays were about.

Everything in our loft was, naturally, in some variant of arena staging. Though our production was much praised, I was personally uncomfortable with *Summer and Smoke,* which I directed. I found it hard to take a lot of it seriously, and I wrote shiftily of Williams' "almost feminine respect for the beauty that perishes, for our incertitude, neurosis, and fragility." There was in the play the poetaster's fondness for chiaroscuro and a gilding of that old *fin de siècle* "eternal silence." Yet, while the doctor was a fabrication and the medical chart sophomoric, there was something lovely about Alma Winemiller, with high giggle and nervous chatter, one of Williams' "shadowy people, unaware of and distrustful of their private natures."

So, too, was Sally Bowles attractive in *I Am a Camera,* through a kind of superficial outrageousness, like green nail polish and Prairie Oysters. In an era in which few of us knew how to live, we could admire her (I wrote this time) "for her undeviating and scrupulous immorality." But it was all too easy and too chic, easy for us to do, easy for the audience to like, easy for everybody to feel charitable in offering a compassion that has become a virtual staple of feeling in the American theater, with its bruised heroes and paper-doll heroines and psychiatric social workers. Weak ourselves, blessed are the weak. And by offering tea and sympathy, we have the illusion of strength. Set in Berlin in 1930, with Nazis on the streets, the play has a subject which could have taken us through the most significant emotions of our time; but what we get is a little bit of recent history and a whole lot of conversational sex, the right ingredients for a popular liberalism better fed since the thirties, and a little sodden after dinner.

"I am a camera, with its shutter open, quite passive," says Chris. "Some day all of this will have to be developed, printed, fixed." True. Only we are likely to find there was something wrong with the film. When James Joyce encouraged passivity in the storyteller, who backed away paring his finger-nails, turning narrative to drama, it was an act of audacity. I don't mean to push the comparison of great things to small, but there is a point: to record everything seen by a Leopold Bloom or even a Wozzeck is to take on the nightmare of history; passivity is an action of great form-giving intelligence. Today, our instinct, weary of history, is to leave the stage with the barest integument of conscience, the merest civil pinprick of remorse. Certainly intelligence is a trial, it always has been—and there was an understandable desire for relief when a young actor in our company said to me recently, after playing two roles that put his mind to the test: "Do you think I'll ever get to do one of those parts where I just have to emote, not think?"

That depends on how passive one cares to be. "And the sky can still fall on our heads," writes Artaud, that wizard of entropic art. "And the theater has been created to teach us that first of all."

We were learning. And the very setting of our work—its *No Exit* atmosphere and the sheer ordeal of keeping things going—cultivated a sense of defiance, like Sisyphus rolling his stone. Everything we did, within or without, there was somebody to say it couldn't be done. Frankly, I didn't really think it could be done, but I was trying hard to believe it. If I wavered in faith and wanted to get out, somebody else was converted by me, and later—when I would despair of it all—I'd remember my obligation to him. Though Entropy was the one concept I remembered vividly from my training as an engineer, though there might be a leak in the universe itself, and we might all want to run, it became a matter of pride—we would not go under!

Wasn't this the central conflict of modern art? The formal problem—the work of art itself—contained all the other problems, economic, cultural, philosophical. When Yeats—late in his long career—created his idiosyncratic *A Vision,* he said it was intended as "a last act of defense against the chaos of the world." The Abbey had been a part of that defense.

Entropy is the enemy, slippery as a demon, lethal at the bone. As I put my study of poetry and my study of thermodynamics together, and brought the resultant imagery into the theater, every kind of inertia, every defecting actor became a measure of fallout. Entropy was the formula for the Cold War, with all its wasted energy—the specter behind the bounty of things, the worm beneath the manicure, paralyzed force, spilt flux. I must have known you couldn't photograph it by merely leaving the shutter open. For out of this sense of Entropy I had written a story, an impossible story about an impossible subject, about a boy who stood for hours before a mirror, trying in vain and not in vain to watch himself die. The best part of the story was the epigraph, from a Shakespeare sonnet:

> Ah, yet doth beauty, like a dial hand
> Steal from his figure, and no pace perceived.
> So your sweet hue, which methinks still doth stand,
> Hath motion, and mine eye may be deceived.

By a curious perversion of thought (like Hamlet tracing the noble dust of Alexander until it stops a bunghole) dwelling on Entropy was invigorating. I saw analogies everywhere, but mostly in the art of the theater itself, that time-serving form with a wallet at its back, given over to what passes and what expires, to "seeming, seeming." Entropy was experience's sleight of hand; it was in the seraphic wildness of Callot's drawings of the *commedia dell'arte,* where obscenity flies like a bird, all the brainy vigor of man poised against his dissolution. Seen again, Entropy was dispossession seeking a homestead, like a haunted Orestes.

If you were looking for something to care about, Entropy taught you to care and not to care. It was an extraordinary lesson to somebody like myself, who was just beginning to direct plays.

For, from the Duke of Saxe Meiningen to Elia Kazan, the director has tried to make the performance a kind of ideal engine, or Carnot cycle, in which all elements work in perpetual harmony, defying the laws of motion. The despotism of the director has accounted for some of the greatest achievements of the modern theater. But as things become more determined, intimidating around us and frightened within, it has become increasingly the director's function (whatever his own problems) to be a depth diver, who must issue warnings or find the release. If the task is more therapeutic, the methods are more pedagogical. The director has tried to become an expert in getting behavior, which wants to behave as the wind behaves, out of its jam, to activate the will, to show even for an instant that it is still beautifully alive—and then to keep it from jumping, like Peer on his buck, over the cliff. As in the other arts, the technique of directing has become both scientific and spiritual—a salvage operation and a mode of salvation. But as always with the will, one learns that one way to make it move is to know when to let it alone. If the actor is devout in self-exposure, the director must know when to respect his privacy. And the inevitable performance of the director— goad and gadfly, counselor and private eye—is like the Duke of dark corners in *Measure for Measure,* who sets things in motion that may or may not go their authorized way.

The director is a man of action reduced to a mote in the middle distance, darkling, critic and ghost, swearing mournfully, "Remember me." Old truepenny, he must learn to sit still. For the theatrical performance is the very image of Entropy, the explicit form of the ephemeral, where reality is assiduously unfixed. The theater is always imperfect, the least manageable of forms because the most contaminated by people. Various sages of the theater have deplored this and tried to create their perfectly suspended systems, like a windjammer in a bottle. They have tried to reform the theater by getting rid of the people or engulfing them—Gordon Craig with his towers of light and sliding screens, Otto Schlemmer with his Dance of Forms, Antonin Artaud with his plague and *mise en scène* as performer. But for the director there is always, even under the mask, the recalcitrant flesh. Satan, it is rumored, was the first actor. For the director, it is one of the facts of life. "*You* will disappear," an actor said to me, as he turned back to the stage—speaking of Entropy.

Though it goes without saying that we must cherish the playwright, the theater always comes back to the actor in the center of an acting area. Even so magisterial a director as Reinhardt had to concede, "It is to the actor and no one else that the theater belongs." It is not, however, a question of which comes first, chicken or egg, priorities, hierarchies, the Platonic riddle. It is a question of *performance*—the final cause, the furnishing forth, the Noh or Accomplishment, the investiture and the offering. If, as Heidegger says, "The human condition is to be *there*," the actor is at the altar—though it has, true, been a long time since he has felt really priestly about it, and though both his technique and his economic plight suggest that he may have been transformed into the sacrificial lamb.

We had founded an Actor's Workshop. The title was singular, in honor of the art; the necessity was plural, if we were to practice the craft. For all my obsession with illusion and reality, in the development of the theater, the world is very definitely *out there*. Theory aside: in the sweep of horrific events, in the cares and business of our age, in the rigor of rehearsals, and in the practical working life of a theater of the 1950s, the question was: *How do you create a permanent company if you don't have the actors?* If you can't afford them? For we were soon thinking of expansion. And San Francisco was no mineshaft of talent. Gertrude Stein had said of nearby Oakland, where she was born, that it lacked *thereness*. For all the money we had to lure actors, we might as well have started in Oakland, or gone to Paris.

In the beginning, as we came out of nowhere—as it were, out of the collective unconsciousness of the American theater—we were part of the provisionally impoverished end of the Welfare State. I say provisionally because there was benevolence on the horizon, though I didn't see it until the theater itself induced us to look closer at the social scene. Fearing we couldn't grow at all, we enunciated a "principle of slow growth"—that is, we would never pretend to be anything more than we were, never reach beyond ourselves, never claim to be professional when we weren't, never undertake plays we could not do (which we quickly violated), and never even ask the audience for money before we were ready to consider ourselves a producing company, and not merely a study group. In a status society this proved to be an accidental advantage to our growth. For, as we did our work in the loft to invitational audiences, and our undercover reputation spread, it became quite a thing in San Francisco to receive an invitation to this mysterious group which was rehearsing in an out-of-the-way part of the city. I blush to add that as soon as we recognized our illicit appeal, we encouraged it. Our mailing list increased, and more actors appeared.

When people say, however, how lucky we were to be in San Francisco, with its receptive audiences and cultural *savoir-faire;* that what we did could not be done in any other city, I can never resist saying that if The Workshop survived there, it was in spite of the general neglect, and even civic suspicion. (The ex-Mayor of San Francisco, an enlightened milkman who recently felt compelled, like Khrushchev, to examine the paintings offered prizes in civic competition, wondered out loud after our eleven years of production what the devil we did that deserved any allocation from the hotel tax.) San Francisco has all the topographic benevolence and the advantages I cited before, but in the old rivalry with Los Angeles, it doth protest too much. At present, Los Angeles is culturally a more vigorous city to the extent it is more aggressive, with looser money that buys, along with the call girls, a good many more paintings, including those by San Francisco artists, who are rarely bought at home. While the city does show more concern than most about protecting its landscape and preserving its "character," it is also a nice place to stay home in, unless there is some reason to be "with it," as when the Bolshoi arrives, or a big name. But the New York City Ballet, which has no very big names but perhaps the best choreography in the world, does not do very well in San Francisco; and I have heard one of the directors of the San Francisco Ballet—which has no place to dance and is losing its best people as a result—say publicly that they may just decide one day to give it up and go elsewhere.

True, we have in recent years received a good deal of support in the press, but subscription grew meagerly—and is still amazingly small compared to the numbers some of the new regional theaters are announcing even before they open. Beyond this, any new enterprise in San Francisco had to overcome the reputation for culture the city had acquired in the past, along with its opera and symphony, and the Civic Light Opera, whose musicals are sold out long in advance. Since culture is culture, the city has felt no urgency— like, say, Oklahoma City or Minneapolis—to buy itself some. Nor, though we well need one, to build us a new theater, even with the foundations standing by with the possibility of matching funds. Indeed, after tearing down the old but gracefully serviceable Alcazar, the best of its class-A theaters, it may have trouble saving the couple it still has. Moreover, we are a home-grown product; having started as a "little theater" we had, unfortunately, to live down that once-honorable name. (Some years ago I said to a reviewer who used the term with condescension that it was true we were a little theater, but that he, compared to us, and his paper, compared to *The New York Times,* were infinitesimal. And that neither of us would become any better unless we started thinking bigger about ourselves.) One hears of a colorful history of old stock companies in San Francisco, but after the war one professional theater venture after another failed, for reasons mentioned, but also for lack of support.

As other cities advance, however, in cultural standing, San Francisco, guarding its reputation, will be pushed to compete—that's inevitable;* and it has the natural advantages. One can also see in my criticism the engaging and comprehensible shape of the city; you can talk about it as a unity as you can never quite talk about New York. And as a major city, it has the additional advantage that, unlike New York or Los Angeles, it is no market place for actors. Within the city we are protected from the Diaspora by the absence of TV allurements and the rat race; but then their absence put a severe limit on the actors available when we started, and even now.

That we were not at first supported may have, if you'll forgive the puritanism, been good for us. It seeded the enterprise with an internal strength. The actors we did have all worked voluntarily. Irving and I did all the technical jobs. Those actors with Equity cards were on honorable withdrawal, but when you're utterly insignificant the unions let you alone. Nobody drew any salary for several years. As we began to clarify our purposes, the sacrifices and refusals of other opportunity increased, in the expectation that The Workshop, where the actors wanted to work, would be able to support them in time. The voluntary character of the theater continued, however, even into the period of a paid full-time staff. It continues today, and it is beneficial. The pattern of sacrifice is not new in the theater, but the intensity and extent of it is relevant to my account of the period. As the prospects of new theaters improve in the present decade, what we did may be neither emulable nor necessary. Let us pray. Still, the character of what was done might be better understood by a further contrast with the Group Theater.

For all that was abandoned, passed up, or conceded by those who worked with the Group, it was never really an obscure organization. Among its members were Morris Carnovsky, Marry Morris, and Philip Loeb, who had already established reputations with the Theater Guild; Stella and Luther Adler of the distinguished theatrical family; and a number of young actors, including Franchot Tone, whose promise had already been acknowledged. The enterprise received attention from the outset. Now, I don't want to minimize the devotion and sacrifice of these people, but with the Group salary was an issue from the outset—and though everybody settled for a good deal less than they might have pulled down elsewhere, the better-known players, such as Tone and Carnovsky, were paid $300 weekly during the first season and, as Clurman records it, "The other salaries ranged from $30 to $140 weekly"

---

* Since I wrote this, a new Mayor has been elected, who has taken the first step toward getting us a new theater, by directing the Redevelopment Agency to secure a site if possible.

during the Depression—salaries which, for some of our actors, would to this day be considered utopian.

I do not contend that all of our people were similarly deserving. None of those with whom we began were well known (my wife, Beatrice Manley, who had minor roles in several Broadway plays, represented our best "credits," as the playbills say). But, not to labor the point, the situation of an actor like Robert Symonds is instructive. Symonds, a protegé of B. Iden Payne at the University of Texas, played there with Pat Hingle and Rip Torn, who are now well known in the New York theater. While they went east, he went to the Ashland Shakespeare Festival, with the intention of going to Broadway afterwards. We saw him do a superb Polonius in Ashland and were surprised, in the midst of rehearsals for *Oedipus Rex,* to have him show up one day in San Francisco. He was merely passing through. But after some conversation he was in the chorus of *Oedipus* and has remained in San Francisco ever since.

He worked then for nothing, as he did for several years, with interims in which he received the most nominal kind of salary, rarely going over $50. For a long while he rehearsed all day, performed at night, and then went to the produce market, where he hauled vegetables to support his family. He is only prototypical, and one may ask: Why did he do it? Why didn't he just go back to New York and fight it out with his peers? Was he scared?

Anybody who has seen Symonds' acting over its full range—and he has developed something of a trade reputation in the American theater—knows that this is not the case. There were other talented people in San Francisco with whom he had chosen to work in a common enterprise. He had opted not only for The Workshop, but *against* the system that was enslaving most of the actors in his profession. Like the Chinese actor screaming in the desert, he *knew* what he was doing. His choice was disciplined, principled, and visionary. And he would not run away.

It was a choice that would have been understood in other days, before the Little Theater Movement was aborted. Whatever caused that revolution to fail, Symonds knew that Decentralization had remained the major goal of the American theater. And he preferred to act out the belief that what is needed are theaters in which an actor can develop his craft by playing a wide variety of roles in the very best plays—and not only that, but behave in his art like a first-class citizen. He liked the idea of a theater in which he could over a period of time find out what he wanted to say as an artist, and say it, and test it, and say it again—in a community where what he has to say is increasingly respected.

I pick up the Sunday paper. There is an article by Symonds on his direction of *Volpone.* Writing on the difficulty of directing himself in so complex a play, he says it was "not out of a desire for a grand gesture, but because there has developed in The Actor's Workshop over the last ten years of work a common experience to draw upon. There has evolved, if not an exact definition of style, at least a touchstone of feeling which supports the individual. . . . In the theater, as in love, there are only those who do and those who don't dare."

No one can deny that a number of his contemporaries have more considerable reputations nationally. Certainly they are better paid. But—and the question is the crucial one—what have they played? Symonds—and I am naming these off the top of my head—has performed Falstaff, Face, Archie Rice, Galileo, Casanova, Undershaft, Sir Toby Belch, Mr. Mississippi; Krapp, Gogo, Hamm; Harpagon; and I mentioned Volpone. And he has been in any number of other plays, including the American premières of *Mother Courage* and Pinter's *The Birthday Party,* which most of his contemporaries are just beginning to hear of, as they become more firmly typed for the kind of roles they have already done. One may contend that becoming a Broadway star opens up new possibilities, and that may be true for the greatest of stars; but it is also likely to be confining. And anyhow, ask yourself how many and what variety of roles even the better known and best of them, like Geraldine Page and Eli Wallach, have done in recent years. Ask yourself, how many become Broadway stars?

What I proposed earlier may still be bothersome: why should an actor work without salary? Equity forgive me, why shouldn't he? if it is possible (as it was with us then) and if it is necessary so that he may continue to act as an artist. Of course, when everybody seems to be eating well and buying much, you can't entirely blame the actor for wanting his portion of the general welfare. I daresay even the most intransigeant *jongleur* of the Middle Ages didn't entirely cherish his impoverished state; but there are few artists so conventional, or backward, as the average actor. Precisely because he is vulnerable, he is liable to be wary of, if not outright hostile to, what has not yet been approved by publicity. Right now, when those cultural statistics make it appear for the first time in his collective life that a good thing is almost in the bag, he is likely to be more cautious and obliging than ever. Gradually, he may even become a commodity in much demand. Few people in any profession are prone by nature to incur risks; this is all the more so in a profession congenitally prone to Willie Loman's ailment, the anxiety to be "well-liked." The chicane and pretexts range today, however, from the laughable to the odious, and pathetically resemble those you hear in exurbia.

Certainly I'd have liked to see most of our people paid well from the very first, as I should have liked to be paid myself. But in the days when sheer exhaustion used to raise the salary issue around The Workshop, as we all came wearily to rehearsals from full-time jobs or, for those who couldn't take it, foraging and dieting, I used to say that if what we were doing was worth doing, what we wanted to do, then we would have to put up with the minor inconvenience of another job until other provisions could be made. Until very recently, I spoke from the vantage point of my own full-time job at San Francisco State College (which has no formal relationship with The Workshop, and where I still teach because I like teaching). Though I knew that teaching literature is not quite the same as selling at Macy's, or lugging vegetables at the market, the principle remained the same. For several years now our Ford grants have relieved the situation (not for all of our people), but when W. McNeil Lowry studied The Workshop for a possible grant he could not quite bring himself to believe we were *really* professional because Irving and I were at the college, and almost everybody else held some kind of job. He used to refer to us as "a theater club." When we objected, he explained that he meant we weren't working at theater full time, that I taught, for instance. I told him that was true, I taught full time *and* I worked in the theater full time. Nobody was sleeping very much.

Here was the place to work, we said, here were the people to work with. The clear-cut issue: did you want to work toward the consolidation of what you said you believed in, or did you want to go off and make a living at your "art"; that is, on radio and TV, if you were lucky; or in stock or Broadway crap, if you were luckier. It was a while before our evangelism was such that we would try to dissuade an actor from leaving The Workshop. In the beginning, without any clear prospects, we didn't feel we had the right. But as we analyzed the cultural scene more intensively and became aware of the drift, we began to exercise all kinds of persuasion, cajolery, and moral intimidation. When one actor who had left us began to write that he was tempted to return (by this time people were feeling guilty about leaving), that what he was doing was trivial compared to what was possible in San Francisco, but that he was earning his living (he had worked constantly) and that he would return only if we could pay him a living wage, I answered to this effect: when we can pay you a living wage we won't need you; we need you now. He came back after a while to do a new play, acted for a nominal salary, and has remained with us since—like Symonds, at nowhere near what he is worth by the standards of the trade, but adequately paid as an artist.

So, too, when our company designer—a painter who had just done his first production—complained in a letter about "the mild slap of insult carried by a sole check for $40," I felt no compunction about replying: "The Workshop may have many reasons for being embarrassed, but what it pays or doesn't pay is not one of them. . . . Your services are in the best sense extravagantly appreciated by the cast, by the rest of the company, by Jules and, as you know, by myself. If this isn't sufficient, I can only remind you that you were laboring in a situation where janitors are paid, and must be, before artists, and where artists are paid not as artists but as janitors. That sole check for $40 was, on the Encore budget, a costly insult. . . . When I first talked to you about design I said nothing about money, partially because it never occurred to me, but partially because we had allocated nothing for a designer at this theater. This is one of the paradoxes with which the theater, our theater at least, has often to live, that we make intolerable demands on those who have already made intolerable demands on themselves in the service of their art."

Eventually we were paying a substantial number of people substantial salaries, but there were always those, unfortunately, who would respond neither to bluntness nor moral persuasion nor money, and our work was periodically retarded by people who, believing in what we were doing, left either because we couldn't pay even more for what they were doing, or because of the recurrent stupidity about having to go through "the experience" of New York. Before that mystical journey there would be remorse, conferences, lamentations, apologies, assurances of love, and then departure—and another name added to the list of those who, with their hearts in the right place, did themselves and the theater—mind you, not only our theater—the same old injury.

I said before we had committed ourselves to a "principle of slow growth." Given the economic dilemma, there would seem to have been no alternative. Actually, we wanted to remain small as long as possible, for artistic reasons. But as a pending institution in the Cold War, not only couldn't we determine our identity, we could hardly control our size. Slowly as we grew, we grew at first faster than we wanted. Though we were generally more discreet than the series of managers who had started "professional" theaters in the area after the war and, one by one, collapsed—slow growth was the process of another era. So long as we remained sheltered, we could rehearse a play until it was "ready" and could maintain the character of a workshop.

Once, however, we decided to move from our studio into larger quarters— an abandoned Ford warehouse that had been used as a church—we had to ask those on our accumulating mailing list for money. And though it was gratifying to be able to raise nearly $10,000 in a few weeks by floating stock among those who had seen our studio work, once we did that, we became subject to the pressures that all small businesses suffered during the Cold War. All the more so when our converted warehouse was run through by a free- way, and we were—after moving a couple of productions downtown—forced to consolidate things in the heart of San Francisco's meager theatrical district. This gave us greater status and, in the mode of the times, greater anxiety.

Part of this is inevitable in the development of any theater out of a non- professional phase. But small business had an especially tough problem during the Reconversion into the Cold War. The only way the small business- man could survive was by going after defense contracts in an even more war- like way than the industrial giants. To remain small was a hazard, next to impossible; the liability, extinction. Though we have had no explicit occasion to put our hands in the armament pot and have become not quite an inter- national cartel, we have shared this experience and have done our scrounging for the collateral bounty that is necessary even for a studio (as Kazan and Strasberg learned in New York). Not content to remain a studio, we made one decision after another that pushed us into the costliness of public life. As Captain Vere put it in *Billy Budd,* we then had to suffer the wisdom of the choices that were being forced upon us.

No doubt we enjoy today the prospect of playing in our two theaters; but the prospect is often enjoyed more than the fact. Our second, intimate theater may seem a luxury, and we wanted it for experimental purposes. But it is also true that we *needed* it so we could have a company large enough to operate our larger theater; that is, to keep sufficient personnel in the area and with us, there must be sufficient opportunity. What we have in effect done is to create a small off-Broadway of our own, lest we lose the already limited talent that there is in San Francisco. And while we offer at our second theater an extraordinary repertoire, we also have the obligation to produce enough to keep the two theaters open.

The alternative, once out of the studio, was to remain a little theater, with unpaid actors and volunteer workers and an auditorium with very few seats; there was no middle ground, and we often talked of retrenching to our smaller theater. Once salaries were paid, however, it was nearly impossible to retrench without losing even our most devoted people. You could only push ahead, trying as best we could to preserve the best attitudes of a little theater.

All things considered, however, we did not want to remain a little theater. Our work was exacting, and we were after the population at large, like Galileo.

There was a good deal of amateur activity in the Bay Area after the war. Little theaters had mushroomed down the Peninsula and up the Sierras. In San Francisco, a group of Quakers and pacifists, some ex-conscientious objectors, started the Interplayers, from which the Playhouse later split off. The old Interplayers did a remarkable repertoire of modern and ancient classics (with the best theater programs I have ever seen, by Adrian Wilson). The Playhouse remains an exemplary little theater, with modest ambitions and relatively untrained actors, but with a faithful audience for an admirable repertoire, including experiments with local writers and artists. If, however, the ambitions grow larger, as ours did; if you want to create a popular theater, as Vilar did—then the problem becomes that of preserving the integrity of "the true amateur" in an economy which encourages largeness as a condition of largesse.

Moreover, America has no repertory-theater traditions. People do not come back to see plays they have seen. They demand the novel, especially when it is not really new. So constant production is forced upon you, without the relief of a regular policy of revivals; not so much to supply a demand but to retain the supply of audience that you have, so you can pay the salaries and accumulating costs. As a theater aspiring to permanence, too, you cannot simply dissolve after each production and raise money for a new venture. Our condition was similar to that of the English Stage Society, described by George Devine: "The regular audience at the Royal Court itself is still regrettably small. Far more people in London support the English Stage Company as an idea rather than buy seats at the box office, except for obvious successes."

Audiences come where audiences come—and desiring to reach the widest possible audience, you learn that attendance at a local theater (we had no obvious international success like *Look Back in Anger*) is to a great extent in proportion to physical growth and external recognition, especially recognition from New York. Quality may ultimately win the day, but it is not always our major achievements that are best attended. In the economic system of "countervailing powers," strong sellers creating strong buyers, you become a victim of the laws of quantity. (Before the Foundation came along, I used to predict it would—hoping it would solve all our financial problems. Our first grant—involving matching funds—actually caused financial problems, and nearly brought us to bankruptcy; first, because it was extraordinarily difficult to raise the matching funds in San Francisco; then, because—while we had more money for more actors—paying those actors meant more payroll taxes and an increased staff to provide for increased production, not provided for in the grant.) Soon you are producing far more plays than you desire, and the luxury of rehearsing a play until it is "ready" disappears. Even the definition of "ready" changes. What was acceptable in the studio was not quite acceptable before a larger public that pays its way. You begin then to yearn for the older simplicity. There are those who want to retreat, just as there are those who will always remain studio actors. But like the archetypal actor in the center of an acting area, something kept us moving: ambition, pride, defiance, foolishness, a sense of Manifest Destiny.

One of our salvational expedients is to keep a "workshop program" going for "internal development." Actually, while it has become a "showcase" for our younger actors, it has kept the critical spirit alive within the company; that is, whenever production demands aren't so severe as to keep everybody occupied in getting productions on. Indeed, given our material circumstances and the lack of a theater building of our own (our main theater is exorbitant and ill-equipped), a large part of the company's energy—and I mean the whole company, not just the producers—goes into activity that has nothing whatever to do with the art of the theater.

If you keep this hazardous cycle going, and continue to grow, then a part of the audience—those who preferred the earlier intimacy—is disaffected; or a part of the company, those who instinctively equate growth with corruption. (To some our Ford grant was a boon, to some a sellout.) If we were to tally up such criticism, our theater would have been dead more times than the Fabulous Invalid. There is an element of truth in the charges that we can't ignore; yet we can't accede to it either. For we could hardly function at all—we might not even exist—if we were to heed the advice of people who constantly wish on us a purity which they could never exercise in the same position. And the position was that we had chosen to be ourselves while playing the game. We were *a producing theater* with an honest desire for developmental training, but without the facilities or the time for any systematic program—so our productions had to be all things at once.

One could reasonably ask: isn't this the best situation anyhow? Some of the great European companies work in that empirical way. The difference is that, whereas the European companies can count on their actors having been certified in the academies, some of our actors *are* in need of fundamental or continued training. By American standards we take a fair amount of time to teach in rehearsals, but unlike European theaters, we cannot rehearse for three or four months or, as the Ensemble does, for nine months to a year or more.

While we were developing our principles, we had also opened a box office. There was no subsidy at first, and the Ford Foundation underwrote our program according to its principles, maintaining the spirit of free enterprise: the box office had to do its adequate share. And though, with Milton, "I cannot praise a fugitive and cloistered virtue, unexercised and unbreathed, that never sallies out and sees her adversary," let there be no doubt about it, beyond that box office the adversaries are legion—and they rally round that pampered jade of the theater, the Public.

"What services does the theater provide?" asked the chairman of a regional planning group. That depends on what theater you are talking about. For me, I said, the theater does not *provide* services, it *is* a service, a sacrament, a Noh, an offering, not to the Public but to the gods, a fifth Veda to be shared by the people if they are so willing—but, as a result, always in danger of worshiping false gods. The most prominent of these remains Mammon, but there are others: the gods of Geniality, Clubbiness, Temperance, Equivocation, Conformity, all of which reduce the admirable objective "to serve the Community" to an agreeable smile, an obliging front, and the deferent ogle of Orgman, converting service to servility.

We have talked of them before, but it's a subject worth examining further.

As a student, and working with actors, I had recited all the platitudes about loving the audience and feeling them there and feeling them love you, and I had theorized in writing about that mystic current and that mysterious consensus of opinion that is something other than mob thought and, by strange subliminal connections, is wiser than any of its members. I suppose I remain in the theater because, finally, I believe this. But there was always something in me that resisted believing it, and I must confess to distrusting audiences more than I love them.

As I became more familiar with the impure collaborative instruments of the theater, I also wanted them to function with the efficiency of the individual artist. To approach this as a limit, it was necessary to make one assumption: the audience is a datum; it is there. To admit any more than that, I felt, was to insult the people in it. I did not want to play guesswork with their capabilities, nor measure them. If the actor came with an offering, a real honest-to-heart offering, what more could he do? Our job was to bring the best we had in us, our fiercest intelligence, our greatest range of compassion, our deepest analytical powers, the pride of disciplined craft, the incremental wisdom of our own life together, our desire to *see* what was really in the text— and enact that with whatever grace and joy we had in our souls. That was what we had to ask of ourselves; that was all anyone could ask of us. And we had to risk believing—and sometimes saying—that it made no matter what they asked. If I could finally yield to the collective good sense of an audience, guarding among them the inherited wisdom of the race, transcending in some way their personal limitations, I still question their initial judgment.

Give an audience a chance, and it will certainly be wrong.

I don't know why we are so timid about conceding this, considering all the errors to which civilization is liable. Shaw worked on that assumption; Brecht based his theory of Alienation on it; and Jarry, not beating around the box office, expressed my own experience: "We know, from our four years' observation at the Théâtre de l'Oeuvre, that if you're absolutely determined to give the public an inkling of something you must explain it to them beforehand." And he was writing about the audience of one of Europe's most *avant-garde* theaters. Jarry could be pretty bizarre, but in my opinion he is not far wrong when he says it is the natural inclination of the Public to reduce the artist to what they might have written "*in collaboration.*" Jarry asks whether it mightn't be better to consider the Public the other way round, as "a mass—inert, obtuse and passive" that needs "to be shaken up from time to time so that we can tell from their bear-like grunts where they are— and also where they stand. They are pretty harmless, in spite of their numbers, because they are fighting against intelligence. Ubu didn't disembrain all the nobles. They are like Cyrano de Bergerac's Icicle-Animal, which does battle with the Fire-Beast—in any case they would melt before they won, but even if they did win they would be only too honoured to hang the corpse of the Sun-Beast up against their mantelpiece and to allow its rays to illuminate their adipose tissue."

When we consider the history of the modern theater or of modern painting, we recognize this as the kind of hyperbole of Alienation which is almost exact prophecy.

And in our day, virtually every public mode of expression, all our obnoxious mass media verify it. So crippled is judgment becoming in the mass that we are now confronted with the phenomenon of "pseudo-events," those which don't even exist unless they are reported or publicized. Ring Lardner used to say when he watched sportscasters, "This is like a double-header. I'm seeing one game and hearing another." But if today at the ballpark you can see the spectator who sees a play but believes what he hears about it from the sportscaster on his transistor, so you can go to the theater—we all know it— and see audience after audience watching a play with the eyes of the review that brought them there. Nowadays prior explanation is not the answer, but prior publicity. If Jarry seems too perverse or hyperbolic, listen to this judicious voice: "Do you think, Socrates, said Agathon, that my head is so full of theater as not to know how much more formidable to a man of sense a few good judges are than many fools?" And do we need to cull passages from Shakespeare to prove he held similar sentiments?

If this seems too cynical a basis on which to run a theater which depends on an audience, let me say you will not run a significant theater unless you appreciate Jarry's attitude and Agathon's advice. And it seems to me far less cynical than to pretend you are deferring to the wisdom of the audience and then treat it like a patient, whose reflexes can be tapped according to up-to-date surveys on its blood count and biases; and treated to plays, as Kepler said of Osiander's preface to Copernicus, "written by a jackass for other jackasses." You will not run a theater at all if you are not interested in an audience; but as no artist is so arrogant as people who are supporting each other's inadequacies, so nobody is so hypocritical as the person who claims, having nothing to say of which the audience might disapprove, that the Public is always right.

I don't think every play need run over an audience with Ubu's unmentionable mop, but I do agree with Shaw, citing Hamlet, that in a genuine theatrical experience, we are "guilty creatures sitting at a play." And while I am charmed, I do not agree with Sabina in *Skin of Our Teeth* that in the theater people's feelings shouldn't be hurt. If you do anything original, they will be hurt—love them as you will. What keeps the actor there should keep the audience there, but let us hope it is not mere self-gratulation. And certainly it is to do an audience nothing but honor if their predispositions are checked soon after the lights go down. The lights may come up with the audience believing what they believed to begin with, but believing it more ardently for the experience they helped re-enact. Edification is one of the natural functions of the theater, but one would like to have it accompanied by awe, wonder, and an awakened intelligence. In a Giraudoux drama, a man sitting on a bus says of some passers-by: "I am sure they saw a good play last night. Perhaps they don't understand it; but, except for the play, today they understand everything, the beautiful weather, the plane-tree leaves, the horse's ears. . . ." Which suggests that behind this skepticism over the character of the Public is a deeper trust in their capacity to *see* if their weaknesses are not entertained; the old desire for mysterious unity, a fantasy of collective reverence.

Who wouldn't want the theater that is implied in the Panathenaic procession at the end of the *Oresteia,* where the life of the drama flows right into the life of the community, clarifying its laws, and the audience were to go home to carry it on.

In Granville-Barker's *Exemplary Theater* there is a dialogue between a Man of the Theater and the Minister of Education. The Man of the Theater says: "Art is constructive, but it constructs from the elements, as life itself does. Refuse it right functioning, and in its neglect and degradation it does become a disintegrating and . . . as I hold the theater of today to be, . . . an anti-social force." The Minister of Education, who is no slouch either as a businessman or a man of culture, says: "And is it only a coincidence that many of you theater reformers are out after reforming the rest of the universe, too?" I have tried to make it clear that I think the theater in America *is* mostly an anti-social force; I have also tried to make it clear that we started our theater with no intention of reforming the universe. The struggle itself brought on the fantasies of reformation.

We refrained at first from publishing a manifesto such as the Provincetown's, but soon we realized that if we couldn't declare what we wanted to be, there were things we were absolutely certain we *didn't* want to be. However ambiguous our aims, moreover, we sensed this: fighting the waves and sometimes floating on them, we were obliged to help restore to the community a better notion of community than it presently had—for whatever combination of prospects and dangers the period offered us, our first years were lived through an oppressive atmosphere of conformity.

There was an outside factor: the loyalty oath had been legislated in California, and as we were organizing The Workshop, I had become embroiled in the campaign to repeal it. In the beginning I managed to keep my politics, like my ontological rage, out of The Workshop, but as the campaign intensified I became aware of the degree to which undercover surveillance had become a national habit. I saw people betrayed, others abased, and principles flung to the wind. Psychic voyeurism had been given social sanction.

We shall never be able to measure the effect our national cowardice had on the generation that grew up in the shadow of the demagogue, when righteous men were not only turning the other cheek but looking the other way when the injustice became rank. The sins of the fathers are visited upon the sons in both the latent violence and the apathy that we worry about today. Yet the great irony of the period was that even the demagogues had nothing but their passion. McCarthy wasn't a fanatic, but a bully. We knew what he stood against, not for. And it had become apparent that he mightn't have stood at all if more of us had gone to the barricades earlier. In the classroom, I did not watch my words, but it was a period in which one had to be diligent not to watch them—for they were being copied down for purposes beyond their wisdom or examinations.

We are not a political theater, but our first minor step toward identity was made with some political consciousness behind it. When we left our loft to become a theater in the community, we wanted a play that would remember the ancient image of theater as a social force and that would, also, point to specific issues that were beginning to alarm us. There were obviously other reasons for choosing Aristophanes' *Lysistrata,* but aside from the bawdy spirit of the old fertility rites, it was audacious enough, we said, "to make political policy a matter of public interest, and with the courage to insist, in defiance of the demagogues, that each citizen be given the right to judge, debate, and to voice his objections. . . . Written over two thousand years ago —before the black market, the Big Lie, and the Kinsey Report—it is perennially and disarmingly modern."

Of course, though we stressed the parallels, it was more disarming than audacious. We would now probably take more license with the text and find other means, in the music and staging, to give the comedy more thrust. Yet the production was, quite properly for our new home, a festive occasion; we presented a large company with our characteristic energy of performance, and the reception was all we could expect.

It would be a while before we did anything, in my opinion, to outrage a flea; but the production of *Lysistrata* was also the beginning of a conception of a repertoire which we have tried to define over the years. At our Elgin Street warehouse—where we did plays ranging from *Oedipus* to a new American play, David Mark's *Captive at Large*—we acquired a reputation for "thoughtful" or "quality" plays; and later for being *avant-garde*. It made no difference that we were never so experimental as people claimed we were, nor that some of our more experimental plays were ill-attended. They were the ones that gave us character, and we did eventually become, like Aristophanic comedy, something of a public nuisance.

We have been attacked for our egghead pretensions and, in one period, with plays by Brecht, Miller, and O'Casey coming one upon the other, we developed a liberal following and aroused right-wing suspicions. (There were rumblings on the board of the building where we had our theater, owned by the Marine Corps.) Later, when we veered bodily into the quicksand of the Absurd, we dredged out allies in the Underground, but upset some of the liberals, who were by then looking to us for drama with "objective social values," like *The Crucible* and *Mother Courage*. As one person put it, dropping his subscription, we should be providing leadership in the revolt against "the revolt against reason." What has attracted some people to our theater has chased others away. Tempers have been aroused. The darker and wilder our comedies became, the more some people thought us humorless. "Why don't you do a *comedy?*" they would say. "*The Cherry Orchard* is a comedy," I would answer, "Chekhov says so. *Endgame* is a howl." Actually, we had done various conventional comedies along the way, but that they were forgotten is an indication that we were, literally, being taken seriously. And perhaps nothing causes so much resentment among those who would advise us or label us is their inability, when they come to the theater, to pin us down or predict what will confront them.

And it was something more than eclecticism. In the absence of Ideology, confrontation had become a norm. To our audience it may feel sometimes like hostility, sometimes like mere caprice, but we have tried to let everybody know what we were looking into when we seemed arbitrarily to change our course. Though sometimes our audience didn't quite know where we were, they knew increasingly we were *there*.

As for the company, in the summer of 1956 I conducted a seminar, which I introduced by saying that the history of The Workshop was like a dramatic action, not conscious of its own working out. We were actors in the center of an acting area—expending all our energy on play production. Though we had occasionally taken pause for a summary soliloquy, we had no real idea of where we were heading. In some ways we regressed, shifted principles, and squirmed to avoid being pinned down. Was that good? These meetings were the result of growing internal demand for reassessment of purpose. Random in origin, the theater had begun to stand for something that everybody vaguely felt, but that needed definition. Our work contained no explicit "message"; our plays were still heterogeneous. But action somehow works its way toward meaning. There was a tension surrounding our work and in relations with our audience (and with people who never even came to our plays) that was clearly different from what most of our company were used to in the theater. What we were was contained in what we had done and what we had not done, what we had said and failed to say—every choice, grown out of conflict with our plays, our audience, our culture, ourselves, had narrowed down the limits under which we could continue to work.

If there wasn't ideology behind us there was inordinate self-consciousness, including anxiety now over the absence of Ideology.

Nevertheless, while I was personally in the habit of seeing analogies between the slightest gesture on stage and the fate of nations, I was not fooling myself that everybody else saw things the same way. I would not concede the analogies, but I also wanted to stay with the facts. To this moment I am wary of using the editorial *we*. Yet Irving and I were acquiring the authority we lacked at the onset. It was an authority acquired from persistence and survival, as much as from anything we said, though I had for some time been saying more and more. I was also directing more and more, and though some of our actors could never quite rid themselves of their image of me as bookish and intellectual, I had done some of the most "theatrical" of our productions —such as *Camino Real* (which I picked for that reason)—and they were coming to admit there was no insurpassable gulf between mind and passion, between a theater and ideas.

If they didn't admit it, that made no difference. I was, in fact, bookish and intellectual—and made a point of it. And, willy-nilly, we were becoming a theater of ideas—even if they weren't always our own. As Louis Jouvet remarked, however, it is the theater's business to be successful, like any other business. And success, to this wounded Philoctetes, is the giant weapon. To assure everybody that we were by no means cloudy idealists, we carried as a preface to a promotion book the remark of Stanislavski that a theater must be a harmonious working instrument in all its parts, including finances. But our people were beginning to realize that the things which were succeeding for us were often precisely those things thought least likely to succeed. They didn't always make the most money, but they were giving us the prestige and artistic distinction which made zealots—in our company and in our audience. They were the things which made it worth striving for existence, considering the hardships. Beyond that was the incontestable fact that of all the theater enterprises which began in San Francisco after the war, we were the only one to survive, however marginally, on a professional level. I could stop almost any argument with that.

Thus, it was possible that summer to talk of what "we" had done and what "we" aspired to. And we could ask the questions, because people were demanding that they be asked, which we could not ask that first night in the loft: Why does The Workshop exist? What does it really want? What does it *mean?* How do *I* fit in? The meeting was, indeed, a reflective pause in a dramatic action, both probable and necessary.

To know what The Workshop means, I said, we had first to review what it had grown out of. And I proceeded to place it historically as a theater; culturally as a growing institution; and sociologically as a group of individuals. Arthur Miller had written about this time an essay on "The Family and Modern Drama." He said man could not find a home in the world of the Cold War. What about the theater? If we were irresolute, did we not also reflect the overwhelming malaise that was baffling the greatest thinkers and statesmen. That did not excuse us, I added, for it remained the function of art to contend with chaos not to yield to it. If our group seemed quite normal and even bourgeois, we avoided the eccentricity of the members of the Group by being more cautious about causes. But we must not delude ourselves about sparing our energy for the art. Our danger was complacency and the moral listlessness of injured will. Yes, yes, exactly, some of our company felt, we had no activist function. But it's one thing to talk about function and another to exercise it. Here we were, a group of relatively earnest and capable people. What was keeping us from positive social action? Never mind society even, what about our art—why didn't we have a common style?

And if we did, what assurance was there that such a style would constitute the sort of affirmation for which some of us longed? For the desire to emulate the Group that was beginning to arise in some of our people reminded me of academic discussions on Tragedy in the Modern World. Some very great minds have tried to revive the form, but though the problem has been explored in all its ramifications, though we have tried surrogates for choruses and imbedded myths in the Living Room, though we have replaced the old language of tragedy with a Poetry of the Theater—all the strategems come down to the old impasse: we don't have classical tragedy not because we don't have the talent or the will, but because we don't have a classical world.

For ourselves, we couldn't proceed to the question of style—to which issue we would constantly return—until we knew what gestures were credible in the Cold War. Whatever else may be involved, style is only born at the limits of the possible. Possible for *us*.

To review the atmosphere in which we were proceeding, I quoted a speech by J. Robert Oppenheimer, "Prospects in the Arts and Sciences." Dr. Oppenheimer was directing himself to the limits of the possible. He would also be persuasive with those members of the company who, nostalgic about the period of social action, still felt there were easy options to be made on the subject of style: "To the artist's loneliness there is a complementary great and terrible barrenness in the lives of men. They are deprived of the illumination, the light and tenderness and insight of an intelligible interpretation, in contemporary terms, of the sorrows and wonders and gaieties and follies of man's life. . . . One thing that is new is the prevalence of newness, the changing scale and scope of change itself, so that the world alters as we walk in it, so that the years of man's life measure not some small growth or re-arrangement or moderation of what we learned in childhood, but a great upheaval. . . . What is new in the world is the massive character of the dissolution and corruption of authority, in belief, in ritual, and in temporal order. . . . To assail the changes that have unmoored us from the past is futile, and in a deep sense, I think, it is wicked. We need to recognize the change and learn what resources we have."

I took it that he meant the immediate past as well. And what resources did we have? Part of the dilemma, whatever our own want of material resources, is that we were otherwise dazzled by possibility. "For the truth is," Dr. Oppenheimer added, "that this is indeed, inevitably and increasingly an open and, inevitably and increasingly, an eclectic world. We know too much for one man to know much, we live too variously to live as one." Yet there we were, desiring communion in a world fearing that with all its apparatus of transmission, it couldn't communicate.

This was already true, though the thirties had the temerity not to admit it, in those fervent years. Clurman describes a philosophical dispute with his father, who said the Group was "doomed to failure" because it "held to a collective ideal in a competitive society. . . ." Said the old man: "It's a very hard job." Said Clurman: "It's an impossible one."

And hadn't the Group failed? Why were we presuming, then, on the edge of Apocalypse, the competition so fierce it would maybe annihilate us? Was a theater, a true theater, really possible except in the most limited sphere of a commodity system so vast it might have to destroy itself to keep accounts? Surrounded by cultural philistinism and cultural snobbism, by sheer ignorance, self-delusion, treacly good will, and phony value—how significant could we be? And were we exempt? I brought up our own duplicities and our own snobbism—and our own silences.

I reviewed the fact that we were not attached to any social movement; we were a dissociated organism. We were not, like the Group, surrounded by any ideological ferment; nor, like the Vieux Colombier, by public spokesmen and aesthetic programs. We had no literary organ like the *Nouvelle Revue Française*. Most of us were brought up with a conception of theater which is actually anti-literary, anti-artistic, hostile to ideas. We spoke only on stage, and then eclectically, and was that enough?

No manifesto came out of these meetings either. But I did recapitulate what the impediments to purpose were, bringing us closer. If we were seeking form and formulas for the anarchy of modern life, it was our business, first, to prepare ourselves for further seeking. We had to recognize, however evasive it might seem, that there could be no decision on style except by some arbitrary imposition of manner. (Another theater in San Francisco which started about the same time we did made this choice; there were other reasons, but it is now defunct.) Style is neither a prescribed mechanism of performance nor a question of heightened makeup. Unity of behavior on stage comes either out of years of organic collaboration, scrapping, battling, devotion—thoughtless as the wind—or a willing assent to some consolidating perception. Our beliefs were too various and our personnel too doubtful, too caught up (like myself) in the *self*-inquiry of the period to count on the latter. We also had to recognize that certain companies with distinctive styles, say the Group or Joan Littlewood's Theatre Workshop, were distinctive by virtue, too, of what they left out. Eventually, we might have to choose to leave certain things out, lest we cripple ourselves; but it was part of my conditioning, at any rate, to be one of those upon whom, as Henry James said, nothing was lost.

It wasn't, then, that we no longer had anything to say, but that the multiple things to be said tended to cancel each other out; and we hadn't found a style by means of which to say everything simultaneously.

Nor did we have a playwright, a Chekhov or Brecht, to unite us. I was reading new plays constantly and carrying on an enormous critical correspondence, but one reason we didn't do more new plays is that we couldn't find any that really pulled the disparate ends of our disorder together. Not that there were so many plays with even the virtues of technical excellence. As I've said, the best writers in America were not writing for the theater. But we would probably have been compelled to do any number of imperfect plays if we could have found not only an authentic voice but a representative one— a voice that spoke directly, as Odets did for the Group, to the collective anxieties and aspirations of the company. That we couldn't designate anything even remotely like that prevented us all from being very partisan about new plays. (As for myself, I was not writing much drama then. Alan Schneider said to me some years later, "Either you run a theater or you write plays, you can't do both." I now try, and the company has shown devotion to my plays which, however, have not yet solved our problem.)

The company's attitude toward the new play was interestingly demonstrated in our production of *Captive at Large* (1955). David Mark's play was unquestionably the best I had come across in about three years of reading. It has the form of an improvised morality drama, with techniques indebted to Pirandello, Brecht, and the *commedia*. Because character was schematic, some of the actors trained in the naturalistic traditions of the Group complained that the play was "using" them. Some later felt the same way about Brecht, and at this writing the old uneasiness is arising with Genet. (With customary scorn, Genet attributes this to "the haughty stupidity of actors. . . . If, on occasion, their boorishness does subside then lack of culture and shallowness become evident.")

Yet *Captive at Large* is a play that was both topical and technically adroit. It is one of those plays of the "self-conscious stage," in which the theater itself becomes a burning issue, and all of us actors, poseurs, participants. Like the plays of Ibsen, it is a play with a Secret; like some of our recent imports, it is a cryptogram and a charade, a comedy of insidiously serious intent. Moreover, it is a play with a message; its message is its secret; and its secret is the terminus of a series of themes arising from a world in which "issues are born confused." They were precisely our themes. The action is even concerned with an actor who is running away. Yet he wants to be confined; he wants security, standards, and authority; but he will not be coerced. He must be his own master, but he must surrender to know how—and in the process he goes through various modes of authority which are represented by parodies of dramatic form and acting techniques.

The play demonstrates how we become our pretenses and suffer the strain of our imposture. Our melodrama and farce (recorded diligently by the mass media—the climax is a Senate investigation covered by TV cameras) become real, and our reality is made ludicrous by the social forces we design to protect it. "Make of it what you will," the author suggests, perhaps too imitatively. But the play is an argument as well as parody—an effort to induce Man (the name of its abstract hero) to have the courage of his manhood; and it burlesques those forms of society and the theater which make his manhood false and almost impossible.

The drama may, however, be more manipulative than emotionally persuasive, and its nonconventional structure runs over a somewhat too-specific delineation of the issues. For all its atmosphere of obfuscation, one does not feel the confusion in the marrow. And it flounders in part because it tries to have it both ways—that is, because it tries to get at the Human Condition, which seems hopeless, while calling for positive social action. And one does not finally know what to make of it, because the humanity called for struggles against the play's own expertise.

Still, the production (in the round) was tumultuous and engaging, and was generally commended, the most influential of our reviewers writing that the satire was "one of the most hilarious efforts in the history of the local theater. . . ." He compared it most favorably with our production of Camino Real, which had caused a lot of excitement and debate, adding: "And whether you like both or either, San Francisco's new renaissance of live theater is well on its way, whether you like it or not."

Unfortunately, he was premature, because there was no audience for the play. We were in the era of the safe bet—with so much to see and do, people preferred to see what was already authenticated. Though we have done about a dozen new plays over the years, we write them off in advance as losses at the box office. As for some of those who keep urging us to do new plays, or complain that we don't do enough, we are prepared for them to be absent when we do. Certain obscure plays have since become very popular, but they —say The Balcony and Godot—had the advantage of previous notoriety.

Despite the relevance of Captive at Large to our own predicament, the company did not rally round it and call for more of the same. About the public response, of course, they could do very little. But their own response had to do with the abstract formulation of the drama, and the fact that character serviced action instead of becoming it. It wasn't until we first produced Beckett that a drama in this mode, which also deferred to behavior, released intrinsic energies. Though not everybody deferred and though Godot came to us with the advantage of an international reputation, it provided a talismanic rhythm for both our company and our audience. Up to that time, only *Mother Courage* had elicited a similar partisanship.

At the seminar I said that since there was not much inspiring us at home, we might have to continue to look abroad. Roger Stevens and David Merrick, who have since wised up, were not at the time buying up all the rights to European plays, and if we remained alert the best of them were almost immediately at our disposal. Of these, I warned the company, many were likely to seem remote and clannish. Some of them, like the modern poet fracturing language into meaning, would be dislocating action into drama. They might be coded, capricious, and mandarin, titivating over secret pools. But they would be likely to take us into unexplored terrain.

As for American plays (outside of originals), though they would be more comfortable, we had to face the fact that even those we would do were likely to seem parochial and thin beside the European dramas we would be undertaking. We had already done one of the best out of the acknowledged modern repertoire, Miller's *Death of a Salesman*—and that was certainly to our purpose. But I pointed out there is also something suspect about the kind of play they entered too easily, as they did with *Salesman*—a play they got with to the point of tears, at the very first reading. I was quite aware as I said this that some of the plays I might think good for our souls possibly wouldn't move them at all.

I also pointed out that some of the playwrights we had done and most of those we were contemplating—Brecht, Eliot, O'Casey, Sartre, Genet, Beckett, Montherlant, Duerrenmatt, Ghelderode, and even Shaw—were dramatists with social views, techniques, and political sympathies hostile to our own. I thought we ought to consider the implications. If they made no difference, we were really in trouble. If we were to court the abyss, we ought to ponder the risks; and if we were to be a forum, then we had to be sure no voice was wholly lost, especially our own.

Improvising our way, it might be necessary to consider various formulas in order to arrive at our own form, but for the while our Superobjective, if I were forced to state it, was "to create, out of the world which we are given, the peculiar style and distinctive rhythm of *intelligence*." It was hardly satisfactory, being so vague, but to do that I knew we should have to dispel false distinctions between what we like and what we should like; that we would be alienating our audience even as we wooed it; and that we would have to widen the areas in which we felt or had been trained to feel—so that plays foreign to us or with strange dimensions would come alive.

We had to recall, moreover, that the Group, even with the limited range of feeling in its repertoire, could not avoid diffusion. And when we resisted some of these plays, we had to ask what and why we were resisting. While tolerance could be careless, rejection could be boorish, or scared. We didn't want to dismiss what came naturally, but in our easiest flushes of feeling, we had to ask whether there was a good deal we did not want to feel, or of which we were unaware. For with all the knowledge of which Dr. Oppenheimer spoke, the universe was constantly expanding beyond our reach. At the same time we had to trust our craft, ourselves, and what we did know, for as he said: "Never before today has the integrity of the intimate, the detailed, the true art, the integrity of craftsmanship and the preservation of the familiar, of the humorous and the beautiful stood in more massive contrast to the vastness of life, the greatness of the globe, the otherness of people, the otherness of ways, and the all-encompassing dark."

Looked at again, here was the basis for another return to classicism, a respect for limits, brought on by the overpowering strangeness (if not estrangement) of a world that had not been wholly remade in the thirties. Yet it was that dark, rather, which would soon command a lot of our attention, and paradoxically give us more direction.

Meanwhile, if we had started out drifting, it was possible to defend drift as a matter of principle. "I do not know," Symonds wrote me when I was abroad, drifting, in 1959, "I do not know what is to become of our theater." Looking at us from a distance, I had apparently regretted that our theater had no *cause* to fight for. (It may have been after I did an article on Littlewood and Planchon.) I must have given the impression that I thought a cause was a necessity, and Symonds said he was skeptical: "This has been true for the last 75 years because the theater itself has become debased and those few earnest persons working in it were grasping for something outside to pull it up. But the true theater stands much more at the center of life reflecting whatever forces play upon it and radiating an energy of its own. I cannot believe that the theater of Molière or of Shakespeare derived its basic vitality from any cause or program. But rather it is the social phenomenon of many artistic individuals under the stress of the times and the need for survival, being shaped together into what becomes a true theater. This cohering of personalities—in Molière's theater, Shakespeare's and our own—is almost as much a biological phenomenon as a social one. There is both purpose and chance in finding compatible types."

With more or less variation in the strain, we had found our compatible types, and in the absence of a program, the biological need for survival has served as a rallying point. Even where the coherence of the company yields to the lure of New York, so that one is tempted to ask in exasperation What company?, there is the *Zeitgeist* into which one steps now, for better or worse, when he joins us—and, as I have said, it is that nucleus of cohering personalities which draws like adamant our faltering hearts. Of course we hadn't a Molière or a Shakespeare to write the time for us—as Eliot once put it. Nor could our time be written in quite the same way. We could see analogies between the seventeenth century's dread of immensity and the terrors of our own leaping universe. We would explore these analogies, but our universe seemed to be leaping in ways that were not wholly dreamed of in the avid skepticism of the Renaissance, with its medieval moorings. Or if they were dreamed, dreaming our own dreams, we had to rediscover that archaic wealth.

In a world of vast momentum and diffused energies, one thing seemed clear: no single play was an adequate abstract and brief chronicle of the time. Or at least, to date, no modern play—as Francis Fergusson observed in *The Idea of a Theater*—has put "all the modes of human action in ordered and rhythmic relationship." There are monuments in our literature. In them, transfigured beyond history, reality may be seen in the round—in myth, dream, trope, and anagoge, as well as the aspiration and beautiful failure of reason. We wonder how to imitate them and where to place them. Unlike the Elizabethan theater, with its architectural Chain of Being, our stagehouse no longer seems to be a comprehensive reflection of the Human City. Or if it does (I am thinking of the theaters we play in), we could despair over the City and desire our own monuments. The glorious heritage makes us more forlorn. We envy the analogues and live by fragments. And as nature assumes more and more the elusive character of unpredictable particles, "our playwrights (like hunters with camera and flashbulbs in the depths of the Belgian Congo) are lucky if they can fix it, at rare intervals, in one of its momentary postures, and in a single bright, exclusive angle of vision." When reality dissipates at the touch of enlightenment, like the electron consumed in the act of measurement, the task of a theater, or rather its only choice, may be to grasp at the emanations.

The trouble with the grasping is that it still left the question of style up in the air. If we could settle on a certain kind of play, we might have solved the problem out of hand. But we chose to do everything. Thus, when I was abroad I was still improvising over the subject of style. R. G. Davis, a mime then with our company, wrote a letter in which he said, "yes we have a style. . . . Naturalistic vague Americana with some presentational leanings, but for me this is not quite satisfying. It's hard I'm sure to put down what the Workshop's style is, it is undoubtedly yours and Jules' but can you (all) nail it down? Can you make a list something like Brecht's—the Don'ts and Do's of the Actor's Workshop Style?"

I might have made such a list, and presently it might have become directive, but it was against my inclination. I preferred to answer with the following parable and the sort of evasive reflection that didn't satisfy me either, but that wasn't too far from the most truthful account of our predicament: "While the Ghibellines and the Guelphs were scrapping over the Tuscan countryside, Catherine, the saint of poverty, rose from her penitence stone and bossed the Popes around. Just before we left Florence this morning for Siena, I read an article on Paul Getty, the richest man in the world, with an Oxford education and a rare collection of French furniture. When asked wasn't he scared to risk a lot of millions on a deal that wouldn't move, he said: 'One must learn to wait.' It's a pretty trite remark, except when you have all those millions to back it up. Though Getty has half the oil in Saudi Arabia and Catherine had nothing but her sackcloth, I respect them equally, as I've always believed in the power of the private vision, whether mad, moneyed, or mystical.

"Vision, sure of itself, learns to wait. For me, that's style. I think it's a little easier for the moneyed or the mystic (even secular mystics, like Marxists). For those of us who have only our madness, our art is the means and process of finding out what our style is. How can I know what I mean until I see what I say? It may be that at The Workshop we've been a long time saying it, but then, as Americans, we have a lot more to talk about, we having their past (the European, that is) and all our uncatalogued present. There is also this: it's harder to be the man in public that you are in solitude, and the theater, more in America than elsewhere, puts up its defenses against private vision. As I've always maintained, the marvel of The Workshop is the unity it has achieved, not that which nobody has—it has its eclectic ups and downs, but you can't put tumbleweed and driftwood together and expect them to come up tulips; even man had to go through all the stages of evolution. This is not beating around the vegetation—the point is you don't make up destinies overnight. If I could have named a style before this, I would have; but every nail you put in my style closes my coffin. . . ."

Given these ruminations, the notion of a program or an ideological solution became even less tenable. I was partially playing with words, but it was the best I could do; and the words were indeed defining a kind of cultivated indecision, a way of perceiving, which was more prominent in my productions after I returned. And the very drift of our theater became another example of the tendency of modern art—imposed by default, fear, and aroused will— to trust itself alone; that is, instead of a program, *process*. The letter concluded: "You know a man by the experiments he chooses to make—that's part of style. Dictum: you are not talking about style when you speak of melodrama, farce or theatrical styles, or getting an actor to smoke cigarettes in each style. Not in my lexicon. Just as to say an actor who can't move can't act is also missing the point. Move how? in what direction? for what purpose? . . . That doesn't mean . . . actors shouldn't be highly trained, as musicians are trained. I believe most certainly in the perfection of skills. But style exists somewhere between a play and what you choose to make of it, somewhere between the lizard and the stone, in the path of perception in a world of only partial rights. Style is risk. Style becomes form with every lucky jump in the dark.

"To cut down whatever excess of chance there may appear in this, let me add I'm betting on the guy who is trained to jump. . . but I might also bet more on the guy who just wants to see what's on the other side."

What a relief it would have been if there were something ideological to grasp at, to cut down the risk! If there were, I'm sure we would have all grasped and been glad of it. In its absence and with this shaky definition of style, the task of creation would remain the same—ardor and labor and technique; no program would change that anyhow, though it might keep us from having to find all the radiant energy of which Symonds spoke in ourselves. As opposed to those among us who wanted to create a program by fiat, Symonds was certainly right, and we had no alternative. But the hazard of "reflecting whatever forces play upon" us is that of the weathervane which merely whirls in the wind.

What would have to govern us, we could agree, is "the true art, the integrity of craftsmanship," and while we deferred to the intimate and the detailed, we would also have to press ourselves to think large and see as far as possible, to make everything human our province, raiding the borders of the invisible —even as we settled back upon ourselves in the social security of craft and the solace of production.

In that same letter which Symonds wrote to me in Europe, he gave a report on the activities of the company during the summer of 1959: "I wish you could have been here during this last month, because in many ways it seemed to indicate what the rhythm of our daily life is to become in the future. Wednesday, Thursday and Friday saw the successful revival of *The Crucible,* Saturday *The Entertainer* at Marines and the Noh plays [modern versions by Yukio Mishima, produced for the first time in America] at the Encore, and Sunday nights we continued with *Endgame.* All had very special and lively audiences. At the same time *The Busy Martyr* [a new play by George Hitchcock] was in rehearsal, *The Plaster Bambino* [a new play by Sidney Michaels] and *Epitaph for George Dillon* in the planning and I had a set of workshops going. The rhythm I speak of, however, is not just that of stepped-up activity. What I really mean is that the actual performing of three such varied and positive dramatic events as *Entertainer, Crucible* and *Endgame* set up a kind of cultural counterpoint within the company. Of course, I was uniquely aware of it because I was playing a major role in each. But I do feel that for each member of the company there was something going on which he could identify with and defend as an artist. Immediately at hand there were points of comparison."

So: in the cracked perspective of the Cold War, the play was not the thing, the repertoire was. It was the consensus of our distracted opinion. It exposed our conflicting emotions. In a period of taxation without any conceivable representation, it represented us partially—and impartially. It permitted us those "momentary postures"; we could take a stand, and change our minds. Any given play was subject to suspicion and chagrin; its limits were our liabilities. If we were confronted with the dark, the theater was a seeing eye. And by engaging us onstage and offstage, kaleidoscopically, with all the main obscurities of the period, it eventually turned our sights on the unencumbered Self, unaccomodated man—whom we also found wanting.

The danger of constant shifting was the powerlessness I have talked about. The constant check on the refusal to choose was the prodding of our critical instincts.

"Tell me, Grumio, how goes the world?"

"It's a cold world, therefore fine."

Some of the plays we have done would pick a quarrel with Grumio, some would defend him. But Grumio is no mere fool. What we have been trying to find out in the most significant of our plays is whether Grumio is telling the truth. Some of these plays go directly to the question, some are more circuitous, some try to refute Grumio by giving other evidence of the world's temperature. In turn, we quarreled with some of the plays, even in the doing, and defended some of them against those who quarreled with us for having done them. Equivocation over Grumio's view, the searching of his tone, became the source of style. One wants to live in his world, whatever the temperature, as best he can, according to his soundest principles, however shifting. If not by program, then by shaping behavior to principle by instinct, clarifying principle as you go. One needn't be an environmental determinist to know that in the theater, more than any other art, the aesthetic temperature is affected by the moral climate of our public life. Though art may be the strongest climate for art, the theater shakes conspicuously in all weather.

I have tried to show how the history of The Actor's Workshop reflected the indecisiveness of a nation in sustained crisis. It could drive you to despair. A year after we began, Robert Lowell wrote of "Inauguration Day: January 1953":

> Ice, ice. Our wheels no longer move.
> Look, the fixed stars, all just alike
> as lack-land atoms, split apart,
> and the Republic summons Ike,
> the mausoleum in her heart.

The inauguration of John F. Kennedy in 1961 was full of promise and proposed audacity, and seemed to announce the entry of style into public affairs. Poets are professional worriers about style, and I'm not sure the performance of the Kennedy administration substantially changed their tune. Nevertheless, it is surely rare when someone in the center of political life brings up the subject in Congress. In Washington, on June 29, 1961, Senator Fulbright made a speech in which he said that America, as leader of the democratic revolution, must be assured in principle, and not wage the Cold War by fighting the fire of the enemy with fire. "It is style—our performance as a nation and a great power—that determines the credibility of our policies. In the present struggle, style is as important as power." One might add—what General de Gaulle and the artists know—that style *is* power. Senator Fulbright listed among American "lapses" in style our shaky position on neutralism, our heavy emphasis on massive retaliation, and the Cuban invasion. *The New York Times* reported that when he rose to speak, after having pondered the question of style for some time, "the floor was largely abandoned. Those present were eager to get on with other work and in no mood to listen. Mr. Fulbright read a few paragraphs and inserted the rest in the record."

Whatever our own uncertainties of style in this period, there was a time when we did plays as almost anybody might have done them. We may not be able to get up a full list of Don't's and Do's, but I don't think this is entirely true now. If there was any evolution toward identity, it came out of the developing sense that much of what was important in our lives was being ignored or merely inserted in the record. Soon, when put the question, I would say the purpose of The Workshop was to save the world. If the theater, however, gave us a platform, we didn't merely sound off, because the plays compelled us to face the issues as they are not often faced in Washington, and the issues in turn, prodded by voices from within us, came back to plague and shape the plays.

Our production of *King Lear* was to be, perhaps, the most majestic expression of this collective self-analysis, which cuts to the brain. Whose brain? Even the most disinterested among us couldn't help but be affected. Our most significant productions were the most threatening. Like John Whiting's *Saint's Day,* which enraged a good part of our audience, and didn't last long, they remained in the atmosphere of our enterprise. The production of *Lear* was for us a momentary terminus of our search in the dark, and the base for new proceedings. Whatever else it may have been, it couldn't have been what it was without our self-conscious history. It offered a provisional style, upon which we still draw. Certain productions before it, such as *Endgame,* stood in relation to it as pilot projects. In that relation lurks a meaning, which I shall trace later as a commentary on the ubiquitous question of style, and its relation to belief.

Our activity is not always so prolific, however, as it was the summer of Symonds' letter. In the 1962–63 season, we abandoned a full-scale repertory schedule, lest the ambition become a mere burden. Artistically, we prefer it and hope to return to it; economically, and physically, it is at present unnegotiable. But there are at least two plays in production and generally two in rehearsal, and very likely others will be maintained for revivals and tours. There are also children's theater plays and a high school program (e.g., comedy from Aristophanes to Ionesco). For all our searching, so much activity has touched on a lot that was merely familiar. If we were to do one or two productions a year, they might be entirely original—but then, we might have to be entirely subsidized. We have chosen certain plays because, following the old saw, they were to make money to support our more "experimental" efforts. Some did, some didn't. We picked certain plays to relieve the distress of our audience. Some of those distressed them even more. Whatever concessions we have made over a given season (and they were concessions only by our own standards), there were still casualties among our subscribers. (If San Francisco was not exceptional in response to us, I recognize that no other city would have responded any more.) And a running dialogue developed not only within the company but with our audience over the nature of the repertoire.

A couple of years ago, responding to vociferous complaints over the difficulty and darkness of some of our plays, I wrote a short piece to our audience on "The Meaning of Repertory." Assuming the unemployment problem as a datum, I examined the revival of interest in repertory theaters in America after the dearth of the forties. The last paragraphs summarize what we had

come to believe about the function of our theater by the end of the fifties—
and what we wanted our audience (and the company) to accept as the bedrock motives behind any concessions we would make: "The desire for repertory grew in the last decade with uneasiness over the way our excess of
freedom and the agencies meant to service it . . . *seemed* to deprive us of a
public voice.

"Repertory, which is not just a lot of plays but a certain relationship
among plays over a sustained period of time, speaks to this anxiety in the
permanent rapport of a particular company and a particular audience. It
directs itself, by inviting diversity of viewpoint, to whatever is most civic and
civil in man, to his essential brotherhood, his social intelligence, and his
instincts for secular communion. Whatever there is in drama of the secret
life of the race is made, presumably by common consent, the subject of a
public spectacle, which is one reason why the theater is a risky medium and
has been at times scorned, attacked and even closed down. It is our belief,
however, that a theater is the one civic institution in which security demands
that secrets be declared illegal.

"There are occasions when the theater must do its work against what
passes for common consent, to appear to say, 'To hell with society!'—as
Mother Courage did in one way, *Waiting for Godot* in another. The theater
must be for the public welfare without being at public disposal; it must act
collectively with the estranged passion of the individual will. In any repertoire
there will be few enough plays which have this unique passion, the curious
sorcery of persuasion that forces what we'd prefer not to see past our common
resistance. We shall do them when we're able, old and new. But this passion,
this will and this sorcery (for what is theater without magic?) must be
preserved whatever form a repertoire takes. And, in our indecisive and
trembling age—pondering Laos, Cuba, Space, and nuclear deterrents—there
must be that kind of imagination withal that brings courage and joy, not
false optimism or uplift, to humanity's constant war against the outrages it
commits on itself."

ENDGAME BY SAMUEL BECKETT

On the cracked landscape of extinction, precision is next to godliness.

Tom Rosqui as Clov, Robert Symonds as Hamm

GALILEO by Bertolt Brecht

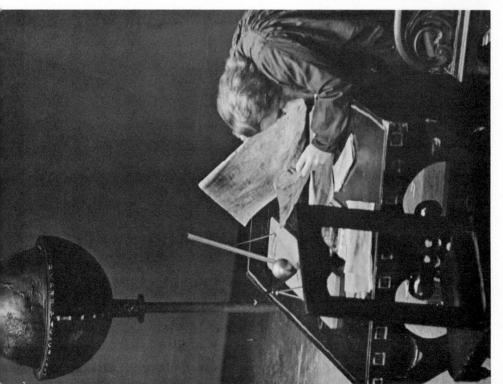

Robert Symonds as Galileo

THE BALCONY BY JEAN GENET

Depravity is a sacrament, . . .

Ray Fry as the Bishop, Ruth Breuer as the Penitent; Irving Israel as the Flagellant, Nancy Bond as the Whip Girl

. the perversions are the basis of Style.

ul Rebillot as the Judge, Sally Ann Parsons as the Thief, Edward Winter as the Executioner

"Crack nature's moulds, all germens spill at once
That makes ungrateful man!"

Michael O'Sullivan as Lear; Beatrice Manley as Regan, Robert Haswell as Cornwall; Lear (behind the map of his kingdom), Regan, and Shirley Jac Wagner as Goneril

Tom Rosqui as Musgrave, Robert Haswell as Atterbury

"We are each one guilty of particular blood."

PLOUGH AND THE STARS BY SEAN O'CASEY

rice Manley as Jennie Gogan, Don Cross as Sergeant Tinley

THE BIRTHDAY PARTY BY HAROLD PINTER
"...it's funny, then it's no longer funny."

Robert Doyle as Stanley, seated; Edward O'Brien, blindfolded, as McCann; also, Robert Symonds, Joyce Lancaster, Barbara Melandry

THE THREE SISTERS BY ANTON CHEKHOV
Nothing is more real than nothing, except people.

Priscilla Pointer as Masha, Winifred Mann as Olga, Susan Darby as Irina

PHOTOGRAPHS BY: Chic Lloyd: *Endgame, King Lear, Serjeant Musgrave's Dance, The Birthday Party, The Three Sisters;* Hank Kranzler: *Galileo, The Balcony;* Ted Streshinsky: *The Plough and the Stars.*

7

To think of an individual fulfilling his subjective needs through social action, to think of him as living most completely when he lives most socially, to think of him as doing this, not as a social worker acting out of conscientious motives but naturally, without guilt or sense of oddness—this is difficult for us to imagine. . . .

—Arthur Miller, preface to *View from the Bridge*

The solution which we are striving towards is only one of the perhaps possible solutions to the problem which is this: How can the theater be both entertaining and instructive at the same time? How can it be drawn away from a place of illusion to a place of practical experience? How can the shackled, ignorant, free-dom- and knowledge-seeking human being of our century, the tormented and heroic, abused and ingenious, the changeable and the world-changing human being of this frightful and important century achieve his own theater which will help him to master not only himself but also the world.

—Bertolt Brecht, "On Experimental Theater"

How much shall I be chang'd
Before I am chang'd.

John Donne's motto at eighteen

COUNTERFORCE I:
The Social Drama

The notion of theater as the public art of crisis, advanced early in this book, derives from the elemental image of the actor in the center of an acting area. He can choose to act out of some rationalized sense of responsibility, or he can waive responsibility as irrelevant and act to stake out an existence, creating himself out of nothing. The motives are not always clearly separable, and in the highest drama they merge in curious ways. *Who am I? Who says so?* (Maybe even, *Who cares?*) The actor may try to deny it, but in his most religious inwardness he knows that somebody is watching.

That image, or conceit, was the aesthetic currency of the period, but it came to focus for me, environmentally, against the blocked window of our Judo Academy loft. "As the Eye is formed," says Blake, "such are its Powers." The loft might have become, given our menacing world and my own fear of the unauthentic, a "nonworld" of introjected abstraction. Indeed, that impulse grew both inside and outside as the power of other forms, par-ticularly Action painting, prevailed upon us. (Again I hesitate to speak for "us." Our older people, generally, were hostile to abstract expressionism—some of them made fun of the exhibitions we had in our lobbies. But our younger people, generally, were hooked. Well-disposed myself, I know we are better off for the resistance.) The impulse remains, but it has never been pure, and our early plays by no means contained it.

As I have indicated, if they weren't from Broadway, they were mainly plays from the standard repertoire. However uniquely we might have done them, they were rooted to a distinct world of identifiable value, even if they were plays of protest. The variable factor was ourselves. But even in a play by Chekhov, personal variation is limited by the character of the action and by our own acceptance of the world it puts in question.

As you move toward what the painters call "breakthrough," the question becomes how much of this world are you willing to give up? It may even become, how much of you really exists about which you can ask Who am I? I have already suggested that while another art may banish all but purely self-bound aesthetic motives, the theater may follow in its wake only so far. I recall when we were rehearsing *King Lear,* our designer Robert La Vigne was doing a huge ravaged bas-relief as an encasing background. It was made of two parallel cycloramas, which he was ripping and tying into abstraction. Alone on stage, demonic, he would stalk the cycs with a jackknife, climb a ladder, and make another gash. Deep in the bosom of the auditorium he would relish those pure forms. Then an actor would cross, and he was outraged. La Vigne is normally responsive to actors and, facing human facts, picks up their rhythms as he works. But for that unnerving instant, he was confronted by the uncontrollable mystery on two legs. For all his vaunted subjectivity, the actor there, the nonobjective darkling splendor was brought to earth.

Axiom for abstractionists: the presence of the actor keeps the theater *objective.*

La Vigne wasn't the first to discover there is a jetty built into the form beyond which you may go if you are willing to give up the theater. Or against which, if you refuse, you may rage. For the seeker of the inviolable Self and the pure creative act, that's what makes the theater impossible. While a Jackson Pollock may extend the canvas into a battlefield, paint searching the psyche in dramatic conflict, he will generally stay out of the theater ("The weather of his stage, himself").

One of the significant tendencies of modern art (the seed of a criticism worth developing) is the way it has tried to appropriate all the powers of the theater without its pragmatic rigors. Which accounts for a new, immensely powerful form of closet "drama." We speak of the dramatic lyric, Action painting, and concrete music, but we mean an art intensely personal and retiring, an infolding vision. The secret powers of this art are now finding their way back into the theater, and I shall discuss the results in our work in the next chapter. But even then, whatever the sense of isolation, whatever the possession by pure Self, one is drawn in the theater to confess the lure of Community, and the conspicuous anxiety that there is no Self without the Other. Whatever the temptation of the solipsistic abyss in a more singular art (and it would not be long after we began that Pollock, Charlie Parker, and James Dean were dead) the theater, collecting disparate and desperate wills, is prone to pause at the brink.

If the repertoire unfolded, then, through one play after another, a bewildering spectrum of motives—as Strindberg says of *Miss Julie,* "the richness of the soul-complex"—it also forced us back, whenever we strayed, to the agitations of Society. In our career, the arc of self-interest swung across the zone of crisis between commitment and disaffiliation, which is not mere indifference. (If memory serves, it was John L. Lewis who said: "We disaffiliate!") At one extreme, a play such as *The Crucible;* at the other, *The Balcony.* Practically every mode of make-believe lies in the territory between. Practically every issue of style, which is an assertion of identity. And every crux and gravity of the Cold War.

Whether the Cold War thwarts the new revolutions or is subsumed by them, the dynamic is so tense and complicated that our sense of crisis is amplified. Moreover, in the twentieth century, we have had bad memories. Ruminating on the wreckage, Jean-Paul Sartre declared in a famous phrase that "Man is a useless passion." On that basis, he developed a philosophy of commitment. Dwelling on the appeal of despair, theologian Paul Tillich urges the courage to be. Psychoanalyst Erik Erikson, confronted with fractures of the psyche, writes: "We will never know what this life was like before it was disrupted, and in fact we will never know what this life was like before we became involved in it." *Involvement* and *Commitment*—these were the clichés of the period; being *in there* and (to use the updated labor jargon of the Action painters) *not to fink out,* to show courage in the absence of hope. Our period moves so fast that, as our most *avant-garde* artists may use anything from clock mechanisms to old condoms for a collage, so our clichés, fecundating, are not exhausted.

Is man a useless passion? He is sure to be if he finks out. Whether he chooses himself or another, the force of a drama depends on the acceptance of rupture in human affairs, and the quality and intensity of involvement. I am not speaking merely of empathy, but what is at stake in the disruption, including the choice to make absolute rupture a way of life.

The drama is a postlapsarian form, born of the Fall. And its commitment to Action (the price of atonement?) makes it responsible to problems of choice and identity. If the theater is an insubstantial pageant, its merit depends on the degree to which—by projecting their changing appearance—it clarifies the disruption of our lives.

In this chapter, I shall be dealing with some plays from our repertoire whose appearance is that of Social Drama; that is, with some definite stake in the existing order of things, even if they incite to rebellion. Every call for change sinks the stake further in established ground. As we shall see, the urgency may be so great that we touch upon bedrock; that is, we may reach a point in any of these plays where it acquires the properties of existential drama. Which need not be surprising, given the true nature of dramatic form.

From here on the focus will be on plays and what they meant to us in production, and afterwards. As before, I shall set them in orbit around the world from which they came and on which they look back, often flashing signals from the unknown. Over the years we have done nearly a hundred productions, some of which were more successful (in various ways) than those I choose to discuss. The ones I shall talk about linger somehow in the life of the company, remaining points of reference, either because they were important to our growth, or because they taxed our craft, or because they embody some theme, theory, or influence I want to explore. I shall follow no particular mode of analysis; the plays were important to us for different reasons—in some instances, for their failure. With some, I shall carry on a critical dialogue. Where I don't talk much about the production itself, it is either because we did nothing unusual with the play or because it meant more to us in other ways.

In the strict technical sense, some of our plays required more stylistic consideration than others. Some we just did, feeling confident they could just be done without our worrying about how. Sometimes, we learned to our disaster, we should have worried. And as a matter of policy, we worry more now, whatever the play. Still, in a generation compulsively engaged with technique, and obsessive about being original, one of the things we had to learn was how to live with our skill when we had it—to have the full courage of our facility. There are certain productions which simply do not tax your deepest resources; they neither open wounds nor greatly extend your range. They are, maybe, valuable as confirmation. True, every play is a new experience, like every day in one's life, but some days are more demanding than other days. I bring this up because, with everyone being zealous these days about organic art, about making things come naturally, it is easy to be embarrassed when they do.

In discussing the productions, I shall want to complete the image of the Cold War as seen through the theater, and my image of the theater as seen through the Cold War. I shall want to develop further the idea of theater as the public art of crisis. For whatever limitations any of these plays may have, or their productions, they were for me part of a Counterforce in that war of humanity against the outrages it commits upon itself.

When Arthur Miller revived the term Social Drama in his preface to *A View from the Bridge,* he was tired of the weeping willowiness of our plays of lyric neurosis. He was also wary of the tougher drama of estrangement, whether elegiac (Beckett) or swollen to grandeur by threat and malice (Genet)— making the outcast into a principle of being. What he wants in Social Drama "is the drama of the whole man." In the introduction to the *Collected Plays,* he said he saw something like it in the drama of Brecht. While he could not agree with his "concept of the human situation" (meaning his politics, I suppose), he did feel that Brecht was working "not on the periphery of the contemporary dramatic problem, but directly upon its center—which is . . .

the problem of consciousness." To achieve consciousness, however, one needs to believe in Society.

If it doesn't assume it, the Social Drama is a drama in search of a body politic. For Miller, a social humanitarian, it comes out of the desire to make sense of the word "individual" in a mass society, increasingly deprived of identity by machines and machine politics and machine values. It also comes from his rather academic preoccupation with the tragic form, where self-realization, the quest of the dramatic hero, is prefigured in the myths and mores of his people. The word "individual," which once meant "inseparable," now usually means "alienated." What Miller is after, almost against the evidence of modern experience, is a drama in which the individual is not an "individual in his own right," but in relation to universal substance and the polity as a whole.

Both tragic drama and the idea of heroism floundered when personal right, becoming a mandate, got lost in the press of the crowd. And even more so when the private life of men became inconsistent with the generally approved definitions of Man. Or when definition floundered in the nihilistic possibility of there is nothing either good or bad but thinking makes it so. The classical trilogy of *Oedipus* shows that, after banishment and disgrace, the final resting place of the outcast is within the City limits. With *Hamlet,* however, the slaughters seem more accidental, the spectators more self-conscious, and it is a stranger who supervises the burial and bids the soldiers shoot. From the beginning, Elsinore is less a City than a state of mind. For a dramatist like Beckett, there is no refuge, as there is only the career of the outcast. We live astride the grave; indeed, we are born to it: "Down in the hole, lingeringly, the gravedigger puts on the forceps." Man's quest for resolution in society is the quest of the psychotic in an armed madhouse, going from one lunatic asylum to another. The only refuge is the closed world of the dispossessed Self, divided against itself; not even the "individual in his own right," for we suffer by nature from impossible dependencies and existential drainage, like the bald patch of Tolstoy's Vronsky, who has pride in himself as a social being. ("Why do we go on tormenting ourselves," says Vronsky, "when everything might be arranged so well?") The drama of Krapp is a drama of the bald patch, mulling over old love. In such a drama Law is a fiction, part of the gibberish of Lucky's speech—a matter of chance, mocked by the firm of "Feckham Peckam Fulham and Clapham."

To Miller, Law is as real as Society. A man may exceed its limits, but the Law is confirmed by excess. Even revolt is dedicated to its preservation. And, as opposed to Beckett or Kafka's *The Trial,* there is access to the Law. Unlike Genet, Miller could never celebrate the frightening dominance of illusion and mutability. The power of change remains in the hands of men; it is a matter of will, operating in a social framework.

Nevertheless, Miller, having seen *The Blacks,* talks now of a Theater of Essences and leads us to anticipate a breakthrough. To date, however, he has been laboring the old forms. He tells us that *Death of a Salesman* destroys the boundaries between now and then in "a mobile concurrency of past and present." But though his argument about the richer scene-changing potential of language as compared to the visual images of film has merit, the treatment of Time in *Salesman* (and in his new play *After the Fall*) seems amateurish compared to that of, say, *Marienbad,* with its multiple series of presences, including several conflicting views of the past, various routes to the present (ambiguously there like hallucination), a realized but contradictory future, and even adumbrations of a reality that may, for all we know, only be wished for. If not flashback, we have in *Salesman* the manipulable Time of a radio drama, "as mad as Willie and as abrupt and as suddenly lyrical," but limited by his derangement so that, wherever he may be, we know exactly where we are.

Now, while this lacks the sophisticated confusion of a *nouvelle vague* film, it may be more of a virtue than we care to remember. And something quite valid is being kept alive in the theater by a playwright who insists, while everybody is relishing confusion as a norm, that the function of drama is to search for "a standard of values that will create in man a respect for himself, a real voice in the fate of his society, and, above all, an aim for his life which is neither a private aim for a private life nor one which sets him below the machine that was made to serve him."

It was another play by Miller, striving to achieve this image in a rather conventional form, that had the most resounding influence on our developing audience. Even to this day, a revival of *The Crucible* will take up slack at the box office. Whatever that may be a sign of, in our theater there was no doubt the reign of McCarthy had a lot to do with its initial success. Miller, however, has tried to minimize the immediate parallel: "It was not only the rise of 'McCarthyism' that moved me, but something which seemed more weird and mysterious. It was the fact that a political, objective, knowledgeable campaign from the far Right was capable of creating not only a terror, but a new subjective reality, a veritable mystique which was gradually assuming even a holy resonance."

The mystique was resonating into an even more subtle shape than Miller had imagined. But while it lacked the terrifying impartiality of greater drama, *The Crucible* had nevertheless the vehemence of good social protest. The play was unevenly cast, put into rehearsal in haste (lest somebody take advantage of the release of rights before we did), the director was replaced after about three weeks, but the actors, upon whom the drama makes no special demands, played it with fervor and conviction if not subtlety. And in our program notes we stressed the McCarthy parallel, speaking of guilt by association and Ordeal by Slander.

The production made us a lot of liberal friends. They are all, all honorable men, but while I have signed the same petitions, that friendship in the theater has always been a little unsettling and subsequent plays have borne out my feeling that if we have the same politics, we do not always have it for the same reasons. While the power of mass psychosis is one of the strongest elements in the play, there is a melodrama in the fervency that always made me uncomfortable. When I brought it up, it made others uncomfortable. But I think it behooves us to understand both the appeal and limitations of those forceful drama—one of those which seems effective so long as it is even middlingly well played, and despite its fate on Broadway.

The Puritan community, as Hawthorne knew in *The Scarlet Letter,* is the ideal setting for a realistic narrative of allegorical dimensions. As Miller puts it, drawing on the annals of the Salem trials: "To write a realistic play of that world was already to write in a style beyond contemporary realism." And there is a powerful admonition beyond that in Proctor's final refusal to be *used.* Like Miller before the congressional committee, he will not lend his name to the naming of names. On this level the play has authority, and it serves as an exemplum. Several critics have pointed out that the analogy between witches and Communists is a weak one, for while we believe in retrospect there were no witches, we know in fact there were some Communists, and a few of them were dangerous. (If Miller were another kind of dramatist, he might claim there *were* witches, but we shall come to that in a moment.) Yet as a generalization, the play's argument is worthy; as a warning against "the handing over of conscience," it is urgent; and to the extent his own public life has required it Miller has shown the courage of his convictions beyond most men—and hence has some right to call for it. One might still wish he were more inventive in form, but in a period where the borders between art and anarchy are ill-defined, we might apply the caution stated in II Corinthians: "All things are lawful, but not all things edify." It is no small thing to say *The Crucible* is an edifying drama.

What the play does not render, however, is what Miller claims for it and what is deeply brooding in the Puritan setting: "the interior psychological question," the harrowing descent of mass hallucination into the life of the individual, where value is deranged, no reason is right, and every man drives his bargain with the sinister. One sees this in *The Brothers Karamazov,* which Miller invokes as that "great book of wonder," and more relevantly in *The Possessed,* where political evil is the reptilian shadow of indecipherable sin. For Proctor, a sin is *arranged,* so that his guilt might have cause. All we can say is: that is not the way it is. For Miller, a psychosis is no more than a psychosis, with clear motive and rational geography. The symptoms are fully describable. His love of wonder is deflated by his desire "to write rationally" and to put a judgmental finger on "the full loathesomeness of . . . anti-social action." The desire is admirable, but the danger is to locate it in advance. Studying Dostoyevsky, Miller had resolved to "let wonder rise up like a mist, a gas, a vapor from the gradual and remorseless crush of factual and psychological conflict." But while that is a good description of the source of wonder in Dostoyevsky, Miller is restive in the mist, which in Dostoyevsky is thickened to nightmare by every wincing judgment and every laceration of meaning, writhing in the imminence of wrong.

By contrast, we know only too well what *The Crucible* means, nor were the issues really ever in doubt. Wanting to write a drama "that would lift out of the morass of subjectivism the squirming, single, defined process" by which public terror unmans us, Miller fills in the record with the adultery of John Proctor and Abigail Williams. He thus provides the rationalist's missing link to the mystery of the crying out. The adultery brings the drama back toward the "subjectivism" Miller was trying to avoid, but its real subjective life remains shallow. Taking up charges of coldness, he says he had never written more passionately and blames the American theater—actors, directors, audience, and critics—for being trained "to take to heart anything that does not prick the mind and to suspect everything that does not supinely reassure."

About the American theater, I think this is exactly so. But my own reservations have to do with the fact that, while moral instruction may be a legitimate ambition of the drama, the play *does* reassure—and it is the *mind* which rebels finally against its formulas while the emotions may be overwhelmed by its force. A play is privileged to reconstruct history for its own purposes; but here we have a play which pretends to describe in realistic terms a community instinctively bent on devotion to God. The Puritans were readers of signs, and the signs, in daily behavior, were evidences of God's will. Hawthorne's novel retains the impermeable quality of that experience by accepting completely the terms of the divine or demonic game. It is yours to choose whose game it really is, according to his strategy of alternative possibilities. But Miller's play makes the choices for you, and its hero does not stand—as one approving critic has said—"foursquare in his own time and place." The records do show that he considered the inquisition a fraud; but though he is bound to the community as a farmer, he does not, in Miller's play, take to heart "all the complex tensions of the Salem community," for he responds to things like an eighteenth century rationalist with little stake in established doctrine. Truer to time and place is the Reverend Hale, who knew "the devil is precise" and saw him in the godly, in himself. He is certainly the more dramatic figure in being compelled to disavow what by instinct and conditioning he has come to believe. Hale resembles Captain Vere in Melville's *Billy Budd,* where the drama is truly divested of "subjectivism" by characters who are, by *allegiance* to retarded doctrine, impaled upon the cross of choice.

One can also see in Melville's Claggart the kind of character that Miller now wishes he had portrayed in Danforth: evil embodied to the utmost, a man so dedicated to evil that by his nature we might know good. Melville saw that to create such a character he would have to stretch his skepticism toward the ancient doctrine of "depravity according to nature," which alone could explain a Claggart or an Iago. He does this by a strategy of insinuation. He suggests to us that there was once such a doctrine, in which intelligent modern men, of course, can hardly believe. The story virtually drives us back to the "superstition," as Kafka virtually restores Original Sin. (I should add that Melville does this in the prose style of the novelette, which could not always be compensated for in the admirable dramatization by Coxe and

Chapman.) Doing so, he takes us back through time, justifying as far as form can reach the eternal intimations of Billy's rosy-dawned execution; a scene which is almost enough to make you believe, with the sailors, that a chip of the dockyard boom "was a piece of the Cross."

Almost. Having proposed to us a possibility just over the edge of reason, Melville writes an ironic coda in which he leaves us to take our own risks of interpretation. Miller, for all his moral conviction and belief in free choice, leaves us none. A master of conventional dramaturgy, with all the skills of building and pacing, he drives past the turbid aspect of social hypnosis to the predetermined heroism of Proctor. Perception yields to sensation and the choice of classical tragedy to its wish-fulfillment. (It is curious that' Billy, *typed* down to his stammer, is a more inscrutable character than anyone in Miller's play.) The final irony is that John Proctor, dramatic hero of the populist mind, might even be applauded by members of the congressional committee that cited Miller for contempt. It is no accident, too, that in temperament and general conduct Proctor resembles our true culture hero, John Glenn, who would be perfectly cast for the role if the astronauts were to start a little theater. One may not have the courage to be a Proctor at the final drumroll, nor a Glenn at the countdown, but no one doubts they are worthy of imitation.

This absence of doubt reduced the import of *The Crucible* for those who thought about it, while increasing the impact for those who didn't. You do a play for its virtues, and one devious aspect of the art of theater lies in concealing the faults. Actually, my belief is that if you know what's not there, you can deal more powerfully with what is. Little of what I have said, however, came up during rehearsals of *The Crucible* (which was not so much conceived as put on), but rather in critiques and discussions of plays done later. Whatever its weaknesses, the production was hard-driving in keeping with the play's rhythm, and performance by performance the actors rose to overwhelming approval. Because we would be doing better productions which would not be so approved, it was important to keep our heads. And, indeed, I think this attitude has made it more possible for our actors to sustain their belief through more subtle plays that have not been so vigorously applauded.

At the time we produced *The Crucible,* Miller was already the most powerful rational voice in the American theater. Questioning the play later, I wanted the company to understand that to criticize him was to take his ideas seriously, and to begin to give some shape to our own. The people we often had to question most were those with whom we seemed to agree. Because we were all vulnerable to easy judgments and that depth psychology of the surface which is so inherent in American drama (and acting), it was necessary to see why *The Crucible* was not really the "tough" play that Miller claimed; I mean dramatically tough, tough in soul, driving below its partisanship to a judgment of anti-social action from which, as in Dostoyevsky, none of us could feel exempt. I wouldn't have asked the questions if Miller didn't prompt them with his reflections on Social Drama and the tragic form. But compare the action of Proctor to that of the tragic figures of any age—Macbeth, or Brittanicus, or Raskolnikov: can you approve or disapprove of their action? Can you make the choice of imitating them? Or avoid it? *The Crucible* may confirm what we like to think we believe, but it is not, as Miller says, intimidating to an "Anglo-Saxon audience" (or actors), nor does it really shock us into recognizing that we don't believe what we say we do. Beyond that, the profoundest dramas shake up our beliefs, rock our world; in *The Crucible,* our principles are neither jeopardized nor extended, however much we may fail to live by them anyhow.

As for the inquisitors, Miller wants us to see evil naked and unmitigated. I am prepared to believe it exists (I am certain it exists), and I won't even ask where it comes from. But—to be truer than tough—if you want absolute evil, you've got to think more about witches. Miller wants the Puritan community without Puritan premises or Puritan intuitions (which is one reason why, when he appropriates the language, his own suffers in comparison). His liberalism is the kind that, really believing we have outlived the past, thinks it is there to be used. The past just doesn't lie around like that. And one of these days the American theater is really going to have to come to terms with American history.

Axiom for liberals: no play is deeper than its witches.

The limitations of *The Crucible* as a Social Drama became more apparent to us when we started to rehearse *Mother Courage* about a year later, in December 1955. Brecht's play is far more ironic, ambiguous, and intellectually subtle. That is why, I believe, some "progressives" and members of left-wing groups who were enraptured by our production of *The Crucible*, and who came out in force to support Brecht as a tribal hero, were disappointed. *The Crucible,* aside from the advance publicity of McCarthyism, catches you up at the beginning and, trying to warn and inform, assaults your critical faculties. Its convention is a modulated hysteria. And if the actors can play with minimum thought, it is because they, like the audience, are caught up in the turbulence. If you know what you think before you come, *The Crucible* permits you to exercise your social passion to the limit. You are not, really, a guilty creature sitting at a play, the other guy is guilty. You are a judge, not judging, but biting your thumb at the judges.

But if *The Crucible* gratifies what you already think, *Mother Courage* lets you feel what you think only long enough to make you judge what you feel. Audience and actors. Moreover, though Brecht's captains and colonels are clearly horrors, and his disposition egalitarian, there is no satisfying celebration of the Common Man. True, there is a vigorous humanity in Mother Courage, who has no respect for the historical moment, the death of a great commander or a victory in battle, for whom a worm in the biscuit is a significant event and the injury to her daughter a major tragedy. But Mother Courage and the Commander are similarly corrupted by the same system. And she does not, like Proctor, make the choice all good men would have her make. She capitulates. Like most of us. And sings a song, rehearsing her fall from romantic grace, to tell us why. It is a nonrevolutionary lyric, a kind of advice to the forlorn, with blood knowledge—cultured by long survival—of the Common Man's inexhaustible capacity for compromise and self-preserving cowardice. (Falstaff's battlefield appraisal of honor is an ingratiating progenitor.) It may not be admirable, but it feels more real.

The capitulation is the chief source of the drama's alienating effect. There is of course the apparent detachment in the acting, the historification of the routine, the juxtaposition of great things and small for purposes of reflective irony, the various interruptive devices. But these are the subsidiary, if inseparable, means of Brecht's drama; they say what he wants to say. When we produced *Mother Courage,* these techniques were still novel, and they were disturbing to many. But what was more disturbing was that the ideological intensity was as complex as the emotional center. Brecht's attitude toward his heroine was (and is) ambiguous. *Mother Courage* is a revolutionary play, precisely because it can't be appropriated without misgivings by any particular cause.

Nor is it reducible to a preachment against war, nor to the commonplace "Life is war." Brecht is saying, if anything, that "War is life"—and since he sees life governed by the economic motive, war becomes the widest and most damaging extension of that motive, grotesque and terrible for all the duplicity it really masks. The war, indeed, is not any old war, it is a holy war, "and therefore," as the Chaplain observes, "pleasing unto God."

In the necessary simplifications of our advertising campaign, we described the play as an anti-war drama and were plagued afterwards by those who declared that it was therefore anachronistic, that after Buchenwald, Iwo Jima, and Korea we do not need to be told that war is bad. One might ask: after such knowledge, what forgiveness? But the truth is *Mother Courage* attacks not only war, but all forms of subservience to the ethics of "business as usual"; it attacks, in sum, the kind of economy we still have, structured on the premise that war is, if not our necessity and destiny, what we must prepare for to avoid it. That is what makes it neither dated nor commonplace. It doesn't tell us what we already know; it tells us what some of us don't want to hear. And for some who share its sentiments, it is disturbing because it impugns us all—because there is no final locus for self-exoneration. At the end of 1955, it was not only iconoclastic as to form, testing our beliefs, it was also an anti-trust suit of our commonest emotions, oscillating finally between a Social Drama and an anti-social vision.

What was true for our audience was again true for our company. I have already described the impression of alienation at our first reading—boredom arising from the feeling that the play was static. Only one scene moved the cast, that in which the dumb daughter Catherine beats her drum on the roof to warn the citizens of Halle of an attack. This engaged the actors; this is what they wanted from a play. It was like *The Crucible.* For the rest, it was a lot of talk.

What we soon realized about the play, particularly as it went on its feet, was that its activity is manifold and unceasing. Where it seemed to stand still, there were countless implicit demands for business: where it appeared to be verbose, there were various stratas of relevant irony, disguised and overt. In Scene 6, for instance, Mother Courage, the Chaplain, the Regimental Clerk, and the dumb daughter are spending a rainy afternoon in a canteen tent, engaged in conversations on the war, the two women taking inventory. The stage, which previously had been rather bare, is now full of sausages, linens, cheeses, belts, buckles, boots, tins, baskets, and shirts, all the innumerable paraphernalia of Mother Courage's enterprise. For Mother Courage, times are good. But the pre-scene projection announces that the great Commander Tilly has fallen in battle. There is funeral music. The scene opens reflectively. And though nothing "dramatic" happens until late in the long scene, the predominant impression, arising out of a lot of talk, is one of abundance, of a steady throb of counting, checking, sorting, tallying, collecting money for drinks—the business of the actors and the business of war forming a single ritualistic image, the business of business, giving point and substance to the conscious ironies of Mother Courage and the ingenuous ones of the Chaplain.

Or take the opening scene, where Mother Courage and her children, traveling with their wagon, are stopped by a Recruiting Officer and a Sergeant, who are interested in her sons, livestock for the war. She identifies herself and, when asked how she got her nickname, explains that she drove through the bombardment of Riga like a madwoman to save some loaves of bread she had in her cart. Her action was not heroic, as some who gave her the name thought (and as some thought when they read our advertising; one woman called for tickets to *Mothers Courageous*). Courage is a pragmatist not a martyr. But the irony is sharper and partially directed against herself. Not only does she discredit the romantic interpretation of her deed, she discredits the deed itself: what a fool, her tone implies, to risk one's life for a few moldy loaves of bread. Business comes first, *except* where it threatens survival. The same attitude prevails in the following scene when, immediately after a surprise reunion, she boxes her son's ears for having too bravely outwitted some enemy peasants. Better always to surrender than to die. (Since, for Brecht, this seems to be a "positive" action, no wonder he outrages certain intensely anti-Communist socialists.)

Set in the framework of great events, the mundane career of Mother Courage is alienated, then, in the various senses that Brecht intends: estranged, put at a distance, made famous (or infamous), historified. Our critical faculties are trained on that part of history which history slights. Tilly wins a battle at Lutzen; Mother Courage loses four shirts. And in the hectic little scene which juxtaposes these two important events, so much happens so quickly that one can hardly keep up with it: onstage some soldiers, taking respite from the looting, are having a drink at Mother Courage's canteen.

Catherine is distraught, running up and down on the periphery. Offstage, a fire is ravaging a peasant's farm. There are cries; wounded people are carried on. The Chaplain runs in, calling for linen. Mother Courage, keeping an eye on the soldiers, one of whom has already stolen a fur coat in the town, tries to protect her goods. She has given all her linen before, she says; she explains to the Chaplain that things are getting worse—taxes, duties, bribes to pay. Furious at her mother's apparent inhumanity, Catherine grabs a stick and rushes at her. Mother Courage shouts her down, but the Chaplain pulls her bodily from the wagon and takes out some shirts which he rips for bandages. There is a cry offstage—a baby is trapped by the fire. Torn between her daughter and her shirts, Mother Courage watches as Catherine dashes off to save the child. Catherine reappears with the baby. Mother Courage, relieved, stalks across the stage to chastise her and tries to take the baby away. Catherine snarls and hugs it fiercely. Meanwhile the soldier with the coat is trying to make off with the bottle of brandy. Mother Courage sees him and, instead of taking back the liquor, snatches the fur coat in exchange, even in the midst of the tumult managing to pull off a deal. The victory music, which had been playing all during the scene, mounts as Catherine joyfully raises the baby over her head.

I have recounted the activity of the scene because so much of it is missed in the reading and because—though it took us hours to work it out—all of it, and a good deal of incidental business that I have left out, happens in approximately one minute.

Thus the initial impression of alienation was mitigated for the actors by the necessity of having to *act* the play. It imposed its will and ways upon them. They could not worry about what they resented when the drama gave them so much to think about and *do*. Gradually they began to realize what Brecht means when he compares Epic theater to the painting of Brueghel. The canvas is large, diffuse, apparently undramatic. But more than in *Galileo,* the minor elements have their unique energy. One looks closer and recognizes that the play is rarely still. The sensation of diversity disappears in the apprehended unity of a common vitality. Degraded and demoralized by the black marketry of war, the people of the play express their consciously rationalized submission with a remarkable vigor. What we have is the caustically robust power of ineffectuality. The stones begin to talk, as one of the projections declares, even before the mute daughter provides the climactic irony with the drum that the war puts in her hands. One feels the rhetorical magic of the contemporary tribunal. A banner with slightly wrenched black (Gothic) letters drops from the flies announcing the place of action: Sweden, Saxony, Bavaria, Saxony, Poland. Why? Because war, like the snow settling over Joyce's Ireland, is general and undifferentiated; it looks the same everywhere. You *need* to be told where you are.

No production we had done until then was so full of discovery. What we all began to sense as rehearsals moved forward was that somehow the diffuse, omnibus, verbal, novelistic character of the play became more active, em-

pathic, concentrated, and dramatic as it approached the end. There was meaning in the graduated contrasts, as in the more obvious interruptions of structure. In the beginning we had the characteristic rhythm and action of apathy
and the materialistic vivacity of survival by bargaining. As in Chekhov—so
different in general from Brecht—we have continual self-justification and
transference of blame by the characters through commentary on public affairs;
in Brecht, commentary beyond their scope as people. The songs, with their
discreetly sardonic music by Paul Dessau, reflect something of this tendency.
Even the Mother Courage ballad suggests with its insistent base the long,
tedious way into the war. There is a sustained relationship with the audience:
Mother Courage talks through the proscenium and there are frequent interruptions in the narrative. One desires very much to participate in the action,
but Brecht makes one stand off and observe it. Later in the play, however, we
are made more fully aware of the human relationships, which should have
been obvious enough before except that we were distracted by a host of
other factors.

Now we pick up events and values by reflexive reference. Back in Scene 3,
Yvette, the prostitute, had sung her Song of Fraternization, prompted by
memories of her unfaithful lover, Peter Piper. Much later, in Scene 8, the
Cook is revealed to be the culprit. The son Eilif reappears, to be executed for
a deed for which he had previously been honored. His armor is new and
burnished, he dies rich. The Chaplain puts on his robe again and sings the
Song of Hours, which suggests the idealistic theological student he must have
been.* In Scene 12, Mother Courage sings a lullaby to her dead daughter, the
only song we did *ohne Verfremdung,* without alienation, although the developing pathos is immediately cut off by the pipes and drums of a regiment on
the march, through which we wove a choral reprise of the Mother Courage
ballad. And Courage, who learns *nothing* from her suffering, makes the last
"deal" of the play, paying a peasant to bury her daughter, and struggles off,
bent as she is, to follow the war, which has not, according to the projected
narrative, reached its end.

One realizes finally that the play of person on person has not been minimized in the earlier part of the drama (for all the to-do about detachment,
the actors had to explore character relations in the usual sense), only it has
not been so forcibly brought to our attention. There was much else to say and
demonstrate, and it is not until we have accepted through action, gesture,
speeches, music, and all the technical elements the unrelenting presence and
localized quality of the abstract war that Brecht lets everybody indulge in

---

* The Song of Hours, done in Scene 3 of the Berlin production, was not used in
  Munich and was not in either of the published English versions. We found the music
  in the Dessau score, asked Eric Bentley to do a version of the lyrics, and placed
  the song in Scene 8. I understand the principle of interruption, but in Scene 3 it
  seemed arbitrary, the only song sung when the focus was not in some way on the
  person singing. Performance bore out our choice; the song felt relevant (but still
  detached) and provided an excellent contrast to the burlesque scene which follows,
  in which Yvette discovers Peter Piper as the Cook.

easier and more rapid dramatic emotions. Hence the preference—at least with our actors and audience, and I think generally—for the latter part of the play. Most of us are still prone to recognize as dramatic mainly that which has uninterrupted momentum, especially if it is fast-paced or violent. But drama exists at the calm peripheries of history as much as it its excited middle, and in the juxtaposition of incongruous elements, such as event, song, legend, rhetoric, or the relaxed flow of ideas.

After the vibrancy of such a play as *The Crucible,* the movement of *Mother Courage* could, indeed, seem too leisurely. But in our anxiety to get on with it, we are likely to skip over a good portion of reality that materializes for a slower pulse. *Mother Courage* was the first of our plays to force us to reconsider the question of Time in the theater, the way it is passed, and the way it gives identity to Action.

At one extreme, there is pure behavior, taking its sweet time; like the bark of a tree, concrete experience in absoluteness. That is the way followed in *The Connection* and certain films of the *nouvelle vague*. The aim: to make tempo disappear in the spatial abstraction of behavior—experience spreads timelessly, becomes graphic, the drama taking on the character of a painting, an Action painting. In Brecht, we also have a spatial form; hence the analogy with Brueghel, whose canvases are mainly outsized compositions of behavior until one examines the parts—or, using incongruously the language of Time, the "events." The eye cannot accommodate it all at a glance (that's life, we may say, and extrapolate from there to the theories behind "pop art"). When we look at a magnified detail of *The Massacre of the Innocents* in an art volume, we are approximating the effect of a scene in *Mother Courage*. The "event" may be violent or casual; two events are united in a total image, not by cause and effect; the whole composition is in repose.

Thus, history diffuses itself through time, resembling space. The dramatist salvages the event from the annals, interpretation, bias, and false report, the mystifications of politics and the decantation of rumor—the obfuscating lens of subjective Time—and places the event before us. In Brecht, the event is not indiscriminately rendered behavior, come what may, life as improvised; but rather, life as judged. The judgment is an aspect of the event, and our emotional predisposition is—in the ideal Brecht performance—redirected by placards, slides, and other appendages that advise us, sometimes ironically, how to take what we see. The event may be named; each scene—as in the ancient Epic—has its argument, which is not a discursive thesis but the logic of narrative. When Weigel is asked about the Method of the Ensemble, she says: "We tell the Story." Story informed by and informing history. The rational intelligence is the chief medium of the telling, and the business of a production is to develop Signs.

The danger (in my discussion of *Galileo,* I tried to show how rapidly this happens) is that the Signs, moving into history, are subject to the same errors of misreading and misrepresentation, and to the ever-shifting perspectives of a relativistic universe. (Genet: "It's the reading that counts.")

Now: consider the concrete fact of performance. What is there is there before you, in measured time. You come into the theater at one moment and go out at another. Moored temporarily before a playing space (whether you pay at the box office or not), you are looking for value received. We know that duration in performance is not necessarily proportionate to tempo. A play that speeds by may seem unendurable; a sudden noise may be dramatic, but sustained, it will become the shrill of tedium. But how much time do you take? In *Mother Courage,* we are already dealing with the slow-building omnibus structure I have described. When you play it "cool," doesn't that take more time? The questions point to the trouble we had in our own productions of Brecht, and to my own feelings of laboriousness in certain productions or parts of productions at the Berliner Ensemble. With Brecht's plays over-deliberated performance may not only feel slow, but like a gloss to a Victorian novel, the redundancy of the didactic—so that while True Believers may be edified, the disinterested will not be so much enlightened as anxious to get on with what they already know. One doesn't have to be vain to say this. If Brecht's plays do resemble the chronicles of Shakespeare, it might be well to remember that with a dialectic no less extraordinary Shakespeare was apparently played more nimbly lest the two hours traffic of the stage run into the dark.

While a play like *The Crucible* may blur meaning in momentum, a production of *Mother Courage* may underline it, too much. The task is to *realize* a scene, the whole crisscrossing motion of motives, so that it might be the better alienated. But here is where Time runs back to behavior. I am aware of Brecht's desire for gestural economy such as that of Oriental drama, and there is sufficient ritual in bourgeois life to muster a telling repertoire of gestures, where one motion may do the job of ten. Yet, to the extent the plays have realistic appearances, a single gesture such as Mother Courage's loud mercenary click of her pocketbook is no substitute for the density that comes of varied particulars. (It may even be, as it clicks shut on a "negative" action, what my young actress would call "indicating.") Nor is slowing down an action necessarily more virtuous than speeding it up—it depends on what you see. Critics used to respond to the introspective studies in the acting of the Group by complaining about pace. People who have nothing else to say often will. We know the factitious excitement of overpacing at its best from Kazan, but the aesthetics of pace has never been sufficiently explored. What I have been trying to emphasize is that it has something to do with the mileage of moments—the degree of *illumination* in each instant. Kazan may be the wiser for dazzling us with emptiness, but there is so much substance in Brecht it needn't be labored. The tedious underscoring of points may have been necessary in the *Lehrstück* for uninstructed workers, but as the audiences become, even in the proletarian East Berlin, more bourgeois and informed, one has to be wary that the determined coolness is not that at all, but a rather dispossessed drag in tempo which simplifies motives and ironies alike. Not only forms, but tempos outdate themselves.

The problem is also a cultural matter. If the Noh actor takes all afternoon to turn half a compass and a Russian company takes four hours to play *A View from the Bridge,* it is no wonder that the rhythm of the TNP production of *Mother Courage* was considerably more vivacious than that of the Ensemble. (Actually Brecht recognized and tried to provide for cultural qualifications of tempo. When his company went to England, he advised them to play more briskly, warning against their own tendency to ponderousness.) As for ourselves, when we did *Mother Courage,* the question of Time was very troubling in all its aspects, and I was never able to separate detachment from drag. I have the impression that as a result, within the unhurried structure that Brecht had laid out, some things were pushed in our playing; part of this may have been due to my own natural rhythm of perception, which made me impatient with the sort of underlining I later saw at the Ensemble. As we might expect, however, the general rhythm of our production ended up somewhere between the French and the German.

Fast or slow, let me stress this: there is a difference between an enlightening succession of "events" and a lustreless sequence of "behavior." To those for whom the brilliance of the rational mind remains a supreme value, the catatonic naturalism of such a drama as *The Connection* may be momentarily engaging, but interest is bound to run out. That is why, despite the throwing of the onus on the audience (by the play and its defenders), I refuse to take the blame for boredom as I refuse to accept the moral equivalence of good squares and good addicts. The anesthesia cannot be aestheticized away. As Baudelaire taught us, Ennui is the cardinal sin of modern life, and art cannot be too cavalier about impacting the situation by outdoing it. When I am told the tempo is the tempo of life itself, I understand the quest for pure behavior, the incessant *now,* but there is behavior and behavior, form and form, and there is a world of difference, because of form, between the behavior of *The Connection* and the behavior of, say, *Endgame,* which is involved in the same quest with an even greater sense of stasis.

I shall say more about the question of Time later in this chapter, and in considering the drama of Beckett. In the end, it may be the essential question of the contemporary theater. Nevertheless, Time is measured out in the theater in accordance with our feelings about it outside the theater. Today, various kinds of disenchantment, aimlessness, a desire for repose, the influence of the Orient have made us distrustful of Time as we normally understand it. But we can also be too cavalier in smashing our clocks because we have the feeling that some elephantiasis of the time-sense is destroying the Western world. In America, true, we may outrush ourselves in being with it, but being with it is not, in itself, a sin (except perhaps theologically); for we are always stuck with the paradox that the enterprise that is corrupting America also made it. While the serene detachment of the East has produced Zen and Chinese landscapes, it has also produced the misery of millions; and that is a nexus we have to be responsible for in our cultural prejudices, just as we have to be responsible for the atrophying effects of heavy industry based on time study.

The throwing over of Time is concurrent with the throwing over of formal conventions. But in the theater we must still come to terms with the discard of all the traditional equipment of dramaturgy: plot, character, consecutive thought, structure, pacing, pointing, symmetrical rhythms, Time—which are testaments to the form-giving power of mind, not incontestable Signs of debility. Brecht certainly knew this; Beckett knows it. Though he works over an excruciatingly narrowed spectrum, part of his power derives from his transcription of the painful cost of discard—the suicidal impulse of which Melville also knew when he had Ahab throw his log, chart, and compass overboard. No matter what it throws away, a great dramatic form has a long memory; and there is inevitably a little bird, or a bit of cloud, in the immensity of the Chinese sky, to keep the mind from drifting to annihilation.

Influenced as he has been by Eastern art, Brecht's is an obdurate Western mind. The theory of Alienation is a specific instrument of judgment, a rational *critique of behavior* which is socially conditioned. "The social effect of the Peasant Wars," he wrote, "was to take the guts out of the Reformation. Cynicism and business were all that was left." Bowdlerizing the Reformation also deprived it of its sense of comedy. And one of the missions of his drama is to restore a comedy which is virile, critical, Rabelaisian, obscene, a mockery of what is worshiped, as in the satyr plays. (It is a kind of comedy to which our company has become most receptive, and at which it has become increasingly adept.) Here, too, Brecht has affinities with Ionesco, Beckett, and Genet, who want to restore to the ritual of art the propriety of the giant phallus. Separating buffoonery and piety the Protestant ethic domesticated comedy and took away its sting. The comedy of *Mother Courage* is another aspect of Alienation and intensifies the dominant severity of the drama. Unlike *Galileo,* which is similarly witty, *Mother Courage* is restrained neither by the dignity of Science nor the historical eminence of its central character, who is a prototypical nobody. Thus, the comedy is closer to the inn scenes of Cervantes and the chronicles of Shakespeare, with their garrulousness and gallows humor, their juxtaposition of bawdry, bloody slaughters, and affairs of state. And their knowledge that the final comedy is the masque of death, passing beyond social criticism into the terrain of human failure, where comedy and tragedy—for all our enterprise and aspiration—rejoin each other in a common doom.

The most astonishing development of Brecht's play is the aging of Mother Courage, whose energy is hideously wasted after the death of her last child into the baleful abstraction of a Chinese mask. As she pulls the wagon in the finale, the musical themes clashing in the blank distance, Brecht's desire for social change is figured in an image of hopeless changelessness. The stage, made to feel more emptily infinite by the disappearance of other properties (property?), becomes an existential platform. And Mother Courage pulling her wagon, alone against a hostile universe, resembles nobody so much as

Sisyphus rolling his stone up the mountain, but with no residue of heroism. In our production her sense of direction was totally destroyed, until her cry after the departing regiments was lost in the twining and imperturbable music, as if in the rhythm of organized nothingness. Still, one can't help being drawn with enormous pathos toward an image of even greater isolation than that of Hamm in the twilight of *Endgame;* for despite the discard of dog and whistle and the complacent terror with which he recovers his face with the bloody handkerchief, Clov remains, however unutterably there.

That final task of the actress also brings into focus all the controversy about acting technique in Brecht's plays. For that mask has to be filled and the emotion of a desperate enterprise that has run down into the mechanical must come all the more from the actress's most secret resources of feeling. If Courage's running after the armies is an emblematic gesture, the most extended image of the play, it is also the inevitable outgrowth of the woman's experience—behavior becoming symbol in a *memento mori.*

The treatment of Courage (played for us by Beatrice Manley) is the traditional crux. The difficulty of preventing compassion for a woman who is meant to be a negative object lesson has been much mused over, sometimes misleadingly. In Scene 3, for instance, after the long modulated movement leading to the death of the stupid son, we did everything we could to "cool" the grief of Mother Courage— to *show* how, under any duress, she would beat the war at its own game. But the scene was undeniably moving in a conventional way; the more expedient Courage was the more moving, until the ironic pipes and drums of the music cut the emotion. The compassion would seem to be unavoidable; yet there had apparently been conflicts between Brecht and his wife, Helene Weigel, about interpretation of the role, its optimum hardness, and the fine line between compassion granted and compassion solicited. When a critic of the original Zurich production compared Courage to Hecuba, Brecht rewrote the play and made the "heroine" more unsympathetic. That's now part of the Brecht folklore.

As we understood Brecht's revisions, they were designed to show as clinically as possible (less ambiguously than in *Galileo*) that experience is *not* always the best teacher—that certain sufferers from catastrophe continue to woo their ruin. Just before he died, Brecht wrote a program note to the London production, meant to allay again false admiration for Courage: "She believes in the war to the last. It never occurs to her that in a war one needs outsize scissors to get one's cut." A camp-following career woman, she was not to be taken as a symbol of the indomitability of humble folk who, as Esslin puts it, "redeem themselves by their courage in the face of overwhelming odds." Courage is as guilty as the warmongers, and the crafty trade around her wagon is our common petit-bourgeois traffic, the natural freeway of which is war and total devastation.

Now, this view of her *can* be given weight in production or, allowing for more than natural compassion, it can be contradicted. True, unseeing as you make her, an audience may *still* not believe the evidence of its senses. But if, in that final moment (for one example), you have the actress square her shoulders and look steadfastly into the future, hauling her wagon like a resolution to survive, ignoring the fact that she is still following the war blindly, then you play right into the sympathies that Brecht didn't want. (It has been done, I hear.) That final *attitude* is crucial, for as I see it, Courage pulling that wagon is by no means indomitable, but a desperate fool reduced to an unthinking beast of burden.

I am reflecting on a production done some years ago, with fewer resources than we have now. In view of what I've said of our approach to *Galileo,* it might seem that we'd do *Mother Courage* differently. No doubt. If there were changes, however, I think they'd be in the direction of articulating every contradiction in the submission of Courage, her good wit demoralized down to that harrowing vision at the end, so that the chances of evading it are reduced. If there were an empathetic response, I would want that final attitude to arouse shame in the audience so that they went home bent with their own complicity.

To say that the acting of Brecht implies an action plus an attitude toward it is to say that an actor should know, beyond his limited intuitions, what there is to be said, in all its contradictions. In this respect, Brecht's method is not so different from Stanislavski's intentions—the Superobjective, we must recall, had its ethical component, a *reasoned* form. Stanislavski stressed the organic factor between what an actor had to feel and what he had to do to feel it; but he assumed there was something objectively there to be felt. Brecht stressed the objective factor between what might be done and what it could mean; but he had himself practiced the ways of obscurantism and was living in a period when any given action could, if not shaped into definition, mean anything. Actually, one learns in comparing the methods that, like so many theories of modern art, technique points to the same end: truth *imbedded in* experience, not concluded a priori, for all the shaping of Brecht and improvisation of Stanislavski. The image, the action, the totem, the happening carries the weight of meaning. Process is the most of it. Thus, the charges of formalism against Brecht in the Soviet Union (and implications of anarchy) while the stream of consciousness of Stanislavski has become the basis of a very objective art.

As a technique for the actor, the Stanislavski method is good for those who have not yet learned to explore themselves for the materials of their art; it is the depth psychology of the theater—a very necessary therapy for those who are inhibited or artificial in their acting, who have no associational powers, who do not know how to tap their memories, for those who customarily borrow emotion as a result. As I've said, the danger is that going down, you may not care to come up again. The technique of Alienation causes a great deal of consternation for the actor, who suspects he is going to be had, trumped up for a message. He wants to know immediately how to "alienate" his role. But he does not have to alienate anything, by reading his stage directions or exchanging parts with the other players, if by nature and conditioning he is not inclined to sentimentalize his behavior or fondle his feelings or merely play himself or float into irrelevance by association. (When I was at the Ensemble I asked about the "He said, she said" technique, and some of the actors could hardly remember it.) What American acting has little sense of is the thing that astonishes you in the acting of, say, Ekkehard Schall, the young, crew-cut, intensely Communist Marlon Brando of the Ensemble, who played Arturo Ui. He is a political actor. And it is really eye-opening to see somebody get so much out of himself by force of *external* conviction.

When we did *Mother Courage,* what we lacked in political conviction, we made up in part through the enthusiasm of enlightenment—the feeling that the drama was an adventure. It's hard to convey how happily naïve it all became after the initial doubts about the play—the alienation, the politics, the sense of mission; naïve in the best sense. There was a general feeling that with this play the theater might earn an effective social role in the community. Yet our optimism was tempered one rainy night at our Elgin Street warehouse, when morale was soaring in rehearsals and everybody was feeling that we might yet change the world. We were ardently exploring some point in the play when suddenly there was thunder and the rain began to beat heavily on the chicken-wire glass of the skylight; and all together as we were, we felt impossibly alone. The discussion stopped. The sense of isolation spread. And our ardor, momentarily dampened, was revived more realistically when I said the production had to contain the knowledge that we were, after all, but a minority group in a minority form in a country pledged to the protection of minorities, in a period in which they needed such protection.

I mentioned before the controversy over the production and cited the reviewer who occasioned an uproar by his disapproval, and his remark that in America there are some who still consider war to be the "great adventure." He also occasioned my first (and only to date) letters of protest over a review. There were repercussions in the company. My letters—one to the reviewer, one to his editor—and the fact that we encouraged some protest (the bulk of it was unsolicited) caused one couple to resign. The greater majority united behind the protest, boosting morale, but what we had to deal with was the strange principle of fair play: that is, you accept good reviews of productions in which you don't really believe, do you have a right to complain about a bad review of a production in which you do? It is a question we have never resolved adequately, and probably won't until we are free of the box office necessity of good reviews.

In my letters to the reviewer and his editor, it was the issue of protest itself that I tried to put in perspective. The bad review had already made its deleterious mark on the box office. Sober heads in the company were warning that a failure of publicity by antagonizing the press could impede the growth of our theater. If that seems overstated, it is also true. (I took note of it in the letter.) We should like to believe that a performance can defend itself if it's good, but there is too much contrary evidence. In our experience, a good review will not make a play, but a bad review will certainly kill it. No important theater of the modern era, responsible for introducing new works, could really go it alone, without the support of other media of expression—especially in America, and especially as isolated as we were, without the support of a cultural movement or other groups. One may see how odd this situation was—and how true to the period of the Silent Generation—in the fact that even Irving and I debated with ourselves the ethical propriety of encouraging those who wanted to defend our production to send on their letters of protest! (When I was in England several years ago, George Devine asked me to write a letter on behalf of *Serjeant Musgrave's Dance,* which had been mistreated in the press. Nobody dreamed it might be shameful to solicit so.) We finally concluded and wrote to the reviewer who had censured us for it that we saw "nothing beyond the bounds of decency and democratic process in suggesting that such letters be written, since we are encouraged to do so on every other issue—social, political, economic. Is the theater to be taboo? . . . It is the old problem of dissent coming to the surface in a field which has been notoriously and unwisely quiet these many years."

In the letter to the editor, I tried to summarize the cultural problem. (We didn't expect it to be printed, and it wasn't, but we wanted our position on record; and it made its impression on the company.) I said The Workshop "does not expect that the *Chronicle* will make an editorial issue of this production, though the *real* controversy is of editorial proportions. . . . That the theater has forfeited its old primacy in the community is due to changes in the structure of the community and the rise of competing media, but also because the theater in our time has accepted its subordination to lesser enterprises and, developing a tradition of discreetly theorized resignation to the 'facts' of modern life, has forfeited its right to speak out on its own behalf. Though I cannot shrug off any longer the treatment accorded *Mother Courage* . . . , I want to make it clear that there is more than a bad review of a particular production at stake." I was referring not only to the flippant dismissal of honest dissent in a Sunday follow-up (which, more than the review, had provoked me) but to the fact that the play, dismissed as dated and commonplace, was a thoroughgoing criticism of our reigning foreign policy, Mr. Dulles' Brinkmanship.

Whatever the cause, it is apparent that since the *Mother Courage* controversy, the reviewers in the area are in general less prone to dismiss plays they know nothing about. They have made an effort to educate themselves (as the very decent observations on Esslin's book reveal), and even acknowledge that The Workshop's repertoire has been the main source of enlightenment. Instead of being curtailed, our publicity has improved; and, indeed, we sometimes thought ourselves confronted with the reverse problem: rather indiscriminate praise of certain productions because the strangeness is intimidating and because, as with abstract painting, misjudgment in either direction can be justified. With all the support we have now received, there is sometimes in the attitude of the press a delayed revulsion of feeling that leads to outright censure. And the brand-new play—one which is not certified either in New York or Europe—remains fair game.

The reviewers are not entirely at fault; they too suffer from a system which is so contemptuous of real criticism that people barely qualified are assigned to the task. If they are zealous, they may grow partly up to the job. But in any case they are not justified as specialists in the art they review, but as representatives of popular opinion—which is merely another example of the cynicism that mocks popular sovereignty with misinformation, and confounds democratic process with the vices of the mass mind.

One longs for the severity of a criticism which deplores, when necessary, the failing of the thing loved, but is able to communicate the love in the severity. What we usually get through bafflement is petulance, or the reprehension that comes of embarrassment by difficulty, or praise that comes out of fear of being wrong. We revere critics like Shaw, James Agate, and Stark Young because they have the eye and the ear—and the language—to record what is really there and the temerity to let us know what they think of it, in principle, without condescension or false humility. I have read scathing remarks by good critics that made me want to see a play; I have read favorable notices by some of our reviewers that would have kept me away. I suppose anyone who has ever worked in the theater has felt a compulsion to sound off on the critics. It should be apparent that I have not used that word for the reviewers, for I have nothing but the highest regard for the art of criticism. I should like nothing better than for our reviewers to turn into real critics— who would really grapple with our ideas as they occur in performance, with what we are trying to say in each production, and from production to production, as they judge our effort to live up to it. See first, judge after. That property, that gesture, that abstraction—why like *that?* That actor—what is he doing? Why that way? And then, absolutely, what do you think? But as there is little dialogue in our press on the crucial issues, it may be too much to expect one on a theater which is trying to find ways to re-enact them with maximum complexity.

A production is a criticism, too. The production of *Mother Courage,* more than anything prior to that time, drove that home—that what we did on stage was a moral commitment. And through the controversy, it gave our theater a feeling for partisanship, whatever our politics.

As the Welfare-Warfare State provides more benefits, real or illusory, and as we become adept in "selective inattention," anybody's ability to take a stand becomes diminished. And one man's outrage may become another man's amusement. This has been the fate of Sean O'Casey in America, where he was *persona non grata* for years but has recently become something of a pet bobcat; as Joxer Daly might say, a darlin' fella. In the theater, people love him who have never really read him all the way through, and for those who condemn capitalism and Broadway alike, he is one of the chief heroes, perhaps the court jester, of the Disestablishment. With all the defusing subtlety of mass admiration, the myth of his iconoclasm has been blurred o'er with the pale cast of respectability. In magazine profile or TV visit, he comes out an amiable old boyo, bespectacled, earthy, full to the brim with memories, minor grievances, and endearing old charms, a family man whose "failure" on the commercial stage is a well-publicized injustice and whose politics is simply another sign of cordial eccentricity. "One trouble," *Life* wrote about O'Casey's communism, "has been that O'Casey's feelings tend to get away from him on the most unsuitable occasions."

While we can agree with *Life* that O'Casey is "a congenital no-sayer to all constituted authority" who might "well be among the first silenced in any standard people's republic," congenital no-saying is the orthodoxy of our own pseudo-intelligentsia. We appropriate the man by discounting what he believes. Unlike Brecht, who has been given the same good-guy-in-spite-of-himself treatment, O'Casey is one of those artists whose charm is, indeed, likely to subvert his anger. He encourages the assimilation. In a recent collection of essays and stories, O'Casey characterized himself as a Green Crow, "a laddo that can't afford any gorgeousness in his feathers," but a "remarkable bird, clever and cute." It is a peppy, braggart, contentious book, mixing the crow's caw with the lark's song on behalf of life, liberty, and O'Casey's plays. It has the refreshing vanity of a plucky man, "making a strange nest from twigs, gay-colored feathers, and a few sprigs of thyme." And it is similar in spirit to his later plays.

Cock-a-Doodle Dandy, which we produced in 1959,* is a play with the same frisky and risky brilliance. And O'Casey's Cock is a gorgeous bird, the black crow's alter ego, dreamed of by O'Casey in his unkempt philosophy. A gay, devilish thing, it is "part of man's right and part of God's pleasure," stirring up a Holy War on the four fields of Ireland.

For O'Casey, who survived poverty, calumny, and civil war, gaiety is a matter of principle. There are those who want to live and there are those who don't want to live—the issue is reduced, extravagantly, to that. The Old Man has grown impatient with heretics. Those who do not want to live he consigns to his own version of Hell, the bleakness and unloved loneliness of their un-chastened piety. O'Casey's jeremiads are not merely against those who would legislate pretty girls out of existence or raise anathemas against dancing, but against those who would destroy man's generous share of God-given joy, particularly by taking the bread out of their mouths. The potato-patch toughness behind the gaiety O'Casey shares with other Irish writers. It is in the sentimental confessions of O'Neill, and it is in that part of Shaw which is willing to kill those offensive enough to be social criminals, or to take pride in their poverty.

Out of indignation, O'Casey brings to the theater an exuberance so naïve

* We had put the play into rehearsal before, in 1955, but O'Casey's agent refused us the rights because—after years of neglect—O'Casey was insisting then, like Saroyan, that he be produced first in New York.

it is a wonder to behold. As he says of Ireland, hope springs infernal in his breast. It is a quality we needed to hold on to, as we went further into the dark. (We were producing *Endgame* simultaneously.) Nevertheless, there were times during our production of *Cock-a-Doodle Dandy* when I had cause to wonder whether all the shaking walls, flying dishes, ducking and dodging, collapsing chairs, disappearing Cock, and the myriad cuckoo calls had a dramatic theme worthy of them. One treasured the joy—for one can hardly think of an American dramatist who is capable of it. And there was no doubt the play was playable, despite the bromides about the unstageability of the late plays. So much gusto, so many effects, may seem, however, like the caprice of a septuagenarian *enfant terrible* who appears to feel that since nobody does him anyhow he can get away with anything. The miracle is that when he is done he very nearly will. That the play went so long un-produced in America is another instance of our theater's driveling wanton-ness.

Yet for all the daring and derring-do, which restores a sense of play too ancient for Broadway, *Cock-a-Doodle Dandy* fights old battles and swears old oaths. The rowdy theatricality comes more directly from the primitive heart than the literary staginess of *Skin of Our Teeth* or *Camino Real,* but one wishes the younger O'Casey had written it. If the older O'Casey did, we may admire him as a fountain of youth but realize he is writing out of the ideological security of a thoroughly celebrated neglect. We have heard him before on the tyranny of the Church, the superstition of the folk, the bigotry of age and the jauntiness of youth. Indeed, we have not only heard O'Casey on these subjects, we have heard all his predecessors, and we wonder as we go along with him whether we have anything more than some very colorful threads of a well-worn piece of the pagan fabric of the Irish Renaissance. As he does to his characters in the play's marvelous wind sequence, O'Casey charms the pants off of us; but we incline to "take no notice" of the play's real perturbations, even when the old rage comes upon it and a lorry driver is struck dead by a priest.

As for O'Casey's voice, in his later plays the natural poet of the prosy tenements finds tongues in trees and melody in everything. The lyrical pro-fusions were once impelled, however, by the immediate passion of common life and the errant lilt of Dublin's tumult. The passion is still there, and the lilt, but they sometimes seem as insubstantial as the fog over the River Liffey in *Red Roses for Me.* From the retreat at Totnes it's a longer way to Tip-perary.

Not that his view of Ireland is altogether out of kilter. While the rest of the world worries about its birthrate, we are told that Catholic Ireland is the only country in Europe in which the population is decreasing. At Joyce's Martello Tower, from which you can see similar towers in the distance, a friend of mine, a Celtic scholar, remarked that they were built to defend Ireland against Napoleon—who never came. One could not help thinking that he knew better. One has only to see the Abbey today—that shabby empyrean of the Irish National Movement, where it is now an event to have a play on a Gaelic theme that is *not* in verse, to understand why it is not only the artists who are deserting. The retarded gentility is as appalling today as it was when Eric Bentley directed there about a dozen years ago, or when Frank O'Connor wrote you can hear the voice of Cuchulain singing "I've Got a Girl in Kalamazoo." Even if the Common Market survives the entry of England, expectations of social and economic progress are not high in Ireland, where an accomplished architect has nothing to build.

While O'Casey's plays can raise the banshees there to this day, for the rest of us he does not seem so immediate as Brecht, nor so tough. If we ask for immediate relevance—that is, a more viable social criticism, one touch beyond nature—it is because O'Casey's early plays have led us to expect it.

A couple of seasons before our production of *Cock-a-Doodle Dandy,* we had done *The Plough and the Stars.* When you return to those first plays, you hear real drums under the window and the effervescent anger of a man who had seen dung carried through his living room and almost had his head blasted off. Those plays seem rabidly a part of a long history of Irish passion and politics. And when O'Casey marches his little legion of characters out of the Celtic twilight into the stiff sun of a Dublin street, his own lyric extravagance is an extension of nationalistic ardor. With *The Plough and the Stars,* we were able to have fun, but there were fewer temptations to fool around. O'Casey had written it with an impartial vengeance.

If the sides are more clearly drawn in the later plays—the golden lads and girls against the forces of darkness—it is not because drama has turned into morality (there is nothing simplistic about morality), but because O'Casey had never been able to do very well with the prime sources of light. In *Cock-a-Doodle Dandy,* Lorna and Loreleen are very inconsiderable characters, the maid Marion has a stereotyped bounce, and the Messenger Robin Adair has a major function in very minor key. The early plays are scarcely free of this naïveté, but they are also more urgent. Nora's insanity has always seemed rotogravure to me, and her love scene with Clitheroe drenched in sentimentality, but she is nevertheless a character whose motives are more complex and whose turmoil is more specific. Like everybody else in the play she wants to achieve a life of greater dignity, but she confuses dignity with respectability and her desires conflict with public passion. "Ireland," cries Jack, "is greater than a wife"—and the drama is still so close to history that it is not exactly corny. Personal anxiety competes with and fortifies the ferocity of national ambition. *Plough and the Stars* is finally not a darlin' play—it is hilariously grim. (I should say that the final moment of *Cock-a-Doodle Dandy,* when the Messenger replies to Marthraun's question about what he should do—"Die. There is little else left useful for the likes of you to do"—is as bitter as anything in O'Casey; but one doesn't feel there is quite as much as stake.) In *Plough,* one feels that O'Casey, laying about objectively, is right in the thick of things.

For Yeats, "A terrible beauty was born" in the Easter Rebellion of 1916. But for O'Casey it was a tragedy that bordered on farce. Writing of the effect of the rebellion in *Inishfallen Fare Thee Well,* he says: "Things had changed, but not utterly; and no terrible beauty was to be born. Short Mass was still the favorite service and Brian Boru's harp still bloomed on the bottles of beer."

That is pretty much the tone of *The Plough and the Stars,* which is an Epic drama in its own right. Though O'Casey encourages all the Brechtian vices of empathy and illusion, the principal ironies resemble those of *Mother Courage.* The heroic event is undermined by the routine activities of common men; great things are shown up by small. We worked hard on Fluther's carpentry, the dressing for the rally, the passing of plates in the family dinner, the sedentary patience of Mollser in the little sun by the walls of what was our most expansive (and handsome) realistic set to date (by James H. Stearns). In Act II, the rally is a shadow of the shenanigans inside the pub; but as the Speaker kept passing by the window (like the funeral of the Commander Tilly in *Courage*), real hostilities were released, and the hilarious battle between Jennie Gogan and Bessie Burgess called our attention to the pathetic absurdities inherent in the revolt. In Act III, the rebellion underway, we do not see the gallant fighting at Liberty Hall or Boland's Mills (where De Valera emerged a national hero), nor are we with Macdonagh and Connolly and Pearse at the Post Office. We see instead Bessie and Jennie with a carriage full of stolen goods, the young socialist Covey with a ten-stone sack of loot, and then (in our production Robert Haswell made this the most stunning image of the play) the "heroic" Fluther Good shouting down the big guns with the cry of "Up the rebels!" as he reels, this genial good man, in a drunken frenzy. Everything ingratiating in the character is obliterated in that moment by the raw brutality of debased nationalism.

O'Casey naturally had mixed emotions about the sacking of the shops. The indignity of the looting is balanced against instinctive approval of those who were, as he said later in his autobiography, "stretching out their hands for food, for raiment, for colour, and for life"—or, as the Young Covey snarls at Peter Flynn, "to ketch a few o' the things that God is givin' to His chosen people. . . ." We tried to keep all these ironies up in the air as the looters sped in and out. Like the Young Covey, O'Casey had been a member of the Socialist Workers Party and, as a member of the lone Protestant family in a Catholic tenement, whose brother was in the trenches on the continent, he knew well the ambiguous and voluble brooding of Bessie Burgess (whose son was fighting also in the Great War, *for* England, with the Dublin Fusiliers). Those who protested, however, against O'Casey's looting scene apparently missed the point (or didn't get to it) of Brennan's anger in Act III—the exasperated wrath of a rebel who sees his cause besmirched by the silly people for whom he fought.

To the American actor, if I can judge from our experience, O'Casey is more immediately appealing than Brecht. He requires gusto and comic ability, but no special technique of feeling, no intellectual wit, beyond knowing how to play and breathe naturally through the racing curiosities of the language. (The dialect: where it is a problem, I believe in working on it separately from rehearsals, by a systematic breakdown of the sounds, even as the character finds the rhythm in rehearsal. I do not believe, as some lazy actors think, that finding the character is going automatically to find the dialect, for all the rhythm, if the actor doesn't pay some attention to it. Irish dialect, however, is easier than most.) Brecht is not above pathos, but pathos is more strategically deployed and surrounded by an iron curtain for conceptual purposes. A sob can be costly. Pity is ground out of the tough logic of plot. In O'Casey it is always just under the skin and on the tip of the tongue. Brecht is mordantly witty, O'Casey unregenerately humorous, breaking into harshness. He reminds us of Hals; Brecht, of Hogarth—at his darkest, of Goya. But O'Casey sings in a register that is rare in Brecht. And when he is aroused, he boils and soars and rages. If he can be appallingly sentimental, he can also shock. The death of Bessie is comparable to the death of Dumb Catherine, and the final tableau of *The Plough and the Stars*—the Tommies sipping tea while the Post Office is being shelled and their comrades sing "Keep the home fires burning" beneath the window—is an irony too calmly bitter to forget. Yet there is a marvelous charity in the desolation, far from the dread loneliness at the end of *Mother Courage,* as the Tommies are included among the chosen people.

The real virtue of O'Casey, in an age compulsively full of enmity, is this charity; and while other artists are compulsively engaged with technique, he also gives you a chance to let go with a big heart. As we run out of ways to have fun, he gives joy—and we need it.

Major Barbara would appear to be an ideal comedy for the Warfare State. For the capitalist Undershaft, whose daughter is drumming up souls for the Salvation Army, the two principles of salvation are Money and Gunpowder. Those of us, like myself, whose artistic enterprise is encouraged by the dividends of our permanent war economy, know how much comfort there may be in those principles.

Our production of *Major Barbara* was done in 1963, following our production of *The Balcony.* Shaw might have been outraged to hear it, and his devotees more so, but we returned to him then as to conventional ground. Despite the ominous subjects, it was a happy occasion. At the first meeting I told the cast that almost all of them were very well suited to their roles and that, as director, I would try to see that their natural sense of play (it was excellently read the first time round) would not be subverted by a false exploratory zeal. This kind of remark might have incapacitated actors in another setting, but it could be taken in its proper spirit by a group that had spent a whole season exploring one demanding play after another. This was not to be a rest. The actors had wit, intelligence, carriage, and a feel for the civilized flow of ideas, that happened to be a fact. Yes, we wanted to root the ideas in developed character, but we also wanted to trust ourselves. Simply, they appeared to know what Shaw wanted said and they wanted to say it with ease, not fearing glibness before it occurred.

It was when we thought about what Shaw wanted said that the trouble arose. And I tried to toughen the good easy familiarity by reminding us that, if some things in the play felt dated (there were people in the company who simply thought it square) it was Shaw who had given us the whole ethical ground for, as well as a warning against, Genet. "I am, and always have been," he wrote, "and shall now always be, a revolutionary writer, because our laws make laws impossible; our liberties destroy all freedom; our property is organized robbery; our morality is an impudent hypocrisy; our wisdom is administered by inexperienced or malexperienced dupes, our power wielded by cowards and weaklings, and our honor false in all its points. I am an enemy of the existing order for good reason; but that does not make my attacks any less encouraging or helpful to people who are its enemies for bad reasons. The existing order may shriek that if I tell the truth about it, some foolish person may drive it to become still worse by trying to assassinate it. I cannot help that, even if I could see what worse we could do than we are already doing."

Nevertheless, the play—taken seriously—was still troubling. There were themes that seemed as true today as they were at the turn of the century: though we may have somewhat less of it, the crime of poverty; the establishment of religions on blood money; the superiority of blood money to no money; the dominance of Undershaft and Lazarus in affairs of state. But as for the making of war on war by making explosives, it seemed to some of us that the limitation of the Life Force is that it could never free itself of Victorian illusions, because gunpowder is not exactly strontium 90.

"Well," says one of the characters, "the more destructive war becomes the sooner it will be abolished, eh?" If the play is just short of being instantaneously modern, it is because the character who advances that theory is at first glance the most oafish. But times change; yesterday's fool is tomorrow's oracle. Today that same character, flourishing his computer, may be advising the administration.

While we were rehearsing *Major Barbara,* William H. Honan published an article in *The New Republic,* "The Peaceful Use of Terror," in which he lists a number of the nineteenth-century scientists and inventors, headed by Alfred B. Nobel, who believed in that idea. "Like Andrew Undershaft in Shaw's *Major Barbara,* Nobel was an 'idealistic' munitions manufacturer. His object was not to advance the art of war, but, on the contrary, to abolish it, as if with a pedagogical *reductio ad absurdum.* 'On the day when two Army corps will be able to annihilate each other in one second,' he once told a friend, 'all civilized nations will recoil from war in horror and disband their forces.' And later, 'I should like to be able to turn out a substance or a machine of such horrible capacity for mass annihilation that thereby wars would become altogether impossible." Honan points out, with no more argument than facing the evidence of history, that "man continues to hope, blindly and sublimely, that the terror of his own destructiveness will repress his warlike nature. It never has."

Actually, the comparison of Nobel to Undershaft needs to be qualified. The latter says he is an impenitent "profiteer in mutilation and murder," though he might have put it thus bluntly to provoke his family, to shake up Wilton Crescent. His motto, however, is Blood and Fire. And he no more believes that the more destructive war becomes the sooner it will be abolished than he does in making excuses for his trade. He agrees with Mr. Honan, and goes one step further: "The more destructive war becomes," he says, "the more fascinating we find it." Which may be why we are not appeased when Shaw seems to urge us to convert Money and Gunpowder to the purposes of social revolution by marrying the daughter of the munitions king to a Greek scholar. We feel then that he lived in a world of more limited terrors, where such Platonic romances could be imagined with reason, and where one didn't shudder when he said, as Undershaft does, "What can blow up people can blow up society." It's hard to keep the explosives straight. Still, if one understands the spirit of Shaw's incendiarism, he realizes there is no solution *in* the play; the characters' brainstorms are left in tension by the drama, and the play's symbolic marriage is in the same realm of zany hope as Giraudoux's Madwoman saving the earth from rapine by pushing the capitalists into the sewer.

Don't mistake me: seeing the play this way, and playing the ecstatic *what if?* of its proposal, did not solve whatever acting problems did arise. But it did stiffen the spine of the comedy and keep it from becoming for us a muddled and anachronistic parable; or, rushing over the imperfect analogy to our own time, mere farce. The atmosphere of rehearsal for which we strove: in technique, fluent conversation and a definition of behavior by time and class; in attitude, to preserve the feeling that we knew what needed to be said, and could say it with ease; as regards what was said, to bring into performance—in Barbara, Undershaft, and Cusins especially—the wild imagination to believe there could be a common revolutionary motive in Undershaft's cannons and our bombs. Which is to say: to make a joyful plea for enlightened men to put aside their "oughts," to seize power where it beckons and act for drastic social change—the sort of change inherent in the more demonstrative and violent impulses of our unfinished democratic revolution.

To this job, or supporting it, there must be absolute will on behalf of humane value. "I am prepared to kill to make my own life worth living. This preparedness," says Undershaft (anonymity of the drama aside, one hears Shaw's voice in it), "is the final test of sincerity." The play, then, turns out to be harder tack than at first appears. And there is a fine existential ring firming up the social consciousness of this prefatory assertion: "We shall never have real moral responsibility until everyone knows that his deeds are irrevocable, and that his life depends on his usefulness." In playing out the conflict with Cusins—who can find no use for himself—and Barbara—who misuses herself, Undershaft had to believe these things with satanic conviction. Yet, in the playing, we wanted that conviction to grow from his first bland and intimidated entrance, when he is baffled by his family and mistakes everybody, to the oracular force in front of his guns, when he mistakes nothing. With Barbara and Cusins, through the final scenes, there is an incessant testing: Cusins admits he shares the Undershaft guilt, which makes him worthy of the Undershaft heritage; and there is a simple human weighing of their choice by two young people, before they dare to do ebulliently what they had every intention of doing anyhow.

As for the minor characters, say those useless denizens of the Salvation Army shelter: in their robust vitality, in their brainy time-serving, they remind us that there was once a world in which even the defeated were indefatigable, a world in which the impossible ringing down the grooves of change stood a faint chance of coming true.

Let me not exonerate the play from Shaw's apparent belief in the benevolence of force. Undershaft is blood kin to those visionaries of peace by threat of violence, like Gatling, Shrapnel, and Nobel, who said: "Let the sword of Damocles hang over every head and you will witness a miracle." After the agreement on the atmospheric test ban, I read statements by more than one scientist who believes in the same miracle. To convey a sense of it in the production, we executed a scene shift in which the munitions plant materialized before the audience out of Wilton Crescent, after Barbara, in *a single sentence* by Undershaft, turned from despair to faith (her spirit still troubled, she says) and asks to be taken to the factory of death, so she might learn something more. As a chorus sang "Praise ye the god of gold!" (from Walton's *Belshazzar's Feast,* the text from Isaiah), a gun-base was rolled on, a cylinder head, and a cannon lowered amid high-rising cable; and in the last image of the production, it swiveled over Cusins' head toward the audience. Which laughed, slightly, with discreet anxiety.

Distrusting the miracle we had helped propose and explore, we could direct our belief to that part of Shaw which had placed the burden on our willingness to be incendiary, to use our brains to control our power, and to attack that in society which made the cannon necessary. What we didn't feel free to do was to cancel the necessity outright, by any false flush of Barbara's enthusiasm for universal salvation. Cusins' trial was our trial, and we meant him to realize in that last Damocles moment that he had maybe taken on more than he bargained for.

The solution remained outside the play, if at all.

It was the apparent failure of all post-Shavian solutions—normalcy, the war, normalcy, Spain, appeasement, the blitz, the Bomb, normalcy, the renewed smuggeries of the stiff-brained Tories, as well as the queer collusion of Blimps and liberals in the publicly owned cant of postwar Britain—that led to John Osborne and the generation of Anger.

Whether one remained socialist or not, angry or not, George Scott (who became a Tory before he was thirty) speaks for all their disenchantment in *Time and Place:* "Socialism created not a universal brotherhood but a clogging, spreading weed of bureaucracy, leading logically perhaps to an authoritarian state." And it was even possible to feel that Shaw's enlightenment by scholarship had led to educated frustration in the uneasy peace. Barbara, not Cusins, had had her way with the munitions workers, and she proved the bloody bore Bill Walker thought her to begin with, a regular earl's granddaughter, naggin' and naggin' about higher things: "Wot prawce selvytion nah?"

Graduated from those red-brick universities with the social gift of education and the prospect of no-future, the sons of the socialist revolution seemed to have three possible alternatives, one relatively modern, the other two classical: male hypergamy (marrying into the Room at the Top), emigration (usually to Canada), or blowing up in outrage. The last may have preceded the other two, or subsided into adjustment and even gratitude for the benefits. Or, into the detached irony of a Kingsley Amis, who muses above the anger with which he is identified—nobody wanting to be classified: "Violence has a good deal of charm for some sections of the intelligentsia (as the cult of bullfighting shows), or at any rate the thought of violence is attractive. It provides a way of getting one's own back by proxy on one's parents and one's old headmaster; one can work off the guilt of having been to a public school and so on by chatting about blowing up the class one was born into. . . ."

Or, since John Osborne was born into the working class, to make others feel guilty—as Jimmy Porter does with his wife—for not committing class suicide. Pusillanimous.

The Welfare State, then, has thrown up a new breed, with competing strains: those who are embarrassed by privilege and long to be stripped of it (ALISON: I was wrong, I was wrong! . . . I want to be a lost cause. I want to be corrupt and futile. . . . Don't you see! I'm in the mud at last! I'm grovelling; I'm crawling! Oh, God. . . .) and those who want, like Arnold Wesker, "to resist the application of manufactured standards, to protest against ugly articles of furniture and tableware, to speak out against the sham architecture, to resist the importation into more and more public places of loudspeakers relaying the Light Programme, to say one word against the Yellow Press, against the best-seller, against the theater-organ," etc., etc. Only those are not Wesker's words nor those of Beatie Bryant in *Roots.* They come rather from "the new hero," Amis' Lucky Jim who, with "a long, jabbering belch . . . got up from the chair where he'd been writing this and did his ape imitation all round the room." One slips from anger into wild laughter or, since there is a wit of good sense even in the most demonic of the British, into satire.

Withal, there *were* the ghouls and gibbers of the painter Francis Bacon to accompany the lower debasements of the Empire: the tubes shrieking with queers, the "models" advertising at the grocery stores, or the zombies of Bond Street, looking like they'd been got up at Madame Tussaud's. The Profumo revelations would be, for Osborne, only the confessed aery of national scandal, which Archie Rice had been singing about for a long time:

> Thank God I'm normal, normal, normal.
> Thank God I'm normal,
> I'm just like the rest of you chaps.

For Osborne, the national failure may require socialist solutions ("Experiment means asking questions, and these are all the questions of socialism"), but the real failure is a failure of Sex. ("Keep your peckers up!") He is the heir of Lawrence as well as Shaw. And when he reviews the plays of Tennessee Williams he sounds as if he were writing an appendix to Lawrence's *Studies in Classic American Literature*: "America is as sexually obsessed as a medieval monastery. That is what the plays are about—sex. Sex and failure. The moral failure of Protestant Capitalism has produced the biggest sexual nuthouse since the Middle Ages."

Yet one source of Osborne's rage is Britain's dependence on America, economically, militarily—and sexually. In the grain. We produced *The Entertainer* in 1959. Two years later, there was a report from England that the oaks in Sherwood Forest—Robin Hood's woodland and Lawrence's childhood park—were being stunted by factory fumes and feeble soil. To replace them, red oaks from America were being planted. The report said: "The American oak will flourish in poor, sandy soil." "I must say," says Jimmy Porter, "it's pretty dreary living in the American Age—unless you're in America of course. Perhaps all our children will be Americans. That's a thought isn't it?" In Nottinghamshire, Robin Hood's oak still stands, but the prospects—even if we discount Osborne's scourge of Merrie England—are not imperial.

Lest we be tempted into racial superiority, mustering our niggling savagery, remember that Osborne said we were in a nuthouse too. And if, looking over the revolution in the English theater of the fifties, we excuse our own impotence by saying Odets did the same thing in the thirties, well, Odets went to Hollywood; and to compare with the Angry Young Men we have had the Beats, who may have talked a good deal more about orgasm, but who were finally more showoff and less educated, and—if I may be allowed, like Osborne, another sweeping statement—more queer. True, one of the oddities brought on by the insurgence of the English Stage Society and Osborne, its chief demolition expert, is the devotion of young English directors to American acting. After almost a century of balanced teacups, kind hearts and coronets, the English stage is become virile with a vengeance. The Method was plumped for in the posh papers; and just as there are poets with clipped accents and measured cadences writing knowledgeably of motorcycles, so there are actors, trained at RADA and speaking the speech of Gielgud, practicing a self-seeking slouch in the American way.

This cult of "truth" and gusto, now qualified by devotion to Brecht, was part of the Americanization not only of England, but of Europe. It partly explains why American ballet, with its swift leaps of modish neurosis (even a little faggoty) wowed them all over Europe, and why the British intelligentsia were crazy about *West Side Story*. American musicals, we know, thrive on the West End, and for a while the new "serious drama" on the commercial stage (for instance, Robert Bolt's *Flowering Cherry*) began to look like *Death of a Salesman,* in line with the British discovery that father *is* to blame.

So, while Osborne requires little from our actors that they don't already know, as actors, the one element that is new (since none of our dramatists have it, except Albee) is the particular wit, not a needle, but a jackhammer. (We hear it in some of our stand-up comedians.) In this respect, Osborne is the dramatist of the age of Teddy Boys and devaluation, a hip foundling with a wicked tongue, incendiary in the tradition of Shaw but blowing up like Dizzy Gillespie. The success of his plays (granted their limitations) may convince us that social breakthroughs are tougher in the American theater, but we could not scorn their bite, their pith, their pertinence, and their full-gutted complaint. The sado-masochism, the scatology, the socialism gone bell-wacky, the pathology of squirrels and bears can be irritating (and Osborne is not so sophisticated in the uses of infantility as Albee or Gelber), but the barrage inspired his contemporaries, as it turns the mind back to society and social change. You could rally round it—and that is no mean thing.

As The Workshop developed, we felt allied to the breakthrough in the British theater, even as we envied it. And we knew that those who used Jimmy Porter's lament that there were no more causes to justify their own delinquency had forgotten to notice that Osborne toted a sandwich sign in Trafalgar Square, and had gone marching to Aldermaston. While a lot of us were living it up, our compeers in London were sitting down. For all the despair and paradoxes in Osborne's generation, it was trying by rage and political action to recreate society with the theater. The Royal Court, directed by a very congenial square, gave egress to the new protest, as well as the new voices from abroad. And Joan Littlewood's Theatre Workshop, more militantly socialist, was one of the most original popular theaters in Europe. While she faced the paradox that the proletarians in the district of her theater didn't come to her plays until she made it to the West End, she never sold out. And after a period of disenchantment with the possibility of a permanent company, dispersed by success, she came out of retirement, collected her people, went back to the East End; and if what we hear is true, has done her best production to date, *Oh What a Lovely War,* a singular achievement of the idea of an ensemble.

The Long Revolution may go on imperturbably, but the passion of rebellion does waver. So with the breakthrough of theater in England. When Kenneth Tynan returned to London in 1961, after his stint in New York (where he complained of almost everything except *The Connection* and Lenny Bruce), he wrote of "The Breakthrough that broke down." But for Tynan—catechist, parodist, midwife, and Prime Minister of the Movement (he saved *Look Back in Anger* after it was doused by the dailies)—that was a way of whipping it up again. If I dwell on the English theater of the fifties it is because, unlike the same period in America and the new "developments" of the present decade, the things happening took the shape of ideas, passions, plays, and ways of working. It led to the formation of the Stratford company, and a conception of National Theater which includes Tynan as *dramaturg* and some of the young directors of the breakthrough working with Laurence Olivier. True, most of the energy has been consolidated in London, and we can afford nothing like that—we must spread over the country, and in our own way. At the moment, we have threads, but no fabric. But the English theater of the last decade has been a refreshing partner in a common enterprise. We could still see that platforms were being nailed up in the theater, revolutions were still possible (the English claim their situation was more hopeless), and passion could still be young. Cries Jimmy, when he is most infectious: "Oh heavens, how I long for a little ordinary enthusiasm. Just enthusiasm—that's all. I want to hear a warm, thrilling voice cry out Hallelujah! Hallelujah! I'm alive. I've an idea. Why don't we have a little game? Let's pretend we're human beings, and that we're actually alive." Yes, yes, in our great running critique of Romanticism, we know all about the dangers and even silliness of misdirected enthusiasm, but what a great lovely productive value it once was—and how our theater needs it.

The achievement of *The Entertainer,* however, was this particular young man's view of the tatty, tawdry, fornicating, shot-load grifter of the music halls who, rising above trade and station, does become an emblem of a nation's self-disgust.

The Entertainer is an elegy with a sting. Its topical background is Cyprus and the Suez Crisis, Mr. Eden's gamble, which represented for many of Osborne's generation the last feckless effort of the Empire to keep its sun from setting. The social urgency takes the form of a Chekhovian plaint of passing seen through the numbers of the music hall. What is rare—say in comparison with our own little wistful plays of decay—is that there is history in the delirium tremens. It is a Social Drama, with far less of the author's self-pity coming through Archie Rice than through Jimmy Porter, and practically none of the ineffectual crying-in-the-cups that one feels in Anderson or Inge. And the coming of the income tax man has, on both the personal and social levels, some of the more dreadful reverberations of Mr. Pereira and the KNOCK KNOCK KNOCK in Eliot's *Sweeney Agonistes.*

In his prefatory note, Osborne writes that "The music hall is dying, and, with it, a significant part of England." What this significance was had been described by Eliot, one of Osborne's most eminent targets, now major poet of the Establishment. That was back in 1923, in his epitaph for Marie Lloyd: "The lower class still exists," Eliot said, "but perhaps it will not exist for long. In the music-hall comedians they find the expression and dignity of their own lives; and this is not found in the most elaborate and expensive revue. In England, at any rate, the revue expresses almost nothing. [He might be speaking of the American musical.] With the decay of the music-hall, with the encroachment of the cheap and rapid-breeding cinema, the lower classes will tend to drop into the same state of protoplasm as the bourgeoisie. The working man who went to the music hall and saw Marie Lloyd and joined in the chorus was himself performing part of the act. . . ."

Osborne might smell out intimations of snobbery here, and there is also something of that highbrow sentimentality about the vigor of folk art, like boxing and six-day bike racing, that—as with Cocteau and even Brecht—often forgets that for every Marie Lloyd there were hundreds of Archie Rices, even in Billie Rice's day. As Raymond Williams has pointed out, there is a direct line of descent from the maudlin chaos of the eighteenth-century stage through the music halls to the variety shows on the telly. To complain about those, or of strip-tease shows and "pop" singers, "and to use the music-hall as an example of contrasting vitality or health, is to ignore the clear evidence that it was the illegitimate theaters and the music-halls which established these kinds of entertainment. If you don't like it in one century, you can't reasonably like it in another, and the attendant features of fashionable booms, fantastic salaries, and high-pressure publicity are all equally evident in music-hall history."

It is to Osborne's credit that while he recognizes the offbeat areas of experience opened up by a Marie Lloyd or a Dan Leno, and while he may long for the old days with Billie Rice, the play puts the music hall there in all its tart, baleful, titty-peering shoddiness. Eliot's prophecy is fulfilled: Paradise Street and Claypit Lane have gone, like England, to seed. Archie Rice plays before an assemblage of sad little drabs and by the reluctant agreement of thirty angry people; or so he says, for there is also the real audience, to laugh it up with this failure who knows he's a failure, the calloused jester of a nation's embarrassment, enthusiasm gone sour, turned into acerbity and self-contempt. Irrepressibly nasty and done to a turn ("Have you ever had it on a kitchen table? Like a piece of meat on a slab."), Archie still lives, he does, he has a go of it, and his family is rendered with a mature compassion.

However harsh and mistaken the drama's social criticism may seem to members of the Establishment, and even to outsiders (we had complaints), it has pity without condescension and the grace of humor. And I don't mean that Rotary sense of humor which, in London or San Francisco, is invoked whenever there is a real kick to be made, and invoked by the most craven, the snivelers and the biggest boors, who would despair of themselves in an instant, if they had the wit to know it.

> Why should I care?
> Why should I let it get me?
> What's the use of despair,
> If they call you a square?

Archie, who *says* he is out for "good old Number One," knows them for what they are, and he who directs or plays him (Irving directed, Symonds played Archie) has got to be able to spit it out. The danger in the playing is to soften the attack by ingratiation. Archie must be winning, but he mustn't fudge.

His banter is never without a slicing edge—and on the verge of full personal exposure. There is decency in the background that comes up in him, and in his wife, who sings lovelily in *her* cups, and helps him on with his coat to meet the income tax man. The image of affection is unashamed, but it comes by default into the rhythm of dependency, out of painful loneliness of heart, with no lectures about forgiving love.

Actually, it is the younger people with whom Osborne has the most trouble in this play. They are harder to act, for they don't have the compulsions of Jimmy Porter to excite them, and they are driven by passivity to provide formulas for what Archie's songs so palpably define. Picking at the putrescence, they are dying for hope. What they end up with is doctrine, borrowed from the Continent. "Here we are," says Jean, who mopes through the play with a sympathetic ear, "we're alone in the universe, there's no God, it just seems that it all began by something as simple as sunlight striking a piece of rock. And here we are. We've got only ourselves. Somehow, we've just got to make a go of it. *We've only ourselves.*"

Where it occurs, it seems redundant, tacked on to the tackiness, which speaks for itself. Archie has something in common with Sartre's hero in *Nausea,* who says for both of them: "The Nausea is not inside me: I feel it *out there* in the wall, in the suspenders, everywhere around me. . . . I am the one who is within *it.*" Nevertheless, I think that residue of dependency, a familial warmth rather than irretrievable alienation is what will keep Osborne's drama from ever developing more than existential tremors, in its darkest plight. In fact, I think there is probably something in the English character— that character which the stuffiest characters in Shaw are always extolling— which kept existentialism from taking real root there after the war, as it did in France. One would think the Blitz would have made a nation of existentialists overnight, but it took only one channel crossing for me, succumbing to Nothingness, to have a sense of British resistance to Nausea.

Jean's existential "choice" to make a go of it seems banal, and it is possible in performance to show that—a platitude added to the passivity, resolving nothing, the last note of collective desperation. But I suspect Osborne means her to mean it, and we played it that way. Never mind. *The Entertainer* is hardy enough to support a little grasping at ideological straws; and when Osborne says, "I shall simply fling down a few statements—you can take your pick. . . . It is too late for caution"—he is young enough to be still privileged to the bravado. There was always something sophomoric in his declaration of war against England, but in *The Entertainer,* the personal thrashing was becalmed and directed more tellingly through the dreary consolations of song and dance, exposing the dissipation of an Empire.

Too late for caution. It is an attitude we could have used more of in the American theater during the last decade. If we didn't make the same allowances for some American dramatists, it was because, having dirty grievances written all over their pathos, they cringed from spitting it out. Their complaint, avoiding direct confrontation, lacked the breadth of social criticism.

It became a whine. So we contented ourselves with hippy sniping in the bistros and did foreign plays. With Albee, one feels the imminence of a more public loosening of tongues and more audacity, but up to date our best social criticism has been way out, almost unhinged. We still have to find a way of leveling with Society without self-exemption, without demeaning people, and without a promiscuous stream of abuse, whatever it opens up. I dig Lenny Bruce as much as anybody, but when we invoke Rabelais to justify every obscenity, we forget that while he had Gargantua piss over Paris to clean the streets, it was over the Abbey of Thélème, a stronghold of humanism, that he inscribed "Do What Thou Wouldst." Which is to say that, like Shaw, he was finally an organization man who understood something more disciplined and provisional in the social use of violence, and that by breaking the bone and sucking "the substantific marrow," he was not prescribing unlimited orgones and experimental kicks. Which is to say that saying it all may still fall short of saying it whole, either about Society or about the Self.

A play which explores directly the social use of violence, and its limits, is John Arden's *Serjeant Musgrave's Dance*. We did the American première in October 1961. Our rehearsals started during one of the larger tremors in the Berlin Crisis. As the situation was not much less alarming than at the start of *Galileo,* we joked about *Musgrave* being anachronistic before it went on. If dread tends to become comic or sanctimonious, that's one of the crosses of living in a world which toys so hugely with our fears. It makes no difference that fear and trembling are built into the Human Condition, or that behind the past lurked earthquakes, the Black Plague, and barbarian hordes. Our terror is both more subtle and omnipresent, as it is advertised more efficiently, than in the Age of Dinosaurs.

Because it fears sanctimony, *Serjeant Musgrave's Dance* is an anti-war drama that, to begin with, and more alarmingly as it goes on, distrusts its own best convictions. That makes for a remarkable tension that will take us to the borders of despair, and into the same region of our black hearts as other dramatists with less hortatory purpose.

Arden has written in his introduction to the play: "Complete pacifism is a very hard doctrine: and if this play appears to advocate it with perhaps some timidity, it is probably because I am naturally a timid man—and also because I know that if I am hit I very easily hit back: and I do not care to preach too confidently what I am not sure I can practice." The first production of the play in London actually led to charges that this pacifist drama was urging a bloody revolution. Arden denies it; examined closely, the play isn't sure.

What is sure is the boldness of its technique, the strength of its dramatic gesture, and the balladlike character of its action. Which reminds us, as we ponder the genteel decay of the Empire, that the English are also, as Arden says, "an extraordinarily passionate people, as violent as they are amorous, and quite astonishingly hostile to good government and order." The ballads document this passion, like Jacobean drama, and if "the modern idea of a sludgy uninterested nation, married to its telly and its fish and chips, has any truth in it . . . it is the business of the dramatist to cry out against it even if there seems to be no hope of his ever being heard. That there is no hope, I do not believe." He is, indeed, trying to write social criticism, and if he has a model in the contemporary theater, it is Brecht—from whom he has learned not only that one must place powerful images before an audience, but also a Story which forms "traditional poetic truths." Brecht, we recall, was a balladeer.

So then: primary colors, heroic gestures, verse, dance, song, and a military drum; a simple theme in a harsh setting; *violence* (as the ballad says, "the cannerin' worm doth chide"). Legend becoming history; informing it.

Four soldiers, presumably recruiters, come to a strikebound mining town, carrying the skeleton of a dead comrade in an army crate. They have come, according to their leader, "to work guilt back to where it began." The town— northern, bleak, suspicious—takes the soldiers for strikebreakers. At the action's climax, in the public square, the skeleton is hoisted from the box, a Gatling gun appears from another crate, and the Serjeant turns his rifle upon the townspeople, demanding from them a revolution: Peace—or else! He does a savage dance to drive home the threat.

It is the piety of the fanatic. We are reminded again that the danger of logical rebellion is the loss of coherence. The high idealist becomes the impassioned murderer. What comes out of the drama—for all the boldness of design—is the incertitude of the Saint, as well as the conviction—the one testing and outraging the other, until we have an action that is frightened by excess of its own peaceable intentions. "I think," Arden has written, "that many of us must at some time have felt an overpowering urge to match some particularly outrageous piece of violence with an even greater and more outrageous retaliation." In a century which has seen so much wanton shedding of blood on behalf of Purity or Ideology, the skeleton is a harsh reminder. "We are each one guilty of particular blood." The play impales us with particular responsibility. But Musgrave, in that final assemblage in the public square, wants to do more than "pay for Billy"; particular guilt turns into a universal death wish. The Gatling gun, we realize, is turned upon *us*. And it takes the Dragoons to save the town from the fate of Lidice.

Things "are restored to order," however, in a gallows dance. The townspeople lock hands in the normal round, driven on by the sniggering Bargee. The colliers capitulate, like Mother Courage. The war machine, represented by the Dragoon Officer, smiles benignly. Our own complicity is defined in the capitulation. But if we are moved to act against it, not knowing how, we may also be evading a deeper strike. Have we not seen a magnified example of the truth that, in our desperate desire for peace, or justice, we might be driven to violence to achieve it? (Think of our racial problem.) The play evokes our darker suspicion that war may be some inhuman form of human necessity— not only a matter of power politics and economic duplicity, but rooted (as Freud hinted at the bleak end of his last books) in the divided nature of man. (The Bargee—a not wholly realized character—points to the lower depths, to pure evil limping as social cunning.) The problem stated by Camus remains: how can we discover in our acknowledgement of universal crime "the principle of reasonable culpability"?

As a study of the pathology of a town, *Musgrave* is far more threatening than *The Crucible*.

The production went on, as I wrote Arden, "with great expectations, a sense of pitch and moment in the cast. It went down, on the very hottest heat-wave night of the year. . . , like a plugged rook." Surmounting approval of the play's eloquence were sneers, apathy, condescension, and outright virulence. As an opener to our season, it was one of the plays that lost us a fair number of subscribers. If the production was praised for its imagination, the play was condemned for being "punch-drunk" and amateur. One reviewer, who said that it didn't take courage but foolishness to produce the play, called for the sponsors of The Workshop to "take a good look at just who is running the theater. And to what purpose." But if the play was scorned as "a soapbox for the social philosophies" of those who run The Workshop, I was scoured else-where for directing it with "intolerable slowness" and bogging it down with psychoanalytic gloom. Whether there were laments over the murk, or assaults on our eggheadism, or the whole thing patronized by some fatheads as a "mildly interesting" first play, there was universal complaint over the length of the production when it first opened. And even those who were favorably disposed called for us "to trim it up and shape it up"; in short, to move it faster.

There were various reasons for the length of the production, including the fact that our shop had been looted (like a scene from *The Plough and the Stars*: whoever broke in proclaimed to the neighborhood that the building was being condemned and everything was up for grabs), and the technical apparatus was late. Thus, when we opened, scene transitions—involving front projections and abstract backdrops—were sluggish. The harried technical rehearsals unnerved the actors, but Tom Rosqui nevertheless gave us an adamant and possessed Musgrave. The transitions were easily corrected (they were actually faster to begin with than in the London production), but the main source of tedium was in the body of performance—the play as played.

Indeed, the question of tedium in *Musgrave* is so complex it brings us again to the idea of Time in the theater. The crucial subject: Time as time-serving, material Time, Time as tempo, Time in its metaphysical aspect. The whole controversy over phenomenology resonates in what used to be accepted as the two hours' traffic of the stage. It is significant that after the production in London, comparisons with film technique were used in its defense.

Criticized also for moving the play too slowly, the director Lindsay Anderson wrote later: "When an intelligent critic makes a comment like that, I don't feel—'Oh, what a pity, it didn't come off, I should have made the whole thing brisker. . . .' On the contrary, I feel I should have made the whole thing *really* slow . . . *boring* the audience into a realisation of what they were seeing . . . ." I read this after we had done our production. By then I had been tempted to the same theory (not boring people to death, but boring them into life) to defend our "intolerable slowness." But I am convinced it is rationalization, and while I concede that a correct inner rhythm must be granted its time, and will be, I am not sure the play can support the urge to make it *"really* slow."

The ballads, to which the play is indebted, are revealing on this point. There is in the ballads a *"poetic concentration on the everyday,"* but those narratives are not *"anti-dramatic"* in the modern sense. While an action may be told and retold, giving the illusion of a spatial form, there is also a swift economy of detail from scene to scene, and a beautiful sense of pacing. If they seem timeless, it's that they cause you to forget time by measuring it out quickly, even the longest of them. The images speak directly to the heart. The strategy is scenic, as in film, but the camera does not hover—except where the action lingers, like the cork-heeled shoon bobbing on the deep in *Sir Patrick Spens.* Above the dead sailors the verse floats in lament, and moves on. The ballads may circle back upon themselves in refrain, but they go about their business, which is the telling of a story, with incessant motion. Even the bobbing shoon are an elision in the telling—a climax not indulged.

So I think the defense of *Musgrave* wants to have it both ways: on the one hand, the simplicity of a ballad; on the other, the unhurried *thereness* of a Dreyer or Antonioni. I think it takes nothing from the audacity of the play to admit there might be faulty construction—and that the long suspended exposition of Musgrave's mission, and the characterization of the town, might be too much there. As for directing it more slowly, the bright tunics, the guns, the crates, the drum, the songs, the monomania of Musgrave—the *Fable* itself —are powerful enough to make their impression without lingering on objects and actions, whose "meaning" is already self-evident. Everything must be given full weight, but without permitting it to retard the narrative. So, too, with the acting.

I was aware of all this when we started rehearsals. I pointed out to the cast that in an earlier version Arden had spoken of a "farcical-melodramatic convention" for the play, which implied a spare psychology in the acting out. Aside from the colonial atrocity which was the cause of his coming, we do not know how Musgrave became the way he is; he reads the Bible, but biography is minimal. Given the way he *is*—a Cromwellian soldier in a colliery town in Victoria's England, by way of the Crimea—we are to understand what he means by what he says and does. Detail of *behavior,* I said, must be rigorously selected. As in Brecht, the play demands some disinterestedness in the acting: not what *you* feel, but what the play *means* you to feel. The actors are images. This was not to say that what they felt had no relevance, only that it could move, in all personal honesty, off into irrelevance. We would, I suggested, explore the play "naturalistically" and organically discover its "objective content." Though Arden used masks in a later play, *The Happy Haven,* we would not do so here. But the actors might remember— the minor characters in particular (Parson, Constable, Mayor, etc.)—that they were defined by *social roles* almost as if they were wearing masks. The actions were to be "real," vivid, unencumbered actions, as in the ballads.

Yet no sooner did rehearsals begin, our own instinct for "exploration" took over. And when I say exploration, I mean psychological exploration, the kind we seem to know best. The actions become more and more "real," and more and more protracted by "truthful" filling in of character. When this happens you may reach a point of no return to selective gesture. I don't think we ever reached that point, but it was true that the play's retarded motion, its expansive development, was aggravated by psychological earnestness in the acting of the major roles. No matter what those who defend the play argue, it cannot be held back too long. We didn't select enough. Even if we did, the controlling factor in Time is perception: what needs to be seen could be seen no better by the most engaged observer if, as Anderson insists, the action is slowed to the point of boredom. And what would boredom be telling us? That the town is slag-ridden, dank, weighing heavily on life? I should think that would be a given; such a town, a type of town, speaks for itself. What wants definition is the conversion of Musgrave's saintly passion into holy terrorism, and the collusion of the townspeople in their own oppression.

In itself, the acting of the major roles was always interesting. To discern where it impeded the Fable is, of course, a relative matter; that depends, finally, on the chemistry of a particular production seen by a particular audience, and the placement of a scene in the great rhythm of the whole play. The love scene in the stable, leading to the murder of Sparky, is a case in point. It was, I think, beautifully played, but because just about that time one was feeling the play's length, it was possible to become aware that it is an old-fashioned "scene," leading to a melodramatic climax. While it had to be given its proper time lest it be unbelievably played, it didn't really have that much perceptual content. Meanwhile, Musgrave, who needed the time in his delirium, and whose ramblings must be assimilated, had to play through a kind of drag in the play's rhythm that we could not overcome entirely—and which did account for the one scene I was conscious of directing fast, too fast, the end of the second act. Constable, Parson, and Mayor rushed on, keeping up the momentum, but artificially.

Nevertheless, we all felt, right after we opened, that the *play* was immediately improved when we went through it and moved other sequences faster. And when I say improved, I am not talking about creating excitement by pace to wake up the audience which likes that. I mean its Fable was more vividly felt, given more meaning, more rhythmic definition, instead of being dissipated in inattention. (In the end, boredom is not the point of *Musgrave*, as it is the point of *Waiting for Godot*.) With that adjustment alone, we felt —though it was a box-office disaster (the reviews had done their work)— that *Musgrave* was one of our best productions. Instead of tedium, there was a suspended intensity that moved, and burst into violence.

Visually, what we tried was only a partial success—but well worth the try. There was a fast traveler on which we projected landscapes, in color, of the north country. Behind this the objects of each scene materialized by "bleeding through" a scrim. These were in extended structural relation to the backdrops, which were black-and-white abstractions of the projected scene (I felt, however, they were too narrow in proportion to the landscapes, so that the stage lacked the density we wanted). The front projections were like the illustrations that might precede a chapter in some narrative of adventure, but bleakly evocative, acid in tone. The abstractions were painted with a rough monolithic stroke (something like Franz Klein). The heavy wooden crates of the first scene, containing the guns and skeleton, were disposed about the stage in the same positions as the gravestones later. There was metal: the rifles, cold, sticking to the fingers; the Gatling gun; the collier's boots, the pick-hefts, the brass bedstead. An industrial town; metallic emotions.

In the graveyard, there was a *trompe l'oeil* subversion of style toward abstraction, as the soldiers ("red uniforms in a black and white coalfield") perched queerly on the gravestones, quite like red rooks, as they tensed to wait the colliers. The Fred Karno sequence, meant to show that the ignorant miners were the type to become good soldiers, was played with the actors drilling in and out of three equally spaced pools of light, like street lamps extended from the front projection. These corresponded to the three rectangular stalls of the stable, defined by light, as Musgrave's bed in the rear seemed suspended in darkness. What we wanted in each scene was a rhythmic image (the means were actually simple) moving visually from a whole landscape to a whole scene to a particular event abstracted from a whole social action.

And everything was meant to focus the movement in Musgrave from apparently rational purpose to an *idée fixe,* in that terrible domain of human passion where obsession becomes possession; that is, where the force of personal will is invaded by a demon. The demon takes possession of the whole town; but it is the point at which Social Drama reels back into the realm of Mystery—and one wonders again at what terrible cost a man finds a home among men.

In the preface to his plays, Arthur Miller writes "It is necessary, if one is to reflect reality, not only to reflect why a man does what he does, or why he nearly didn't do it, but why he simply cannot walk away and say to hell with it." He adds that a play is "a species of jurisprudence, and some part of it must take the advocate's role, something else must act in defense, and the entirety must engage the Law." The Law may be represented by snaky goddesses or a Button Moulder; by a Beggar Woman or a Creditor; by a Bargee or a Dragoon, *or both*—which immediately puts in question the lawfulness of the Law. Still, the punishment for infraction may range from loss of job through social ostracism to suicide or the gallows. However it is represented, the Law functions in mysterious ways, and the Last Judgment of the finest drama takes us back to the arcane, where the drama was born.

Whatever is is right, but it may be impossible to understand it—just as it may be impossible to explain fully why a dramatic character cannot walk away and say to hell with it.

"Why seems it so particular with thee?" asks Hamlet's mother, after the unnerving but common saw: "All that lives must die,/Passing through nature to eternity." "Seems, madam! Nay, it is. I know not 'seems.'" Yet there is always a gap between the impertinence and the reality, which is seeming, seeming. Precisely. It is the gap that makes things more particular.

Axiom for psychiatric social workers: the dramatic character is beyond adjustment, as he is beyond bargaining.

Which is to say, whatever his social role, as dramatic agent he cannot be bourgeois. Lord of the bourgeois, the Troll King says to Peer Gynt: "Man, to thyself be—enough." The Troll King is the purveyor of seeming; so is Iago; so is Judge Brack. They all have bourgeois values, but they are masters of their class, exceeding it. Unclassifiable, Peer, mountebank of Free Enterprise, is full of the momentum of a century careening through its fantasies of change; he cannot rest. (Nor change.) Until he comes home roundabout or is gathered into the artifice of eternity, the dramatic hero insists on following things out to their inevitable end, or to that unmathematical and ready middle of experience that resolves "To be or not to be" in "Let be."

The motive—what? Will? Moral Purpose? Fate? History? Providence? The Dignity of Man? Or all these working interweavingly and impossible together, as in the mat-making incident of *Moby-Dick,* where Chance, in the indifferent blade of the pagan Queequeg, has "the last featuring blow at events." The cost: mainly self-destruction—calamity, catastrophe, the fall of the sparrow, accidental slaughter, a plague on both your houses, the shadowy waters, the dark root of the scream, the mill race, Birnam Wood, and the bleeding eyeballs. The effect: Catharsis? Maybe. More likely woe and wonder, the hieratic emotion of what the jazz addict means by *stoned.*

The excess of the instinct for bearing things out to the edge of doom turns tragedy to comedy. We are in such an impure way now, with our ambiguous Cold War. "What is right for us is comedy," says the Swiss dramatist Duerrenmatt, with native impartiality making the best of a bad job. "Our world has led to the grotesque as well as to the atom bomb, and Hieronymus' madness is with us again, the apocalyptic vision has become the grotesquely real. But the grotesque is only a way of expressing in a tangible manner, of making us perceive physically the paradoxical, the form of the unformed, the face of a world without face; and just as in our thinking today we seem to be unable to do without the concept of paradox, so also in art, and in our world which at times seems still to exist only because the atom bomb exists; out of fear of the bomb." Dread prolonged *is* laughable—a commonplace long before Baudelaire, but a collective fact of our time. Or, as the banished Edgar, resting from his role as Mad Tom, puts it in *King Lear*: "the lamentable fall is from the best/The worst returns to laughter."

If comedy is what happens when tragedy fails, tragedy is what happens when comedy fails. Duerrenmatt knows that the tragic (if not tragedy) may come out of the comic "as a frightening moment, as an abyss that opens suddenly"—as when Buster Keaton, directing the Rebel artillery with a sword that flies off the hilt, notices his comrades falling, mysteriously, one by one, about him. Discretion being the better part of valor, he runs, brandishing his terrible sword, blade leaving hilt in a high lyric arc, impaling a Union sniper. At the limits of the credible, the Absurd, an *O altitudo!* in reverse. "The point about tragedy," says Harold Pinter, "is that it is *no longer funny*." In *Musgrave,* the townspeople guzzle their beer and dance around the public square—a dance of death. For a moment, "it is funny, and then it becomes no longer funny."

Which brings us to those disturbing and Januslike "anti-dramas" that, annihilating social value and dancing with death, make a fine art of having it both ways.

8

There is nothing so stimulating as nothing, at least now and then.
—Max Frisch, *Diary*

You could not be born at a better period than the present, when we have lost everything.
—Simone Weil, *Gravity and Grace*

HORATIO: *Oh, day and night, but this is wondrous strange!*
HAMLET: *And therefore as a stranger give it welcome.*

COUNTERFORCE II: Notes from the Underground

A woman once asked Chekhov: "What is the meaning of life?" He replied, "You ask me, what is life? It is just as if you had said, what is a carrot? A carrot is a carrot; that is all there is to it."

I have a feeling he really knew there was more to it than that, but a goodly amount of art in our time has been created or talked about to put off people who are always looking for meaning. That is why so much of it has acquired the reputation of being without meaning. The artists encourage this. Eliot says he would tell us the meaning of *Sweeney Agonistes* if he knew; Beckett says he would tell us who Godot is if he knew. In a discussion after our production of *Godot,* a chemist insisted it couldn't be a good play because there was no meaning, no message. "I want to know the message," he said, pounding the table.

Well, all you can say to that is, if there is a message it's not glad tidings. And when you're really aroused you may insist in return that an empirical scientist ought to know better than that—that a carrot is a carrot is a carrot, overstating the point.

Even so: after we satisfy our aesthetic egos and get rid of the boors by saying the thing *is,* or "nothing happens, twice," we can settle down and say a good deal about the meaning of *Waiting for Godot,* as we could about the carrot if pressed to it. If, however, you work on the assumption that "A carrot is a carrot; that is all there is to it"—nobody dramatizes the idea better than Beckett.

As for the despair which is the "objective content" of Beckett's plays, he has given the best answer to that: if it were all dark, everything would be easy, but there is the light too. You might say Beckett begins where Chekhov leaves off. I remember a drawing by Robert Edmond Jones of the last moment in *The Cherry Orchard* as produced at the Moscow Art Theater: a brooding pointillist darkness; a sliver of light, like the vertical beam of the Cross (which you complete in your mind), the slumped figure of old Firs crawling toward the couch to die. Look again: it might be the opening of *Endgame*. Adjust your eyes to the darkness. Now you see the closed shutters, the covered furniture, the spaces on the walls where the pictures had been. The decrepit motion of the servant is the last residue of pure behavior. It is the gravitational field where Beckett works. If you stay with it, it may even become lively. I recall a speech by an official of the Peace Corps, who said that people today *do* want to act. He quoted Confucius: "Better to light a single candle than to curse the darkness." A Beckett play lights a candle *and* curses the darkness.

For a man who has *chosen* loneliness, there is something unreal about the theater, a betrayal: the public premises, the assumption of a contained space, actors, others, an audience. As though in penance, the drama contracts to a needle's eye. The action crawls through the eye out of time, "in the dark, in the dark mud, and a sack—that's all"; or there is "a voice which is no voice, trying to speak" (I am writing from his conversation), then the crawling, the mud, "the form of weakness." When you try to imagine the play before it comes off the printed page, you may think of Beckett's favorite sculptor Giacometti, whose figures yield, in metal, as much to the air as the air needs to surround them.

The true rhythm of Beckett's plays: "I can't, I must." When the voice rises it can be apocalyptic: "Mene, mene? Naked bodies. . . . Your light dying! Listen to that! Well, it can die just as well here, *your* light."

One might say about Beckett in the theater what Walton said about Donne, who slept in his winding sheet but appeared to preach in Saint Paul's when he should have been on his deathbed: "And, when to the amazement of some beholders he appeared in the Pulpit, many of them thought he presented himself not to preach mortification by a living voice: but, mortality by a decayed body and a dying face." Donne, like Beckett, was a man of great erudition. His most searching devotions were born of the Plague. So in *Godot*, the tramps look over the rubble of the audience and say, "A charnel house! A charnel house!" In one little diabolic canter, we have the decay of Western civilization and Beckett's opinion of the modern theater. If, however, the cultural diagnosis seems merely misanthropic, let us go back a few years before *Godot* to another voice, renowned for grandeur and hope: "What is Europe now? It is a rubble-heap, a charnel house, a breeding-ground of pestilence and hate." It is the atmosphere out of which *Godot* was born—the despair, hunger, and disease of postwar Europe—being defined by Winston Churchill.

As Beckett didn't invent despair, neither does he rest in it. Salvation is a fifty-fifty chance ("it's a reasonable percentage"); his favorite parable: the two thieves, one of whom was saved. Because Chance leads Power in the end —Pozzo tied to Lucky—the protective device, the living end, is laughter, "down the snout—How!—so. It is the laugh of laughs, the *risus purus,* the laugh laughing at the laugh, the beholding, saluting of the highest joke, in a word the laugh that laughs—silence please, at that which is unhappy." So Nell: "Nothing is funnier than unhappiness, I grant you that. But. . . ." The laughter dies like the funny story told too often. The trick, perhaps, is to find another way of telling it. Technique again, to baffle the fates, and Time. But when technique fails—as it must—more rage. So Hamm: "Use your head, can't you, use your head, you're on earth, there's no cure for that! (*Pause.*) Get out of here and love one another! Lick your neighbor as yourself!"

The message is clear—but the message is not the meaning. As we wade through the boots, the gaffs, the bicycle wheels, the ubiquitous pipes and spoools, the circular dogs, the colossal trivia and permutations of loss, the spiritual mathematics of his withered heroes and amputated clowns, you may be bewildered. But then you accept them as a matter of fact: fact—each world to its own protocol. For instance: a man needs a hat to think. "How describe this hat? And why? When my head had attained I shall not say its definitive but its maximum dimensions, my father said to me, Come, son, we are going to buy your hat, as though it has pre-existed from time immemorial in a pre-established place." Where did Lucky's second hat come from? It was just *there.* In our second production of *Godot,* when Didi and Gogo were terrified by the invaders who never came, Gogo hid behind the tree and Didi jumped into a hole we had cut into the front of the stage. Then, using a technique borrowed from the cowboy movies, he tossed his hat in the air to test the enemy. No shot, all clear. One picks up his hat and proceeds. On opening night, Didi threw his hat into the air. No shot. But nothing came down. It was perfect. One picks up Lucky's old hat and proceeds.

For those willing to play the game, the acrostics are alluring, the virtuosities entrance. But at the end of the wild-goose chase we are entangled in the net of inexhaustibility. That, rather than exhaustion, is Beckett's real subject. "You're right," says Didi, "we're inexhaustible." That, too, is terrifying. It's funny, but then it's no longer funny. Lest we think the universe too inscrutable to bear: the hat thrown up by Didi (Ray Fry) had stuck in the light pipe above. "So much the better, so much the better." It's the proceeding that counts.

One learns, in doing them, that the plays—with their whoroscopic revelations and buried performances—are always looking in on themselves, throwing up readings, telling you how to do them. If any dramatist has the right to speak of drama as an ado about nothing, it is Beckett. And he means what is *there*. The picture waits to be turned. The window asks to be looked out of. The tree is meant to be done. The empty landscape waits to be recognized. The boots wait to be worn. Beckett may say (at a café in Paris) "that cup, that table, those people—all the same." And yet which of the New Wave—hovering over images with the camera's mind—can invest man-as-object with so much humanity? Why, tree, boot, bowler, and black radish seem more human than the people in other plays.

As for uncertainty of meaning, just perform what he tells you to perform, and you will feel—as if by some equation between doing and feeling—exactly what you need to feel, and in the bones. Climb up the ladder like Clov, backing down the rungs as he must, and you will know why he walks as he does. Speak the speech of Lucky trippingly on the tongue, clutching through all the eschatological gibberish at the loose ends of Western philosophy, and you will know—if you follow the rhythm—the full, definitive exhaustion of thought. Let the tramps and Pozzo pummel you at the same time, and you will know what it is to be "finished!" Try keeping Hamm's chair *exactly* in the center of the stage, and you will know what a tortuous thing it is to wait on him. Try to hang yourself upon the tree—go ahead, try it—and you will see, decidedly, the degree to which the tree is useless. Eat Gogo's carrot and try to carry on a conversation, and you will know quite materially that a carrot is a carrot.

On the physical level, the inexhaustibility of the plays is just plain exhausting. Even thinking is a physical task, not only for Lucky. Look at Didi's face agonized with the effort to use his intelligence. Our actors discovered the physical investment demanded of them in this apparently intellectual play, as they discovered a new conception of character-in-action. Indeed, Beckett has fulfilled on stage the idea of character advanced by Lawrence in his famous letter to Edward Garnett. Not character defined by "a certain moral scheme," but character as a "physiology of matter, . . . the same as the binding of the molecules of steel or their action in heat. . . ." Not what the character *feels,* for "that presumes an *ego* to feel with," but what the character "is—inhumanly, physiologically, materially. . . ." Lawrence speaks of another ego with allotropic states, in which the individual goes through transformations "of the same radically unchanged element. (Like as diamond and coal are the same pure element of carbon. The ordinary novel would trace the history of diamond—but I say, 'Diamond, what! This is carbon!')"

Like Lawrence, Beckett is out to recover *wonder,* the mysterious harmony of man-in-nature, man-as-nature. But characteristically, like chipping a hairline in marble with a nib, he does this in the form which puts character—in all its flux and transformation—in *separate bodies* before you. By an act of histrionic juggling in which they perform no-action, the two tramps convince us they live one-life, Between them—urinating, eating carrots, putting on boots, scratching the head, playing charades—they compose an identity. While habit may be the great deadener, bare necessity gives energy. The rhythm is a continuum of crossed purposes and lapsed memory. How did they get that way? As Gogo says, unable to recall what happened the shortest time before: "I'm not a historian." For the actors, identity has to be rehearsed into being. As there is no biography, there is no other way.

Nevertheless, instead of demeaning men by reducing them to tramps in an inscrutable dependency, *Godot* restores the idea of heroism by making the universe their slave. They are, as Simone Weil says of Being (in a book with a title that describes the play, *Gravity and Grace*), "rooted in the absence of a place." What would it be without them? "To see a landscape as it is when I am not there," she muses. Unimaginable. "When I am in any place, I disturb the silence of heaven and earth by my breathing and the breathing of my heart."

Because the waiting, for all its avowed purpose, is purely gratuitous, it is bound to look comic—especially when, as with Pozzo, the heart seems to stop. If, like Chaplin, the tramps are victims too, there is a comparable sweetness in the terror. And unconscious power: Godot is concealed in their names.

The movement is circular, like a worn-out wheel of fortune at a deserted fairground, mysteriously turning. Having come out of history like shadows, the tramps are nothing but, and something more than, the concrete fact of the time they pass. And the question of Time in the theater is limned in their every gesture. Time-in-space. If the landscape needs one of them, the one needs the other. And, as we sit superior to their impotence, our whole past vibrates in their ready presence. Patience. The future stirs in the magic circle, wheels within wheels within wheels.

Do they also serve who only stand and wait? There is an exemplum in the stasis. To a country always in danger of floundering in its industry, *Godot* is a marvelous caution.

And with all its pretended anti-drama, we know it is brazenly theatrical—an occasion for Talent: the Noh, the pantomime, the music hall, the circus, the Greek messenger and the medieval angel; the play is a history of dramatic art. There is even the Secret of the well-made play, Sardoodledom's ultimate question: Who is Godot? Will he come? But above all, there is Racine, the great dramatist of the closed system and the moral vacuum, salvaging exhausted *données,* illuminating what was at the beginning almost entirely known.

Someone cries, another weeps—by the sorcery of form Beckett defies the Second Law of Thermodynamics. Energy is pumped back into the dead system by having it come back from the other side of the stage, crippled and much the worse for wear, crying pitiably for help, and then behaving like an Ancient Hero, wisdom come from suffering: "Have you not done tormenting me with your accursed time! It's abominable! When! When! One day, is that not enough for you, one day he went dumb, one day I went blind, one day we'll go deaf, one day we were born, one day we shall die, the same day, the same second, is that not enough for you? (*Calmer.*) They give birth astride of a grave, the light gleams for an instant, then it's night once more. (*He jerks the rope.*) On!" In the great mystique of modern helplessness,

Beckett's strange achievement is to provide us, exploring the rubble, with the most compelling theatrical image of the courage-to-be.

As character grows fabulous, so does nature—with the same paucity of means. The tree grows leaves, the moon appears in an instant. In this effect and in the knockabout farce, there are similarities to Brecht, who admired the play and wanted to write an answer. The difference: Brecht's moon is hung on a chain; Beckett's "bleeds" out of the sky. If Alienation means to be made strange, coercing you to look again at the familiar, salvaging it from history, Beckett is the most conspicuous dramatist of Alienation. It is another way of describing his subject.

In discovering a style, the effort was to extend the natural into the un-natural, to create the reality of illusion *and* the illusion of reality, to make the theatrical real and the real theatrical, to test the very limits of style and stage. Thus, the actors, who might be going through the routine motions of anxiety, as natural as possible, would move, almost without transition, into the shoulder-to-shoulder, face-front attitude of burlesque comedians. Or Gogo, wandering about the stage in irritation, would suddenly strike the proscenium and cry: "I'm hungry!" The motive was personal, the extension theatrical, the biological urge becoming the aesthetic question. The prosce-nium had, in our production, no "real" place in the "environment" presum-ably established by the scenery, but it was an immovable fact in the topog-raphy of the stage. It was part of the theatrical environment as a painter's studio is an environment for his painting. Our task in performance was to make such gestures believeable moments of action, to reassert the oldest criterion of dramatic truth, to make the improbable probable. Gogo's strike was a criticism, encapsulating years of protest, as if he'd be less hungry if the proscenium didn't exist. The character's problem, the actor's problem, the theater's problem, the philosophical problem were rolled into his fist.

Needless to say, the proscenium didn't fall.

When we played in New York, an actor who had studied truth objected to another extended gesture by saying, "People don't do it that way." What be-guiled us—aside from his certainty about how people do what they do, the different conceptions of reality and style involved—was that he thought we didn't know it.

Godot, indeed, gives the definitive turn to the idea of Alienation. A sub-terranean drama, appearing to care for nothing but its interior life, it searches the audience like a Geiger counter. No modern drama is more sensitively aware of the presence of an audience, or its absence. There is this conscious-ness in its most delicate dying fall, when the actors are most intensely self-absorbed. Empathy is controlled with diabolic precision. The Chekhovian silences, the residue of aimless doing, are measured as carefully as in Webern. It is then, in silence, that the whole emotive tapestry of the theatrical event can be *heard.* The music is the most artful polyphony. Listen to the awakened boredom, the very heartbeat of the audience in this superb threnody on desire, mortality, and Time:

> All the dead voices.
> They make a noise like wings.
> Like leaves.
> Like sand.
> Like leaves.
> (*Silence.*)
> They all speak at once.
> Each one to itself.
> (*Silence.*)
> Rather they whisper.
> They rustle.
> They murmur.
> They rustle.
> (*Silence.*)
> What do they say?
> They talk about their lives.
> To have lived is not enough for them.
> They have to talk about it.
> To be dead is not enough for them.
> It is not sufficient.
> (*Silence.*)
> They make a noise like feathers.
> Like leaves.
> Like ashes.
> Like leaves.

I am talking of *action-to-be-played*. Gogo and Didi are like dully dressed bower-birds in what the ornithologists call a "tight arena," absolutely attuned to each other, but waiting for someone else. Here they are actually engaged in a competition of sound and image, two *performers* trying to top each other, while character disappears in the metabolism. If nobody comes, together they are (the word was said with a beautifully syllabified sibilance) *sufficient,* constituting a rhythm. The rhythm is their bower. And as they sit side-by-side, staring out into the dark auditorium, listening to nothing, who can avoid hearing more of himself, and thus becoming a participant in the drama?

"The air is full of our cries," loudest in silence. To live is to be dubious, the acting is a revelation, we are all exposed: "At me too someone is looking, of me too someone is saying. . . ." The play-within-the-play was never so poignant, so particular, in its quiet dignity.

For our company, in the midst of the Silent Generation, Beckett's silence was a considerable shock. And the actor, associating through his own anxieties, had to submit to the rhythm. If *Waiting for Godot* was another testament to the decay of language, it was no mere pantomime of impoverished rhetoric, a mere autotelic gabble of words, words, words. Beckett worked like an engraver or a diamond-cutter. And in the best classical French tradition, he was purifying the language of the tribe, by referring words back to things, by making things of words. Despairing of communication, some of us were getting our kicks from silence. Thus catatonic jazz, thus dope, thus Zen. I don't mean to simplify these phenomena of the period, but Beckett knows well how deceitful, and lazy, they can be. His personal addiction is to the hardest task. "It is all very well to keep silence, but one has also to consider the kind of silence one keeps." As Roger Blin has pointed out, Beckett is not only prudish, but "In daily life we are confronted with a positive personality; a man who has fought indignities."

If *Godot* was the most authentic revelation in our theater's history, it was some time before we could get to do it. By then it had become a *cause célèbre* in New York, when Michael Meyerberg asked the support of eighty thousand intellectuals to keep his production going. In San Francisco, we could parlay the notoriety into something of an event, but it was more than likely to be a hapless one. Even the actors were wary of the play. Others were revolted. Several weeks before it opened, a sense of disaster circulated around the company. Irving asked me whether I wanted to go ahead. This had nothing to do with rehearsals, where the rarity of the play mostly prevailed. The meaning was becoming plain below the level of meaning. If the play seemed at first sight appalling or remote (and we forget how remote it was a short time ago), it soon acquired the queer presence of the utterly familiar, the beauty of a manipulable thumb trying to undo a shoelace under water.

Some of us became so engaged with the play that when one of the actors baited me at a company meeting until I dropped him from the cast, another one ran down the hall after him, pinned him to the wall, and shouted, "You bastard! it's like running a knife through a painting. You hear, it's a desecration!" We made a replacement, and in about a week I talked him through the play like a catechism, directing by hypnopaedic suggestion. He is a Catholic, and was suspicious of the play's despair, but no movie director ever had an actor who succumbed with such simple faith.

"On this soil of Europe, yes or no," André Malraux once put the question quite bluntly, "is man dead?" "No," Beckett answered in his novel *Watt*, "but very nearly so." If we were exempt from that question, *Godot* nevertheless broke through the hostility of our company and our audience. And there was a time when I was almost convinced that this very European play, written in French and translated into English by an expatriate Irishman, was by some miracle of cultural diffusion meant expressly for Americans. As a keynote to his book on *The Theater of the Absurd,* Martin Esslin has already described our experience with the production at San Quentin, where fashion could hardly have been the reason for the play's success. The word Godot has since become a clinical term at the prison, where a good portion of the inmates had, before our production, never seen a play of any kind. They knew nothing of the play's notoriety. Nor did it appeal only to their sense of confinement. As a teacher at the prison remarked: "They know what is meant by waiting . . . and they knew if Godot finally came, he would only be a disappointment."* *Godot* was the very subtext of an "International Style."

Though the San Quentin experience was, in the performance, almost surrealistic (I sat among the inmates, who tossed matches in the air), and in the response one of the purest we have ever had, it was a while later that I had occasion to define our own relationship to the play. In 1958, we were invited to represent the United States regional theater at the Brussels World's Fair, and we chose to play *Godot*. Prior to the trip abroad, we were to play six weeks in New York. I went there with the cast, but returned to San Francisco after two weeks to start on another production. At the conclusion of the run the cast was to go on to Brussels without me.

Unlike the performance at San Quentin, the opening in New York was a terrible disappointment. To begin with, there were murmurs before our arrival about letting this pessimistic foreign play be performed as an American offering at the Fair. The New York representatives of the State Department's Performing Arts Program, possibly rattled by newspaper criticism of our selection (adverse publicity makes everybody quaver in New York), didn't even show the courtesy of greeting us before we went abroad. Heat and humidity were high that summer; we felt the coolness. As for the performance, it began (I thought) with all the verve and precision that had been so triumphant in San Francisco and on other tours, but the audience seemed frozen too. Through the whole first act there was hardly an audible reaction to any one of the reliable lines or pieces of business that had enjoyed more than a year and a half of success in our own theater. Could San Francisco be *that* provincial? The actors nearly panicked, but by sheer doggedness they aroused some response in the second act. When I had gone backstage at intermission, one of them said, "We'll show the sons of bitches!"

The reviews were mixed, the talent of the actors couldn't be denied, and the houses were as good during those six weeks as anybody expected. But during my stay in New York no suggestions I could make, no dressing-room critique could restore full confidence and spirit. Maybe we had been playing it too long. In any case, the actors were going through the motions, showing mainly technical skill, and I left New York with misgivings about the appearance in Brussels, wondering too whether in our previous revivals and in rehearsals before the trip there hadn't been a mechanical set that I had hoped would disappear in the excitement and purpose of the tour.

About a week before their departure for Brussels, after they had been plagued by the snub and the heat, and then a State Department ban on our stage manager for unspecified reasons, I decided to write the actors a letter, in an effort to review the basic impulses of the production. The affair with the

---

* Following our appearance there, the inmates formed their own Drama Workshop and, after a year or so of preparation on other plays, have performed both *Godot* and *Endgame* themselves. They have since put out a Commemorative Edition of the prison newspaper containing reviews, commentary, and letters on our presentation of *Godot*.

State Department had made the Brussels trip all the more meaningful, because we were now going under protest. After he was first informed of the ban, Irving (who was playing Lucky) and I exchanged long-distance calls and decided, after much legal counsel and because the choice of *Godot* was already an issue, that the strongest action we could take was not to refuse to go—we had the impression they would just as well have been rid of the play—but to go to the Fair and make the production work, and to publish widely a denunciation of the ban. When the State Department—to which we showed the protest in advance, hoping they would change their minds—tried to persuade us against publishing it, saying it would be embarrassing to the Performing Arts Program at the Fair, we said that if America wanted a good reputation abroad it ought to learn how to behave at home. To which we added: "We have no political character, except that we cannot abide political censorship of our work."

The protest was, indeed, picked up by the news services and the foreign papers, and when the company arrived in Brussels, there was a great deal of extra-aesthetic attention to the production. As for the eyebrow-lifting over the choice of *Godot,* we had contended before that the risk was worth taking, that Europeans would prefer it to *J.B.* or *Carousel* and soda fountains, that the play was one of the seminal dramas of the postwar era, that Europeans would not only be interested in seeing an American company perform it, but they would be impressed that Americans could have some sense of the peculiar anxiety and dread underlying the European recovery.

Our view was confirmed. The performances were wonderfully applauded. The interpretation occasioned much discussion by theater people, who remarked especially on the Chaplinesque comedy of it. Moreover, it outdrew everything—we were told by the State Department—except Harry Belafonte and the jazz concerts. As I do not believe the protest was responsible for that, let me not imply that my letter to the cast remade the performance. I quote from it at length now because neither my notes nor my production book will convey more immediately the directorial problem involved, the character of our work on the play, and the ultimate motives behind its original production. What the letter demonstrates is the degree to which *Godot* had provided us with a vocabulary for our own condition:

". . . . At this distance I can hardly pretend to be an authority still on your performances. But I am restive with intuitions and would like as usual to have the last word—this time before you take off to Brussels. These are my considered reflections and my blessings. If they range beyond *Godot* itself, they may by indirections flush directions out.

"I was, not to begin too solemnly, disappointed by our reception in NY and by our initial response to it. The response was natural enough; pride only makes me wish it could have been otherwise. Perhaps that was impossible under the circumstances of heat, hostility, and what seems to be a proprietary interest in Beckett or a naive contempt for him. But your disappointment had its fly open; it was profoundly on stage at most of the performances I saw, either in a sluggishness that verged on resignation, a caution unbecoming your talents, or a determination (admirable enough) that made you strain to show the bastards when you weren't saving yourselves. You never quite showed them what I have seen, and I suppose the most irritating result was not the intolerable comparisons . . . but the faint praise and blind phrases that hurt all the more because they were kind. You were not, we all agreed, so brilliantly received as in our richest fantasies. The fantasies were natural, too; something makes me wish they could have been otherwise.

"For I should like our work to be more pure, more selfless (hence deeper to the Self), less deluded, and more durable. I don't think we have reached the point yet in The Workshop where we are perfectly at home with this grand conception of our vocation. But I hold these truths to be self-evident, that neither fame nor fortune means as much as the personal integrity of art and that to lose faith in the face of disapproval of what you have believed to be good and true is not itself good and true. This happened, however briefly. You were stricken. So was I. I hope you have recovered, because you are not going to Brussels merely out of dedication to The Workshop or to prove anything to the world. . . . I should like to believe you are going to perform— as the word generically implies, to complete, to carry out to the finish, to perfect, the action you have begun. . . . You are committed, personally, each to yourselves. I should like us to reach that serenity in our collective work, someday, when we are proving nothing to anybody, even ourselves. Here we are. On the stage. We begin to act, for whoever happens to be looking, but more, for the sake of the action itself. . . .

"I used to think of our production as a Noh, an accomplishment, with something ritualistic and devout about it. I don't mean to be sentimental; I think you have all felt something of this yourself—and our audiences too. . . . But there are dangers to devotion; you close your eyes. I think we have, through negligence and necessity, and through intimacy, come to take the play for granted and moved away from its nature.

"Let me clarify this. Remember in our first discussions of the play (Gene was not there)* a drawing by Paul Klee that I showed you, of an Egyptiac-Negroid woman with a rat growing out of her hair? The effect was grotesque and funny at once. I said then that unless you grasp the play's morbidity (seriousness is not the same thing), you'll never gain its humor. Intimacy has made the play less strange and less repulsive, and whatever gain that may be in catholicity of taste, it may be necessary to recall your first experience of it to perform it again with maximum force. The performance needs a sense of wonder. You have to be alive to the landscape of the play and its many

---

* Gene Roche, who was the replacement I talked of a moment ago. And who, despite my letter and with that remorse of conscience I have described before, has since left the company, for New York.

marvels, for it is an Odyssey of a kind, though it stands still. Its action is a beautiful tension of buffoonery and gathering darkness, inevitable refrains and seizures of truth, asceticism and acerbity, and a ruefully inadequate humanity. I remember Gene telling me before we left SF that someone had told him that the play was not, when he saw it, serious enough, and Gene defended it by saying that we saw the comedy in the play. We did. But we saw much more. Only I think that Gene, with his alert and vivid sense of humor, slights, as we all have, the remorseless pessimism of Beckett. The drama, take it or leave it, offers very little in the way of salvation and you must, for the duration, live with the pittance it offers. Without accepting the next-to-nothingness that Beckett gives, you will never achieve the proper intensity of desperation. Didi and Gogo are incurable patients locked in an eternal Patience, sad, lonely, dreadful, without avail, two hands clasped in numbed fear and trembling:

> We are the hollow men
> We are the stuffed men
> Leaning together
> Headpiece filled with straw. Alas!
> Our dried voices, when
> We whisper together
> Are quiet and meaningless
> As wind in dry grass
> Or rats' feet over broken glass
> In our dry cellar
> Shape without form, shade without colour,
> Paralyzed force, gesture without motion. . . .

Pozzo and Lucky are gesture with motion, motionless. Beckett's sense of the human condition, what makes it ironic and universal is not that they are trapped or condemned, but they are condemned to be free. Any way you look at it condemned sounds like damned, and you have a world with all the symptoms of original sin and neither cause nor recourse.

"The rhythm and the meaning, the power and the glory, are in total surrender to this state of being; one's own optimism, negligence, or cosmic indifference cannot be imposed upon the plaintive and static anxiety of the play. And since the play was created so obviously with piety, like a stylistic prayer, you betray it by carelessness. And betray yourselves. In literature of this sort, precision is next to godliness. . . .

"I think you've had your fill of NY, but be sure you've had your fill on aesthetic grounds too. Ask yourself what you might have thought of your stay if you had been much better received. I am as much concerned about your return here as your stay in Brussels; each time I go back to NY I am more than ever convinced that with all our frustration and floundering, we know better what we are about, and that a theater worth the effort of decent artists cannot be built without vision. . . .

"At the risk of wandering, the trouble with the NY theater is not merely that everybody acts alike, as they do. The more serious trouble is that they act alike because, minor reservations aside, they see alike. At Stratford, there is in my opinion no grasp of Shakespeare not because American actors have not been taught to gesture gracefully or tell a pike from a halberd, but because the American theater, even when it speaks trippingly on the tongue, gives only lip service to the Shakespearean reality, which includes an allegiance of spirit to the absurd, the destructive, and the demonic, that is at the heart of *Godot,* and that is systematically expunged from the Broadway theater as we mostly know it. Broadway has ejected the Devil; it had made fashionable peace with evil by labeling it. *Godot* has the real devil, the good old-fashioned Devil that floats on the face of the deep and grins like a blessed idiot. Its sympathies are not with the party in power, with the belongers, even when they are social liberals; but with the outsider, the way, way outsider. Broadway . . . pretends to love the outsider . . . but really patronizes and insults him. We are a culture given to delusive togetherness and the most frightfully egocentric group therapy; we are a culture playing it safe because we know no other way to play it. But we are not safe. Like it or not, we are on the edge of the absurd and . . . the direst problem of our time, in a labyrinth of power politics and infinite bureaucracy, is to make yourself known, to be felt, to let somebody know you are here. 'You do see me, don't you?' That, in a country given to knowing people by statistics and cocktails, is the heart of the matter. The problem, I know I am repeating myself, is not who is Godot, but who am I? And I do mean you. And as you assess your stay in NY and your purpose in Brussels, your purposes indeed as actors in the American theater, the foremost question in your minds should always be: Who, really, am I? What, really, do I want? What am I doing here? . . .

"True, by all popular and conventional American standards, Beckett is on the Devil's side. But remember, as the Reverend Hale said [in *The Crucible*], an instant before the Devil fell God thought him beautiful in heaven. I am twisting the point as the devil's advocate, and maybe obscuring it too. Simply this: as regards *Godot,* we have made our choice, let's live with it, beautifully. And whether they like you or not in Brussels, if you have done what you have done with courage and conviction, 'Be secret and exult,/Because of all things known/That is the most difficult.' "

I would eventually be qualifying my position as the devil's advocate, but it was that spirit of secret exultation that was even more wondrous in *Endgame* —in my opinion the most profound drama in the modern theater. It was also probably the most perfect production we have ever done at The Workshop.

Endgame is a play with a tenacious memory. One may understand more about it by contrasting it with *Godot*. For some the difference may be marginal, but in Beckett, a dramatist of the selvedge and salvage, the margins are immense. If the characters in *Godot* suffer from lapses of memory, that has certain disadvantages for behavior trying to place itself. Rational discourse depends on propositions that have gone before; you have to have something to refer to in order to proceed. All consecutive argument depends on memory and when, exasperated by an empty stomach, you refuse to be a historian, that's the end of consecutive argument.

Still, not being a historian has compensating advantages for behavior, which also likes to take its head. The lapses of memory are liberating. Unimpeded by custom, form, tradition, ceremony, canon, and code, all the restrictive appurtenances of the past, behavior becomes vital, improvisational, with a childlike sense of wonder, a thing unto itself. It is. A pebble in a shoe is a catastrophe, that carrot is really a carrot, never to be forgotten. Or so one thinks. Whatever one thinks, *Endgame* puts it to the test. The title taken from chess—the crucial, deadly terminus of the game—one has a sense of looking back through thousands of years of cultural history at almost every instant. One feels inside those grey walls, as amid the odalisque splendors of Stevens' *Sunday Morning,* the dark encroachment of old catastrophe. History dank and stagnant, ineliminable, the characters forget nothing. Thus, we have an intensification of the Hamletic condition, the maximum impediment of what Coleridge described as a "ratiocinative meditativeness." All motives present at once, moved equally in opposite directions, Clov can barely act. (There were times in rehearsals when Tom Rosqui, playing the role, nearly passed out by concentration to brain fever.) The choices are marginal; the stance is indifference; the effect is excruciating. We are in Artaud's Theater of Cruelty, at the dark root of the scream, unbearably humane. What is amazing about the play is its magnitude. Haunting the limits of endurance, it finds grandeur amid the trash, trivia, and excrement of living. More than any modern drama I know it creates explicitly that place where Yeats said Love has pitched its mansion. And it does this by converting an enormous sense of loss into a retrospective vision, reaching back through the failure of a culture to its most splendid figures: Hamlet, Lear, Oedipus at Colonus, the enslaved Samson, eyeless at Gaza. This vision turns up in the acting out, affecting style. The characters are savagely solitary and dreadfully engaged, the engagement impacted by paralysis. In comparison, Didi and Gogo—having forgotten their history—live moment by moment improvising, as though Time didn't exist, astonishingly active in a static scene. In *Endgame,* Time is the measure and the Plague. Every action seems the consequence of immaculate preparations mounting moment by moment through unnumbered years. Again Patience, but fevered and fierce, moving by delayed reflex of the characters through stages of decantation, down corridors of hopeless end. And there is rage, rage, against the dying of the light.

At our first rehearsals, I kept emphasizing the savage dignity of the play and the great figures in the background. But in looking back through the grotesque image of the master Hamm, whom Clov attends with his rage for order, I had forgotten to mention another character, of whom I was reminded in the foyer of the Comédie Française. There, encased in glass, is a large chair, its leather long worn—the chair in which Molière was supposed to have died while playing *The Imaginary Invalid*. (Biographers tell us he died after performance, but the other is the kind of story which, if not entirely true, should be.) Now, if in some way the mind creates its world (nothing either good or bad but thinking makes it so), you can become sick by playing sick long enough. Blind and paralyzed in fact, Hamm is in this sense an Imaginary Invalid. He is given to an excess of that self-dramatization which mars and aggrandizes the Shakespearean hero; like Othello or Lear, he savors his grief and his role.

After the dread pertinacity of Clov's opening mime and the mournful cadence of his first lines, Hamm stirs and yawns under the bloody handkerchief which covers his face. In the production, we decided to meet head-on the problem of stasis in relation to Time: the opening mime, before the ritual unveiling of Hamm, took anywhere from twelve to fifteen minutes without a word being spoken, with hardly a sound in fact. When Clov, after about ten minutes, opened the curtains of the small windows with a sudden jerk, the scraping of the curtain rings on a brass rod was a major "event." That one action was prepared by improvisations in which, at times, he took several minutes to pull the curtains apart. The single gesture was an expressive condensation of all the remembered effort. Since there was as much reason for not pulling as for pulling, by the logic of the play the action might have taken an eternity.

In this context, the stirring of Hamm was a "miracle"—and it was waited on as such. If Clov revealed the ashcans by some untraceable canon law, lifting the sheet like the cloth from a chalice, he folded Hamm's sheet with devotional care, painstakingly each fold, and the actual unveiling before that had all the grace of a matador in his moment of truth—the physical feat was to remove the cloth in one swift gesture, without disturbing by more than a dove's breath the handkerchief on Hamm's face. It was grueling for Clov. It seemed to be, for no reason, his duty. But the privilege of lifting the handkerchief itself—always a temptation to Clov—that was Hamm's own.

"*Very red face. Black glasses.*" Under the glasses, the blank eyes ("they've gone all white") like the hollow sockets of a pagan statue; the face red from congested blood, suppressed rage, and the intensest narcissism: "There's something dripping in my head. (*Pause.*) A heart, a heart in my head." If Didi and Gogo listen to the atmosphere and hear the pulse of the audience, Hamm bursts out at the audience and loses himself in his pulse. The actor takes his cues from the throb of his temple. Action: listen to your life, damn you! The issue of subjectivity in the art of the actor comes to its dead end, vitally. He is his own object. (Or so he says, thinks):

> Me—
> (*he yawns*)
> —to play.

(*He holds the handkerchief spread out before him.*)
Old stancher!
(*He takes off his glasses, wipes his eyes, his face, the glasses, puts them on again, folds the handkerchief and puts it back neatly in the breast-pocket of his dressing-gown. He clears his throat, joins the tips of his fingers.*)
Can there be misery—
(*he yawns*)
—loftier than mine? No doubt. Formerly. But now?
(*Pause.*)
My father?
(*Pause.*)
My mother?
(*Pause.*)
My . . . dog?
(*Pause.*)
Oh I am willing to believe they suffer as much as such creatures can suffer. But does that mean their sufferings equal mine? No doubt.
(*Pause.*)
No, all is a—
(*he yawns*)
—bsolute, . . .

And with that yawn, indifferent and cosmic, Hamm fractures the absolute. There is a sough of history in that joke, the crossbreeding of satanic laugh and sonic boom. It is the somnolent zero of the Cartesian abyss, the penultimate sigh of romantic irony. Can things be that bad? It is to laugh, as they say. Beckett—and to a large extent Hamm—is precisely aware of the possibility that the world may turn into his own worst fears, if it is not that already.

In exploring the beauty, let us not minimize the gloom, the antarctic frost of vast emotion. There is reason for withdrawing, and as our production gathered devotees, I felt like Hamm, enraged by the ritual performance of those who came to it for negative kicks, without the discipline of Clov, who would not pull back the lids and look at the eyes while Hamm was sleeping. The play is indeed forlorn, taking place as it does—water out one window, land out the other—on the cracked landscape of extinction. "Finished, it's finished, nearly finished, it must be nearly finished." Dread and desire, in contemplation of the imminent "little heap, the impossible heap." (How does Clov read the phrase "must be nearly finished"? Speculation or aspiration? There are countless choices like that to be made. The actor may stress the first and think the second.)

Endgame deals with "abstractions" of character (allotropic forms), but abstractions attached to our nerve ends. Once again we are dealing with man without a local habitation and a name, dispossessed and deracinated, apart from the propriety, promise, and facile redemptions of region, home, family, custom—which are not absent, but cut down to their stumps. Its memories of the past are, however laughable, full of regret for its passing; and it reminds us of a heritage, worthy, but next to impossible to sustain. The actor must be very aware of these resonances, they must come to mean something to him.

In one facet of its being, a play like *Endgame* is so appalled at the human condition, it can hardly speak. The compulsive talk, when it occurs, is the distress signal of silence. The language of excommunication. Its view of the future is the whisper of the faintest perhaps. In this respect, it is the consummation of other dramatic visions of our century, from disparate sources: the final words of Mr. Kurtz in Conrad's *The Heart of Darkness,* "the horror, the horror"; the desperation of Willie Loman's "I've got no seeds in the ground"; the image of Mother Courage careening through the void of the empty stage, with its attendant feeling that "the world is dying out"; and the more genial despair of the early O'Casey, "the whole worl's . . . in a terr . . . ible state o' . . . chassis!" The parallels are endless, going back in nineteenth century drama to, say, the old wives' tale of such a schizoid play as Buechner's *Wozzeck,* where the universe is like an empty pot, and "everyone was dead and there was no one left in the whole world."

It's an old Story, no less truthful for its repetition, but encouraged by its repetition (thinking makes it so). It's funny, but then it's no longer funny. Ubu mourns, and becomes Clov. The laughter turns elegiac, fading through the twilight of the gods. A friend of mine once objected to *Endgame* because "You can't call the characters on the telephone." True. But if you could, you'd only be talking to yourself. *Endgame* is the crisis of exhaustion playing itself out in the suburbs of hell. It has the eloquence of blood beneath the eyelids of the nearly dead. It comes out of the world of men and affairs like a scarcely audible bell out of the enshrouding fog—no less alarming for its remoteness. It is just such a story as Horatio might tell if he tried to fulfill the impossible burden placed on him by Hamlet in those exquisite dying lines: "Absent thee from felicity a while,/And in this harsh world draw thy breath in pain/To tell my story." How tell it? Where that story really took place, Horatio never was. To tell it, he'd have to re-enact the play, he'd have to *become* Hamlet. But wasn't it he who said, " 'Twere to consider too curiously to consider so." Failing to tell the story, he'd become Hamm.

In such a play, rehearsing visions of greatness around "the insane root," the magic is blacker than we might like; but you can't run away because where in the world would you go? No modern drama comes closer to making you feel what Socrates meant when he spoke of "a doctrine whispered in secret that man has no right to open the door and run away. . . ." There is no more poignant moment in our theater than when Clov, responding to Hamm's request for a kiss, says no; there is no braver moment than when Hamm discards his properties, his dog and his whistle, retaining only his stancher to support his Self in defiance of Nothingness. Yet, choosing estrangement, he is dependent in bristle and bone—and the play's black art awakens our will to survival by cutting us to the quick.

There was nothing more regenerative in our repertoire.

And this was also true of Style. If *Godot* made us significantly aware of barriers to cross, with *Endgame* we made a decided leap. I am talking of the whole visceral life of performance, which was to a large extent prompted by the scenic idea. For it was with *Endgame* that the eye-opening blitz of modern art came most subtly and vividly into our theater.

We did a second production of *Godot* after we did *Endgame*. The first, designed by Robin Wagner, was enchantingly "seen," but it was more deliberately "symbolic," with the clean Gothic line of a romantic ballet. There was a huge black backdrop with raggedly-etched streaks of white and gray cloud. It was somber, but very handsome. There was even a certain luxury in the bare tree, bent like a willow (or a question mark), two low branches twisted into the shape of Rosicrucian crosses; or, since there was nothing exactly to be read, a pair of crossed fingers. Above two molded levels there was a hint of barbed wire strung from three stakes. They might have been telephone poles on an abandoned road; the perimeter of a junk yard; or a concentration camp; even, vaguely, a circus. The action, suited to the impeccable bleakness of the open spaces, broke out of deepest melancholy into dance: a gavotte of musing. If nothing were to be done, it could be done with the most meticulously orchestrated activity. *Endgame* was similarly orchestrated, but every move was made at great cost—and the reason could be read in the nonobjective surfaces of the walls. How they came to be the way they were is worth looking into, in view of all the current urgings for our theater to catch up with the discoveries of painting and sculpture. For there are dangers, particularly as the "anti-form" of Beckett develops into a new Ashcan School, with ragtags of cadence and attitudes that are gratuitously worn, as though carrying by some willful assumption of feeling the burden of thousands of years of culture. With Beckett every discard is deeply felt. (I remember Roger Blin saying, after he dropped out of the role of Krapp, that he was tired of the Absurd. Coming from him, the most relentlessly disaffiliated *régisseur* in the French theater, that was quite an admission. Beckett had worn him down. When I returned from France, I asked Bob Symonds—who had been playing constantly in *Endgame*—how he felt. He said: "I feel terribly old.") Innocence having ended, however, some of our young artists try to sound as if they were born to a dying fall, prematurely ancient.

Axiom for Absurdists: in art, even decay has to be earned.

About the time of *Endgame,* I had been rereading Mann and thinking much about modern painting. Ruminating on Beckett, I thought of Cézanne. There were other places from which to look, but you could see the Magic Mountain from Aix. As I mused over Sainte-Victoire, I could see Hans Castorp aloft with his *petite tache* and Cézanne below with his *petite sensation*—the Wound and the Suture, the one a symptom of cultural disease, the other of the technique which, pat by inexorable pat of pigment, tried to seal it off against itself. (They came together in Hamm's stancher.) Rilke describes how Cézanne, aging, went about his little town between furious labors, guessing at the horrors without from the slightest deterioration within :*"Ca va mal . . . C'est effrayant, la vie."* For some, it was better not to look. The nineteenth century, with its passion for analysis, had looked too much. But if looking could take away, *seeing* could restore. It was a more stringent optical analysis—the oscillant contours and the facet-planes, the packed mosaic of the incorruptible gaze—that salvaged the reality of the apple from the wear and tear of history.

Not only life but the technique had something hermetic about it. The risk was tyranny. Cézanne's was one of those astonishing efforts of modern art to avert the time-serving disaster of experience by bringing form to its knees. At its most harrowing, there was a strange airless beauty about it, like James' Millie Theale, "heiress of all ages," who was also the "survivor of a general wreck." Like Proust (whom Beckett studied). A little grace goes a long way, and for all his doggedness and insularity, Cézanne opened vistas for the Cubists and others. Yet, through no conscious fault of his own, there seemed to be a dead end in the middle distance. The record is there, and I am no authority. But despite the ferment of all the *isms,* after two wars it no longer remained a question for some artists of redeeming the apple, but rather what do you do with the funeral baked meats?

Cézanne tried to see things into being; now we can hardly believe our eyes. Max Ernst said "the object sees itself in me"; now the object, whatever it may be, may have reasonable doubt that we exist.

Thus: a good deal of our visual art is Lidicean, dreaming on vacancy. Born of relativity, rapes, and incinerators, it studies lasers and talks of "breakthrough." It has the texture of fallout. Look at it: the abscessionist canvas, the collage, the combine-painting, the whole Tachist and tacky assemblage of gouge, slice, muck, and slime. The best art, Louis Aragon once said, might be produced by placing a stick of dynamite under a cathedral. Our most advanced art is a connoisseur of the rubble; annihilating the past, it lets nothing go to the junkyard. The stove pipe, the gear boxes, the slime of glue, the fur-lined teacup, the prophylactic, the umbrella ribs, and the severed hands of dolls—everything has its history, inescapable. We have made a ceremony out of what Artaud calls "the revenge of *things.* . . ."

I am not being pejorative. Art has its own reasons. And its own defense policy. In its fierce sluice and savage thrust it may appear to contend with the social wound by doing injury to itself. But by the perverse logic of the new logistics, self-abuse is a mode of deterrence. In its desperation to keep things alive, some of the art reminds us of the fertilizer marches of backward countries. I have talked of it before: salvation by excrement. (They say that in Communist China some of those who march with leavings in their hands refuse to wash as a badge of honor.) In its remedial aspect it is the art of proctological science. As *mythos*—and this is the dramatic image behind its hallucinated forms—it is the manger without the Magi, but maybe a couple of deadbeat clowns. It believes, by compensation, in Magic. And it has a sense of humor, because all the horrendous incongruities sink to the base court of comedy—which, the most artful of forms, thumbs its nose at art. Appearing improvident, it practices a frugal economy. "Thrift, thrift," said Hamlet about those funeral baked meats. Collage and combine, like Beckett's plays, are the lumpen-heirs of Poor Richard's Almanac: junk-wise, crap-happy, they save everything.

There are many sources of the new anti-drama, from *To Damascus* to Harpo Marx, but one of them is Duchamp drawing a mustache above the Giaconda smile. It has something in common, too, with the self-destroying creations (or is it self-creating destructions?) of Tinguely. It stands between the old Dada and the new "Happenings." Cézanne could make monuments of sensations; we make sensations of monuments. A student of mine—a sculptor in a playwriting class—wrote a drama in obeisance to Artaud's "No More Masterpieces": the chief scenic artifact, aptly conceived, was a huge anus, up which at one climax went Michelangelo's David (in the orchestra pit was a summer camp for survivors of Auschwitz). Another student (now studying architecture) announced he was going down to the Palace of the Legion of Honour—with its resplendent view of the Golden Gate—and desecrate a painting. I understood the fertility rights involved. As Sweeney said of the woman drowned in Lysol, every man has to, needs to, wants to, once in a lifetime, do a painting in. I had talked of the ethics of outrage and the virtue of "the destructive element"—now, by my green candle! I had thrust the un-mentionable mop into the hand of Ubu.

The trouble with Ubu is he can also be a terrible bore. Yet through all the clichés of "breakthrough," we prowl the new frontiers for signs of order. In the beginning was neither Word nor flesh, only the beginning. He who was there first looks classical. So Pollock: study the Blue Poles—they take a lot of heart out of a lot of Happenings. The miracle of motion, however, has become an icon of the Id; postlapsarian turbulence is brought to a godlike halt. *Ur-mensch* of breakthrough, Pollock is now an Idea of Order. Through which we try to break through. The drips and blobs become "draggings" and the great rough beast slouches to the scrap heap to be born.

When art turns itself loose on art, the result can be monstrous. And the predicament is curiously described in a news item from Dar-es-Salaam in Tanganyika, where natives are warned to be on the alert for the bloodthirsty lion-men of Singidia, who are taught by witch-doctors, usually women, to walk on all fours from childhood. They wear lion skins and kill at night with their claws. All the efforts of the government to wipe them out have failed. Reported on the rampage again, they caused the regional commissioner of the African National Party to call for their extinction: "Those still posing as lions and walking on all fours and killing others must be routed out. We must bury the traditions of the past."

Serious as it is, the whirligig is laughable. Breakthrough, as always, breaks down in parody.

Parody is the gamble made by Robert La Vigne, the painter who designed *Endgame*. His own "Black Art," a series of collages done after he had been with us for several years, owes a debt to assorted lions: Ubu, Beckett, Genet, and Cézanne. "I am the thief in the night," he wrote to me once with dark humor, "Beware my shifty voice." He meant it in a mantic way, but given the nature of the collage as an art form, there is a relation between prophecy and pillage. What you see depends on what you turn up, and the reverence you have for it. For all the desire of this neo-Dada art to take off like the Bird, La Vigne is an incurable stylist, even a collector. "Standing away from myself," he wrote, "what do I observe? Another 'curator.' But what painter today is not?"

Still, there are collections and collections; and the style he cares for is agape in the blood, the trill of wonder. Though he presses down on nature with the optical nerve, La Vigne has a longing to be surrealist—against, he feels, the grain of the American temperament and language. Like Blake, he tries to see "through the eye, not with it." The art, thus, is not analytical, but alchemical, like the theater imagined by Artaud. It is a matter of leashing spirit until, as Artaud says, "it has passed through all the filters and foundations of existing matter. . . ."

Whatever La Vigne picks up in his wary passage through the night (during rehearsals of *Endgame* an amazing pile of junk accumulated in front of the stage), forage and style go—when he is in control—through the crucible of a fine sensibility. There is the liability of a lot of thrashing about, an impulse to desecrate, but La Vigne, with a French ancestry, has Taste. Painting, he says, "is an old man's art." La Vigne himself is still young, but has an instinct for the ages. And that is why I remembered him when the idea struck me for the scenic image of *Endgame*.

Beckett's stage direction calls for a *"Bare interior. Grey light."* Nevertheless, as in *Godot,* I wanted a landscape. We are beginning to realize that much abstract expressionism is fundamentally landscape painting, collage being its most urban manifestation. Beyond that, it attempts to put time into space. And I wanted a temporal landscape—a cultural geography, allusive, visual quotations from history, crepuscular, rhythmic, emblems of decay, bleedings, rot, scum, fragments shored up eloquently in the general ruin, blending into the nonobjective surfaces of gray walls. I took my cue from the Japanese Noh, which is a kind of dramatic collage, impacted with allusions remote beyond memory of its oldest connoisseurs—*Endgame* was of this nature. There was also Beckett's essay on Proust, in which he speaks of personality as a "retrospective hypothesis": "The individual is the seat of a constant process of decantation, decantation from the vessel containing the fluid of future time, sluggish, pale and monochrome, to the vessel containing the fluid of past time, agitated and multicoloured by the phenomena of its hours."

So the walls, washed by the hours: the color of epochs coming back to gray. That's all to begin with: gray walls, and hardly a real object in sight. Only shapes: Hamm's shape under a sheet; the shape of ashcans under a sheet; Clov's stooped shape in the rear, barely discernible even as a shape. Bulk. Undifferentiated mass. Then more light. Two rectangles in the rear (the windows); the door; a patch on the wall (the picture turned in, waiting to be turned). The sheets removed: Hamm's stancher like a Veronica; the flutings of the ashcans, sulfated, like stumps of Corinthian columns, but ashcans. Collage was not only the principle of the scenery, it was also in the costumes and makeup. Clov, for instance, was virtually sealed into leather, as if preserving himself from whatever air was left, his face swollen red by concentration of his rage for order.

For all the implication that the drama takes place in the brain, the walls were rigidly squared, for chessplay and precise measurement, a graph in three dimensions—adjacent to a kitchen ten feet by ten feet by ten feet. Nevertheless: with a collage made of hundreds of nails, lace, paint, brocade, corrugations, glue, and grit, there was history for Hamm to look at (though he couldn't see) when Clov pushed him on his Oriental journey amid these walls (the walls of the brain, the eyes of the mind) to the end that was hollow, hollow. It was a diffused, indecipherable sort of history, not easily read, but appropriate for such a journey (counterclockwise, like the movements of Krapp). When Clov finally brought him back to the dead center of the stage, gray light laving from above, one had the feeling they had gone through a rite of passage lasting untold years. It is near the end, as at the beginning. Something has taken its course. And it had a profound influence on the way we conceived our plays from that time on.

When, for instance, we revived *Godot* at our small theater, La Vigne did a new design. As we were discussing possibilities for the play, I happened to read an account of an underground nuclear test, in which the released megatons accelerated the process of mineral evolution, so that artificial jewels were imbedded in the ground. It was such a landscape I had in mind for the new production. The audience would be in the cave (our little theater has a low ceiling); the stage would look as if it were blown away from the end of the building by a blast. The whole landscape would be *man-made*. Junk would either be impacted in the ground, or look like it were growing out of it, like vegetation. The mound was a "found object," a gas tank rigged on a curved pipe; it looked like a toadstool. The entire floor (on which the audience looked down) was covered with foam rubber painted with black latex, so that the ground, tarred and tactile, would impede motion. The background was a collage of cloud forms and found objects, and the hole we cut in the front of the stage served numerous functions, a hiding place or a trap in an obstacle course. The floor of the stage was so inviting, like marrow, like mud, like pus, like the "bubos" which Artaud celebrates and children explore with their fingers, the bubos which appear "wherever the organism discharges either its internal rottenness or, according to the case, its life."

The floor led to one sequence where, after abusing the crippled Pozzo and trying out the names Cain and Abel, the tramps lay down to sleep, and all four actors became part of the total collage. Immobile. Time erased. The waiting reduced to inertness. Pre-totemic. (*Silence.*) Geologic birth. A setting for "the truthful precipitates of dreams. . . ." Then slowly the collage comes to life, motion festering in the inorganic, ontogeny recapitulating phylogeny. In their movements the actors rehearse both the natal cycle and the process of evolution: Didi crawling in and out of the hole, luxuriating in the landscape, a reptilian form; Pozzo twisting, flopping in agony, like a wounded mammoth; Gogo rolling into a foetus; and Lucky there, still, a fragile crustacean, his white hair like some sun-bleached fungus in the Encantadas. A preverbal poetry born of the death instinct, and the Plague; carrion man restored. The conscious waiting resumed in a rebirth of action marked by the completion of a game and the line: "Child's play."

It was in this production, too, that we did one of our first experiments with front curtains, in warfare with the proscenium (another Totem, with its own Double). Again the cue was taken from abstract expressionism, where the painter's desire to escape the constricting boundaries of the frame is equivalent to the director's desire to escape from the proscenium stage. The painter "solved" his problem by widening the canvas so that the verticals and horizontals of the edges were out of his ken in the act of composition. He could work toward them, but they were, if he battled close in, no *a priori* imposition on his impulses—they were a periphery out of immediate sight. On the stage we were doing just that, working inside the box to lose sight of its limits. But once the director moves out of the frame and sits back in the auditorium, there is the Totem again. So, in our losing battle, we tried to violate it with a floating nonobjective form, with apertures—and when the lights came up on Gogo on his mound, he became part of a sculpted image. When the play began, the curtain jerked up once; no rise; then again; no rise, and then slid indifferently to the floor—a failure, disgraced. "Nothing to be done."

This action and the blitzed landscape were prepared for by a score of Sound Blocks by Morton Subotnick, electronic music composed directly on tape. The audience walked into this barrier of sound, this ambiance, as they entered the auditorium. They could not adapt to it because of its atonality and the accidental occurrence of its sequences, until, like a disarticulated Pied Piper, it led them directly into the play. Or so was the intention. For while I think this worked, and the revival was much applauded, there was, for me, a failure of harmony in the production. It lacked the "completion" of *Endgame*. One of the hazards of collage is its prodigality—the difficulty of resolve in the art of waste. In La Vigne, while it releases fantasy (loot and lust making for restorations), it also encourages a natural equivocation. Though one never knows when a theatrical composition is finished, you can feel when it is unfinished (I do not mean under-rehearsed). And so far as the scenic investiture went, it suffered from a desire for total mastery that, in principle, doesn't give a damn—by which I mean the collage, however permanently built, is a tribute to impermanence. It isn't quite a Happening, but doesn't know why it shouldn't be. In *Endgame* the possibilities were limited by the walls.

As for the acting and directing, it might have been submitted to a more ruthless scourge, in keeping with the landscape. The pocks should have secreted entirely new ghosts. I don't mean that it wasn't a compelling production, only it depended somewhat too much on findings from the first; and the balletic motion of the original sometimes stumbled on the more cluttered stage. At the same time some of the exploration induced by the new environment tortured some of the old rhythms out of shape. When we played at the Seattle Fair in the summer of 1962, we returned—because of the larger playhouse— to the old set, and the actors felt liberated by greater space. There may have been one additional factor: by the time of the revival, we had become accomodated to Beckett, exhilarated, possessive, dilatory over the nuances. I was also intensely engaged in the effort to find our own hieroglyph—a theatrical style that would stretch every action to the limits of the credible. The *mise en scène* was becoming a more powerful motive force in my own work; and I was talking then—conditioned by our production of *Lear*—about "risking the baroque."

Meanwhile, we were becoming more and more adept at the new "Comedy of Menace." (I am still speaking alchemically, productions varied in quality.) Aside from Beckett's other plays, they ranged from Duerrenmatt to Albee and Ionesco. If Ionesco's plays encouraged the elephantiasis of theatrical metaphor, our production of *The Chairs* was marked by an extension of the notion of interchangeable character: the Old Man and the Old Woman were both played by men. The décor for *Jack* gave vent in La Vigne to a kind of Caligari glee which one finds in the assault of combine-painting on conventional value, in the no man's land between real-space and art-space. In our most advanced art, total war against the totems of the squares has become a sort of demon-lover's quarrel. Inspired by the vast rummage sale of modern life, with old values going at a song, the new abstractionists have taken off again, with a pillow trailing from the canvas.

Billboards, comics, TV, supermarkets—if you can't beat them, use them. Such art, like Ionesco's short plays, has the weird glitter of a silent film running backwards at high speed, the whole world gone out of whack, actors and props sucked back in the hopper, recapitulating to a dead stop. Our relation to it at first is likely to be that of the cop on the street corner when all the cars charge by in reverse. It's wild and exciting, and a little terrifying, and one wonders where it will go next. The probability is it will repeat the same cycle. Having learned to distrust labels, we are now painting them with reverent accuracy. If it is true that crimes are committed in the name of words, "I love potatoes with bacon" is not only the "absolution" of Jack, it is the credo of "pop art." Parody becomes realism becomes orthodoxy.

While Ionesco, attacking Brecht, says that "ideological theater risks being only a theater of patronage," he is himself by nature a publicist and an ideologue. Fortunately, he is also a great inventor, and when actions take the place of words—as in the game of chairs—he can dazzle us with the virtuosity of vacancy. Things sing, luring us into the abyss. More than any other modern dramatist, Ionesco has illustrated Artaud's dictum that a stage is a concrete place to be *filled*. As he demonstrated that life may engulf us in its dead forms, the fossils of language and being, he also restored to us the dynamism of play. Three noses may be grotesque, but the horror is impacted to hilarity before it returns to dead silence—the cadaver floats away on a balloon, as *we* fall into the black hole.

The direct sense of play is not so conspicuous in Duerrenmatt. The zaniness is less improvisational, more designed, like a giant cuckoo clock. Nevertheless, the pyrotechnics of *The Marriage of Mr. Mississippi* gave us the chance to put some Expressionist devices, including film, back into operation on a large scale. The production's best reward, however, was a negative recognition—for the play churned to impasse over the fact that you still cannot get much mileage on the American stage from a straightforward conflict of abstract ideas. Duerrenmatt likes to talk politics, we really don't. "The state today," he has written, "cannot be envisioned for it is anonymous and bureaucratic. . . . Any small-time crook, petty government official or policeman better represents our world than a senator or a president. Today art can only embrace the victims, if it can reach men at all; it can no longer come close to the mighty. Creon's secretary closes Antigone's case. . . ."

This being so, Duerrenmatt—like a good neutral—mediates between the Underground and the Social Drama. Around all the discreet murderousness of the private life, "the beast, which calls itself society, survives." *Mississippi* is the tragicomic Hitchcock-thriller of the True Believer. We find him in various avatars—born of revolution, degradation, squalor, "the scum of cities" —in the bourgeois parlor, a museum of antiquities, whose taste stinks to high heaven—the menace in the manners. By curious transformations, the setting becomes a political arena and an amphitheater for a psychiatric congress (whose members, in our production, were a series of bespectacled masks popping over circular walls). In fact, it was from the beginning rather "freakish in appearance," as if "built for giants above and dwarfs below," the powerlessness of men seen down the funnel of eminence of the old gods. There are two windows, as in *Endgame*: but if Beckett's strategy is poverty, Duerrenmatt's is extravagance. His windows are enormous: through one we see an apple tree and the snow-covered roof of a cathedral; through the other, a cypress tree, a Greek temple, and the deep blue sea. The windows are actually the boundary of a giant, mechanized, artificially anarchic public area, where Salvation Army processions pass, ministers conduct their insidious work, and revolutions go their crazy round. We would not be surprised, under the circumstances, to see Ionesco's Mother Peep, warning us of demystifiers reviewing "mystifications demystified long ago. . . ."

Indeed, that is one way of looking at the action which takes place, purporting to show "what happens when certain ideas impinge on people who *will* take them seriously." The messianic strain is distributed in the comedy, which is a way of reducing Power to size. But Duerrenmatt would agree with Ionesco's exhortation to the True Believer: "I beg of you. We've had enough civil wars already, and blood and tears, and iniquitous trials, and 'just' assassins, and 'ignoble' martyrs, and ruined aspirations, and prisons." As the action circulates around the adaptable Vanessa, the Whore of Babylon, one may ask whether the human mind can "change—in any way—a world which merely exists, vegetates without a guiding idea?" Through Count Ubelohe we are taken on an "adventure of love, that noble and divine enterprise," which, mortified and absurd, survives quixotically the bloody idealisms of Justice, Political Utopianism, and Sex—to have the last word in a world of Power.

But that is only fantasy, as the ideas are rehearsed mystifications. Within the fantasy, as Ubelohe is given his loving due, the ideas are submitted to constant debate. In America, that's a different story. Though the spectacle of the play arouses interest and the bizarre events were often funny, *The Marriage of Mr. Mississippi,* more than *The Visit* (a better play), depends for maximal effect upon an audience in which you have a reasonable chance that some might even be Communists. St. Claude and Mississippi are "the last real moralists"—Mosaic and Marxist—who slug it out to the end of dogma. In the absence of the right sort of divided audience, their confrontation seemed talky and overcharged. I had instructed the actors that they would have to make the experience of ideology real. But it was, in the specific terms of Duerrenmatt's play, too much for us; and we strained to fill out emotionally an argument that might have been more immediately engaging if played more dispassionately in another country, which had really suffered the catastrophe of true belief. All I can say in defense is that when we played it so, it was simply dull.

In the cyclic chaos of a whorish world, in which ideas return to plague us, Ionesco seems to be moving toward the position of Duerrenmatt: if we are helpless as regards eternity, we must act in the changeable present to resist ideals when they become debased, lest we fall prey to "rhinoceritis." We have frequently been asked why we haven't done either of Ionesco's long plays, *The Rhinoceros* and *The Killer.* In Berenger, as in Ubelohe, we have that willingness for maximum self-abasement, the Johnny-on-the-spot naïveté which is, in an overorganized polity, the apparent condition of social intercourse. Yet I have never been able to understand the enthusiasm for the Berenger plays, except as overelaborated formulas of the Absurd, demonstrating a thesis in precisely the way to which Ionesco normally objects. In the most nauseous cavity of the two plays, when Berenger is confronted with the silent killer, what we have is the catechism of the Absurd, mimicking *The Trial,* Nothingness by rote. And while this provides us with a rationalistic terror, the end of *Rhinoceros* offers us the sentiment of self-exoneration. With everybody turning into rhinoceros, I am glad as the next fellow to be offered a way out, but it is a play which has lost its nerve; and I prefer the wilder, inexorable malice of *The Chairs* and *Jack.*

Ionesco is surely the most productive dramatist on the modern stage, and he continues to amaze us with the brilliance of his theatrical conceits. If there is a limitation, I don't agree that it is his renunciation of "objective reality," toward which he seems to be drifting. I think it is a limitation in the *subjective* life of the plays, I realize he is not interested in character in any conventional sense, but if I have not yet been mortally struck by his plays, it may have something to do with that—the superiority of the mechanism to its subjectively felt life. For while Ionesco is constantly invoking the structure of dreams, the personal imagery of his childhood, "disarticulating" the world and its languages to get *inside* existence, where "anything is conceivable," it is the heated physiology of matter, the full allotropic human presence, which is missing, the inner swell of the ancient wound.

Ionesco is right in saying to his critics that "The heart is not worn on the sleeve," but his mystery is in the sleight of hand; and it is in the ascetic Beckett that something primordial and profoundly moving forces its way between the craft and the hat tricks, so that one truly feels, wherever it may be, the heart has its own reasons.

As we ran the gamut of anti-plays, the most palpable hit, after *Godot* and before *The Balcony,* was Harold Pinter's *The Birthday Party,* which we produced in July 1960. It was directed for us by Glynne Wickham, head of the Drama Department of the University of Bristol, where Pinter's first play, *The Room,* was done in 1957.

We did *The Birthday Party* after it was, as Stanley says of his concert, carved up in London and before anybody knew of Pinter in America. Since *The Birthday Party,* we have done Pinter's short plays, *The Dumbwaiter* and *A Slight Ache,* and next season will produce *The Caretaker.* While he has certainly contributed to the *Zeitgeist* around The Workshop, I was already, by the time of *The Birthday Party,* having personal tremors over a certain tawdry and suffocating aspect of the anti-drama. I had never felt it with Beckett (that malaise was always deeper). And what I describe is still mainly personal, and if shared, shared for other reasons by conservative members of the company, who have deferred to these plays by now, but never really got with their premises in the first place.

Nor, when I confess these tremors, is my admiration for the talent and promise of Pinter any the less. He has an extraordinary command of the lyric possibilities of the mail-order catalogue; the weird responsory of social brainwashing; the prolix deceit and the crushing platitude. He writes like an actor, with a natural sense of play. He can elaborate a joke about the Englishman, the Irishman, and the Jew into a commentary on the anti-human collaboration of the Judaic-Christian tradition with the mechanized vanguard of the Organization. In *The Dumbwaiter* he shows himself capable of a zany conceit as threatening in its way as the best of Ionesco's. He knows the excruciating boredom of the tea cosy and the horror of the fly in marmalade. He can appal us with a virtual autopsy of our inadequacies, our isolation, our moral claustrophobia, our panting repressions, our deadly *non sequiturs.* And he has given us effective characterizations of those smiling agents of bureaucracy, or the haunted thugs, who converge on us, with instructions from unknown sources, to deprive us of Being. There is in Pinter a subtler crackdown on the hypocrisy of an Empire than one finds in Osborne; he has a subtler model—in Samuel Beckett. By ear and craft, he seems a worthy follower. But while he raids our dreams, divests us of safeguards, deprives us of refuge, and reduces us to ciphers, he has not yet learned to do justice to the forces of resistance. And while he knows the cleansing action of the scourge, he does not—as Beckett does, as Artaud's Theater of Cruelty portends—exalt.

The most degraded fantasy in Genet redeems itself by exaltation. If Pinter has something in common with Kafka, his victims do not, like Joseph K., have the obdurate conscious power, the almost religious passion to understand the System which does them in, and which—in frightened acquiescence —we may acknowledge as the state of life itself. Beckett forces such an acknowledgement. His tramps are not merely victims, but patients who suffer —which implies consent. As an image of existential torment, they act out all the psychic ramifications of the concluding line of Pirandello's *Henry IV*: ". . . here we are . . . together . . . forever!" Though Beckett denies such interpretations, their fate can be read as social parable or political allegory. A particular reading will be reductive, but *Godot* has formal cogency on those levels. Didi speechifies while Pozzo groans, and there is parody of social humanitarianism—but the fact is that the tramps *do* lift him from the ground and carry him on their shoulders like caryatids. Their stumbling is as moving as it is apparently aimless. If Didi finally asks whether the waiting is all a dream, one feels that Beckett has the right to wonder, the tramps doing what can be done, whether or not the doing is all in vain.

It is this positive (nasty word!) side of the victim that one misses in Stanley of *The Birthday Party*. Wickham wrote in his program note that "the 'little man' under scrutiny is an artist trying to come to terms with the fact that contemporary society has little time or use for art or artists. Faced with the alternatives of devoting himself to the money-making routine of 'keeping up with the Joneses' or of espousing some political or evangelistic cause, he succumbs to a nervous breakdown." If one feels that these are false alternatives (or that contemporary society is becoming too zealous about the artist), one might pull a Brechtian negative lesson from Stanley's impotency—he has earned his "punishment" by delinquency of will. But Gogo is made of sterner stuff, as he is more expeditious about declaring his profession. When Didi says he should have been a poet, he says: "I was. (*Gesture towards his rags.*) Isn't that obvious?" And goes on from there. In *The Caretaker* we have a more promising sketch of the poet-out-of-commission, but the social indictment leads to a set piece on Aston's experience in a mental hospital— reminiscent of the lobotomy in *Suddenly Last Summer*—turning existential innocence back toward case history.

All of this may be simply to say that Pinter is much younger than Beckett, and his *Angst* more inherited, without the same experienced fund of disillusionment to constitute an authentic vision. While he has mastered the rhetoric of the Absurd, it is still a rhetoric—a demoralizing one to be sure, but we have heard it before with even subtler cadences. And it is becoming apparent that some of the forms (we see it in painting) which deny value for the sake of emancipation can become as oppressive as the medieval syllogism. By which I don't deny the power of the syllogism; a form is valuable as long as it is enlivened by fresh permutations. Playing over the same themes, the sonnet died only when it couldn't accomodate new passions; or when, moldy with inherited rhetoric, it kept certain things from being seen, even by young men. The knowhow may be extraordinary; the sense of tension may be very great. But as the Web of Tensions (a favorite phrase of the New Politics) entrenches itself as a vocabulary, it must find a more humane voice, lest it become an official barrier to even deeper perception. And this is as true of drama as it is of presidents.

At any rate, my tremors came to a head one night at our production of *A Slight Ache,* when I had to suppress an urge to stop the performance and proclaim my guilt for promulgating an imagery in which I was beginning to disbelieve. And when I say this I am quite aware that disbelief may not be the word for an attitude toward what palpably *is*. I am not talking of what can be justified, I am talking of what I felt. I wasn't convinced that that's the way it is, and if it is, I didn't want it that way. And wasn't my thinking making it so? The rage that night might have been mere reflex against one of Pinter's lesser plays if it wasn't for the fact that even with Beckett I was becoming uneasy.

If I express reservations about those dramatists who have so illuminated our theater (more, I would say, than Brecht), it is precisely because capitulation is easy. For one thing, they are great entertainers. Though nausea, *Angst,* fear and trembling are the dusty void of their stock in trade, there is something fundamentally liberating in their techniques, their basic way of seeing things, their ability to extrude from a closed situation infinite possibilities of action. In discarding or parodying the worn-out gestures, they have brought us back to the *dromenon,* the nuclear act behind the words; but I think it is misleading to say, as they break into gibberish or fracture vocables, that they have despaired of language. They obviously hear better and see better and use the language better than almost any of the dramatists working in more conventional forms and conveying more palatable "messages" from the world we think we know. If in going behind the words to the mimetic instinct, they return us to a world of infantile sexuality and a kind of abandoned foreplay, they also have—whether in the prodigality of Duerrenmatt or the puritanism of Beckett—the kind of childishness of which Rilke speaks in his description of the artist: "Not any self-control or self-limitation for the sake of specific ends, but rather a carefree letting go of oneself: not caution, but rather a wise blandness; not working to acquire silent, slowly increasing possessions, but rather a continuous squandering of all perishable values. This way of being has something naïve and instinctive about it, and resembles that period of the unconscious best characterized by a joyous confidence, namely the period of childhood."

We may miss the joyous confidence, but what is strangely rewarding is that so much should come of despair; a proof, perhaps, that the way down is the way up. Nevertheless, one can't be too prodigal about this "continuous squandering of perishable values"—where do you stop? Are they all perishable? Or are those false questions? I don't think so. There is something binding in the purest mud. When my wife played Winnie in Beckett's *Happy Days,* buried up to her neck, I was asked openly in a review whether I considered myself Willie. I'm not sure I could really carry on a dialogue with somebody who would actually ask that question; but I don't rush to say—as some of my friends and Beckett's admirers thought I should—that I *am* Willie. If my wife played Lady Macbeth, I would not automatically turn myself in as a murderer, but I would surely be more aware of the possibility that at some level I am—as I would of the disease of moral imagination that puts murder in our bravest minds.

If you are really game, then the so-called Theater of the Absurd asks you to doubt, and I presume that if it is more than technical exercise, we must doubt it too. Those who believe nothing may be distraught with Nothingness; they are likely to be the same people who believe anything. Their recoil from these plays is too unenlightened to mean anything. Yet if the anti-drama can be liberating to those willing to be exposed, it has its own wily dogma and overbearing technique. And as I watched some of them, I often found myself thinking, rightly or wrongly, of Cippola in Mann's "Mario and the Magician," another fabulous entertainer; and of Mario, who at some deep level of his innocence, felt violated. As compared to the general run of goons in the modern theater, the dramatists of the Absurd have shown intelligence, novelty, and charm; but because Beckett, say, has been so captivating, there has always been a fundamental suspicion, as I direct his plays, that I am trafficking with the realest devil, a foreign devil, who is all the more alluring because he knows more about the nature of my uneasiness than anybody but myself has a right to know.*

Outside of O'Neill, there was hardly an American dramatist in our formative years who really touched upon it. (Williams might have if he weren't so horror-stricken by his own infirmities.) The satanic laughter of the Absurd followed on the resumption of the pipe dreams in *The Iceman Cometh.* Each of the vagrants was unfathomably panicked by the necessity of encouraging their self-deceits. Still, that play is less ruthless about the old questions, the old values than an *Endgame.* There are similarities of feeling between Harry Hope's saloon and Beckett's ashcans, but while Nagg remembers Turkish Delight and Nell muses over the depths of old love, there is nothing in any of the Absurdists quite like the unabashed good cheer, the sentimental affec-

* There are others who think we are trafficking with a foreign devil. Our current unsavory reputation with the Right comes largely from our anti-dramas. A couple of weeks ago a Hearst columnist syndicated from San Francisco spoke of "the hard-left fixation of people in and behind the avant-garde theater who have made it their ideological captive."

tion of the lovely genre scene of Harry's birthday party, the unpremeditated robustness. Adulation may have fooled him into believing in his profundity, but O'Neill never welshed in his conviction that, because its material blessings offered the greatest hope, America is an outright failure. Whatever its faults, his drama gives a clue to what is missing in the anti-dramas, for there is a qualitative difference between American despair and European despair, due to the fact that ours came not from the noxious clutter of civilization, debacle in our midst, but from the dwindling of the American Dream, the Lost Eden, from the repeated betrayal of enormous open possibility.

If I was restive about that difference, I was also inclined to agree with Lawrence that, given our own heritage of the diabolic, we were involved in a queer reverse lend-lease: "Truly, European decadence was anticipated in America; and American influence [say that of Poe on Baudelaire] passed over to Europe, was assimilated there, and then returned to this land of innocence as something purplish in its modernity and a little wicked. So absurd things are."

The new end of innocence: a painter friend of mine, not yet thirty-five, says the end of art is to teach us how to die. We can be glib in either direction, but have we been sufficiently instructed in how to live? In any case, such questions were troubling me as we made our way through the new anti-dramas. The dark was liberating, yes, but it may become, I felt, at some point in the absurdity, a trap.

"Death requires sacrifices or else it comes at once." There is a fervency behind that voice which, tracked down, verges on paranoia. While Pinter and Ionesco rack butterflies upon a wheel, and Beckett leaves man in a suspended patience, we had gone back to a dramatist—the Father of them all—who had will enough to burst out of a strait jacket.

"Sometimes," says one of Strindberg's characters, "I'm seized with a raging desire to say all I think. But I know the world would go to pieces if one were completely candid." Strindberg has taken that chance, and, from the standpoint of the Absurd dramatists, the world has survived, barely. Their plays, following in his candid wake, are testaments to bare survival—sacrifices to death. In that sense, they are undeniably life-giving, the flowers that, astonishingly, "grow out of filth," like the children out of the horror of *The Dance of Death,* which we produced because it seemed a natural development of our life in the Underground, with its counterclockwise movement.

In *The Dance of Death,* we first encounter these children over the telegraph apparatus, with the irreality of the child out the window of Beckett's *Endgame.* One wonders whether they exist. But if, as in *The Ghost Sonata,* "Everything is dug up!"—it is also true that "Everything comes back!" And not only hidden guilt, the mummy in the closet, but the Sunday children as well, the sources of light and rebirth.

Death, true, our dead end. But, as Hamm says vehemently, "To think perhaps it won't all have been for nothing!" I was longing for a form in which that would be more than an ironic sado-masochistic moment, without invalidating all the evidence on behalf of nothing. Brecht was close, but foreign too. Though I have no intention of discussing my own plays here, when we produced *A Gift of Fury* in 1958, not long after *Godot,* the disturbance was already there. I indicated in the program that the play was in part a response to the experience defined by Beckett, an effort to deal with people you *could* call on the telephone, but also " 'caught in the savagery of the trivial,' beset by violence from within and without, trying so desperately to escape that they fall prey to that final ironic violence—spiritual dryness and self-contempt. . . . 'Nothing to be done'—that was the metaphysical premise of *Waiting for Godot;* really, a very undemocratic sentiment, but one to be contended with." I have pointed out that doing nothing can, at second glance, encompass even images of positive action; but there is still the tone and cadence of despair to baffle resolution. And I added that my play would try to explore "the margin between democratic desire and existential doubt," so that, while we may not ultimately reclaim ourselves from the abyss, we might repair the will for further duty here.

If the Action of Strindberg's plays is mainly concerned with "the labour of keeping the dirt of life at a distance," forstalling Creditors, bloodsuckers, moral vampires, and monstrous Cooks in whose kitchens "the seed-leaves of the children are nipped," he was one of the great examples of the regenerative power of the destructive element. It may say something of our own state of mind, however, after our constant experience of the Absurd, that we did only Part I of Strindberg's *Dance of Death.* It seemed more immediate and more believeable, as if, under the influence of Hamm, we preferred to keep the child in the ambiguous distance: "If he exists he'll die there or he'll come here. And if he doesn't. . . ." I said before there was a resemblance between Beckett and John Donne, and we were in that wintry and withering phase of the analysis of despair, in which Donne had written:

> I hate extremes; yet I had rather stay
> With *Tombs,* than *Cradles,* to weare out a day.

Perhaps, like Hamm, we were only Imaginary Invalids; but if it seemed like fetish, it was a fact that our most favored plays, those which seemed most real to us, continued to improvise over the terms of the equation set up by Strindberg at the end of *The Ghost Sonata*: "this madhouse, this prison, this charnel-house, this earth. . . ."

The Dance of Death, with all the detail of an intense naturalism, explored further the idea that "Crimes and secrets and guilt bind us together. We have broken our bonds and gone our own ways, times without number, but we are always drawn together again." It had the apocalyptic rhythm of an *Endgame,* enormous will in the figure of catalepsy:

> CAPTAIN. It *is* the end. Just enough left to wheel out a barrow and put
> on a garden plot.
> ALICE. All this fuss for a garden plot.
> CAPTAIN. Well, that's how it is. It's not my doing.

There is vitality in the mold, and the redemptive self-consciousness, the
play's subtle sense of play, that one finds in Beckett. When the drama begins,
we find the Captain and his wife, rigid with boredom, in a cluttered living
room of a stone fortress, whose walls outside resemble a prison. Prolonged
silence. Then:

> CAPTAIN. Won't you play something for me?
> ALICE (*indifferently but not crossly*). What shall I play?
> CAPTAIN. What you like.
> ALICE. You don't like my repertoire.
> CAPTAIN. Nor you mine.

Out of this unpromising liaison, the diminuendo of possibility, comes a drama
of immense will and passion, anticipating every motif and perturbation of the
contemporary dramatists in whose plays we were becoming reputed specialists: the despotism of dependency, the oscillation between Eros and
Agape, the sado-masochistic forms of devotion, the psychic relief of role-
playing, the erotic pleasure of torment, the seesawing ambiguities of power,
the *No Exit* phenomenology, a sense of life as quarantined ("for plague,
cholera, and so forth") and Society as a refuge for brainless scoundrels;
creation itself accursed—and yet, after the Fall a terrible rage for survival,
cruel humor and dark humor, the black grace of humor, which has always
made the pessimism of these plays more inspiring than all the witless
prescriptions of love and good cheer in the havens of positive thinking.

Elizabeth Sprigge says that *Dance of Death* is something of a tragic farce,
like the plays of Ionesco. But I think the play has exactly that depth of profoundly felt life that I have always found wanting in Ionesco. And though
there is a temptation to "stylize" its playing, as in Beckett the style comes
from squeezing realism to unbearability, and finally back to comedy. In *The
Ghost Sonata,* the Girl reports her father's view of his relations with his wife:
"What's the point of talking, when neither of us can fool the other?" The
Captain and Alice might be the father and mother. Comedy results from
doing what has no point—and the powerful ending of Part I of *Dance of
Death* comes from their refusal to stop talking until the curtain falls. In
the deepest sense, a refusal to relinquish their humanity, even when they'd
lost faith in the forms that support it.

In our production, the setting was as realistically concrete as the acting;
yet the room, jammed with properties marking the time, was like a museum
of found objects. The telegraph apparatus was the prime artifact, a character
—actor and object apparently equal in status, until the actor rebelled against

inertness. "How insipid life is now!" says the Captain. "One used to fight; now one only shakes one's fists. . . ." And then he imagines the absurd comedy of their silver wedding, at the image of which Alice giggles. "Makes you laugh, eh?" Encouraged, he remembers another silver wedding in which "The bride had to wear the ring on her right hand, because in a moment of tenderness the bridegroom had chopped off her left ring-finger with a bill-hook." The brutal humor enlivens them both. Alice has to stifle her laughter with a handkerchief, "Are you crying? No, you're laughing, surely. Yes, child, that's how it is for us—part laughter and part tears. Which it should be, don't ask me! The other day I read in the paper that a man who had been divorced seven times and had married again seven times, finally eloped in his ninety-ninth year and remarried his first wife. There's love for you!" He doesn't know whether life is serious or trivial, but he does know that "if you finally decide to take yourself seriously, someone comes and makes a fool of you." He asks Alice whether she wants a silver wedding. When she is silent, he urges her to say yes: "They'll laugh at us, but what does it matter? We'll laugh at them—or else be serious—just as we choose." As in Beckett, in the very midst of apparent impotency (but with characters you can call on the telegraph), we have a superb assertion of the will to be what one must. "So silver wedding it is. . . . (*Rises.*) Cancel out and pass on! So—let us pass on!"

Watching this last scene, I always felt very much as I did when I saw the impotent Lear comforting Cordelia before the victorious armies of the bastard Edmund: "Come, let's away to prison./We two alone will sing like birds i' the cage." Catastrophe may follow hard upon, like a grisly joke, but there is exaltation in the pathos:

> Wipe thine eyes.
> The goodyears shall devour them, flesh and fell,
> Ere they shall make us weep. We'll see 'em starve first.

The Dance of Death is one of those plays in which—when all illusions are peeled away, life clawed to the bone—we come to understand more about the spiritual resources of fantasy, too. The imagination of the silver wedding, a protective ritual, moves past delusion to identity. It may seem absurd, but the joke is more profound than meets the eye.

Which brings us to Genet—a changeling in whose work identity confounds itself in fantasy, and nothing that meets the eye is trustworthy.

In Genet, full exposure reaches an orgiastic apotheosis. Freud held that people were not made to contain secrets: "Self-betrayal oozes from all our pores." What oozes out of one person seeps into another. There is a perverse frugality in nature—the Maids live by sucking secrets from each other's pores and from the pores, the gowns, the lipstick, the sweat on the telephone, the dalliances of the Madame whose dominance depends on them to the extent it is sucked from them. In Genet we have reached the beautifully hallucinated end of true confession. In his latest play, *The Screens,* "you feel it too—that the air and the space and the time now circulating about us are like any other. The brothel's no longer the brothel and, so to speak, we're fucking in the open." Saved by the ritual breath of that "so to speak," we have still confessed so much and exposed so much that we hardly know what to believe; and we have come so far since Ibsen in the dredging up of secrets (as in the development of Ekdal's photographs) that "mirror on mirror mirrored is all the show."

Genet has made a ceremony of that process—a ceremony of relativism wrought by a demon.

The Blacks, which we have not produced, is a kind of handbook to the theater of Genet. The play proceeds, as the master of ceremonies explains to the audience, under circumstances which are designed to make communication impossible. It is a necessary civility, learned by the Blacks among the Whites. "The distance which separates us originally we will augment," he adds, "by our pomp, our manners, our insolence—for we are also actors." The action will take place "in the delicate world of reprobation." Out of this world grows a jungle of absolute scorn. Nobody is spared, not even the Blacks. Nor the actors.

To the social meliorist who dreams on universal brotherhood, Genet implies that the only communion is out of history, in utter darkness; that he, Genet, is black, and so are we all. Whiteness is the outcome of Time, of the institutional processing of the human. Bleached by history, we are White. And the theater of Genet is no mere effluvium of despair either, but a regenerative assault on every mask, totem, habit, lie, base truth, and hypocrisy, and every mode of judgment thrown up by history through Time. Kierkegaard proclaimed a "clearance sale" of value, Genet is scourging the customers out of the stalls. *The Blacks* is, literally, a Black Mass played by Blacks on the theme of human blackness. It ends with a call for the annihilation of the Whites.

In this assault, in the equivalences of real murder and fake murder, real devotion and fake devotion, revolutions and perversions, maids and madames, gasmen and bishops, worship and sacrilege, he moves toward a drama of total appearance, in which every apparency cancels every other apparency. The plays enact a scabrous dialectic, all terms of which, thesis, antithesis, and synthesis, are synthetic. And in this process he gives us the most direct *sensation* of the experience modern drama has been defining since the more rationalistic dualities of Pirandello, forms straining against forms that are straining against forms in a closed system of illusions that is opened, perhaps, in death. There is in Genet's vision not only the Hamletic mousetrap but the Hamletic rub, the fear that even the country from whose bourn no traveller returns is the final seeming of the reality of illusion. Whose color appears to be black.

It can make you scream. And it is this scream, gangrenous and atomistic, which makes Genet's theater the most scrupulous realization to date of

Artaud's vision of a Theater of Cruelty. Insolence is the tone of alienation, the formality of blackness. (In *The Theater and Its Double,* Artaud writes: "If we think Negroes smell bad, we are ignorant of the fact that anywhere but in Europe it is we whites who 'smell bad.' And I would even say that we give off an odor as white as the gathering of pus in an infected wound.") Yet, coming out of the Underground, Genet may be our most astringent social dramatist. Certainly he does not write about "the Negro problem," but it is no accident that he became meaningful for us about the time that problem had reached the limits of the tolerable. If Beckett's cadences have the passive resistance of Martin Luther King's "all, here, now," Genet's aggression, like his rhetoric, resembles the Black Muslims. His piety is almost too severe. If Beckett writes for the dark, Genet writes—as his translator says— for the dead. And the scream is a prayer that comes from the devastation of Artaud's Plague, when "all the perverse possibilities of mind . . . are localized," and the theater reborn in horror "to drain abscesses collectively. . . ."

It was a considerable way from the languid, Lost-Generation despair of our first play *Hotel Universe* to the savage relativity of *The Balcony*—like leaping off Barry's terrace into the benign indifference of the universe to find ourselves floating on the face of the deep. For some in our company, it was like servicing a mortal enemy. Every performance was an outrage. But while the experience may be infernal, nobody denies the service has splendor. If Beckett seals us into our deepest selves, weaving the nerves around their dead ends, Genet offers us an infinitude of masks with which to effect a release. The diabolism is such that we are entangled in escape routes. But the labyrinth is strangely ennobling; and at the end of the dark passage a hand signalling through the flames.

"What is he really seeking?" asks Sartre in his study *Saint Genet: Actor and Martyr.* "*To be like others,* nothing more, and precisely because others are good and just, just because they are right to be what they are." And because they are helpless to be anything else. We feel the scorn, and look for judgment. Genet's drama laughs at our partiality. It asks no quarter, and makes no overtures. The condition of communion is warfare; it is a battle none of us can avoid. The warfare is within. With Genet, the barbarians are always at the gates; the hordes are loose. They cannot be denied, they can only be propitiated. Thus, the ceremonies to which he invites us—for he is as courteous as he is corrosive—are sovereign feasts, tributes to Dissolution. In *The Screens,* he writes that "the thing that kills is grease paint on a skeleton of precise gestures"; but through the decay and the caked makeup, embalming the hordes, we are looking for the spark of life.

The plays are rituals of delectable innocence born out of long disease. They are also funny. In *The Balcony,* the curtains part on large solemn fantasies which are pure extensions of our own. The comic reward of life is nightmare. After two thousand years of Western history, civilization is an execution. But there is laughter at the gallows, and erections. Pillaging the past for signs, Genet mocks up effigies which he torments, embraces, and devours. The action oscillates between the barest human feeling and the stiffness of perpetual metaphor. If all the scenarios end in death, the drama is a Tomb, a royal monument, built on the same principle of Beauty as Keats' Grecian Urn: "For the royal idea is of this world," he writes in *Our Lady of the Flowers,* "and if he does not hold it by virtue of carnal transmissions, man should acquire it and adorn himself with it in secret that he may not be too debased in his own eyes."

In Genet, we think Greek and feel Elizabethan. Or we remember that the perverse glory of Jacobean drama came from characters who would be waited on in death. The grisly comedy had the queer dignity of a dirge. So the Horse Girl leads a procession for the Hero who died with his boots on. It would be funny if we hadn't become aware—by some transcendence of perversion—that it is a sacred duty to honor the dead, and the dying. (Then it's funny, too.) In the funerary arrangements of Genet's play, there is a strange energy; and we may recall that during the Renaissance the verb *to die* was a way of describing the sexual act.

I have said a play's conception may be enriched by its inclusion on a continuous repertoire. Just before we did *The Balcony,* we had produced Ben Jonson's *Volpone.* At the first rehearsal of *The Balcony,* I pointed out that the distance between Genet and Jonson is not nearly so great as that between Genet and many of his contemporaries. Genet's drama is more self-consciously hieratic, but the plays are consanguineous across time. *Volpone,* written by a man in dead earnest, is a lacerating farce about a man who plays at dying. If Falstaff is the Spirit of Carnival, red with sack, Volpone is its concupiscence, bent on fraud. His career incorporates those devious connections between Money, Power, and Sex which are the undertow of Genet's fantasies—in which even revolution becomes a carnival, an orgy.

In our constant seizures of culture, we concede a lot of libido, but Volpone has no truck with repression. He is a voluptuary, a magnifico, a superb actor. Like the Renaissance itself, he wants it all ways: love and lust, greed and glory. While Galileo's world revolved around the sun, even the priestly revolved around wealth. A man could be his dreams of glory if he could afford it, and had audacity enough—or until Fortune or comedy showed him his proper measure. How infinite in aspiration! How vainglorious in fact!

On the rim of the open platform for our production of *Volpone,* there were gilt effigies of the seven deadly sins, reminding us that the archaic face of comedy was the death's head.

And through the sockets of death's eyes, one sees the fantasy of free enterprise in a world of villainy. The action takes place in an atmosphere of conspiracy; the ethics of rumor are in vogue. Sir Politic Would-Be not only believes in subversive pumpkins, but "oranges, musk-mellons, apricots, lemons, pome-citrons, and such-like; sometimes/in Colchester oysters, and your Selsey cockles." He warns us to be "reserved and lock'd" and "never speak the truth." In a world of exploits and exploitation, "swimming in golden lard," with so much hidden, what else can we expect but "parasites or sub-parasites"? If Volpone is unbridled Eros playing the market, Mosca is the middleman, living off the fringe benefits and secretly cornering the stock. "Is our trade free once more?" says the parasite to his lord, after their "masterpiece," the turning of bought justice on the innocent and pure of heart.

But, in principle, Jonson's world is a moral world. And if Mosca, for all his braininess, is only a voyeur, Volpone is finally a libertine and not a lover, lavish of wooing, offering "the milk of unicorns and panther's breath" but rapacious, a "libidinous swine": "Yield," he says, "or I'll force thee."

Of course, he is punished. Like those he spurns, the birds of prey, who plunder the earth. But the trouble is, like other comic heroes, Volpone also comes back. And we, in our innocence, are asked to applaud him. As he stands before us to deliver the epilogue, the moral comedy is subverted by —what?—illusion? or the breaking of illusion?

The Balcony and *Volpone* are both plays that store up a lot of wisdom about the hallucinated way of the world. There is no great alchemical distance between Jonson's humours and Genet's perversions. The visitors to Volpone's sick chamber are playing out fantasies of Power that almost, like the customers of Irma's brothel, consent to be duped. Exploring our dirty linen, both plays make an enchantment of disenchantment. Would Genet be worth our effort otherwise? if there weren't wonder in the savagery and meaning in the opacity? True, the closest we get to the purity of Celia is Carmen's fantasy about her child in the garden. But then, the pipes of the brothel are stuffed with the slime of two thousand years, including the incredible scum of the present century. No wonder it needs a plumber. Still: there is an amazing order to this world without a moral center, with its own Central Intelligence Agency—and its Andromeda network, ruled by a withdrawn, self-possessed, implacable Queen, who is there and not-there.

In doing the play, the hardest task is to preserve its Mystery; that is, to show that life, moving through the brothel's depravity and the "shit and darkness" of the revolution, is a sacrament. The lies are exposed, the masks ripped, the secrets bared—but the faces, fictions, and allegories which contain our depredations and seem born from our very nature, ripped untimely from the womb, return.

The task of the actors is to fill these archetypes by assenting to the fictions, and thus raising to the dimensions of their makeup and costumes the full range of expressive gesture that history has attached to their roles. This requires not only—for the Allegorical Figures—fullness of voice and technical stamina, but strength of inner being. Metamorphosis exhausts the Self. Sartre has pointed out how Genet finds within himself the Sadist "principle of delicacy," and that his inner tempo strives toward that-which-is-not. "He never dreams." Which is to say he practices corrosion upon the real. So with the actor: his role is not realized, but de-realized; personality falls away like the skin of a snake. But there must be a personality to fall away. Ceremony, Genet says, is not a mere masquerade. He wants an ideographic theater, "a theater of shadows," replication *ad infinitum,* in which "the characters on the stage would be only metaphors of what they are supposed to represent." In Genet, as in the Noh, the drama "speaks to the mind"—and to the extent the actors are embodied ideas or signs "charged with signs," their work requires discipline and self-renunciation, a willingness to behave within the terms of rediscovered ritual. As Seami says in *The Book of Criticism:* "Forget the theater and look at the Noh. Forget the Noh and look at the actor. Forget the actor and look at the 'idea' and you will understand the Noh."

Nevertheless, the actor cannot resolve overnight to be a walking symbol when he prefers to be a human being. And Genet's theater is easier to discuss than to embody. It may be true that among the Mau-Mau, as in Bali, we could get to it more directly, but *The Balcony,* let us face it, is no primitive ritual, it is a Daedalian drama, almost overwrought by language, and while Genet scorns the limitations of Western actors, he is too cunning not to absorb what he knows about them into the structure of the play. Just as in Brecht one learns that Alienation is finally a state of mind, provoked into action, so in Genet the hieratic is a way to "tease us out of thought/As doth eternity." It is the result of unceasing transformations in the process of the drama. Instead of a stable ego to explore, there are fecundating roles and images of roles to be played out, and character is discovered by decantation. If there is a Self to come to in the unraveling of dependencies—as the actors lock egos—one comes to it, if at all, by default. The Bishop, for instance, left alone with his function, may look right through the mirror images of his role, in exhaustion of function, to the actor who plays him—who may be surprised into identity when he is ready to relinquish it. But such a moment— what the studio actor calls "the private moment"—will vanish in its occurrence. Life is trapped between extremities; pure form and pure self are its untouchable limits. To act is to move in a magnetic field or—if you prefer the mythopoeic to the scientific—the Andromeda's web between them. The Queen lives in absence, dwelling on vacancy; she also "picks her nose, examines the pickings and lies down again," like the archetypal Method actress.

"Haunted by a quest for immobility," *The Balcony* is also trying to have the last word in Diderot's dialogue on acting. That is one of the significances in the Envoy's description of the Queen's embroidery. In the old controversy between objectivity and subjectivity, the Mask or the Face, the play suspends us in the experience of incessant paradox: "In the middle of the handkerchief, embroidered in pale blue silk, will be a swan, resting on the water of a lake. That's the point about which Her Majesty is troubled: will it be the water of a lake, a pond or a pool? Or simply of a tank or a cup? It is a grave problem. We have chosen it because it is insoluble, and the Queen can engross herself in an infinite meditation."

Distressed by insolubility, deprived of a continuous *persona,* feeling himself divested of coherent being, the actor is likely to feel violated. Trained to a drama of behavior, why should he respond to the emanations of myths? Who wants to be only a metaphor in a symbolic structure? No actor I know will ever be satisfied by the notion of literary critics that in the architectonic design of a play a character is a convention like an oxymoron. Even if he accepts the premises that life is a dream and personality fractured into provisional relations, the actor has still to be convinced that there is a better tradition of drama than character-in-action. Tell him to pick up a glass because he wants to toast the woman he loves, and he may be moved to do it; but it will take a lot of brainwashing before he will pick it up with reverence because the rim of the glass is a circle and a circle is a symbol of eternity. (I should say there are a few actors in our company who will, indeed, respond to this kind of direction far more amply than they will to units and objectives.) He may accept that, too, as a playable action; but he will want it rooted in character. Which is to say that the most imaginative of Western actors are not, as one is led to believe, intimidated by symbols or frightened of archetypes; rather they *choose* the inadequacies of their manhood to the certainties of the *Anima Mundi*. You can prod them into risking individuality and pursuing the archetype as an exercise of their personal gifts on behalf of some challenging vision, but you will not attract many of them, even those with suicidal impulses, by saying, "How would you like to be an effigy?"

Like other innovators who have tried "to bring theater into the theater," Genet has created a drama which is a corrective to limited notions of coherence; he is looking for significations of behavior beyond psychology. That may be hard for our actors to understand given their training and their beliefs, but it is hardly beyond their range. You may remind them that when they were children they played effigies quite naturally; why, when they were shot in the game of cowboys and Indians, they even played the corpse. It doesn't take long either to remind them that there are other cause-and-effect relationships—that in the fairy tale the bear-skin dropped from the True Prince at the Lady's awakening; or, to be more sophisticated, that the pirate ship in *Hamlet* is a phenomenon of Mystery rather than probability, that it seems pressed into service by Providence, chance completing necessity.

But even when this sense of childhood play is restored, arbitrariness welcomed back to reality, and psychology put in some larger perspective, the actor lifting his glass as if it were a chalice *may actually prefer* that it be a glass. By which I mean he may be quite aware that it has symbolic and subliminal values, but as he runs his finger over the rim thinking either Vagina or God, he may sincerely wonder why ceremony should be so privileged. Our world, he may feel, has its secular troubles, but he does not feel haunted by the quest for the hieratic, for he remembers what slaves the hieratic once made of men, and still does. The pyramids may be truly magnificent, but does one really want to accept everything else that went along with worship of the dead? The Egyptians building the Aswan Dam have made another choice.

True, Genet goes beyond the historical and social significance to man's unappeasable dread of death. But those who persist—against all evidence— in believing in the rational continuity of institutions and the human family, may be able to deal with that dread with less insistent mortification. Illusion for illusion. Indeed, the game of annihilating value is played better with a two-edged sword. Scorn for scorn. Genet, in fact, needs our scorn. And while people who know little about acting rub their hands over Genet's contempt and run down the actor for preferring the slackness of his own nature to the stiffness of an icon, *The Balcony* goes after the actor more subtly. (Again I should say that those for whom this is not a problem at all must work and think so that it may become one.) Genet's drama courts the actor's suspicion and makes the experience of violation the main action of the drama: the characters want "to be both legendary and human."

That's the true Genetic rub; an impossibility. Genet lures the actor by daring him to be the cynosure of a regal procession. The actor may not be up to it, but he may also feel he is being used. So the preordained formality is usurped by the thinking blood. The actor resists his scenario, and should. The drama gains intensity of meaning from encouragement of the actor's natural grievances. In directing the play, I found myself exhorting the actors to rise to their "roles," sometimes defending the play, and at others urging them on in their criticism of it, and of Genet. For the truth of his hostility is contingent on the depth of ours. Hasn't he shown us that the act of serving risks the liability of hate? A ceremony needs its proper emotion. As we worked on the play, it was only natural (and useful) for the question to arise: at what point does a service become a servitude? If the strategy is ceremonious, the play is finally about rebellion, how it fails, and renews itself.

Thus, when the Envoy says, "We've reached the point at which we can no longer be actuated by human feelings," the human feelings are ripest. And when he says, "Our function will be to support, establish and justify metaphors," he may be speaking like Genet, but the action is running away from him. Irma, playing the Queen, does not want to be an abstraction on a postage stamp. And the Envoy—another role being played, for all its oracular qualities —is experiencing a shadow of the dread of Pirandello's director, who has to contend not only with the life of the characters, and the life on which that life is predicated, but also with the real life of the actors playing the characters who are playing their fantasies. "I love love," says Irma, "and I love power and I want to experience them with my body." Up from the reservoirs of her secret life the actress gives that particular substance. She wants, as the Envoy says (accurately?) of the rebels, to "dominate by personal qualities." Furious with Genet after one rehearsal, our Irma cried: "Who is he to run me down? I am not make-believe! I am not a square! I am me, me, Beatrice Manley!" And what was more enraging was that he forced her to feel defensive about it.

So: the rebellion continues. For all his clairvoyance, the Envoy is speaking only a provisional truth. Lose touch with human feeling, and the metaphors— like the revolt—congeal. Without the metaphors, the feeling may congeal. As for "the providential fixity," which does away with Time, it is back in the dilemma of all artifices of eternity: its imagined permanence depends on the idiosyncrasy of what is past, and passing, and to come. The Chief wants his impersonation to accord with Eternal Principles, but his face must be recognizable. He goes into his Tomb with grub for two thousand years.

It is only appropriate in this "sexual" play, that form seduces feeling. And because we know that feeling will show through the interstices of form, we watch the watchers watching for signs of betrayal. The Judge watches the Executioner and the Thief, lest they improvise another justice around his scenario, while all three are being watched by Irma through her viewer; and she, mistress of ceremonies, feels excluded when something "real," that is, unanticipated, spontaneous, seems to be happening between the whores and the clients, who reach out into the Andromeda network with its spies and counterspies. (Genet has written: " 'A spy that looked like a spy would be a bad spy,' a dancer one day said to me. . . . I don't believe it.") So complex is the maze of voyeurs that the spectators become aware of themselves watching too; and if—as in our production—mirrors are actually used on stage, even more wary that they will be able to see themselves watching the actors, who may be watching themselves acting and being watched. And so on.

As for the scenarios, since they all end in Death, or the image of Death— whose scenario are we playing at any time? It is possible, as we occasionally did in rehearsal, to think of the Judge's scenario as if it were the Thief's. Or even Arthur's. In the whole interlocking directorate of this "imposing funeral-pile," with its endless mutations on the process of dying, you may want to take up the Envoy's dare and "gaze at the world tranquilly and accept responsibility for your gaze, whatever it might see"—but there is always a leak in the hieratic universe of the brothel; always motion, like in Eliot's still point of the turning wheel; always another reflection—the whole structure, like Brueghel's Babel, about to topple in its replicated magnificence.

Every gaze must of necessity be deceived. Which, for the cowardly, may be the last alibi for inaction. "Who," says the Chief, "will assume real responsibilities?" But how do that in a world with no end to the hierarchy of imagination? It is only for an instant, or the illusion of an instant—when one imagines himself into the Nomenclature—that the earth stops rotating.

As Ithamore says in *The Jew of Malta,* "The meaning is in the meaning." Obscurity, drawn from the nature of things, is designed back into it, like the Queen's embroidery. A production may be conceived in its image; or rather, a production may be a reading of the embroidery. (In Beckett it's the *doing* that counts; in Genet "It's the reading that counts.") So the *mise en scène* is a magnifying glass with many facets. One seeks for clarity not by indulging but by defining, through proliferation, the reflections to infinity.

Ideally, the machinery of the brothel should be a cornucopia of fantasy; a Chinese puzzle box, or an abstract miniature of the Tomb (crowned by a diamond sentry box) with which the Envoy tempts the Chief of Police. What we finally improvised were three navigable mirrors, built so they could tilt within the columns and pediment of a classical frame. The stage was opened to the back wall of the theater. A huge white square was bordered there in black plastic, and away from it the wall was painted brick red. The front curtain consisted of four black lace hangings, with large nubile women collaged in lace, black on black. Similar hangings appeared later in Irma's room, but upstage. In the first chamber scene, the mirror units were in haphazard arrangement, at the disposal of the Bishop—who swung one majestically, to hide behind it. As the scenes proceeded, the mirrors moved into more symmetrical patterns, and when we came to Irma's room—of which all the chambers seemed to be extensions—they formed the back wall. Later they slid apart to reveal the Mausoleum Studio. With a very large amount of clear glass, we were able to get reflections and cross-reflections in which the action could be studied front and back and in several views at once. (Odd how we prefer to watch an action from behind, or rather its image.) It was impossible to see the play in even approximately the same perspective from different parts of the auditorium. And even so, what we had was only a reasonable facsimile of the reflections implied.

So with the sound: ideally, endless reverberations. In performance, a test of perception. Take the screams: false screams or real screams? If, as Brecht says in *The Threepenny Opera,* "Natural scars are never the same as artificial," we soon discovered that taped screams could be more frightening than real ones; or at least the audience couldn't distinguish them—and, since we mixed them up, the "real" ones often seemed fake. Since the bells proclaiming the Chief's consecration come from Irma's apparatus (like the machine guns? —we used only one machine gun sound), why not the screams? Live fake screams or real taped screams? Screams because a whore is really being hurt in an adjoining room, or screams because she is acting at being hurt? And what do we mean by really being hurt? Aren't we dealing with an actress acting? A scream that started real might, because of poor recording (or deliberate recording?), end fake. It is an extension of the dilemma we confront in a world so highly instrumented it can manufacture reality. The variations were, unfortunately, too numerous for us to explore in our rehearsal period; the hardest part of doing the production was, at any point—in the acting or the surrounding atmosphere—to make a workable choice.

For even in a world of total illusion, doing a play demands that you proceed *as if* choices were possible—so that illusion might reign with greater truth.

When I say a production may be a reading of the embroidery, I am not slighting altogether the explicative function of the Envoy. In the abstract relations of form and feeling, being and becoming, permanence and change, life and death, and the indiscernible shadings of death-in-life, the Envoy may have the answers—but, as another "character" in this play of appearances— what warrant do we have to trust him? "Do you really know what's going on?" asks Irma. "What about your spies?" "They inform us," he says, "as accurately as the peepholes that peer into your studios." But we have already seen that the peepholes do not quite give us "a true image of a false spectacle." In the midst of the ritualized fantasies there is always a moment of secret accord between the "actors" that exasperates Irma at her viewer. Something is taking its course that no image can ascertain. So, in the overall rhythm of the production, it was important to understand what the appearance of each character brought to the repercussions of illusion.

The Envoy—who, as the Chief remarks, appears anemic toward the end—appears after the revolution scene. He seems to have some insidious connection with the unseen Central Committee. But seemings are not facts, and there are no facts to go on, only a network of rumor and association, of Power behind Power behind Power, with no final source ("No one has power," says the Bishop), except the absent Queen, who will eventually be impersonated by Irma. Is the Queen there? She is embroidering. And the Envoy's function—he is a surrogate for the Minister of the Interior—seems pressed out of the anarchy of the first six scenes, when even the "real" world of the revolution seems as illusory as the chamber scenes of the brothel. An explanation is called for; the Envoy comes, embroidering around the embroidery, expert in all the types of ambiguity, caressing chaos into a work of art. Taken all in all, he does not bring enlightenment, but mystification. He is a master obscurantist: Yogi, Poet, and Commissar. And I think it is the greatest stroke of Genet's genius—to the extent we identify him with the Envoy—that he shows him also as a thug. A death-bringer. Moreover, if we are to believe Carmen, he is also impotent; and if his taste coincides with the Minister of the Interior, his perversion is the most profound in the play. When we came finally to the Funeral Studio (prepared by "the Wisdom of Nations"), our great mirrors tilted, and there came floating out of disembodied darkness three images of the bare hulk of the Executioner (Apollo Belvedere on a slab): "The Minister desired a fake corpse. But this one is real. Look at it: it's truer than life."

In our production of *The Balcony*—which has many philosophical corridors—the perversions were the basis of style. (I say perversion because, as the Judge cannot exist without a Thief, the brothel cannot exist without piety. When the Chief announces that he wants to appear as a giant phallus, the Church is less disconcerted than Irma, who says her house "is reputed for its imaginativeness, it's known for its decency, and for a certain tone as well.") Voyeurism, masturbation, animal buggery, flagellation, homosexual necrophilia—one can choose to conceptualize around them, or above them, in analysis of the play, but one has to go down to the perversions in *doing* the play. What, specifically, is the charity distilled under the carapace by the Bishop when his hand begins to dream? What are the distorted ramifications of the three-way dependency of Judge, Thief, and Executioner? As we sought out every unsavory possibility, we asked how it could be redeemed in form. The task was to transform the most repellent act by ritualizing it, as in Indian statuary. So the swell of the Bishop's cope in the gestures of onanism had a luminous beauty that caused even Irma to relent in trying to evict him. Born of ancient need, the perversion became a piety. Irma and the Whore, indulging the gas-man, found themselves involuntary witnesses at a ceremony. As the Judge feels the "arm, hundredweight of meat," without which he says he'd be nothing, his fingers and the Executioner's entwine and open like a lotus bud.

One begins by pitying, scorning, or laughing at the poor souls who come to the brothel for perverse satisfactions, only to discover there is an exquisite release of energy in their fantasies. Enviable. On the most basic level of the actor's psychology, he who throws himself into his role to the furthest limit of debasement achieves an extraordinary power. Self-debasement is the spring of charity. And the actor who hesitates really to crawl or really to lick, who won't ardently "make the gestures" or follow a perversion to its sacerdotal root, is more than likely to offend us; for the play is, indeed, on the edge of cheap sensation and hard-core pornography, for all its cerebral potency. Yet there is something immaculate in its sins, as in the towels, folded like altar-clothes, which Irma shows to the Horse Girl before leaving her with the General. Or in the way the Penitent laves herself and wipes off her scorn for the Bishop whose needs solicit *her* fantasies. We tried to convey the piety of this scorn in the opening image of the play, the cleansing action and self-love of the Penitent foreshadowing the ritual of their resumed dependency.

The production must not only explore the serenity of the Queen's embroidery, but the pipes of the brothel as well, putting its fingers in the muck, in order to create an environment in which "evil is impossible"—so that, as in the trial scene, we understand that the desire is "not to condemn, but to judge. . . ." To discriminate. Confounded by translucencies, our reality is opaque. In the midst of thorough exposure, the agony is unknowing. The brothel is "the universe of the irremediable. It is the same as the one we were in, with this special feature: that instead of acting and knowing we are acting, we know we are acted upon. A gaze—and it is perhaps of our eyes—has the sudden and precise keenness of the extra-lucid, and the order of this world—seen inside out—appears so perfect in its inevitability, that all this world need do is disappear." Only it doesn't. Street noises obtrude on the fantasy of Roger, who castrates himself because even in the brothel there is no final purity, only its illusion. And as Irma closes the brothel after the revels to prepare for another day, the lights come up slowly in the auditorium. The audience is startled by other images in the mirrors. They are exposed. Irma tells them to go home, where everything will be even falser than here—less perfect, less reverent, more confounding.

Starting with the perversions, we extended each scene through its dominant imagery. The trial, for instance, moved from the courtroom to Hell, hate and forgiveness oscillating in the antiphonal responses of Judge, Thief, and Executioner—who played through all the emblematic modes of inquisition, from torture to brainwashing to seduction to rape. No *one,* truly, had power. Their task was to find the Self in the unison of their dependency. Like actors, they would shake off distractions and get back into their roles. *As* actors they would *use* the voyeuristic expectancies they could feel in the audience. Stalled,

an artificial rhythm might turn them on. The scenario gave them the opportunity of mythological grandeur. As they moved in the perverse harmony of
inquisition—a love feast of crime and punishment—the Judge grew into the
archetype, becoming Minos, weighing the dead. The Executioner, imitating
Cerberus, barked in a dance around him; and the Thief—suspended by a
chain from the flies, her hair glowing in a virgin crown—turned like a victim
in the flames, beyond pain, her moans rising above the growls of Cerberus in
eternal woe, like a plainsong; first performing a function, then loving her own
sounds, her chthonic role, then becoming it, lost in the cadences of ever-
lasting pain. The "real" action behind the fantasy, and the "fantasy" itself
became an allegory of Divine Judgment; and for that moment, in the phantasmagoria of this created Hell, the scene took on the qualities of that other
mad scene in which Justice is scourged and transcended by dispossession: the
great scene on the heath in *King Lear*. "What then? What then?" cries the
Judge, as he gapes at the nothingness of Self, and the absence of any principle
of order in the universe, and throws himself to the ground like a giant icon,
a world falling, like Chaliapin as Boris or like Lear trying to annihilate himself
in the storm as a protest against "the intense inane," all "germens" spilling
at once.

In Genet, the question of Identity which we had been tracking through our
entire repertoire, the chief psychic question of the Cold War, is tortured on
the unreadable wheel of outrageous fortune. Whirling impermeably in the
human mystery, we are back for an instant in "a clearing where suicide at last
becomes possible." It is the natural egress of life in the Underground, a
"region of exact freedom." The discipline of defilement is harrowing. And the
final outrage against the infamy of a life that cannot be shattered in hallucination is the urge to die out of it. In that process, the Bishop who "precedes"
the gas-man reconquers a domain. Reduced to the absurdity of his own
dimensions after the fleeting dignity of the cothurni, he beleaguers "an ancient
place" from which he was driven. One is reminded of the lunatic Lear as he
studies Mad Tom. There is the shock of recognition as we confront the thing
itself, unaccomodated man. "Off, off, you lendings!" cries the King, as he
tears off his garments. But the madness is also a masquerade. The most
dazzling of illusions. And if Genet takes us back, in that instant of dispossession, to the marauding priest in the sacred grove, there is also that other
moment when he shoves us out onto the Balcony—that is, when the clearing
becomes the open stage of public life, and by some cosmic provenance you
have been given a role and you have to summon from yourself, in fear and
trembling, the resources to fill it. We are back with the actor in the center of
an acting area, where tragedy and comedy meet.

Suicide, then, remains an open possibility. But there is also the feeling
expressed by Freud (quoting Christian Grabbe) in his *Civilization and Its
Discontents*: "Out of this world we cannot fall." Inadequate as we are to life,

the wonder remains when we don't run away. Honoring the dead, our task is to learn to live with the irremediable.

Aside from its techniques and the clinical analysis of the deracinated Self, the drama of the Underground has restored enormous energy to the theater by showing us, in a deranged world, that man is his own disease. By total exposure, by probing the wounds, it has tried to insure us, or inure us, against further breaches in nature. It has courted madness for our mutual benefit. "Every work that makes us feel its aesthetic value," Malraux has written in *The Voices of Silence,* "links up the dark compulsions it expresses with the world of men; it testifies to a victorious element in man, even though he be a man possessed. Indeed we may soon come to wonder whether these voices of the abyss have any value other than that of making man more vividly aware of his prerogative as Man."

Extending the strategy of Pirandello's *Henry IV,* these plays speak with lucid consciousness of "those desires where the will is kept within the limits of the possible." In doing so, it has extended those limits, or rather recovered powers which have long been lost. The perversions were once part of the adventure of our childhood, as they remain to this day the honorable practices of other tribes. And we are only now—in our most sophisticated therapy—trying to reincorporate them, somehow, into the life of adults. As for the ambiguity of the Queen's embroidery or the inscrutability of Godot, it encourages us to live in doubt by offering endless possibilities of inquiry.

If these dramas still seem peculiarly frightened and paranoid, they are behaving—in a world threatened with total annihilation—with the ingenuity of a Galileo threatened with personal extinction in the years of the Curial decree. They think in a theatrical language which is as cunning as it is baffling, and which is a natural response to intimidation and dread. So that he might the better proceed, Galileo was even willing to describe his own theories as "dreams, nullities, paralogisms, and chimeras." And who was to say they weren't?

If these plays cultivate these properties, they also descend through trance back, as the Bishop says, to "the laws of visibility." There is no body of drama since the Jacobean period that tells us more about the internal processes of our world, the neurology of institutional man whose habitat is the stink of the body politic, and the temptations to an exalted psychopathy. It was no mere coincidence that the first spontaneous protest in which the non-political members of our theater ever engaged was over the fate of Caryl Chessman.

Taken with Cuba and the Congo, the Chessman case gave a social mooring to the obscurantism of Genet. Aside from arousing humanitarian sentiment against capital punishment, Chessman's career in prison seemed to some of us an act of existential courage. As Elizabeth Hardwick described it: "He had to bring himself forth from the void of prison, from nothingness, from non-existence. The condition of his nothingness, his nonexistence, makes his remarkable articulation, his tireless creation of himself as a fact, his nearly miraculous resurrection or birth—which it was we do not know—a powerfully moving drama." To the extent that was an enterprise of personal salvation, the social tear over his death was misguided. The dignity of Chessman was not that he gave normally uncommitted liberals a cause to which they could rally, but that he made himself worthy of execution, as if life were not too much to spare for his manhood. It was Dostoyevsky who had demonstrated some time before that, as we don't understand the harrowing processes of crime, we don't understand the redemptive nature of self-punishment. In Chessman, as in Genet, we are confronted with demoralizing evidence that amazing powers of creative performance, and an astonishing piety, could come from "the insane root" of the apparently unregenerate. Normality is dismayed. And when Chessman went to the gas chamber it was possible to feel that society needed his death to avenge itself for being confounded by his strange resources of will, and for having failed to provide in its law—as Aeschylus did in *The Eumenides*—for the rightful claims of the infernal gods.

Whatever latent fury there may have been in society's refusal to commute his sentence may have been increased by the fact that Chessman spoke with the uncompromising logic of Genet: "No, I wasn't guilty of the crimes for which I was sentenced to death. I was not the red light bandit. . . . Yes, I would say I was not the red light bandit even if I were." (It is the same stupefyingly cunning voice one hears in the black politics of the twentieth century, to which Chambers' *Witness* is a Dostoyevskyan testament.) By such assertions—out of depredations, violence, cruelty, self-torture, and unaccountable lust—there came the semblance of a man. Our present justice does not quite know how to forgive him; that would take a charity too gratuitous for us to bear. Even if he had been spared, it would probably have been for the wrong reasons.

Yet: it was a negative reality one admired in Chessman. So, too, with Genet. While every truth—however debased or obscure—might find its place in his scheme of things, we were dealing with a drama which was devoted, any way you redeem it, to the diabolic, which is privation. For ourselves, while Milton was of the devil's party without knowing it, we were in danger of becoming card-carrying members. In defending these "nefarious" plays against the merely self-righteous, the wholly deluded, the ignorantly threatened, or the proponents of Mental Health, we could argue with Blake that everything that lives is holy. Or we could even show there were American antecedents in our national poet, Whitman:

> Let murderers, bigots, fools, unclean persons, offer
> > new propositions!
> Let faces and theories be turn'd inside out! let meanings
> > be freely criminal,
> > > as well as results.

But in all the rage and outrage, the hostility against established forms, the demystification, the incendiarism on behalf of fresh perception, the discard of conventional properties, the hallucinatory effects, the provision for the infernal, we felt neglectful of another dispensation. If the Grand Balcony is the most artful and "decent house of illusions," having the integrity of utter fantasy, we may still feel it is holding something back, whose presence is more painfully suggested, if not realized, in Beckett. Carmen says: "All the same, it must be nice in a real house." "Who knows!" says Irma, nervous over her investment in demoralization. "But Carmen, if my girls start bothering their heads about such things, it'll be the ruin of the brothel." It is precisely such things, however, over which we *were* bothering our heads. We have hardly lived our way through the illuminating secrets of the Underground, but we are anxious to come up for air. And by some instinct of counterillusion, we were reluctant—some of us—to give up the old conventions of language, logic, character, and plot, and the squandered values which upheld them. The world of Genet could be mightily convincing, but some of us wanted realler frogs, realler children, and realler queens in our imaginary gardens.

These demonic plays submitted all the old ideas to the test of horrendous fact; now the new fact had to be submitted to the test of fact. The archaic horrors may remain constant below the surface, but the face of the world, these last couple of years, seemed to be changing again. And new emblems release new energies. According to Genet. If the old plots were exhausted (and one wondered), then the imagination would have to be taxed to dream us a more compelling story that *could* be played out to the bitter end. Like the medieval demon, Genet had almost overwhelming power in the domain where he exists, but even genius can be severely limited in its existence:

> For there's a kind of World remaining still,
> Though she which did inanimate and fill
> The world, be gone, yet in this last long night,
> Her Ghost doth walke. . . .

John Donne, ruminating beyond Tombs, had written about a girl he had never even known. He might have been talking of Cordelia.

Seduced by the dark powers, we were wondering about other gods.

9

A strong egoism is a protection against disease, but in the last resort we must begin to love in order that we may not fall ill, and we must fall ill if, in consequence of frustration, we cannot love.

—Sigmund Freud, *On Narcissism*

A Piece of Sea-Weed serves for a Barometer; it gets wet and dry as the weather gets so.

—William Blake, letter to Butts

It is of the actual, however, that we pretend to speak, and not of the possible or impossible.

—Henry James, *The Scenic Art*

THE CLEAREST GODS

An aged King—martial, vain, Druidic—enters in savage pomp. A ceremony has been prepared. The kingdom is to be divided among his three daughters. They have only to play out the scenario, improvising, but formally, on the theme of paternal love. The Queen is absent.

Invisibly in her place, there is Hecate, the dark goddess. Thwarted, the King will invoke her with the outrage of inveterate sovereignty. Whether from her or "the sacred radiance of the sun," or some weird collusion of radiance and darkness, he assumes his power comes directly from Nature. "Meantime," he begins the ceremony, "we shall express our darker purpose." A giant map is spread on the ground, and the King, treading this image of the land, draws great lines through the kingdom with his sword. He has possessed the land by Divine Right; now he is giving it away in bounteous portions, by dispensation of his own, in perpetuity and validity. Or so he thinks. They told him he was everything.

And so he is—in ways he is still to understand. "Do you smell a fault?" We might already have had forebodings from the prosaic little scene that preceded the splendid entrance of the King. If there is wit in his benison, there is truancy in the darker purpose, and chthonic stirrings in the blood. There is also politics in the background. The King is a statesman. He is publishing his "daughters' several dowers, that future strife/May be prevented now." If we have been listening carefully, it is clear that the apportionment of the kingdom has already been made, and now has only to be ratified theatrically, to put the sacred seal of ritual on the diplomatic arrangements. Still, the King is by original consent an absolute King, who can take away what he has given, and who—when Nature's inscrutable purposes rise to meet his own (" 'tis our fast intent/To shake all cares and business from our age")—converts the political ceremony to a gift-giving in his own honor, a patriarch's rite of passage.

Is he paranoid? Is he irresponsible? Our psychology hasn't the word for it, our morality fails. (And the word *Superobjective* seems a little inadequate for the Action being played.) Say what we will of the King's pride, it is his due; and what he does *seems* rational. Power will be conferred on "younger strengths while we/Unburdened crawl toward death."

But if love eludes ratification, can power be conferred? As the Bishop says in *The Balcony,* no *one* has power. And surely, one cannot "retain/The name, and all th' addition to a king," without the baser power—the "sway,/Revenue, execution of the rest"—which supports the name. What is the true source of power? And if the King's purpose turns darker than anyone has expected, what is the reason? "No cause, no cause." We shall return to the charity in that instinctive denial of judgment, but if the youngest daughter cannot speak to begin with, perhaps it is because she sees herself as a loving pawn in a complex necessity. No cause, or too many causes? Among them the political game; the matter, manner, and subtle felicitations of her sisters; and the pride inherited from her father that turned to a ponderous tongue what might have been a saving grace. But what if she had been solicited first and was spared following the artful duplicity of the other two? The motives of the scene become as raveled as the Queen's embroidery.

"The King is coming," the sennet had declared—feel the weight of that noun; an impregnable Presence, reigning substantially, mythically, divinely over State, Family, Tribe, and Self. In an instant, we are staring into vacancy. The Great Figure crumbles, the Metaphor bleeds.

"Speak," the King commands, most gently, his favorite daughter. "Nothing, my lord." "Nothing?" "Nothing." "Nothing will come of nothing." The exchange reverberates with all the paradoxes of the abyss. The Word has failed; Love is silent. The ceremony smells of mortality. Nothing becomes the subtext of the Action to be played.

Full of vainglory, the King is nascently suicidal. Mortified by power, he cannot turn back. Cynosure of all eyes, he must press his claim. Once magnificent, he is now the exposed actor in the center of an acting area, proceeding from nothing. Before he is through we are back behind all the fantasies of Power, cutting through all forms, to the Womb itself: "Thou know'st, the first time that we smell the air/We wawl and cry." In the pain and absurdity of Birth, we smell the fault. The King's darker purpose is fulfilled more expeditiously than he wished. The scenario ends in Death.

If there are aspects of *King Lear* which resemble a Genet fantasy, conferring illusion on illusion to the point of madness, our production was also impregnated by our work on other dramatists of the Underground, especially Beckett. It was after producing *Godot* and *Endgame* that I began to see most luminously those great bleak scenes after the storm, when the play researches for truth in the waste land: "World, world, O world!" Madness, the liability of too much life, is astonished by bloody eyes and scours the universe for Identity. Beckett and Genet may have given us a new dramatic vocabulary for the reading of *Lear,* but we were also working out of internal necessities of our own. I don't know how we would have come to *Lear* without them, but we would have come, as we came to Beckett and Genet through a world which, when we started our theater, felt remarkably like that of *Lear.*

Beyond any indebtedness, the production was a provisional summing up of the disturbed questing of our entire theater in a period infected by the demoralizations of the Cold War—which gradually forced us to do our own crawling in the muck. It was a world remembering strategic slaughter and threatened with total annihilation. However tranquilized, we always came back to that. If we were dramatizing Apocalypse, we were encouraged by the wild alarms of the daily news, which literally drove us into the dark corners, even as it tried to woo us back with all the seductive apparatus of selective inattention, the public fantasies of the Good Life in an Affluent Society, creating terror in abundance and abundance from terror.

It was surely possible to forget about it (and almost, to function, necessary to forget about it), but the presence of the Bomb seemed at some point of awareness to make a mockery of our enterprise, as it shattered all belief. In the councils of the world, in domestic politics, in religious and secular institutions, in the home, education, everywhere, in all the arts, we were improvising new forms in response to a world which was drifting off in all directions from the horror at its center. An expanding macrocosm, an infinite microcosm. Those were our prospects. But while we had to recreate our institutions and techniques to explore them and reflect them, one had the correlative feeling that there was no choice in the matter. We were caught in the centrifugal force of dissolution which Yeats had prophesied in *The Second Coming* ("Things fall apart: the center cannot hold"), and if we didn't explode our beliefs, stretch our politics, change our tunes, the sky—as Artaud warned—would fall on our heads.

As in the Renaissance, the major irony of our raid on the unknown, our immense repositories of knowledge and our knowing about knowing, is that as we move toward the secrets of the universe, we are frightened to death of the possibilities. Who does not, at some margin of personal fantasy, have some vision of the world disintegrating, either through scientific carelessness or its sheer inability to carry its population? Man, the minister and interpreter of nature, has become its fearful master. So is it any wonder that when the Chilean earthquake was reported in San Francisco, about the time De Gaulle went ahead with testing in the Sahara, that there was an epidemic of sharks at our beaches, followed by a report that a whale had been washed ashore, with ulcers. Given all this, and the additional liability in San Francisco of living on a major Fault (along which an atomic reactor was going to be built in proximity to an already disturbed balance in nature, the pollution of our wild life), it was not hard to have sympathy for the Elizabethan world picture, with its Chain of Being and cosmic correspondences which, through the years, we had tried to dismiss as pathetic fallacy: the idea that disorder in the soul is accompanied by disorder in nature, disorder in the body politic, disorder in the stars, disorder in the whole universe. A mere mystique? A fancy? One feels like Bernard Shaw in his preface to *Saint Joan,* deriding the smart guesses of science as equally untenable. And surely we have come to know (our relations with doctors aside, at least the medicine men danced!) that science has its exasperating mysteries too.

No matter how we were cheered by rising expectations, we also felt that the forms created to accommodate them were also necessary on a more elemental level: to protect us from premature extinction. To trouble us further, there were the Genetic excesses of the colonial rebellions, and the shifting power relations among the Red Enemy, the great bleak mystery of the Chinese, refusing to renounce warfare, and pursuing the idiot atom on their own. It is a very ironic world, indeed, when the approval of a "hot line" between Washington and Moscow is welcomed as a symbol of improvement in international affairs. If the twentieth century's spilt flux and subsequent absurdities put all value in question, like the action of *King Lear,* the wonder is that we have not only survived it, but that we may even learn to live with it—though we shall probably never be able to estimate the effect on the collective psyche of all the subliminal terror, as we shall probably never be able to estimate the effect of fallout on subsequent generations.

It was with such ideas afloat that we undertook our production of *King Lear.* When we were asked why we should begin to do Shakespeare with the most formidable of his plays, I would say in all honesty because it seemed the most immediate. The whole question of realism, like the question of style, got lost in its relevance. What is important is not to do (as they used to say before we had done one) *a* Shakespeare, but to do a play. And the problem of such a play as *King Lear* is not—given minimal proficiency by the actors— a question of training in speech, body movement, fencing; updating to make modern, space-staging to make Elizabethan, festivalizing to make an occasion, or gimmicking to make laughs—the main problem, the determining problem, is to take the risk of really *looking* at the play. I say "risk" because you cannot look at *Lear* without wondering why Shakespeare is suddenly so popular in the plushier suburban communities. The eighteenth century knew that *Lear* was intolerable, and for good reason, so they revised away the horror. Even Dr. Johnson, appalled by Cordelia's death, said he would never look at the play again. And Dr. Johnson was neither a fool nor a coward. To do the play in the twentieth century, confronted by the possibility of capricious extinction that we see in the death of Cordelia, is to realize how awfully, "Thy life's a miracle."

We began, then, not with a Shakespeare, but with a certain kind of experience. "Nothing will come of nothing. . . . All's cheerless, dark, and deadly." Granted our new horizons, our common markets, our revolutionary promise, my world (and not only my despair) is packed copiously between such lines. Behind the munificence of Lear's gift-giving, there is barbarism and *Realpolitik*. The civilized world, proud of its contained energy, is shocked into realizing how close it lives to the anarchic id. "The blood-dimmed tide is loosed," wrote Yeats, "and everywhere/The ceremony of innocence is drowned." It doesn't take much. The action develops like a cosmic joke, tragedy proceeding from a trivial source. Comic. An eschatalogical farce. Look at the disproportion between what happens and what caused it to happen. Can a mere domestic quarrel shake the universe? "Ha! I think the world's asleep." The temptation, to begin with, is to project the disorder upon the world. But as life becomes increasingly a dream, and derangement rips at the incriminated Self, one wonders: is it the world asleep? or me? "Ha! Waking." But waking to what?

As I conceived our production, its problems resembled those at the begining of the film *Hiroshima Mon Amour* (which I saw later). As Marguerite Duras wrote in her screenplay, the initial exchange of the man and woman— waking after "the ashes, the dew, of atomic death"—is allegorical. *"In short, an operatic exchange."* This does not mean it isn't played with the intensest realism. Operatic because predicated on something almost unspeakable, because the cause is not really—as meets the eye—trivial, but almost beyond containment by the rational imagination. "Impossible to talk about Hiroshima. All one can do is talk about the impossibility of talking about Hiroshima. The knowledge of Hiroshima being stated a priori by an exemplary delusion of the mind." What seems to be historical fact cannot be adequately documented; neither can that cause in *Lear;* not as our historians and our sociologists customarily think of documentation. The only way to document some things truly is to re-enact them in some way—as the Eichmann trial re-enacted the experience of the incinerators.

I am not talking of a "right" interpretation of the play nor of what the audience saw at first sight (though many saw it right away), but what they finally saw feelingly because it infused the play—became its atmosphere and its metaphor. Recent history spread its terrors behind the scenes. In the cellarage. For us, the opening ceremony, blasted, was the ritualized Hiroshima of the play, an unprecedented explosion, an obscene event transformed into "an exemplary delusion of the mind"—after which no value was safe. After Hiroshima, what could you believe in? And not only Hiroshima. Gloucester, his eyes gouged out, is thrown out at gates to smell his way to Dover. After Belsen, what benediction?

The aim of the film was "to have done with the description of horror by horror . . . but make this horror rise again from its ashes by incorporating it in a love that will necessarily be special and 'wonderful,' one that will be more credible than if it had occurred anywhere else in the world, a place that death had not *preserved*." The miracle of *Lear* is that it rediscovers and nourishes such a love by proceeding from horror to more horror. In a country that was preserved from death, it was as close as we could come to really talking about what we had caused. And in view of it, to look again at the possibilities of our own nature—and what we thought we believed. For it was conceivable, if one really took *Lear* to heart, that love might be a derangement at the summit of derangement. Which doesn't mean it doesn't exist.

In such a play—as with Hiroshima—motives oscillate between the two questions: how did this happen? why in heaven did we do it? Pulverizing morality, the drama is obsessively redefining the moral fact. It is that definition which has to be acted out—the objective: to see what is really there. Kent, looking at the bastard Edmund in the very first scene, says, "I cannot wish the fault undone. . . ." But one begins to realize that the fault cannot be undone even if he wished it. There is a savage economy in nature. Edmund, tolling his life's blood with his fingers, says after the duel: "The wheel has come full circle; I am here." Whether one is more sinned against than sinning, or renounces sin as a fraud, it is a universe in which you cannot retract a fault. Existence is a mortal wound. Man is his own disease. And one must learn to live with that.

What is replenishing, however, about the universe of *Lear,* in which consequences seem to exceed the faults, is that it offers no alibis. What is most frightening is that it makes each of us—always searching for moral exits—totally responsible for what we do, and what we do not do. It favors neither sins of commission nor sins of omission. It deals harshly with equivocators. If Gloucester's personal revulsion over the brutality of Lear has to await the encouragement of political opportunity to take action (his outrage can act a little more safely when powers are afoot from France), he is thrust out at gates for his tardiness. (Recalling the form of action that led to the concentration camps.) But when Gloucester, smelling his way to Dover, asks the madman to lead him to the cliffs, he is posing the problem which Camus said was the "one truly serious philosophical problem" of our century: given the rational barbarity, the civilized reduction of men to things; given our common complicity—why not suicide? If the gods do kill us for their sport, certain generations forget about it more easily than others. In our time, it became possible to ask again about the death of Cordelia, not why should she die? but why should she want to live?

It may seem an absurd and melodramatic question, but it can be asked by very sane and fortunate people, as Tolstoy asked it in his *Confessions* in the middle of a prospering career and healthy family life. Given the question, the necessity is to rediscover the grounds upon which to live; all things conspiring against it, to salvage the human. The task is achieved in the play by the yea-saying resonance of a "Never, never, never, never, never!"—a sort of absurd leap from denial of life, like Gloucester's mock suicide, after which Edgar says:

>   . . . therefore, thou happy father,
> Think that the clearest gods, who make them honours
> Of men's impossibilities, have preserved thee.

That "therefore" has no logical foundation whatsoever, except the audacious life-giving logic of the imagination which is Shakespeare's, and which is Lear's on the heath, when the lucidity of his madness makes him every inch a king.

But where in the world—with plenty of evidence of "the fiend, the fiend" and of those other gods who kill us for their sport—are those "clearest gods" invoked by the outcast son? The whole effort of our production was to *see* them somehow, by means even of derangement, and especially by trafficking with the fiend in ourselves, providing all the evidence we could that they *didn't* exist. Lear says: "Nothing almost sees miracles but misery." The body picks up derangement in the syntax. Nothing. Miracles. Misery. Which sees what? The mind knows what it is trying to say, but the inner ear is distressed by other resonances. The subtext feeds on that distress. "No cause, no cause." The actors had to make that causelessness explicit. Which is to say the process of performing the play became a dark voyage through the anarchic id; creating the subtextual world was not merely a matter of building a rational stream of consciousness underneath a series of rational objectives—the two moving, according to Newtonian laws, in equal and opposite directions. We are speaking of a *world,* with an atmosphere and a subterranean life; an environment informed by the dark gods. Out of the appearance of absolute form, hallucination; out of hallucination, form.

So, there was an empty platform, encased in that collaged nonobjective bas-relief, twisted and gashed, as if wrought upon a wheel of fire—disorder amazed by its own coherence. The relief, explored during the action by light within, released its subliminal imagery. The costumes, worn in a world of madness, sought a similar coherence. The Fool was not, for example, in conventional motley; outside of time, prehistoric, the Fool was the first Fool ever, a loving and hostile parody of the King, having to invent himself, and what he wore. Why did Edgar choose to become Mad Tom? In such an atmosphere, what else could he become? "Edgar I nothing am." What he is is deciphered through all the permutations of Nothingness. But, to begin with, he is not merely composing a disguise; he is feeling what it is like *to become nothing.* He is not only trying to escape, he is trying to disappear; the body mimics nothing, and is left with its own minimal basest shape, held together by "Pins, wooden pricks, nails, sprigs of rosemary. . . ."

The problem of Identity gravitating to Nothingness was the major problem of even the minor characters, such as Oswald. With no previous history of animosity to Lear, Oswald embodies in himself the whole human career of a toadying, fawning, and resentful servitude. A Genet servant. He knows by birth the smell of mortality. He tries constantly to wipe away his own stink. Detesting the nothing he owns (he lives by lendings), he wants the accoutrements of those above him, as he would possess the mistress who treats him like a dog. When he encounters Gloucester protected by a "peasant," the whole accumulated rage of dispossession, congenital nothingness, leads him to make the one ardent physical gesture of his life. He swings wildly, screaming like an idiot, forcing Edgar—who does not want to kill—to divest him of his sword and be his murderer. And as he dies, he beats the ground in rage for having failed to kill himself into being. The final indignity: to be dragged to oblivion, a mere hulk, stripped of his message, not even knowing that the peasant who killed him is a nobleman in disguise.

Every nerve of the action, tortured by illusion, was bent upon moral nakedness. In attiring the actors, we remembered that we were dealing with lendings. The lendings were collected in the dimmest memory of recorded time; our intent was to drive backward, through time, behind forms, making our way through a disintegrated past to invent a culture of our own. Thus, all the regalia of the play came out of improvisations on motifs drawn from archaic lore, but not only Anglo-Saxon. There were strains from Achaean, Celtic, Mycenean, Polynesian, Columbian, and even American Indian art. And there was a remarkable harmony in the incongruities, just such a mélange of intuition as occurs on the edge of barbaric darkness when the hordes subside, cultures cross and, exposing what is in them of the brute, somehow preserve, as if by a transmission of *mana,* what is residually human.

In the opening procession, which filled the stage with a fierce, venatic energy, we wanted to give an image of a primitive court impacted with ceremony, as if to hold off the hordes within. Regality seemed encrusted with power. Yet one might smell a fault. It was *in* the ceremony. It was in the very essence of ceremony, which is an imposition on Nature. Cordelia's nothing made it apparent, through all the hieratic lendings of magnificence, that forms of authority had still to invent themselves, discovering their true nature. (What kind of Fatherhood is it, for instance, that demands absolute devotion? . . . Lear, raging at Cordelia, turns to his throne to see the bastard Edmund—a stranger—behind it.) The garments were ripped away in the descent through chaos down to the poor bare forked animal of the storm. At the end of the sulphurous and thought-executing fires, there is the cheerless, dark, and deadly truth—that the final lending is life itself.

Lear was the first of our productions in which there was an extensive collaborative effort among various artists in the community. About a dozen of them worked within La Vigne's general design, and in collaboration with the actors. They used the idiom of found objects and free forms. Helmets were invented of plaster, collaged and improvised upon with animal motifs; Lear's robe was made of thousands of chicken feathers, plucked, bleached, sewn, and hand-painted; bodice pieces and breast-plates were made of bone, bead, wood chips, bean, and glue. In all the costumes and properties there were emanations from the imagery of the mutilated relief which was the action's formal background. (What you saw on the actors determined what you might see in the relief.) The cast always had the feeling that things were being created from a *tabula rasa,* from the ground up. A forge was set up in our shop for the sculptor Robert Hudson. He hammered out weapons of spring steel. Beautifully wrought knives, spear-heads, and swords—for which we invented our own rules of warfare. Take the swords: they had real heft, but not necessarily perfect balance; the more he made, the better the balance —like the first swords that might have been forged. I gave them to the actors. Never mind fencing instruction. Here's a weapon, feel how heavy it is; now use it. So we swung hard at each other, until we found the sword's potential rhythm in ourselves. I took it as a tribute to the clearest gods that when the weapons were used with power and belief they sang and showered sparks as they clashed.

So with the music: order out of disorder. It was an electronic score by Morton Subotnick, who set out to create space. The great technical problem of the play is always the storm. In ours, the basic sound was a kind of drone of vast amplitude; moving through time, but unmeasured, expanding, extend-ing the regions of the possible. Subotnick composed this sound of three elements: the sound of Lear's voice saying the word "I" into an open piano; a single pure pitch; and a cello note—which was a subliminal factor, buried in the storm as an impulse of healing. The cello note emerged later in the paradisal sleep music of Lear, in the reunion with Cordelia. Exquisite, lovely then. But in the storm it was part of the ground swell of derangement. The three elemental sounds were imbedded in tape, improvised upon, compacted, swollen, until the drone appeared, like the troubled breathing of the earth projected by Lear upon the universe. Imposed on this was another sound track of accidental electronic sounds; during the whole sequence, perhaps about thirty-five minutes, during which the sound never stopped, these occurred at unpredictable moments. They came whirling or hissing or singeing out of the atmosphere, making the actors play with them, so that the scene could never be the same. Then there was still another sequence of sounds, orchestrated explicitly with Lear's "Blow winds" speech—in which the synchronization of language, sound, and action was meant to establish a perfect harmony of chaos, Lear and the storm locked by sound in a kind of cosmic embrace. Some of these sounds were fierce, frightening, indescribably active; and the Fool danced half-witted in their jet like an hallucinated light-ning bug, an epileptic shadow electrified by the storm, alternately drawn to the King as to a sanctified oak, or repelled in terror lest he not be hallowed after all—panicked in the effort to keep his reason dry in a world so flooded with derangement. Later, as Lear fell asleep from exhaustion, the storm breathed in unison with him, like the relief of Nature.

What was important in the relation between the sound and the acting was that the storm was not merely a background, but a steady presence. When some of the actors first hear Subotnick's music, they are likely to be intimidated. Those accidental sounds were pretty wild. But like an actor, the music had to rehearse. They got to know each other intimately. And for an actor, that opens up possibilities which no thunder sheets can achieve. For it is important to remember that the storm was *music,* with its own properties of perception, and its own interior life—including, at some impalpable level of estrangement, the presence of Cordelia to Lear; and intimations of the clearest gods.

Artaud speaks of the *mise en scène* as actor. What we wanted was for the actor to create the *mise en scène* as it was creating him. The atmosphere dictated the possibilities; the actors, struggling against the storm, became it. No matter how the action was planned, there was always a pressure to improvise. In those mad scenes on the heath, the actors played close to the ground in a perverse animism of rapport, having nothing but themselves to cling to, the storm coming out of nowhere, sparing no man, as we strove for total exposure in the cracking of Nature's molds.

The task was to maintain the barest semblance of sanity in the realm of unleashed id, Entropy running wild. It is one of the miracles of dramatic art—and an inspired convention of Shakespeare's drama—that in the midst of universal chaos, words do not fail, they spout cataracts and hurricanos, in a titanic effort of the mind to raid the abyss, to be engulfed by it, and yet defy it in the end, controlling the tempest by making it beat "there," in the mind, reduced to nothing: "No, I will be a pattern of all patience;/I will say nothing."

Before and after that momentary silence, however, the problem remains—given our own heritage of realism in the theater—how to say the words while letting all germens spill at once. Those who tell me that Shakespeare's verse ought to speak for itself are never convincing—though they may be content, as I have never been, with an orotund sobriety on the heath, rhetoric competing with Nature, in the imitation of an imitation of an imitation of derangement. In my scholarship, I revere the text as much as anybody, but on stage we are dealing with suicidal rage and earth-shattering self-contempt; with a vengeance so awful it penetrates through chaos; and with the maddened clairvoyance of a pariah king—personal injustice cutting to the brain. The play offers us the energy of its conventions—the hysterically swift prose of the Fool's good sense infuses the lucid rumblings of the demented king —but it has also racked us on the wheel of its compulsively brilliant psychology. Unlike the Noh drama, there is no emblematic shorthand for developing characterizations in the Shakespearean tradition. There is no gesture for storm except the whole being of the actor, checked by the skepticism of our realistic expectations. Mythopoeic it may be, but the storm has to be *realized in behavior,* lest it singe us not at all. It may be true that the play, therefore, is (according to the tradition) ultimately unplayable on the stage; but if we choose to play it we must get at the sinew of its onomatopoeic immensity.

If the words are, as I believe, the life of the design, they direct you to an anterior and submerged, pre-verbal reality that has to be filled by the actor's living presence. If the storm has not been conceived with the elliptical relief of pure ritual gesture, it cannot be approximated either by impassioned recitation. What is self-annihilatory in Lear must be *there,* palpitant in the actor, who may indeed try to shatter himself on the stage, as he goes down and down to his own self-destructive demons, striking at the Nothingness within in order to give substance to the Nothingness without, in "that vast passion which," in Kierkegaard's words, "disdains the fury of the elements and the powers of creation in order to do battle with God."

If Lear has never been perfectly realized, it may be as much a problem of audacity and self-revelation as of technique and rhetorical strength. What we were after, in any case, in that nightmare middle of the play was a total image, rhythmic and muscular, of "the thing itself," the naked essence of man in contest with the divine principle—and if in the process we lost some of the words, as we did, it wasn't that the actors didn't strive for clarity, nor that they lacked training in good speech. Nor was it merely another example of the studio plague, the betrayal of language to private impulse, or the triumph of mumble over meaning on behalf of questionable selfhood. There was, indeed, some of that, whether we intended it or not; our actors are not exempt from the *Zeitgeist.* But I would say we selfishly sacrificed verbal clarity to imagistic and psychological meaning if, given what we wanted to show, there were really a choice.

If we all grow more in command of ourselves, and our craft, it may be that someday we could realize everything at once in this fabulously demanding play, to the last syllable of recorded chaos. But given the audacity and full physical involvement of the acting on the heath (by Michael O'Sullivan as Lear, Tom Rosqui as Mad Tom, and Robert Doyle as the Fool), the wonder was how much of the language was not only projected but clarified; that is, extended into an orchestration of sound, image, and movement that made wildly objective this masque of unreason with the marvellous lucidity of madness—the life to which the words gave life.

What I wanted was for them to work as close to *pure behavior* as they could possibly get, turning the inside out, their "five wits" (wit, fancy, imagination, estimation, memory) utterly alive. They were to become each other's prickly skin, exchanging clothes, baubles, voices, sense, fantasies, and identities. A metamorphosis. A sound would screech down from above, Tom would pluck it out of the air; Lear would lurch as if he created it. The Fool would slither between them, recovering the cloak which Lear had bestowed on Tom, jealous that his function was being preëmpted by a madman. Synesthesia. A precise disorder of sense impressions; a stimulus here would produce an unexpected effect there. For Lear, in fact, we came to these scenes not by a subtext but a *fantasy* (or *shadow*) *text,* trying to set loose a whirl of association back to the original fault, a ceaseless internal replaying of the whole unhinged logic of events in the present stream of consciousness, so that if Kent touched his arm in the storm, Lear might say "Wilt break my heart?" to Cordelia, or see her in the Fool; behavior dislocating save for the exactness of what "beats there," until only Lear knows what he sees in each indefinite "that" when he says, "O, that way madness lies; let me shun that./No more of that."

What I prize in an actor—beyond training, beyond talent, beyond brains, beyond the "spine" of performance—is mystery, the ability to bring out of nowhere an action that is incredibly strange and perfectly right, so that one feels, after it is performed, that he has witnessed an enchantment, and can only ask in admiration, "Where did *that* come from, it was so true?" What we wanted to establish in the superflux of Lear's disorder was an atmosphere in which behavior became its own mystery, until finally madness not only descends to prayer, but the action of one actor becomes the appearance of another. "Fathom and half, fathom and half!" Poor Tom, in all his "looped and windowed raggedness," seemed to appear from the lowest depths of Lear's plaint. The Fool screams. Tom screams. The Fool screams, the Fool outfooled (in a moment he is up to his old riddles, but half-witted). Lear screams—a concatenation of brainless sound signifying nothing—as if the earth had thrown up for his soul's benefit an outcast image of his broken heart: "Didst thou give all to thy daughters? And art thou come to this?"

Out of pure behavior, then, we wanted to create a unison of derangement that struck down all forms, plunging deeper and deeper into the amoral fact, to the meaning of nothing. King, Fool, and Madman rediscovered their baser nature as the actors coursed over their own shadows, through every bog and quagmire of their exposed selves. And as they annihilated it, they were resurrecting value: they supported, clung to, competed with, and protected each other—and saner men, like Kent and Gloucester, could only boggle at their responsive lunacy. Out of their anarchy, however, came intimations of very old forms, a charm, a blessing, a ditty, an incantation, or even a very long and dilatory exit, such as Kabuki actors make when they are leaving the stage along the ramp. As Edgar sang "Child Roland to the dark tower came," the madness subsided for a moment into a bizarre and fetching dance of pilgrimage, in which the actors turned back constantly, as they moved diagonally across the stage, to the reality of where they *had* been, coaxing each other into mock silence, encouraging each other's fantasies, lingering, before they let themselves be led by Gloucester ("a walking fire") further into the mad abstract dark.

By the time of the trial scene—the fierce arraignment of the daughters which leaps to incriminate the universe—they were hallucinating in ensemble, and even the famous joint-stool (there was nothing there) was invented by the improvising Fool, who was soon abandoned to the silence of a bare stage, as Lear was led to safety. Emptied of his utility, the Fool dissolved into darkness before our eyes, with—for the while—the fiend, the fiend.

The whole play was conceived as a phantasmagoria of identity, behavior passing from one character to another. The Fool wants to be King, the King a Fool. The three daughters compose the absent Mother, but when you anatomize Regan you find Lear. In the clotted web of associations, the Fool has become a surrogate for Cordelia. He was not present at the ceremony, but turns up when she is banished, by psychic need; as he disappears by psychic exhaustion, when she is about to return.

L'acte gratuit. No cause, no cause. What we also tried to do was create an environment in which gratuitous action became increasingly possible. By gratuitous, I mean the sort of action which comes unpredictably (and absurdly) from the lower depths. Like that first nothing, out of nowhere. From the dark gods. When Cornwall gouged out one of Gloucester's eyes, he might have spared the other, except that in that moment, he saw what Gloucester saw with that one remaining augur eye, the horrid shape of his own deformation. When he went for that eye the force of his assault gave the impression that his finger went wrist up the channel right into the brain. Artaud said the modern actor has forgotten how to scream; Gloucester tried to remember.

As regards the method of acting, certainly we talked about objectives and such. But we worked mostly by *atmospheres,* or *spheres of influence.* Lear runs into the storm, shouting, "O fool, I shall go mad!" The cadences of the storm begin (filling out a line of verse). The others are left in a trough of complicity. What has to be said? That was the King. They speak with the trepidation of ambitious risk, feeling each other out, daring discreetly the one upon the other to lock the gates of their crime. The civility of it is terrifying. Gloucester is alone on the empty stage, in residual guilt—but without a lapse in the rhythm of desertion—and then he leaves. The storm breaks forth in nightmare.

King Lear, and its production, is too enormous to discuss in detail, but I should like to return to that scene on the cliffs of Dover, when Edgar—contending with the despair of his father—tries to answer Camus' question: why not suicide? (It may say something of a new community of feeling in the theater that Peter Brook's recent production of *Lear,* also influenced by Beckett, took this as its germinal scene. One of the things it also points to is a better understanding of the nature of "subplot" in Shakespeare's drama, not analogy in a minor key, but reality seen as cross-reflection through space —and a modern sense of distributed heroism.) On the bare stage, at land's end, with nothing but his unprovided self, Edgar practices a desperate therapy, which turns out to be a model for the salutary use of hallucination. It is a purgatorial scene on the edge of Nothingness.

The two men come before us, son leading father by the cudgel which protects them. "When shall I come to th'top of that same hill?" On the flat stage, Edgar presses down slightly on the cudgel, to which his father stoops. "You do climb it now. Look how we labor." As Gloucester's "senses grow imperfect" by his "eyes' anguish," Edgar is more hypnotic about where they are and what is to be seen. They circle the stage in their long labor, like the journey in *Endgame.* Time and Space are contracted in the movements between each line. Step by step, suggestion by suggestion, the son leads the father to the figurative tip of the cliff. "Stand still." The word *stand* is crucial, we shall hear it again.

Quite literally, Edgar is giving the old man the ground on which to live before he dies. He has become his father's eyes. If through adversity, out of fear and trembling, he has learned to improvise, now he has all the eloquence of an artist who knows that life is born of precision. If we were in any way prodigal with words on the heath, here the necessity is exactitude of language. Out of love, the world is recreated by the Word. With exquisite delicacy of feeling and the most searching imagination, Edgar restores the landscape from the vacancy of the abyss. To avoid vertigo, the most particular image; for verisimilitude, the image adrift in space, a mote to trouble the mind's eye: "The crows and choughs that wing the midway air/Show scarce so gross as beetles." The mind moves like a telescopic lens, a magic camera, from particularity back to immensity; as the tall anchoring bark diminishes to her cock, the cock becomes a buoy "Almost too small for sight"—and then, in a virtual conjuration of cosmic harmony, sea washing land in an eternal process of mysterious beauty. "The murmuring surge/That on th'unnumbered idle pebble chafes/Cannot be heard so high." It is the natural history of the clearest gods. Lest the spell of meaning in nature be broken, Edgar allows himself only one emotional judgment, a commiseration with the man who gathers samphire, "dreadful trade," suspended between heaven and earth. And he knows precisely when to end his survey, when vision can take no more, and the brain turns back to the abyss.

We have come through the most violent drama in a great spatial form, through all the commotion of the heath, to the stasis of the lyric—lyric becoming drama. There is, for this moment (the violence is not done), only one more move to make. "Set me where you stand," says the father. And then, in a ritual identification of past and present, age fertilized by youth, the father is placed where the son stands. Not there, or there, but exactly there, where the son stands. As in the centering of Hamm's chair, the actor must know that the meaning is in the accuracy of placement. With love, words mean even more than they say. We are standing on hallowed ground. The ceremony is prepared. And the gesture must be made. But even as he kneels for the symbolic suicide, his mind reeling with the pain of perception, Gloucester is already beyond despair. The blood has caked on the cruelty of the gods who—whatever their ultimate nature—are surely mighty. And Gloucester says to the poor man who has led him to the cliff, in a reversion to a time of innocence: "Fairies and gods prosper it with thee." As he falls, transfixed in the grace of self-destruction, there is a slight retraction of his body.

For Edgar the task is over. He has another role to play. As he has created the way down (St. Augustine: "My love is a weight, a gravitational force."), he must now (as the tramps do with Lucky) raise his father up. "You stand," says the son. And then, by describing the beggar he was as if he were the monster of a fairy tale—reversing their roles—he creates out of the beautiful concreteness of the abstract fiend, the absurd presence of those clearest gods, verified by the fantasy and role-playing of his own desperation.

What we have seen is not mere positive thinking but the hard-earned triumph of Imagination over disfigurement and Nothingness. Yet this is a very real world, and the will-to-believe is impaled again on appalling fact. No sooner does Edgar urge his father to "Bear free and patient thoughts," there enters the ravaged monarch, the abandoned father, bedecked with weeds. And what we see is that Gloucester, ready now to bear affliction till it cry out for his death, is prepared to see feelingly what he has been blind to before; and what Lear has tracked through the waste of his cut brain to the sulphurous pit.

As the two old men, absolutely humiliated, are brought to communion on their knees, they have become all eye. And the King relents, chooses sanity, but only long enough to summon more evidence for his nihilistic vision. Fondly, he takes the miserable man's head in his hands and, looking down the gored sockets of Gloucester's being, he comes to the pit again, the horror, the horror—and there is the consummate rage of that "kill, kill, kill, kill, kill, kill!"

Born of abated fury, there are other paradisal moments in this amazing play when the clearest gods appear, out of the Plague, behind the wheel of fire. But the worst does not return to laughter, it goes on to worse. Except for *Endgame,* and even then, there was nothing so devastating to play through. Reading the play, even seeing it, is not the same as doing it, living with it, especially if the doing grows out of the kind of darkling inquiry I have described in these last chapters. As we moved in our repertoire through one diabolic phase or another, *Lear* stayed in the memory as a warning against a facile nihilism. As André Malraux said in *The Voices of Silence,* "Nothing conveys more vividly and compellingly the notion of a destiny shaping human ends than do the great styles, whose evolutions and transformations seem like long scars that Fate has left, in passing, on the face of the earth." Like children—in Beckett, in Genet—we were pulling back the scars and peering through the wounds to see if that same destiny was really there. To really experience their plays was to feel like Gloucester with his one eye gouged out, seeing for the first time right through his assailant to the possibility of another truth. In our own dangerous and phantasmagoric world, there is always the fear of another Cornwall standing above us, ready to gouge out the other eye. Which may say no more than that in this life even the intensity of partial vision is perilous.

If we are engaged today in an extension of Kierkegaard's "clearance sale of value," Lear forces you to re-examine everything; and leaving you beyond fear and trembling, it makes you remember what Kierkegaard also wrote: "Whatever the one generation may learn from the other, that which is genuinely human no generation learns from the foregoing. . . . Thus no generation has learned from another to love, no generation has a shorter task assigned to it than had the previous generation. . . . In this respect every generation begins primitively, has no different task from that of every previous generation, nor does it get further, except in so far as the preceding generation shirked its task and deluded itself." When that happens, the generation that follows—like Edgar with his father—may have to instruct backwards.

Nevertheless, whatever Edgar lived through, whatever madness, whatever love; whatever he learned from his father's fate or taught his father in the risks of love, there may always be more to come: "We that are young," he says at the woeful end, "shall never see so much, nor live so long." If we have to see again what he has seen, we may certainly hope so. Those last lines had a special meaning for us, for the history of our own generation seemed similar to Edgar's; and when we lacked his charity it was easy to feel that "the preceding generation shirked its task and deluded itself." If, after two world wars and Korea, our "present business" is no longer "general woe" but peaceful coexistence and new frontiers, how could we proceed in good faith? Life, we had been told by our best thinkers and most powerful dramatists, guaranteed nothing more than nothing; pipe dreams; mendacity. So be it: we would proceed if necessary even without faith—trusting that we have the courage, as we seek the means to live intelligibly in a status quo of peril, to do as Edgar says: "Speak what we feel, not what we ought to say."

There is, we should remember, nothing certain in that either. For how do we know what we feel? Or find the words for it? Look at Cordelia. In that moment of crisis, did she speak the truth? That nothing on her ponderous tongue may have been a destructive vanity. Yet who can deny—never mind the ambiguities for a moment—there is something better in that nothing than all the hypocrisy, the "matter" and "manner," which went before?

And that applies, if I may stretch the point back over this whole book, to the state of the American theater as well—and our own theater in particular.

I have tried to show how and why my theater moved through an eclectic repertoire from original doubt to experimentation with the abyss. I have tried to show how the plays we did became a sort of wide-angled lens on our world which, the lens reversed, could scorch the ground on which we stood. There was no strict chronological development, but of the many plays we performed, there was no question that those which upset our notions of what the theater is about were the most informative, because the most crucial; that is, they kept reminding us that below the apparent stability of our lives (and we are in many ways a bourgeois theater) there was a most conspicuous and deadly fault.

It would provide a neat coda to this book if I could say the production of *King Lear* not only created a full-blown impregnable style, but also exhausted all the anxieties of our more "maimèd rites," getting the fiend out of our system by catharsis. It would be even better if I could say, as Granville-Barker's Man of the Theater said to the Minister of Education, that after we had "murdered the artistic conventions" we "sidled for bigger game, and instead of the present paltry misuse of energy you complain of, you might have had to trace a whole social revolution back to—say—a production of *King Lear*. . . ." I have already confessed that such a revolution is now part of my own darker purpose. But in fact, what the production of *Lear* did was to suspend us in a finer doubt, while the fiend rages with more intelligence. And urged on by the largesse of its deadly wisdom, we have gone back to the abyss and the wheel of fire, again and again, to study the distress signals, as if atoning for the fault. Some of us.

Some of us grow more disturbed that we do so. There are times we may feel, as I felt the night I wanted to cry out and stop *A Slight Ache,* that we are merely vomiting vacancy and regurgitating the slime. Around us, we have encouraged thinking and writing, and behavior, along nihilistic lines. Many of the manuscripts coming into our office, half-instructed, are full of dogmatic outrage, orchestrated obscenities, calculated illogic, and all the acquired paraphernalia of existential protest. Constant nausea throws up confounded nonsense. Circling the Sphinx, we have run like Peer Gynt into wild-eyed seekers of "The Emperor of Exegesis—based on Self," who have seized the moment to declare—as we exclaimed "God help us!"—that "Absolute reason expired at eleven o'clock last night!" Running through these new devastating forms of unreason, we suddenly discovered, like Peer, that we had been appointed guardian of the madhouse. And here we really were, impregnable squares, believing (with Freud) that instinct is essentially conservative, and only wanting to come home roundabout. (Some of us, alas!— for all the chance for adventure in our theater—never left home in the first place.)

Yet, if it took us past the seers to the fanatics and parasites of madness, there were deeper reasons for being unsettled by the new anti-drama. Replacing plot and character with riddles, acrostics, allegories, cerebral gibberish, and the mystery of the Queen's embroidery, these plays—taken seriously, not for fashion—do force us back to a clearing where suicide at last becomes possible. They cause some of us to take more thought than we can stand. "Humankind," said Eliot, "cannot bear too much reality." And if you follow the best of these plays to where they really go, you may want to protect yourself against psychic shock by throwing up your hands against the legislation of despair. While I have fought our audience (and company) on behalf of these plays, I have felt what they felt. Is that what the theater should be about? There are times when the natural reaction to a theater form that tries to accommodate all the terrible emotions of the twentieth century—on the assumption that the theater, unlike politics, must move to crisis, that the function of the drama is to be dramatic, that to be most intensely dramatic is to direct the will to our most insoluble dilemmas, to exalt our common anxieties to the point of dread—the reaction is prone to be like Johnny Tarleton's in Shaw's *Misalliance*: "Anybody on for a game of tennis?"

That question is not only the expression of another, formerly legitimate mode of drama, but a mode of self-defense, another view of reality, a *Weltanschauung*. It is also prompted by the fact that these dramas, for all their mimetic fundaments, are in other ways highly cerebral; in Beckett, say, full of learning; in Genet, impounded with paradox. Johnny's question comes in response to Lord Summerhay's rhetorical question: "How can you dare teach a man to read until you've taught him everything else first?" The exasperation of good sense concurs with Johnny. And—as the savage Old Man says of us in Yeats' last play, sciolists all, pickpockets of culture and opinionated bitches, members of assorted book clubs—we cheer Johnny on when he replies to his father's charge that he doesn't cultivate his mind: "Yes I do. I bet what you like that, page for page, I read more than you, though I don't talk about it so much. Only, I don't read the same books. I like a book with a plot in it. You like a book with nothing in it but some idea that the chap that writes it keeps worrying, like a cat chasing its own tail. I can stand watching the cat for two minutes, say, when I've got nothing better to do. But a man soon gets fed up with that sort of thing. The fact is, you look on the author as a sort of god. *I* look on him as a man that I pay to do a certain thing for me. I pay him to amuse and take me out of myself and make me forget. . . . And if I find that the author's simply getting at me the whole time, I consider that he's obtained my money under false pretenses. I'm not a morbid crank; I'm a natural man; and, as such, I don't like being got at."

Now, who wants to be a morbid crank? Who doesn't feel got at in the plays of these bizarre dramatists? Who needs it? Even those who, like myself, are messianic about the theater, who are in it to create the possibility of a valid public life, to save the world in fact, are weary of alarm and dread, and we are tempted to go along with Johnny rather than off the deep end. Live and let live, and stop crying havoc. Manic and abused, I'd like to concede the point, lest I seem merely paranoid, as Johnny thinks I am (today he reads a little psychology), when I point to the Bomb as the objective extension of the Human Condition. As that protector of the Establishment, *Time,* remarked (Johnny is now a subscriber), all the despair is really a comforting view of reality, and "The Bomb is merely a handy device, welcomed almost with relief, for the release of anxiety and guilt that have little to do with the subject as such. For many Bomb worriers, it seems to be a true phobia, a kind of secular substitute for the Last Judgment, and a truly effective nuclear ban would undoubtedly deprive them of a highly comforting sense of doom." Perhaps. I'm willing to be tried. It might be a relief to be left simply to one's very own (probably illusory) dread, but in the absence of that ban and real disarmament, one still hears those voices from the Underground asking to be recognized, ruminating over the breach in nature, sending up desperate signals in secret code, spreading misanthropy and cosmic alarm—and taking much too seriously the idea that we are "guilty creatures sitting at a play."

Too serious. It is a charge which has, as I have indicated, circulated around The Actor's Workshop. But as some of our plays suspend judgment in dismay, by exploding its convenient grounds, they also, by confronting our doubt with inscrutability, insist upon making us responsible human beings, created by and creating our world. To many of our audience it has no doubt seemed that we were—as in the strange action of *Measure for Measure* (a dark comedy we intend to do)—"Groping for trouts in a peculiar river." But in actuality we have only been catching up with the other arts, which have long been following the rich trajectory of the intense inane, discovering reason in madness, while the theater in America has been coasting through intense fog, discovering it is going nowhere. In our music, in our décor, we have been trying recently to get the energy and adventure of the other arts back on the stage, and the madness we have been exploring in our plays is the insurgence of an awful passion to render meaning to the unmeaning. In the cracked absolute of the static Hamm, as in the flailing anarchy of Lear on the heath, there is something consummately lunatic and terribly sane, the royalty of madness, which we have been trying also to restore to public service.

In the process, I was willing to make peace with the Johnny Tarletons of the world, but I didn't want to become one. For the more I looked at him (and he sometimes came to see our plays, we *were* becoming fashionable), the more I couldn't help feeling that however amiable and forthright he is, however competent, Johnny Tarleton is still a barbarian. He needs to be got at because he is dangerous. He is dangerous because he is appealing, because he distracts us from our larger purposes, because he makes us distrust our own deepest anxieties which—however deranged they may be—"by indirections find directions out." And he proposes for an alternate end the tyranny of the good guy and the straight talker, the insufferable deceit of the apparently sane.

He embarrasses me when I want, in my own art, to exercise my fullest possible humanity, to preach, to pray, to naysay and yeasay in the same breath, to dissent, mock, outrage, contradict myself, and even to entertain. For there are areas of being in which Johnny simply doesn't exist, and if he asks reasonably why he should go to the theater to be worked upon, all I can say is one way or another he'll be getting his money's worth. It is a glib answer, I know, but the fact is I see no reason for patience with Johnny— the damn fool, if he's indulged, will kill us all.

Even so—as the ancient choruses intoned—Fate moves in mysterious ways. Whether Johnny is indulged or not, things may be farther gone than any of us have imagined. Genet, for all his abrasive scorn, is not the first artist to cry doom and be dismissed as a special case, with a professional instinct for catastrophe. I suppose they said the same about Euripides when he wrote *The Bacchae* (another play we must do), where the gods avenge themselves on a people who no longer know which gods to worship; or *The Trojan Women* (still another), where the proclamation that Troy shall be no more must have sounded like the start of a countdown for the spectators. The fact is—let us not forget it—Euripides was right; Athens perished soon after. And the artist's greatest fear, like Hamm's, is that what seems to be true will be true. His greatest mission is not to believe it.

For, if it is not the obverse side of a wish for Nirvana to worry too much about the Bomb, it is true that we may have done too much of the worrying amidst Tombs. They used to say that in the days of innocence, before the closing of the old frontiers, Americans never thought about Death. I seriously doubt it, and even Huck drifted down the Mississippi with his dead father. But if we left our dead behind and thus seemed not to honor them, it is because we were, indeed, too full of the possibility of life. And now, if innocence has truly ended, we are in danger of overcompensating in a repressive society by automating our instincts and taking Thanatos to our bosom. It is a way, too, of winning the rat race against Time. Our freedom martialed and almost paralyzed by an overorganized society, we now find ourselves taking our deepest pleasures not from remembrance of our most vitalizing glories, but from a sense of natural defeat and improvisations on the theme of dying. Death, we are reminded over and over—by our most subtle artists—is an instinct, the great beckoning beauty herself. The Sick Rose has become a standard and clarion. That, I take it, was neither the will of Blake nor the real significance of Lear's "Howl!" If his dying was a release from the misery of existence, brought on by the vicious betrayal of what he bred, he also brought his house and his universe down upon himself. Before he was through he was thoroughly responsible, and one felt his going was a full, natural exhaustion of being. (We see how "right" his dying was when we recall that the eighteenth century restored him to his throne and married off Cordelia to Edgar.)

Let me follow out this issue by returning to Genet. I trust I have sufficiently expressed my admiration for his sheer theatrical brilliance, and for his exploration of that continuum of illusion which is the field in which the theater lives. But there is, indeed, something of the overweening mortician in his plays; and one aspect of their recent acceptance here has to do with the quiet desperation behind the Forest Lawn sensibility of American life. When I returned from Europe to write the first report on *The Blacks,* I pointed out that in the Paris production Roger Blin had trouble keeping the Negroes in his cast, for they felt threatened by the play; and I predicted that when *The Blacks* was produced here it would offend everybody, "not only segregationists, but the zealots of civil rights, the NAACP, and the Negroes themselves"; instead, it won prizes off-Broadway, and is still running as I write. That may say something about the theater advancing, but it also has its seamier side.

Nor am I deluded by the sensation *The Balcony* caused at my own theater. Somewhere behind the gaping, however, there is a more illicit appeal. Repressed sexuality is enticed by dying. Genet knows this; but he is too ready, I think, to bury us. While I honor both his apostasy and his perversion, something keeps reminding me that his dominion is a Fairyland, of which he is the absent King. And while he has—as Shelley says in *The Triumph of Life*—created out of "a world of agony," it is the instinct of his genius, overpowering where it exists, to transform everything to its own compulsive image: "Everybody was a fairy," he writes in *Our Lady of the Flowers,* "that is, isolated by the halo of an unapproachable, inviolable existence, through which all I could see was gestures whose continuity—hence whose logic and thus element of reassurance—escaped me, and whose every fragment raised a new question for me, word by word: disturbed me."

While those new questions are stimulating, they can also be paralyzing. We grow dizzy over the Queen's lake or pool, even if it turns out to be a cup, and only embroidery to begin with. Metamorphosis may be our reality as miscegenation is our destiny, but the final illusion may be Genet's illusion of total illusion, frightened by appearances into a runic and intimidating nihilism, subtle as a spider, sacred as mummy's-cloth. Dreading he may not exist—or playing that game—he is apparently haunted by the astonishing possibility that others might, at some inaccessible limit of his diabolism. It is what caused the serpent to sneak invisibly into the garden. The hope-lessness of vision turns into hypopyon, that vision arising from infection of vision; "the Eye altering alters all," including itself, pus accruing until the eye bursts with the force of vision itself. The result, wondrously, the vision of blindness, of the seer who doth not see. And as we see what he sees, the danger is that, treasuring our "inviolable existence," we do, indeed, become "absolute for death."

When the Duke of dark corners urges that upon Claudio, however—in the searching action of *Measure for Measure*—he is two avatars removed from his function at the center of the State: he is disguised in the prison as a friar. The Duke knows that Claudio's awareness is incomplete, his identity un-formed, without the *felt experience* of life as a constant process of dying. The Duke is on a pilgrimage of his own among the dark powers, so that he may the better know how to provide for them when he returns to govern the affairs of men. In that great nether-comedy on Justice, human and divine, the desire for Community is checked, then, by the enormous evidence of the Absurd; refreshed by it, informed by it. But whatever powers one worships, the one value that emerges clearly from the veils of illusion is that represented in the figure who comes out of the depths of the prison, drunk, toward the place where "prayers cross." In the marvellous social action of *Measure for Measure,* there is Barnardine, the prisoner, "careless, reckless, and fearless of what's past, present, or to come, insensible of mortality and desperately mortal," and who says when summoned to his execution: "I will not consent to die this day, that's certain."

We can pay Death no more tribute than that, however the scenarios end. *King Lear* acknowledges the underworld of death, but it has no special affection for mummy's-cloth. As we admire Genet or Artaud, we must re-member it is a monument that is neither Byzantine, Aztec, nor Egyptian. That is why, ritual lendings aside, *character* lives in Shakespearean drama as its vitalizing principle. Nature's molds are cracked and personality fractured, but the human figure returns to sustain the "gored state," knowing it must be done among overwhelming appearances; those who are ready to go, like Kent, going, and the others determined to live it out just the same, each one cherishing his particular freedom, whatever illusions society perpetuates around him. So, if we worry a lot about the Bomb, it is because the great indictment against civilization is—as Herbert Marcuse has said in *Eros and Civilization*—"Not those who die, but those who die before they must and want to die, those who die in agony and pain," like Cordelia. It is death such as that—have we not seen a lot of it in our century?—that reminds us how culpable we have been, and shocks us into asking of the order of institutions and the cosmic order itself: why should it have been so? why couldn't it have been otherwise?

When, however, we see death as the governing principle of life, then we may find ourselves cooperating with the repressive order of civilization, even when we dream we are annihilating it. As Marcuse says, "In a repressive civilization, death itself becomes an instrument of repression. Whether death is feared as constant threat, or glorified as supreme sacrifice, or accepted as fate, the education for consent to death introduces an element of surrender into life from the beginning—surrender and submission. . . . Theology and philosophy today compete with each other in celebrating death as an existential category: perverting a biological fact into an ontological essence, they bestow a transcendental blessing on the guilt of mankind which they help to perpetuate—they betray the promise of utopia."

From Artaud I have learned much about the liberating terrors of ritual, the relief of *petrification,* the ecstasy of the whirlwind, and the desire of the spirit for purification by fire, offering oneself to the devouring gods. In the Buddhist monk who recently burned himself to death, I have seen a convincing demonstration that one can divest oneself of the need for life—and use one's wasting body on behalf of it. The manifestations of sacrificial agony are always impressive, overpowering, and for most of us who are merely devoured by Time, our perpetual false strivings are exposed by such glorious renunciations. Yet Artaud's purity was his madness, and the monk's death . was his choice—to some extent made necessary by the ethic of renunciation which is the vow and perhaps the penalty of his culture. When life becomes unbearable, we wish it into fiction, and all the passing of men in this world is but a whispering fugue, the patina of a shadow, a dream's dream. If it is the essence of Asiatic experience, we are not unfamiliar with it in the West, when free enterprise fails in reason and comes to the dizzy rampart of despair, poised over non-being. Hamlet felt it; and I need not recite the monuments that have come of it. As Malraux remarked, "As much genius was needed to obliterate Man at Byzantium as had been needed to discover him on the Acropolis."

But whatever it may say of the limitations of vision in me, I take it our present quest is to keep Man from being obliterated, and to rediscover him from the Byzantinism of art as well as the mechanism of society. Cordelia's death would have meant nothing if she had wanted to die; and if she is a sacrifice to the human mystery, she also suggests that beside our false strivings, the fretful fever, are our legitimate claims on life. Our art—our poetry, our painting, and our sculpture—has gone through a Byzantine period which our theater is only beginning to experience; if with more shock, because it is a public form. We are confronted with a passion for ritual purification. There is a cleansing of the ego; dark energies are released. The metamorphosis resembles some novitiate's stages of preparation. This is one of the virtues of Genet. But when I work on his plays, as when I look at certain paintings, what I look for and cherish is the hand signalling through the flames.

As for the salutary effect of opened wounds or the deification of shit in *The Screens,* I find myself assenting at some point in total exposure to the noble anger of Yeats in his last years, when he said of a famous poem of Rimbaud "that the picking of lice was a good lawful theme for the Silver Age. . . ." Nobody appreciated the glory of Byzantinism (or the power of excrement) more than Yeats, but he prefaced that remark with this: "I say against all the faggots that it is our first business to paint, or describe, desirable people, places, states of mind."

That is easier said than done, and an art languishing in the Stone Age, as the theater has been in America, still has much to learn from the lice. But Yeats' remark brings us to another aspect of Genet worth considering in relation to *King Lear.* One of Genet's great contributions to the modern theater is to have carried to a savage extreme—as Lear did on the heath—that critique of moral value which has become a virtual mode of being in our highest art, and which extends in *Lear* and *The Balcony* to the very processes of nature. Genet's indictment is made, however, by also taking to its extreme that banishment of "the ethics of pity" which, for Nietzsche, had become "the most sinister symptom of our sinister European civilization." As the Dionysiac drama of Nietzsche's "gay science" took us behind "the herd instinct" to the ritual power of "nobility and distance," Genet's allegories— adorning that distance—have taken us way beyond the drama of inept sympathies back to a pregenital, pre-oedipal world of the primal Mother, culminating in the castration rites of *The Balcony,* as well as the exaltation of shit (the environment of the cradle) in *The Screens.* It is the domain where our neo-Freudian analysts are beginning to tread. For there, as Marcuse points out, "the 'maternal' images of the superego convey promises rather than memory traces—images of a free future rather than a dark past."

This is by no means the erogenous zone of prepubic sexuality which has broken out on Broadway. It is, as I have shown, an order of fabulous design. But there is something glacial about it too. To use an old-fashioned term, there is something heart-felt, and artless, in the excoriations of Lear that is rare in Genet, who flays his mutating characters with the ornate implacability of the priest holding the knife over the sacrificial victim; or, as if he were himself not Lear but one of those gods who kill us for their sport. "Cruelty," says Artaud, explaining his theater, is no mere "desperate love of blood";

the identification with "tortured victims is a very minor aspect of the question. . . . Cruelty is above all lucid, a kind of rigid control and submission to necessity." That one suffers with his victim, however, does not break the iciness of that control. Genet is one of those instinctive tyrants of art who wants to conquer his form; and hence, even when it is most powerful, trying to show that everything that lives is holy, there is something inhuman about it. It is still another variant of the idea of Alienation: in terror we may laugh away compassion.

Beyond the indictment that Lear makes on the heath, there is another lesson to be learned, or relearned. As a genealogy of morals, *King Lear* is what Nietzsche had in mind, a vast panorama of "strange and vertiginous possibilities," with every variety of suspicion, distrust, rage, demystification, and fear. But at the end of the lunatic career, which has taken us back (in the absence of the Queen) to the anatomy of the daughters, the consumptive womb, the stench, the pitch—there is a restoration of that same "ethics of pity" which Nietzsche banished for whatever good reasons, and which makes of Lear's death an unfathomably moving experience.

Shakespeare had written a sonnet defining an ideal character who, moving others, is himself as stone; there is a sublimity to this grand actor, one of those who are "lords and owners of their faces," combining self-knowledge and Spartan virtue, that Zarathustra could approve. But in *King Lear* the abstraction of human feeling let loose in estrangement doesn't wait on self-conquest for forgiveness. Beyond good and evil, we see again that everything that lives is holy, including the new cardinal sin of self-pity. The posture of existential austerity reels before the fury of the play, which rips open the soul, flooding it with compassion.

For all that the drama of Beckett purports to be no more than *what is there*, "all, here, now," one finds in him the operative force of this same "ethics of pity." Genet astounds, Beckett also moves us in a conventional way. While he understands the curative powers of the plague, he can treat human weakness without mockery, going beyond parody to a more compassionate form of homeopathic magic. While he knows, too, that all the scenarios end in death, he drains all the life-blood from the lethal rhythm, all the rage and all the tenderness, and weeps for the passing with as little shame as amazing self-consciousness allows. He gets everything felt that we are afraid to feel. So Hamm: "You cried for night; it falls; now cry in darkness. (*Pause.*) Nicely put, that. (*Pause.*) And now?" The critique of pity continues, measured and darkly humored, but the pity is there anyhow. And through all the nuances of hallucinated and interfusing personality, there is finally somebody there who is heart-breaking and whom Beckett won't abandon to Nothingness; for he remembers the past glory and virtually wishes it back into being.

At the end of Antonioni's film *Eclipse,* when the camera wanders back through the environment of their vain courtship, we feel the lovers by their absence amid the objects of their love. So, in Beckett, we feel presence in vacancy, the hand of friendship in isolation. And the drama wrings out of us, with exquisite and painful nostalgia, the desire to restore what is lost: "Look! There! All that rising corn! And there! Look! The sails of the herring fleet! All that loveliness." And beyond the fault, beyond Kierkegaard's "fear and trembling," something akin to the old Aristotelian "fear and pity." Not tragedy, perhaps, but very close. The most existential of our dramatists in the way his dramas *feel,* in their very cadences, he has the quality one senses finally in *Lear's* universe of total responsibility, with no alibis: "Oh I put him before his responsibility."

That line occurs a moment after Hamm regrets the absence of the lost child. It seems touched by the clearest gods.

> Nativity, once in the main of light,
> Crawls to maturity, wherewith being crowned,
> Crooked eclipses 'gainst his glory fight,
> And Time that gave doth now his gift confound.

What Time gave, we are still trying to rediscover; but in the process we have become experts of the crooked eclipse, trailing clouds of glory in despair. There are dangers which I've tried to describe, particularly the loss of compassion, with character-in-action, in the destructive element or the mechanisms of parody.

I have also tried to show how my own theater crawled toward maturity through the catacombs, until it started to gasp for air. Recently, I have said at company meetings that we have to learn again to become America First. There was some dismay when I first said it. But what I had in mind has to do with the fact that Americans were once natural-born existentialists. As de Tocqueville observed, "America is . . . one of the countries where the precepts of Descartes are least studied and best applied." What he meant is that, having no institutions to begin with, we learned from experience, from the doing, by plunging after the White Whale or drawing a bead on the bear.

So we did. Those last images are out of the demonic side of our pragmatic tradition, the despair of which one could trace even in the revolutionary optimism of Whitman. There was nobody deeper in blackness than Poe, there is no more frenzied consciousness than Melville's, and E. A. Robinson has said: "You have done your best work when you have forgotten what a rotten place the world is." But before we could start forgetting again, we had to be reminded by sharing to its depths the disillusioned experience coming from Europe. As we developed institutions changing into a bureaucratic maze, we *are* now studying the precepts of Descartes. Our theologians, philosophers, and psychologists are possessed by them, and they fertilized the plays we were doing. We had gone behind muckraking—of which we had our tradition—to the black art of demolition. Confronted with the monstrous, were were back with the monsters. But there were times we felt strange amid the folklore of the existential and in our self-appointed role of savage destroyers; and we'd want to put despair behind us to sing praise, sing praises out, to love our country and our time and have done with it, whatever came.

That, too, is easier said than done, but it was in this spirit that the novelist Mark Harris wrote a play for us, *Friedman and Son,* in which the central character, a writer, "decides he wants to perform a patriotic, reverential service, see. . . . That's going to be the whole theme of the evening: Get off the tiger." We were beginning to feel the necessity of such gestures, however imperfect, lest the limerick turn true and our despair in rage helps create the world it doesn't want. The play was performed with more or less exuberance; yet, in a company seminar, it seemed clear that among the younger people especially there was skepticism, even disdain, over its optimism, and the way that determined character and the rest. Emblematic of the continued feeling the gesture had to overcome was one young actress who said to me that of all the plays we are doing next season, the only one she really wants to be in is Webster's *The White Devil.* And I must confess, my moments of optimistic desire aside, I share her feeling that it is the kind of classic—scathing, a night-piece, a torturing wheel, studying a long silence—that still feels the most relevantly modern.

So be it. When we have occasion to celebrate, we shall celebrate. Meanwhile, without deluding ourselves, we accept the obligation to help wish the world back to sanity, bringing to our desire for joy the intensity of Artaud's scream. To those in the irremediable grip of existential despair our behavior may seem at times like that of the misanthropic Alceste in his appeal to Célimène, the high comedy of maximum desperation:

> Pretend, pretend, that you are just and true,
> And I shall make myself believe in you.

Well, we shall take that chance. And to keep belief from going blind, we shall try to keep developing our sense of the theater—derived from the plays we did—as the Public Art of Crisis. If that keeps taking us back to vacancy and despair, we shall try to reap their perverse rewards. If the world won't give us a better world, we shall try to give it a better theater, in which no man's honesty need feel ashamed. Out of our own indecision and the questing of the plays—both the social dramas and the subterranean—we have become assured of certain certainties, the chief being that without taking on our deepest crises, the most palpably moral and the most inaccessibly psychic, a theater isn't much of a theater.

One day I came to the theater to find that our lobby had been designated by Civil Defense officials as a fallout shelter. There was no warning. But whatever they make of our lobby, I am more and more determined that nobody be able to take shelter in our theater.

We tried to conceive our production of *King Lear* so it would take on all the spiritual, moral, political, and personal exacerbations of that play. As it flailed at our world, we tried to pack our world into the play. I think it is significant that in the various Shakespeare festivals in America, it is usually the tragedies which falter. I am not the first to remark it, and I believe it has had something to do with the muting of crisis in our public life—the refusal to meet issues head on, the encouragement of escapism, the tendency to soften the blows while arousing the fears; and a weakened sense of irony, which comes from recognition of multiple oscillating possibilities in every event. Our scholars tell us that the great perception in *King Lear* is Edgar's line "Ripeness is all." I agree. Ripeness: maturing, coming to fruition, the image drawn from nature, suggesting fulfillment of the human, achieved only in crisis and hastening teleologically to an end. "Blest fig's end," says Iago. One forgets there follows upon the wondrous idea of ripeness in *King Lear* a sense of its absurdity, its death's-head intuition, in Gloucester's equivocal remark: "And that's true too." Something like the enigmatic comedy of the gesture, no less spiritual for its scatalogy, of Leonardo's young Saint John the Baptist.

Gordon Craig thought the conjunction *and* one of the richest words in the language. "And that's true too." That's the real meaning of a theater's repertoire, to let the plays have it out within themselves and against each other. In the acting out, in gesture, intonation, image, character, rhythm, and deed: "And that's true too." Born of conflict. If in Socrates it is the un-examined life that is not worth living, in Shakespeare it is the uncontested. Even in the sonnets, the boughs do not quiver in the cold, they *shake against* it. The serenity of *The Tempest* and the green world of *Cymbeline* follow the blood and blackness of *Macbeth,* the dazzling scrofula of *Troilus,* and the misanthropy of *Timon.* Even when the terror undergoes a sea-change, strong in the memory of the Brave New World is the mudcaked animality of Caliban and all the assimilated rage of the great tragedies up to the very horror of that "kill, kill, kill, kill, kill, kill!" A great drama raids our memory; it does not let us off easy; it may replay what we'd rather forget, like the trial of Eichmann. Even from his grave, Shakespeare speaks with the dramatist's god-given sense of conflict:

> Good friend for Jesus sake forbeare,
> To digg the dust encloased heare;
> Blessed be ye man yt spares these stones
> And curst be he yt moves my bones.

The last warning struck me all the more when I saw the same epitaph in the parish church of Chipping Camden, the curse removed, as the eighteenth century revised away the "multitudinous seas incarnadine" or the unimaginable horror of Cordelia's death. I had visited Holy Trinity in Stratford on a day in late autumn. Leaving the grave, I returned to the churchyard, a perfect sonnet of morning frost and bare ruin'd choirs. There, looking toward the Avon, I saw in the middle of the gentle river—like a footnote from the Underground —a large sign in red block letters: GREAT DANGER, WEIR BELOW.

All the drama that means anything is committed to that DANGER, and to the mystery of that WEIR. Crisis and Change. The dullard Kuligin, in Chek-hov's *The Three Sisters,* tells the story of a schoolmate who was "expelled

from the fifth form because he could never understand *ut consecutivum*. Now
he is frightfully poor and ill, and when I meet him I say, 'How are you, *ut
consecutivum?*' 'Yes,' he says, 'that's just the trouble—*consecutivum*' . . .
and then he coughs . . ." The anecdote is part of that whole mystique of
malfunction and irrelevance that gives Chekhov's studies of provincial life
a longevity that *Middletown* and the Kinsey reports never have. Words, words,
words. "Balzac was married in Berdichev." (*Pause.*) Nothing is more real
than nothing, except people. Look at the following passage from *The Three
Sisters* which, when we produced it, reminded us of Ionesco:

> ANDREY: In Moscow you sit in a huge room at a restaurant; you know
> no one and no one knows you, and at the same time you don't feel a
> stranger. . . . But here you know everyone and everyone knows you, and
> yet you are a stranger—a stranger. . . . A stranger, and lonely. . . .
> FERAPONT: Eh? (*Pause.*) And the same contractor says—maybe it's not
> true—that there's a rope stretched right across Moscow.
> ANDREY: What for?
> FERAPONT: I can't say, sir. The contractor said so.
> ANDREY: Nonsense. . . .

Yet, for all his virtues in the enlightenment of a *non-sequitur* reality, Chekhov
protects the essentially human. Though Nothingness is confirmed, neither
Andrey nor Ferapont is denied; they are not ciphers, even if the one's intelligence and the other's impotence come to the same end. The drama occurs
at that impasse of human relations, no less human for the impasse, where
the rest is silence, for the time being. History remains, a vague possibility.
"It doesn't matter, it doesn't matter," says the doctor, reading the newspaper and humming "Tarara-boom-dee-ay!" "If we only knew, if we only
knew!" says Olga, the music of the military band fading. Andrey pushes the
perambulator in which Bobik is sitting. *Consecutivum*—that's the trouble,
not stasis. WEIR BELOW.

However it ends, drama begins with those who won't "Let be." "*L'audace,
encore l'audace, et toujours l'audace.*" Not all heroes are up to Danton's
ethic, and if Hotspur is not entirely right that "out of this nettle danger we
pluck this flower safety," at least we pluck from the drama's dedication to
danger the courage to live in peaceful coexistence with the irremediable. In
drama—how often have we heard it?—action is all. Though it may return
us, inevitably will, to the mystery of that weir.

Andrey's lament is echoed by a village woman, cautioning her child at the
end of John Whiting's *Saint's Day*, a bizarre, incoherent, and lovely play
set in the English countryside: "Stella! We are strangers here, Stella." The
child is performing a "grave dance" around a corpse who bears her name.
It is impossible to say what it means, nor to resolve it. Nor is it necessary.
Predecessor of the new wave of English dramatists, socialist or angry or
both, Whiting (who died recently) was not searching for causes, because he
believed that all causes are failures. There is an Eliotic tone in the assertion

of one of his characters that "it is not a question of finding but of losing the pieties, the allegiances, the loves"; but the final consideration for Whiting is not a matter of orthodoxies or ideologies or postures or platforms, rather, literally, life and death. With or without the Bomb, "our fear is that the unknown hand is already at the switch." The sin of previous generations, with their passion for social exposé (the play's chief character is an octogenarian muckraker, now disgraced), was misinformation on the Human Condition, the failure to remind us as we convert history to the service of men that "the purpose of any memory—of any experience [is] to give foundation to the state of death." Truth and glibness mixed. It is the child who does the grave dance. Death-in-life. Death *and* life. Whiting knows that one of the *chosen* voices of intellectuals in this century is that which seems, prematurely, to have passed through nature to eternity. The sin of the present generation is the disaffiliation it brings on, and which Whiting shares. *Saint's Day* reflects in action, and in a certain anarchic failure of form, the cost of setting limits on obligation, the risk of neutrality on aesthetic grounds, and the catastrophe of partial commitment. "There is always the responsibility —it must rest on someone."

Once we have put *him* before his responsibility—that is, paid tribute to what is essentially human—the responsibility remains. Where courage fails, Society like Nature revenges itself. Disaffiliation invites the demonic. Indifference, recoiling into action, becomes the dupe of accident, as after the graveyard scene of *Hamlet*. The result: promiscuous slaughter. Today, in mass withdrawal from the horror behind, we are likely to be passive before the horror ahead. When we look back, there is more guilt than we can bear. If the great philosophical problem of our time is suicide, the great practical problem is how to avoid deferring to solutions which are suicidal. Or, as Gerard Piel, editor of *Scientific American,* said in a speech in San Francisco, we become victims of "the authors of frauds by computers. . . ." Nothing will come of nothing. Yet where, again, to begin? Every profit a loss, every deterrent a possible disaster. Would that the mystifications of modern society were even so imaginable as that weir. One hears the splashing of Grendel's dam everywhere, within and without. Whatever there is of ontological anxiety passes over to the structures we create, so that we find paranoia and schizophrenia in institutions. Heorot quivers in the cold. Is there some grim poetic justice in the fact that Mies van der Rohe's bronze consummation of the Bauhaus, which aimed to turn the blight of modern industry to art, was built for Seagram? Bodger thrives on Undershaft's economy. The whores sing in *The Rise and Fall of the City of Mahagonny:* "We must have whiskey, O you know why!"

In our time who can avoid serving the enemy? If Ionesco's *Rhinoceros* had had the full courage of its excellent conceit, Berenger would have gone on protesting his humanity while changing, willy-nilly, into a beast. The comedy would have been realer if more repellent by denying egress to those in the market for evasion. We all go under. It is the way we go that counts.

One hopes he will go when he goes like Ahab's Pequod, taking a living piece of heaven with him. But there we have it—that skeleton-beneath-the-skin sensibility, part of the higher criticism and one of the clichés of chaos, missing the issue in its own way, dodging crisis. Given my prior acquaintance with Yorick's skull, my own scholarly discipline of despair, the temptation was to overstudy a long silence. The struggle of creating a theater during the Cold War kept pushing me back to action, even as we leaped into Ophelia's grave. That leap is a kind of rhetoric, which we must somehow live down. If T. S. Eliot did teach us anything of value, it is to learn to live with our illusions by improving their quality. Not what do we do as we go under, but what do we do while we're here, I'd say, on the assumption the going under (yes, Old Possum, we must still give foundation to the state of death) will take care of itself.

So, too, with guilt. It can make us passive by appalling us. As we do look back, we must remember that there is an enormous conceptual difference between the Karamazovan idea that "we are all murderers" and that we are *nothing but* murderers. If the theater brings conflict to crisis, it's because our conflicts are aggravated by the plague of choice, the most tortuous of which is, indeed—in an age where everything, not only the nefarious but the benign, conspires against it—the choice to remain human. Which includes facing up to crisis without hypocrisy and without snap judgment.

Where drama really takes place, judgment stops short. The Eichmann trial, which sent Portia packing back to Belmont, demonstrated this in an unexpected way. One could be predictably stupefied by Eichmann's discriminating between the assertion of one witness that it was 4,000,000 and another that it was 5,000,000 Jews he was responsible for killing. What monster was this? Yet when the prosecutor Hausner asked Eichmann whether he was guilty, the trial took a sharp turn into the special stupefactions of drama. Eichmann, with wondrous control, it seemed, started to distinguish between moral and legal guilt, whereupon Hausner raised a finger at him and thundered: "Answer yes or no!" I don't know to what perverse instinct I may be testifying, but *at that moment* loyalties were annihilated for me, and I was with Eichmann. I believed in the trial and believe the crime should be replayed again and again, as in a Pirandello drama, so that we may understand it in all its remembered and imagined horror—but for me that moment was its most valuable experience.

Drama being a perpetual present moment, it may cut *you* to the brain. You are there, defenseless, guilty creature sitting at a play. What you lose by way of status and self-possession (*Einfühlung* or *Verfremdung,* drama sucks you in), you make up by the intensity of exposure. You are confronted with— what else?—yourself. That doesn't mean everybody else is excluded; if they were, you could escape the issue by claiming discrimination. The theater is nothing if not universal. Yet in a real Theater—I have not been speaking of that politic convocation of worms where people meet for self-edification and digestion's sake—there is no safety in numbers either. Death or a lemon pie, you must face the issue. You are responsible for your foolishness as for your atrocities, and you may be horrified at the way one brings on the other, as when Lear asks his daughters to say they love him. And there is sorcery in the way, facing it all, brought nearly to exhaustion as *Lear* brings you, you become more available to yourself.

"You live badly, my friends. It is shameful to live like that." The charge may be gently reproachful, objective, as with Chekhov. It may be partisan and partial, as with Arthur Miller. "Attention must be paid!" You may hear a false accent in the voice, but you pay attention because the play insists on forcing its conflict to crisis, as when Biff forces Willie, already half-beaten, to confront himself. Whipping out the gaspipe, Biff says: "All right, phony! Then let's lay it on the line." The drama might be deeper if Miller did the same for Biff, who is clear about his failure but a little wooly about his aspirations. Still, we may be thankful for half-truths in a world of manifold illusions. Real drama, at some point, insists on laying it on the line—like O'Neill's Hickey, to the misbegotten limit of his own delusions. There are times when we may want to run away—but you will know it when you hear it, the authentic voice.

It is this sense of the theatrical event that must have kept the audience in their seats at the first performance of Euripides' *Trojan Women,* which was, indeed, one of the bravest plays ever written. In full daylight, Euripides said to the assembled Athenians, a people proud of being the most civilized in the world, that they were essentially a bunch of barbarians. They had just finished the siege of the innocent island of Melos, which they had assaulted for commercial reasons. Not content with victory, they had sacked the place. The play's prophecy of retribution on the Greeks was actually fulfilled in the Sicilian expedition. All the traditions of the Greek theater permitted Euripides to deal with such a crisis, because the theater, as we have been told, was central to the culture. Aristophanes could in turn be critical of Euripides. Now that the theater is only marginal, it may have to clamor more to get at the issues, but it will be trivial if it doesn't—even if, as with *The Trojan Women,* getting at the issues doesn't save us.

As our theater grew, on the barest hope, we learned that the most formidable and energetic drama of our time proceeded virtually without hope. The so-called Theater of the Absurd has been fighting a guerrilla war. It is the form of the Resistance, coming out of Kafka's Burrow. Its passion is bare survival, and it uses every beanbag, brass knuckle, and Molotov cocktail that can be salvaged from the wreck of theatrical history. It has the scapegoat *noblesse* of the Underground. And it awaits the time. The theater, it knows, needs more than piddling heroes and tight little emotions; it needs actors who, honoring that other, more inhibited, underground activity of the studio, *can* tear a passion to tatters; and it needs plays with a wildly civilized insurgence. It must seize with exuberance the task of being the public art of crisis in an age where crisis is a social and moral norm. And it must not merely escape into the apparatus of ritual and incantation, compounding the spiritual plague by making a mere ceremony of it. "I then asked Ezekiel," writes Blake in *The Marriage of Heaven and Hell,* "Why he eat dung, & lay so long on his right and left side? he answer'd, 'the desire of raising other men into a perception of the infinite. . . .' " He then explains that the Indians of North America practice the same technique. It is the stuff of Myth, an act of Style. But Blakean Innocence can twist the experience of noble savagery into a pretext for sheer Ignorance. One can be square in ritual as in realism, and the best of those dramatists whose guardian angel is Artaud avoid the deadbeat of an easy demonism.

More than anything, the theater needs to learn again to contend with the world out of which history is made, men creating events, events determining men—real men, not ciphers; a world of *Realpolitik,* sneak attacks, and holy wars, no less hieratic for its industry and no less hallucinated for its systems and categories, bureaucrats and dossiers; and—with the revolutions of rising expectations extending now to infinite Space—new possibilities of heroism before us. If character has been deadened by exhausted forms, we must re-vivify the forms to rescue character. And while technical sincerity is the beginning of heroism, we must strive to go beyond the heroism of technique. The Queen must be wooed out from behind her embroidery. The Figure in the Carpet must begin to take the floor. Even talk politics. If man is a thinking reed, he is also a political animal; and one has only to look at a chronicle play of Shakespeare or an Aristophanic comedy to realize the dominion our drama has lost by having no political dimension. His politics may not be, as all the paradoxes of his drama show, the whole story in Brecht; but without the politics, there'd be less of a story, and less ground for paradox. Still, as Sartre noted, there are shadows of the subjective life which are not wholly provided for in his objective form. And the primary virtue of the Under-ground dramatists is that they have provided us with a subtext for a new Social Drama, which has its eye on the heroism of the dark corners and pays its tribute to the dark gods.

The best drama of our generation has been foreign. While recognizing that our world is international beyond retreat, we must also learn, as Whitman said in *Starting from Paumanok,* "to report all heroism from an American point of view." I don't mean point of view as constrained by technique. Our art offers us another tradition: you see it in Whitman; you see it in Melville. Desiring to contain multitudes, we must not be outfaced by the living fact. Our ritual addiction to the particular you see in images from Nick Adams' running a fishhook through the thorax of a grasshopper to the junky in *The Connection* putting the hook to his arm. They have the intensity and es-capist limitations of immediacy. But Faulkner's Yoknapatawpha County, seeing the life of Man in the life of men, has a passion for continuity, sur-rounding the singular with the largesse of history. At its profoundest, Ameri-can art brings the fact into the service of the eternal. Melville, writing of Hawthorne, knew that greatness or genius does not exist without "the indispensable equipment of . . . a great, deep intellect which drops down into the mind like a plummet."

Intellect. It has rarely been respected in the American theater. But we must bolster our failing hearts by using our minds. As a public form, the theater has an illustrious history of plays and people that have thought themselves past false silence and false security. Attention must be paid to that history. We must accept the very nature of our form as a challenge. The theater knows about crisis as other forms don't because it is virtually a State of Crisis—material, time-serving, collaborative, and adulterated by competing claims as by competing temperaments. More than any other form, it calls constantly for its own purification. When Duse said, however, that "the actors and actresses must all die of the plague," it was because their ignorance was making art impossible. Gordon Craig says in his preface to *On the Art of the Theater* that he didn't really want "to see the living actors replaced by things of wood. . . ." Like Genet's Allegories, his Ubermarionette was meant to restore mind and fire to the actor, to cut down on the degeneration of the ego into trivia. Degeneration, Craig felt, was all around him. So with Copeau when he swept the boards or took young blood into the country to kiss the soil. The Craigs and Copeaus never succeed wholly, but they live out the issues for us—the perennial issues. If they incline to tryanny, they are like the superego itself, urging us back to what is liable to be lost in the desperate enterprise of our ambitious art. Because it aspires to function, however marginally, at the dead center of community, the theater is more subject to compromise and adjustment than other forms. That is its shame and—when, somehow, in the strange bipartisanship of personal will and cultural ripeness the theater's inherent corruption is mastered—the source of its formal glory.

It is my conviction that the theater has greater possibilities than other forms because it takes greater risks with more vulnerable means. This is a matter of nature as much as choice. God bless the medium! it is individual and protestant to its corporate bones and cannot help but look for trouble. Yet for every saint who wants to purify the theater, there are thousands who think they love the theater and unwittingly, or pusillanimously, betray it. *You who work in the theater: learn to trust the trouble as it sings!* For the real theater, intimate with catastrophe and "memorizing another Golgotha," cannot be appeased by either evasive optimism or official realism. "After all, life—public or private—can often be carried on," said the Prime Minister of England, "with reasonable satisfaction on what a cynic once called a healthy basis of mutual distrust." Then the scandal broke. In the theater, distrust is distrust, there is finally no hidden agenda. The theater is responsible to that distrust—where it comes from and what it does, its real sources, its real motives, its real consequences. Those declared, the theater leaves us—as far as humanly possible—to our own resources.

Axiom for all of us: "Speak what we feel, not what we ought to say."

And trust to the clearest gods.